TRAVELS

by

Michael Crichton

"Startling and informative . . . I was swept away not only by [Michael Crichton's] richly informed mind, but his driving curiosity. . . . He seems bound and determined to explore every single mystery in the universe. . . . His ultimate concern is that we recognize why we need the insights of the mystic as much as we need the insights of the scientist. There's plenty of both in *Travels*."

The New York Times Book Review

"Satisfying . . . Memorable . . . What a traveler [Crichton] is!"

The Kirkus Reviews

"[Crichton] circumnavigates the currently trendy spiritual-how-to genre, with humor, sensitivity, and didactic honesty as his guides. . . . His sense of wonder and awe, his gentle encouragement toward 'direct experience,' and his simple yet graphic prose will stir the wanderlust in many a reader."

Booklist

"Crichton's curiosity and self-deprecating humor animate recitals of his adventures.

Publishers Weekly

TRAVELS

Michael Crichton

Ballantine Books · New York

Portions of this work were originally published in *The Condé Nast Traveler* and *Esquire*.

Grateful acknowledgment is made to Harper & Row Publishers, Inc., for permission to reprint an excerpt from "The Way In" from *The Selected Poems of Rainer Maria Rilke*. Translated from the German by Robert Bly. Copyright © 1981 by Robert Bly. Reprinted by permission of Harper & Row, Publishers, Inc.

Library of Congress Catalog Card Number: 87-46040

ISBN 0-345-35932-1
This edition published by arrangement with Alfred A. Knopf, Inc.

Manufactured in the United States of America

First Ballantine Books Edition: August 1989

In self-analysis the danger of incompleteness is particularly great. One is too soon satisfied with a part explanation.
—SIGMUND FREUD

Existence is beyond the power of words to define.
—LAO-TZU

What you see is what you see.
—FRANK STELLA

Contents

Preface

For many years I traveled for myself alone. I refused to write about my trips, or even to plan them with any useful purpose. Friends would ask what research had taken me to Malaysia or New Guinea or Pakistan, since it was obvious that nobody would go to these places merely for recreation. But I did.

And I felt a real need for rejuvenation, for experiences that would take me away from things I usually did, the life I usually led.

In my everyday life, I often felt a stifling awareness of the purpose behind everything I did. Every book I read, every movie I saw, every lunch and dinner I attended, seemed to have a reason behind it. From time to time, I felt the urge to do something for no reason at all.

I conceived these trips as vacations—as respites from my ongoing life—but that wasn't how they turned out. Eventually, I realized that many of the most important changes in my life had come about because of my travel experiences. For, however tame when compared with the excursions of real adventurers, these trips were genuine adventures for me: I struggled with my fears and limitations, and I learned whatever I was able to learn.

But as time passed, the fact that I had never written about my travels became oddly burdensome. If you're a writer, the assimilation of important experiences almost obliges you to write about them. Writing is how you make the experience your own, how you explore what it means to you, how you come to possess it, and ultimately release it. I found I was relieved, after all these years, to write about some of the places I have been. I was fascinated to see how much I could write without reference to my notebooks.

There were also some episodes from medical school that I had always intended to write about. I had promised myself I would wait fifteen years, until they were thoroughly ancient history. To my surprise, I find I have waited long enough, and so they are included here.

I have also included experiences in the realms that are sometimes called psychic, or transpersonal, or spiritual. I think of this as inner travel, to complement the outer travel, although that distinction—between what is internal sensation and what is external stimulus—often blurs in my mind. But I've found the effort to disentangle my perceptions useful in a way I had not anticipated.

Often I feel I go to some distant region of the world to be reminded of who I really am. There is no mystery about why this should be so. Stripped of your ordinary surroundings, your friends, your daily routines, your refrigerator full of your food, your closet full of your clothes—with all this taken away, you are forced into direct experience. Such direct experience inevitably makes you aware of who it is that is having the experience. That's not always comfortable, but it is always invigorating.

I eventually realized that direct experience is the most valuable experience I can have. Western man is so surrounded by ideas, so bombarded with opinions, concepts, and information structures of all sorts, that it becomes difficult to experience anything without the intervening filter of these structures. And the natural world—our traditional source of direct insights—is rapidly disappearing. Modern city-dwellers cannot even see the stars at night. This humbling reminder of man's place in the greater scheme of things, which human beings formerly saw once every twenty-four hours, is denied them. It's no wonder that people lose their bearings, that they lose track of who they really are, and what their lives are really about.

So travel has helped me to have direct experiences. And to know more about myself.

Many people have helped me with this book. Among those who read early versions of the manuscript and gave me comments and encouragement were Kurt Villadsen, Anne-Marie Martin, my sisters, Kimberly Crichton and Catherine Crichton, my brother, Douglas Crichton, Julie Halowell, my mother, Zula Crichton, Bob Gottlieb, Richard Farson, Marilyn Grabowski, Lisa Plonsker, Valery Pine, Julie McIver, Lynn Nesbit, and Sonny Mehta. Later drafts of the text were read by the participants themselves, who offered valuable suggestions and corrections.

To all these people I am grateful, as I am to my beleaguered travel agents of many years, Kathy Bowman of World Wide Travel in Los Angeles, and Joyce Small of Adventures Unlimited in San Francisco.

In addition, certain people have had a major influence on my thinking, although they do not appear much in this book. I am thinking in particular of Henry Aronson, Jonas Salk, John Foreman and Jasper Johns.

By design, I have limited the scope of this book. Freud once defined life as work and love, but I have chosen to discuss neither, except as my travel experiences impinge upon them. Nor have I undertaken to assess my childhood. Rather, it is my intention to write about the interstices of my life, about the events that occurred while what I imagined to be the real business of my life was taking place.

It remains only to say that certain changes have been made to the original text. Names and identifying characteristics of physicians and medical patients have all been changed. And in later chapters, some names and identifying characteristics have been changed at the request of the individuals involved.

Medical Days

1965-1969

Cadaver

It is not easy to cut through a human head with a hacksaw.

The blade kept snagging the skin, and slipping off the smooth bone of the forehead. If I made a mistake, I slid to one side or the other, and I would not saw precisely down the center of the nose, the mouth, the chin, the throat. It required tremendous concentration. I had to pay close attention, and at the same time I could not really acknowledge what I was doing, because it was so horrible.

Four students had shared this cadaver for months, but it fell to me to cut open the old woman's head. I made the others leave the room while I worked on it. They couldn't watch without making jokes, which interfered with my concentration.

The bones of the nose were particularly delicate. I had to proceed carefully, to cut without shattering these tissue-thin bones. Several times I stopped, cleaned the bits of bone from the teeth of the blade with my fingertips, and then continued. As I sawed back and forth, concentrating on doing a good job, I was reminded that I had never imagined my life would turn out this way.

* * *

3

I had never particularly intended to become a doctor. I had grown up in a suburb of New York City, where my father was a journalist. No one in my family was a doctor, and my own early experiences with medicine were not encouraging: I fainted whenever I was given injections, or had blood drawn.

I had gone to college planning to become a writer, but early on a scientific tendency appeared. In the English department at Harvard, my writing style was severely criticized and I was receiving grades of C or C+ on my papers. At eighteen, I was vain about my writing and felt it was Harvard, and not I, that was in error, so I decided to make an experiment. The next assignment was a paper on *Gulliver's Travels,* and I remembered an essay by George Orwell that might fit. With some hesitation, I retyped Orwell's essay and submitted it as my own. I hesitated because if I were caught for plagiarism I would be expelled; but I was pretty sure that my instructor was not only wrong about writing styles, but poorly read as well. In any case, George Orwell got a B— at Harvard, which convinced me that the English department was too difficult for me.

I decided to study anthropology instead. But I doubted my desire to continue as a graduate student in anthropology, so I began taking premed courses, just in case.

In general, I found Harvard an exciting place, where people were genuinely focused on study and learning, and with no special emphasis on grades. But to take a premed course was to step into a different world—nasty and competitive. The most critical course was organic chemistry, Chem 20, and it was widely known as a "screw your buddy" course. In lectures, if you didn't hear what the instructor had said and asked the person next to you, he'd give you the wrong information; thus you were better off leaning over to look at his notes, but in that case he was likely to cover his notes so you couldn't see. In the labs, if you asked the person at the next bench a question, he'd tell you the wrong answer in the hope that you would make a mistake or, even better, start a fire. We were marked down for starting fires. In my year, I had the dubious distinction of starting more lab fires than anyone else, including a spectacular ether fire that set the ceiling aflame and left large scorch marks, a stigmata of ineptitude hanging over my head for the rest of the year. I was uncomfortable with the hostile and paranoid attitude this course demanded for success. I thought that a humane profession like medicine ought to encourage other values in its candidates. But nobody was asking my opinion. I got through it as best I could. I imagined medicine to be a caring profession, and a scientific one as well. It was so fast-moving that its practitioners could not afford to be dogmatic; they would be flexible and open-minded. It was certainly interesting work, and there was no doubt that you were doing something worthwhile with your life, helping sick people.

So I applied to medical schools, took the Medical College Aptitude Tests, had my interviews, and was accepted. Then I got a fellowship for study in Europe, which postponed my start for a year.

But the following year I went to Boston, rented an apartment in Roxbury near the Harvard Medical School, bought my furniture, and registered for my classes. And it was at the registration that I first was confronted by the prospect of dissecting a human cadaver.

As first-year students, we had scrutinized the schedule and had seen that we would be given cadavers on the first day. We could talk of nothing else. We questioned the second-year students, old hands who regarded us with amused tolerance. They gave us advice. Try and get a man, not a woman. Try and get a black person, not a white. A thin person, not a fat one. And try to get one that hadn't been dead too many years.

Dutifully, we made notes and waited for the fateful Monday morning. We imagined the scene, remembered how Broderick Crawford had played it in *Not as a Stranger,* growling at the terrified students, "There's nothing funny about death," before he whipped the cover off the corpse.

In the amphitheater that morning, Don Fawcett, professor of anatomy, gave the first lecture. There was no corpse in the room. Dr. Fawcett was tall and composed, not at all like Broderick Crawford, and he spent most of the time on academic details. How the dissections were scheduled. When the exams would fall. How the dissections of gross anatomy would be related to the lectures in microscopic fine anatomy. And the importance of gross anatomy: "You can no more become a good doctor without a thorough understanding of gross anatomy than you can become a good mechanic without opening the hood of a car."

But we could hardly listen to him. We were waiting for the body. Where was the body?

Finally a graduate student wheeled in a gurney. On it was a blue denim cloth, and an underlying shape. We stared at the shape. Nobody heard a word Dr. Fawcett said. He moved from the podium to the body. Nobody listened. We waited for the moment when he would pull aside the cloth.

He pulled aside the cloth. There was a great sigh, a great exhalation of breath. Beneath the cloth was a heavy plastic sheet. We still could see nothing of the body.

Dr. Fawcett removed the plastic sheet. There was another, thin white cloth beneath that. He removed this cloth. At last we saw a very pale form. Limbs, a torso. But the head, hands, and feet were wrapped in gauze like a mummy. It was not easy to recognize this as a human body. We slowly relaxed, became aware that Dr. Fawcett was still talking. He was telling us details of the method of preservation, the reason for protective wrapping of the hands and face. He told us of the need for decorum in the dissection room. And he told us that the preservative, phenol, was also an anesthetic and that it was common to experience numbness and tingling in our fingers during the dissection; this was not a dread paralysis we had caught from the cadavers.

He ended the lecture. We went to the dissection room, to choose our bodies.

We had previously divided ourselves into groups of four. I had given this group choice a lot of thought, and managed to link up with three students who all planned to be surgeons. I thought budding surgeons would be enthusiastic about the dissection, and would want to do everything themselves. With any luck, I could sit back and watch, which was my fondest hope. I didn't even want to touch the body, if I could help it.

The dissection room was large and, in September, uncomfortably warm. There were thirty bodies on tables around the room, all covered with sheets. The instructors refused to let us peek under the sheets to choose the bodies. We had to pick one table and wait. My group chose the table nearest the door.

The instructors gave a lecture. We stood beside our bodies. The tense feelings rushed back. It was one thing to sit high up in an amphitheater while a body was shown. It was another to stand close to a body, to be able to reach out and touch it. Nobody touched it.

6

Finally the instructor said, "Well, let's get to work." There was a long silence. All the students opened their dissecting kits, got out their scalpels and scissors. Nobody touched the sheets. The instructor reminded us we could now remove the sheets. We touched the sheets gingerly, at the edge of the fabric. Holding our breath, we pulled the sheets back from the feet, exposing the lower half of the torso.

We had a white female, but she was thin, and very old. The hands and feet were wrapped. It wasn't as bad as I had imagined, although the smell of phenol preservative was strong.

Our instructor told us we would begin the dissection with two people on each side of the body. We would begin on the leg. We could start cutting now.

Nobody moved.

Everybody looked at one another. The instructor said that we would have to work quickly and steadily if we hoped to keep on schedule and finish the dissection in three months.

Then, finally, we began to cut.

The skin was cold, gray-yellow, slightly damp. I made my first cut with a scalpel, slitting across the area where the thigh meets the body, and then straight down the leg to the knee. I didn't cut deeply enough the first time. I barely nicked the skin.

"No, no," said my instructor. *"Cut."*

I cut again, and the flesh opened, and we began scraping away the skin from the underlying tissue. That was when we began to realize that dissection was hard work, both meticulous and strenuous. You did most of it with the blunt end of a pair of scissors. Or with your fingers.

As the skin spread apart, what we first saw was the fat—a broad expanse of yellowish tissue surrounding everything we wanted to see. In the heat, the fat was slippery and runny. When we stripped away this layer, we found the muscles, enclosed in a milky, cellophane-like covering. This was the fascia. It was strong and resilient; we had trouble cutting through it to the muscle beneath. The muscles looked like what you'd expect: reddish, striated, bulging in the middle and tapering at the ends. The arteries were easy: they'd been injected with red latex. But we had no idea what

7

the nerves looked like until the instructor came over and found one for us—white, tough, cord-like.

The afternoon wore on, and took on aspects of a nightmare: everybody working, sweat dripping down our faces; the smell, pungent and indescribable; the unwillingness to wipe the sweat away because you'd only coat your face with phenol; the sudden horrified discovery that a bit of flesh has been flicked away and landed, sticking, to your face; the ghastly drabness of the room itself, bare, hot, institutional gray. It was a cheerless, exhausting experience.

Just the names we had to learn were difficult enough: superficial epigastric artery, superficial external pudendal artery, pectineal fascia, anterior superior iliac spine, ligamentum patellae. All in all, forty different structures that had to be memorized for the first day alone.

We worked until five, and then sutured the incision, squirted liquid over it to keep it moist, and left. We hadn't managed to finish the dissection, as outlined in the lab manual.

At the end of the first day, we were already behind.

Nobody could eat much at dinner. The second-year students regarded us with amusement, but we weren't making many jokes in the early days. We were all struggling too hard to handle the feelings, to do it at all.

The autumn heat wave continued, and the dissection room became extremely hot. The fat deposits melted; smells were strong; everything was greasy to the touch. Sometimes the doorknob was so greasy that we had trouble turning it when we departed at the end of the day. Even when maggots got into one cadaver, causing the instructors to run around the room with flyswatters, nobody made jokes.

It was hard work. We were just trying to do it.

The weeks passed. The heat wave continued. We were under terrific pressure to keep pace with the dissection, not to fall behind. The first anatomy exams were getting closer. Two afternoons a week, we worked in the dissection rooms. And again on weekends, if we had to catch up. We began to make sour, grim jokes.

One joke made the rounds:

A professor of anatomy addresses a woman in the class:

"Miss Jones, will you name the organ of the body that increases four times in diameter under stimulation?"

The woman becomes embarrassed, hems and haws.

"There's no need to be embarrassed, Miss Jones. The organ is the pupil of the eye—and you, my dear, are an optimist."

After the first anatomy exam, I got a letter in the mail:

Dear Mr. Crichton:

Although your performance on the recent Gross Anatomy exam was satisfactory, you were sufficiently close to the borderline that it will be to your advantage to talk to me sometime in the near future, at your convenience.

Yours sincerely,
George Erikson,
Professor of Anatomy

Panic. A cold sweat. I was shaken. Then at lunch I discovered that lots of other people had received letters, too. In fact, almost half the class. I went to see Dr. Erikson that afternoon. He didn't say much; just some encouragement, some hints on memorization. Talk to yourself, he said. Say things out loud. Pair up and quiz each other.

Pretty soon everyone in the anatomy lab was talking out loud, repeating mnemonics to help them remember.

"S 2, 3, 4, keeps your rectum off the floor." That told you where the nerves to the levator-ani muscle originate, in the second, third, and fourth sacral segments.

"Saint George Street." For the order of muscles inserting around the knee.

"The Zebra Bit My Cock." For the branches of the facial nerve: temporal, zygomatic, buccal, mandibular, cervical.

My lab partner developed a new one: "TE, TE, ON, OM." Two eyes, two ears, one nose, one mouth.

They quizzed us constantly, calling us "Doctor" even though we were first-year students. One instructor came in and threw up an X-ray of a skull. I'd never seen one before. A skull X-ray is incredibly complex.

"All right, Dr. Crichton, what would you say this is?"

He pointed to a whitish area on the film. It was near the face, and horizontal.

"The hard palate?"

"No, that's down here." He pointed to another horizontal line, a little below.

I tried again, and suddenly it came to me: "The inferior border of the orbit."

"Right."

It was a great feeling.

Then he said, "How about this?" A small, hook-shaped thing near the middle of the skull.

That was easy. "The sella turcica."

"Containing?"

"The pituitary."

"What is just lateral to it?"

"The cavernous sinus."

"Containing?"

I rattled it off: "The curving internal carotid artery, and the ocular nerves, three, four, and six, and two branches of the trigeminal nerve, the ophthalmic and the maxillary."

"And this dark space, just below?"

"The sphenoid sinus."

"And why is it dark?"

"Because it contains air."

"Right. Now then, Dr. Martin . . ." And he turned to another member of the group.

I thought, I'm getting it. I'm finally beginning to get it. I was excited. But at the same time, the pressure was building. Every day, building.

The jokes got worse. One guy wrote "Al's Body Shop" on the back of his anatomy lab coat. And the cadavers began getting names: The Jolly Green Giant, The Thin Man, King Kong.

Ours had a name, too: Lady Brett.

After two months, on a day when the instructors were out of the room, several people played football with a liver. "He's going out, he's deep in the end zone, the ball is in the air . . . and . . . touchdown!" The liver flew through the air.

A few students pretended to be horrified, but nobody

really was. We had by now dissected the legs, and the feet had been unwrapped; we had dissected the arms, the hands, and abdomen. We could see that this was a human body, a dead person laid out on the table before us. We were continuously reminded of what we were doing—we could see the form clearly. There was no way to get the necessary distance, to detach, except to be outrageous and disrespectful. There was no way to survive except to laugh.

There were certain jobs in the dissection that nobody wanted to do. Nobody wanted to cut the pelvis in half. Nobody wanted to dissect the face. Nobody wanted to inflate the eyeballs with a syringe. We portioned out these jobs, argued over them.

I managed to avoid each of these jobs.

"Okay, Crichton, but then you have to section the head."

"Okay."

"You remember, now. . . ."

"Yeah, yeah, I'll remember."

The head was in the future. I'd worry about it when I got there.

But the day finally came. They handed me the hacksaw. I realized I had made a terrible bargain. I had waited, and now I was stuck with the most overt mutilation of all, to divide the head along the midsagittal plane, to cut it in half like a melon so we could see inside, inspect the cavities, the sinuses, the passages, the vessels.

The eyes were inflated, staring at me as I cut. We had dissected the muscles around the eyes, so I couldn't close them. I just had to go through with it, and try to do it correctly.

Somewhere inside me, there was a kind of click, a shutting off, a refusal to acknowledge, in ordinary human terms, what I was doing. After that click, I was all right. I cut well. Mine was the best section in the class. People came around to admire the job I had done, because I had stayed exactly in the midline and all the sinuses were beautifully revealed.

I later learned that this shutting-off click was essential to becoming a doctor. You could not function if you were overwhelmed by what was happening. In fact, I was all too easily overwhelmed. I tended to faint—when I saw accident victims in the emergency ward, during surgery, or while drawing blood. I had to find a way to guard against what I felt.

And still later I learned that the best doctors found a middle position where they were neither overwhelmed by their feelings nor estranged from them. That was the most difficult position of all, and the precise balance—neither too detached nor too caring—was something few learned.

At the time I resented the fact that our education seemed to be as much about emotions as about the factual content of what we were learning. This emotional aspect seemed more like hazing, like a professional initiation, than education. It was a long time before I understood that how a doctor behaved was at least as important as what he knew. And certainly I did not suspect that my complaints about medicine would eventually focus almost entirely on the emotional attitudes of the practitioners, and not their scientific knowledge.

A Good Story

The first part of a student's clinical work involves interviewing patients with various diseases. The resident on the floor says, "Go see Mr. Jones in room five, he has a good story"—meaning that Mr. Jones can give a clear history for a specific disease. Off you go to find Mr. Jones, take his history, and diagnose his illness.

For a student beginning work in a hospital, there is considerable tension in interviewing patients. You're trying to act professional, as if you know what you're doing. You're trying to make the diagnosis. You're trying not to forget all the things you're supposed to ask, all the things you're supposed to check, including incidental findings. Because you don't want to come back to the resident and say, "Mr. Jones has a peptic ulcer," only to have the resident say, "That's true. But, what about his eyes?"

"His eyes?"

"Yes."

"His eyes, hmmm . . ."

"Did you check his eyes?"

"Uh . . . sure. Yes."

"Notice anything about them?"

"No . . ."

"You didn't notice his left eye is glass?"

"Oh. That."

To avoid these embarrassments, and to make the job easier, all students quickly learned certain interviewing tricks. The first trick was to get someone to tell you the diagnosis, so you wouldn't have to figure it out for yourself. Knowing the diagnosis took a lot of the pressure off an interview. If you were especially lucky, the resident himself would let it slip: "Go see Mr. Jones in room five; he has a good story of peptic ulcer."

Or you could throw yourself on the mercy of the nurses: "Where's Mr. Jones?"

"Peptic ulcer? Room five."

Then there might be relatives in the room when you arrived. They were always worth a try. "Hello, Mrs. Jones. How are you today?"

"Fine, Doctor. I was just talking with my husband about his new ulcer diet when he goes home."

And, finally, the patients generally knew their diagnoses, and they might mention it, particularly if you walked in, sat down, and said heartily, "Well, how're you feeling today, Mr. Jones?"

"Much better today."

"What have the doctors told you about your illness?"

"Just that it's a peptic ulcer."

But even if the patients didn't know their diagnoses, in a teaching hospital they had all been interviewed so many times before that you could tell how you were doing by watching their responses. If you were on the right track, they'd sigh and say, "Everybody asks me about pain after meals," or "Everybody asks me about the color of my stools." But if you were off track, they'd complain, "Why are you asking me this? Nobody else has asked this." So you often had the sense of following a well-worn path.

But even if you figured out the diagnosis, there was always an exciting uncertainty about interviewing patients. You never knew what would happen. One day the resident said, "Go see Mrs. Willis, room eight; she has a good story of hyperthyroidism."

I walked down the hallway, thinking, Hyperthyroidism, hyperthyroidism, what do I know about hyperthyroidism?

Mrs. Willis was a thin thirty-nine-year-old woman, sitting up in bed, chain-smoking. Her eyes were bulging. She was edgy and appeared unhappy. Her dark tan highlighted

14

the many slashing scars on her arms and face, presumably the result of a bad automobile accident.

I introduced myself and started to talk to her, focusing on thyroid questions. The thyroid regulates general body metabolism and it affects skin, hair, voice, temperature, weight, energy, and mood. Mrs. Willis gave me all the right answers. She couldn't gain weight no matter how much she ate. She was always hot and slept with the covers off. She had noticed that her hair was brittle. Yes, yes, yes, everybody had asked her these things. She was quick and impatient in her responses. She often seemed on the verge of tears.

I asked her about her suntan. She told me she had been staying with her sister in Alabama. It was all right because her sister's apartment was air-conditioned. She had been with her sister in Alabama for three months. Now she was back in Boston.

Why was she in the hospital?

"For my thyroid, it's too high."

What had brought her to the hospital?

A shrug. "I came and they said I had to stay. Because of my thyroid."

"How did you get the scars on your arms?"

"Those're cuts."

"Cuts?"

"From a knife, most of them. This one here's glass."

The scars seemed to be of different ages, some recent, some older.

"Yes. This one is about five years old, the others are newer."

"How did they happen?"

"My husband."

"Your husband?" I proceeded cautiously. She seemed close to tears now.

"He cuts me. When he's, you know, drinking."

"How long has this been going on, Mrs. Willis?"

"I told you: five years."

"Is that why you went to your sister's?"

"She says I should call the police."

"And have you?"

"Once. They didn't do anything. They came and told him to stop it, is all. He was *mad* after that."

And she burst into great sobs, her whole body shaking, tears streaming down her face.

I was confused. Emotional lability is characteristic of hyperthyroidism; patients frequently burst into tears. But this woman appeared to have been seriously abused by her husband. I talked to her some more. She had initially come to the hospital because of her wounds. The doctors had admitted her for hyperthyroidism, but that was clearly an excuse to get her away from her violent husband. She was safe enough in the hospital, but what would happen once she was discharged?

"Has anybody talked to you about your husband? A social worker or anybody like that?"

"No."

"Do you want somebody to talk to about your husband?"

"Yes."

I said I would arrange it, and I left, filled with outrage.

In those days, physical abuse within a family was not really acknowledged. Everyone pretended that wives and children weren't beaten. There were no laws, no government agencies, no homes, no mechanisms at all to assist these people. I felt strongly the injustice of this situation, and this woman's dangerous isolation—sitting alone in a hospital bed, waiting to be sent home to her husband, who would stab her again.

Nobody was doing anything about it. The doctors might be treating her thyroid, but nobody was dealing with the real, life-threatening problems she faced.

I went back to the resident.

"Listen, did you see Mrs. Willis's wounds?"

"Yes."

"Those are knife wounds."

"Yes. Some of them." He seemed calm.

"Well, here we are treating her hyperthyroidism and it seems to me she has a much bigger problem."

"All we can treat is her hyperthyroidism," the resident said.

"I think we can do more. We can take steps to keep her away from her husband."

"What husband?"

"Mrs. Willis's husband."

"She doesn't have a husband. What did she tell you?"

I told him the story.

"Listen," he said, "Mrs. Willis was transferred here from a private sanatorium in Alabama. Her family is well-to-do, but her husband divorced her years ago. She's been in and

16

out of institutions for a decade. All those cuts are self-inflicted."

"Oh."

The resident said, "Did you ask her whether she'd ever been in any mental institutions?"

"No."

"Well. You should have asked. She's not that crazy. She'll tell you, if you ask."

Another time, the resident said, "Go see Mr. Benson; he has a good story of duodenal ulcer."

I went to see Mr. Benson, first stopping at the foot of his bed to read his chart. This was another trick. The bedside chart contained only nurses' notes on fluid intake, things like that, but it could still be helpful. Also, it made you look professional if you came in and read the chart first.

"Ah, Mr. Benson, I see you're in your second day of recovery from surgery." Thinking that if he had had surgery for his ulcer, it must have been severe.

"Yes."

"And putting out good urine, I see."

"Yes."

"How're you feeling, any pain?"

"No."

I thought, Just two days after surgery and no pain? "Well, you're making an unusual recovery."

"No."

For the first time, I really looked at him. He was sitting in bed wearing a bathrobe, a small, precise, tense man of forty-one. He had the detached look that many postoperative patients have, when they turn their focus inward to heal. But it was different in his case, somehow.

"Well," I said. "Tell me about your ulcer."

Harry Benson spoke in a flat, depressed voice. He was an insurance adjuster from Rhode Island. He had lived with his mother all his life. She was sick and needed him to take care of her. He had never married, and had few friends outside work. He had had severe ulcer pains for the last five years. Sometimes he vomited blood. Sometimes a lot of blood. He had been in the hospital six different times for this pain and blood. He had had several transfusions for blood loss. He had had a barium swallow that showed the ulcer. The doctors told him last year that they would have to do

17

surgery if the medication didn't heal the ulcer. The bleeding continued, so he came back to the hospital and underwent surgery two days ago.

That was his story.

As the resident promised, it was a classic story, and after so much medical attention, Mr. Benson told it clearly. He even knew physicians' jargon, like "barium swallow" for an upper-GI series.

But why was he so depressed?

"Well, given your history, you must be glad to have the operation over with."

"No."

"Why not?"

"They didn't do anything."

"What do you mean?"

"They opened me up, but they didn't do anything. They didn't do the operation."

"Mr. Benson, I don't think that's right. They did an operation to remove part of the stomach."

"No. They were going to do a partial resection, but they didn't. They took one look and then closed me up again."

And he burst into tears, holding his head in his hands.

"What have they told you?"

He shook his head.

"What do you think is wrong?"

He shook his head.

"You think you have cancer?"

He nodded, still sobbing.

"Mr. Benson, I don't think you do." He had no swollen glands, no history of weight loss, no pain in other parts of his body. And I was pretty sure they wouldn't send a student to talk to somebody who had just found out he had inoperable cancer.

"Yes," he insisted. "It's carcinoma."

He was so upset I felt I had to do something immediately. "Mr. Benson, I'm going to check on this right away."

I went back to the nursing station. The resident was hanging around. I said, "You know Benson? Did they do a gastric resection?"

"No, they didn't."

"Why not?"

"When they opened him up, his blood pressure went to hell, and they decided they couldn't go through with the procedure. They just closed him up as fast as they could."

"Did anybody tell him that?"

"Sure. He knows."

"Well, he thinks he has cancer."

"Still? That's what he thought yesterday."

"Well, he still thinks it."

"He's been told specifically," the resident said, "that he does not have cancer. I told him, the chief resident told him, his own doctor told him, and the attending surgeon told him. Everybody's told him. Benson's a weird guy, you know. Lives with his mother."

I went back to Mr. Benson. I said I'd checked with the resident, and he did not have cancer.

"You don't have to kid me," he said.

"I'm not kidding you. Didn't the chief resident and the other residents come to see you yesterday?"

"Yes."

"And did they tell you you didn't have cancer?"

"Yes. But I know. They won't tell me to my face, but I know."

"How do you know?" I said.

"I heard them talking, when they thought I wasn't listening."

"And they said you have cancer?"

"Yes."

"What did they say?"

"They said I had nodes."

"What kind of nodes?"

"Aerial nodes."

There was no such thing as aerial nodes. "Aerial nodes?"

"That's what they called them."

I went back to the resident.

"I told you he was weird," the resident said. "Nobody ever said anything about nodes to him, believe me. I can't imagine how he—wait a minute." He turned to the nurses. "Who's in the bed next to Benson?"

"Mr. Levine, post-cholecystectomy."

"But he's new today. Who was in that bed yesterday?"

"Jeez, yesterday . . ."

Nobody could remember who had been in the bed the day before. But the resident was insistent; records were pulled and checked; it took another half-hour, and still more talks with Benson, before the story finally became clear.

On the day after his operation, Mr. Benson, worried that no surgery had been performed, had feigned sleep while the residents made rounds. He had listened to what they said, and he heard them discussing the patient in the next bed, who had a cardiac arrhythmia involving the sino-atrial nodes of the heart. But Mr. Benson thought they were talking about him, and his "aerial nodes." And he had been in enough hospitals to know that nodes meant cancer.

And that was why he was so sure he was dying.

Everybody went back and talked to him. And he finally understood that he did not have cancer, after all. He was very much relieved.

Everybody went away. I was alone with him. He beckoned to me. "Hey, listen, thanks," he said, and he gave me twenty dollars in cash.

"Really, that's not necessary," I said.

"No, no. Give it to that guy Eddie in room four," he said. And he explained that Eddie was a bookie, and he was placing bets for everybody on the floor.

"Put it on Fresh Air in the sixth," he said.

That was the first sign that Mr. Benson was on the road to recovery.

"Go see Mr. Carey in room six; he has a good story for glomerulonephritis," the resident said. My elation at being told the diagnosis was immediately tempered: "In fact, the guy's probably going to die."

Mr. Carey was a young man of twenty-four, sitting up in bed, playing solitaire. He seemed healthy and cheerful. In fact, he was so friendly I wondered why nobody ever seemed to go into his room.

Mr. Carey worked as a gardener on an estate outside Boston. His story was that he had had a bad sore throat a few months before; he had seen a doctor and had been given pills for a strep throat, but he hadn't taken the pills for more than a few days. Some time later he noticed swelling in his body and he felt weak. He later learned he had some disease of his kidneys. Now he had to be dialyzed on kidney machines twice a week. The doctors had said something about a kidney transplant, but he wasn't sure. Meanwhile, he waited.

That was what he was doing now, waiting.

He was my age. I talked to him with a growing sense of shock. In those days, kidney dialysis was still exotic treatment, and kidney transplantation more exotic still. The statistics were not encouraging. If the transplant worked at all, the average survival was three to five years.

I was talking to a doomed man.

I didn't know what to say. For a while we talked about the Celtics, about Bill Russell. He seemed happy to discuss sports, glad to have me there. But all I wanted to do was run from the room. I felt panicky. I felt I was suffocating. What could I *do* here? I was a medical student faced with somebody who was going to die, just as surely as the basketball season would end in a few weeks. It was inevitable. It didn't seem like there was anything I could say.

Meanwhile, he seemed so pleased to talk to me. I wondered how much he knew. Why was he so calm? Didn't he know his situation? He must know. He must be aware that he might not walk out of this hospital again. Why was he so calm?

Just talking away, sports. Baseball season. Spring training.

Eventually I couldn't stand it. I had to leave. I had to get out of that room. I said, "Well, I'm sure you'll be up and around in no time."

He looked disappointed.

"What I mean is," I said, "you're definitely on the mend, you'll probably be out of here in a week or so."

He looked *very* disappointed. I was saying the wrong things. But what should I be saying? I had no idea.

"So cheer up, I'm sure they'll be arranging for you to leave any day now. I've got to go now. Rounds, you know."

He looked at me with open contempt. "Sure. Fine."

I fled, closing the door behind me, blocking out the view of this man my own age who was close to death.

I went back to the resident. "What're you supposed to say to someone like that?"

"That's a tough one," the resident said.

"Does he know?"

"Yeah, sure."

"So what do you say?"

"I never know what to say myself. It's a bitch, isn't it?"

In retrospect, it seems inconceivable to me that in four years of medical education, nobody ever talked to us, formally or informally, about dying patients. Arguably the most important item on any medical curriculum, death was never even mentioned at the Harvard Medical School. There was no consideration given to how we might feel around a dying person—the panic, the fear, the sense of our own failure, the uncomfortable reminder of the limits of our art. There was no consideration of what a dying patient went through, what such a patient might need or want. None of this was ever discussed. We were left to learn about death on our own.

When I think back, I imagine the horrible isolation that young man must have felt, sitting day after day in a room that nobody wanted to enter. Finally some poor medical student comes in, and this young man has a brief chance to talk to another human being, and he's delighted. He would like to talk about what is really going on in his life. He's worried about what will happen to him. He wants to talk—because, unlike me, he can't avoid the realities. I can run from the room, but he can't. He is stuck with the fact of his impending death.

But instead of talking about it, instead of having the strength to stay with him, I merely mumbled platitudes and fled. It was no wonder he finally regarded me with contempt. I wasn't much of a doctor: I was far more worried about myself than about him, but he was the one who was dying.

I was still pretending that I was somehow different—that he wasn't like me—that it would never happen to me.

The Gourd Ward

Four o'clock in the morning, and I am stumbling around in the closet of my apartment in the darkness, trying to find everything I am supposed to bring, my stethoscope and my doctor's bag and my notebook and everything else, because finally the day has come when I am no longer working part-time in the hospitals, pretending to be a doctor. My clinical rotations begin today. From now on I will work every day and every other night in the hospital. I am tremendously excited and nervous and I keep dropping things in my closet. At last I have everything but I can't find my car keys. It is 5:00 a.m. I am going to be late for my first clinical rotation—neurology at the Boston City Hospital.

The old brick buildings of the Boston City looked more like a prison than anything else. I found the parking lot, and made my way through the basement corridors to the correct building.

I said "Good morning" to the elevator operator.

"Hiya, Doc," the operator said in a deep voice. His name tag read Bennie, and he was acromegalic, six and a half feet tall and easily three hundred pounds, with long arms, thick fingers, and a long nose and chin.

"I'm going to Neuro," I said.

Bennie grunted and closed the rattling cage door. The ancient elevator started up.

"Nice weather," I said.

Bennie grunted again.

"Worked here long?"

"Since I was a patient."

"That's nice."

"Did a operation on me."

"I see."

"In my head."

"Uh-huh."

"Your floor, Doc," Bennie said, opening the cage door. I went onto the floor.

The first view of the neurology ward was startling. There were patients sitting in chairs, writhing in snake-like movements known as choreoathetoid. There were patients strapped in chairs, staring forward into space, drooling. There were patients lying in beds, groaning from time to time. Distant screams of pain. It was like something from the eighteenth century. From Bedlam.

I was going to spend the next six weeks here. I headed for the nurses' station to report in. I passed a large man sitting up in bed, with the sheets pulled to his chin.

"Hey, Doc."

"Good morning," I said.

"Hey, Doc, can you help me?" Just to make sure I did, he gripped my arm powerfully. He was a very large man; he had hands like slabs of meat. Beneath a grizzled crew cut, his face was scarred. He looked dangerous. He glared at me.

"Nobody's helping me around this joint," he said.

"Gee," I said.

"Will you help me, Doc?"

"Sure," I said. "What's the problem?"

"Take my shoes off for me."

He nodded toward the foot of the bed, where his feet stuck up under the sheets. I wondered why he was wearing shoes in bed, but he was so big and fierce, it didn't seem worth asking.

"No problem," I said.

He released my arm, and I walked to the foot of the bed. I lifted up the sheet.

I saw two large, bare feet. Ten toes—or actually nine,

24

because one big toe was missing. There was just a dark stump.

I looked back at the man's face. He was watching me carefully, glowering. "Go ahead," he said.

"What did you want me to do again?" I asked.

"Take off my shoes."

"Are you wearing shoes?"

"You can see 'em right in front of you!" he shouted angrily.

I pulled the sheet back, so he could see his own bare feet. But he just nodded. "Well, go ahead!"

"You mean these shoes here?" I pointed to his bare feet.

"Yeah. The shoes on my feet. What are you, blind?"

"No," I said. "Tell me, what kind of shoes are these?"

"Just take 'em off!"

He seemed so volatile. I had no idea what was wrong with him, or how to proceed. I decided I would go along with him.

I pantomimed taking his shoes off.

"*Jesus!*" he shouted, groaning.

"What's the matter?"

"Don't you know *nothing?* Unlace 'em first!"

"Oh. Sorry." I pretended to unlace the shoes. "Better?"

"Yeah. Jesus."

I pretended to remove the first shoe, and then the second. He sighed, and wiggled his toes.

"Oh, that's better. Thanks a lot, Doc."

"Don't mention it." I was eager to get away. I started off to the nursing station.

"Hey! Not so fast." He grabbed me again. "Where do you think you're going?"

"To the nursing station."

"With *my* shoes?"

"Sorry."

"Sorry, hell! I wasn't born yesterday. You leave 'em right here!"

"Okay. There, is that okay?"

"Gotta watch you guys every minute." Then his expression abruptly changed. He looked down at the sheets. He became panicky, frightened.

"Hey, Doc. Can you help me?"

"What is it now?"

"Just get that spider off the sheet, okay? Both them spiders. You see 'em there."

25

"Have you been seeing spiders?"

"Oh yeah, lots of 'em. Especially last night—they're all over the walls."

He was an alcoholic in the midst of the DTs. I said, "I gotta go to the nursing station."

He grabbed my arm again, and he pulled his face close to mine. *"I'm not touching those spiders any more!"*

"Good idea," I said. "I'll be back later."

He released me. I went to the nursing station. There were some nurses and a pinched-faced man of thirty-one who was incredibly turned out, sharp creases in his trousers and jacket, pressed tie, immaculate haircut. He glanced at his watch. "Dr. Crichton? Or should I say, *Mr.* Crichton? I'm Donald Rogers, the visiting chief resident in neurology, and you're late. When I say I want you here at six, I mean six and not six-oh-three. Is that understood, mister?"

"Yes sir," I said.

That was how my rotation in neurology began.

It never got better.

Clinical neurology is basically a diagnostic specialty, since relatively few severe neurological disorders can be treated. The clinical neuro ward at the Boston City reflected that depressing state of affairs; in essence, cases were admitted simply so the young doctors could see them. The thirty-seven patients on the floor all had different diseases. The staff never admitted a patient to the floor if there was already one with the same disease. It wasn't a hospital ward—it was a museum. Most people referred to it as the Squash Court, or the Gourd Ward.

But we pretended it was a normal hospital floor with treatable patients. We did all the regular hospital things. We made rounds, we drew bloods, we ordered consults and diagnostic tests. We carried out the charade with great precision, even though there was little we could do for anybody.

Besides myself as the sole medical student, there was an intern named Bill Levine from New York, a first-year resident named Tom Perkins, and Dr. Rogers, the visiting chief resident. He was a Southerner from Duke who did everything by the book. Rogers was always immaculately turned out; his "presentation," as he called it, was awe-inspiring.

26

One day Levine, who loathed Rogers, asked him about his ties.

"You like these ties?" Rogers asked, in a soft Southern accent.

"Well, I was wondering how you managed to keep them so smooth and unwrinkled, Don."

"My wife does that. She irons them."

"Does she?"

"Yes. She gets up with me at five in the morning, and after I have dressed and tied my tie, she irons it for me. While I am wearing it. She does that."

"No kidding," Levine said.

"Yes, she's okay," Rogers said. "Only once she scorched my shirt, and then I had to get dressed all over again. But she's never done *that* again."

"No, I'll bet," Levine said.

"No. She learned her lesson that time," Rogers said, chuckling.

Rogers was a bit of a sadist. He kept a series of straight pins in the lapel of his jacket, near the buttonhole. On rounds he liked to stick these pins into the patients, "to check their responses." There was a kind of insane pretense in all this. None of the patients were getting any better. None of them were changing at all, from day to day or week to week, except for the two who had inoperable brain tumors. They were slowly dying. But no one else was changing at all. The patients were indigent, extremely ill patients who were shuttled from one state institution to another. As we made rounds each morning, there wasn't really that much to discuss. But Rogers stuck pins into them anyway.

Levine only had to spend a month of his internship rotation on the ward. Levine was a heavyset, smiling guy of twenty-five who was almost bald. A warmhearted soul, he despised Rogers and the ward. He expressed his distaste by lighting a joint every morning before rounds.

I didn't find out about this until the second day. I passed by the men's room, smelled the smoke, and went inside. "Bill, what're you doing?"

"Having a toke," he said, sucking in his breath. He passed the joint to Perkins, the resident, who took a long drag, then held it out to me.

I pushed it away. "Are you kidding? What are you doing?" It was six-thirty in the morning.

"Hey. Suit yourself."

"You mean you guys are *stoned on rounds?*"

"Why not? Nobody can tell."

"Sure they can."

"You couldn't tell, yesterday. And you think Pinhead can tell?" Pinhead was what Levine called Rogers.

"Hey, relax," Levine said, taking a deep drag. "Nobody cares. Half the nurses are loaded, too. Come on. This is great stuff. You know where we get it? Bennie."

"Bennie?"

"Bennie. You know, in the elevator."

It was the medical student's job to draw bloods from the patients daily. Every morning I would show up at 6:00 a.m. and go to the nursing station, and the night resident would read off the list of bloods to be drawn for the day. So many red tops from Mr. Roberti, a red and a blue from Mr. Jackson, a pink and a blue from Mrs. Harrelson, and so on. I had to draw about twenty tubes of blood in half an hour, to be ready for morning rounds at six-thirty.

The only trouble was, this was my first clinical rotation and I hadn't ever really drawn blood before. And I tended to pass out at the sight of blood.

In practice, I'd go to my first patient, put on the tourniquet, get the vein to puff up, and try to get the needle in without passing out. Then, when the blood gushed, I'd stick on the vacutainer tubes and get the required number of tubes, breathing deeply. By this time I would be very dizzy. I would quickly finish up, pull out the needle, slap a cotton ball on the elbow, dash to the nearest window, throw it open, and hang my head out in the January air while the patients yelled and shouted at me about the cold.

When I felt okay again, I'd go on to the next patient.

I couldn't do twenty patients in half an hour. I was lucky to do three patients in half an hour.

Fortunately, I got help. The first day, I went up to a huge black man named Steve Jackson. He could tell I was nervous.

"Hey, man, what're you doing?"

"Drawing blood, Mr. Jackson."

"You know what you're doing, man?"

"Sure, I know what I'm doing."

"Then how come your hands are shaking?"

"Oh, that . . . I don't know."

"You ever draw blood before?"

"Sure, no problem."

" 'Cause I don't want nobody fucking with my veins, man." And with that, he snatched the needle out of my hands. "What you want, man?" he said to me.

"Some blood."

"I mean, what? What tubes?"

"Oh. Red top and a blue top."

"Gimme the tubes, come back later, you got it?"

And he put the tourniquet in his teeth, tied off his arm, and proceeded to draw the blood from himself. Now I understood: Jackson was an addict and didn't want anybody poking around in his veins. So from then on, every morning I'd just drop the stuff off at his bed. "Yellow and a blue top today, Steve."

"You got it, Mike."

And I'd go on to the next patient.

The patient alongside Steve was unconscious most of the time. Steve watched me fumble to get the blood, and I guess it offended his sense of finesse. So he said he'd draw blood from himself and from Hennessey, too.

The nurses took pity on me, and they helped out and drew a couple of tubes for me. And Levine, if he had been on call the night before, would draw a couple of tubes for me. And as the days passed, I didn't have to hang my head out the window quite so long each time. So, with everybody's help, I was eventually able to get the job finished by the start of rounds.

"Nice to see you on time for once, *Mr.* Crichton. Seems you make a major production out of drawing a little blood."

I started to hate Rogers, too.

In this way, the weeks dragged on—the medical student passing out whenever he drew blood, the residents stoned on rounds, and Rogers sticking pins in everybody while we looked away. And always the patients drooling and writhing in the corners, the alcoholics brushing off invisible ants and spiders. It was a kind of loony nightmare, and it took its toll.

Finally the house staff had a party one night, and everybody got drunk on lab alcohol. Around midnight, we decided it would be amusing to draw bloods on ourselves, and send them in for liver-function tests. We used patient names, and sent them off.

The next morning, the nurses were puzzled. "I don't get it. Mr. Hennessey has sky-high LFTs. So does Mr. Jackson. And their blood alcohols—this can't be right. Who ordered these tests, anyway? It's not in the books."

"Oh, *those* tests," Levine said, very pink-eyed. "I remember. I'll take those." And he passed the slips around to us. It turned out we all had evidence of acute liver damage. And we certainly had roaring hangovers.

"Ready for rounds?" Rogers said briskly. He was greeted with a chorus of groans. "Come, come, we're already four minutes late." We started off.

Rogers was in an unusually cheerful mood. He stuck lots of pins into people. Finally he came to Mrs. Lewis. In the ward, Mrs. Lewis's bed was always curtained off, because this elderly woman was semicomatose and incontinent, and from time to time she threw her excrement in spastic movements. There was always a slight feeling of danger when we went up to Mrs. Lewis's bed. And this morning, with hangovers, we weren't looking forward to it.

But her bed was clean, and there was no smell. Mrs. Lewis seemed to be sleeping.

"She seems to be sleeping," Rogers said. "Let's just see how responsive she is today." And he stuck a pin in her.

The poor comatose woman winced.

"Hmmm, there seems to be a little response," Rogers said. He put his pins back in his lapel and pressed his thumb over the bony ridge just below Mrs. Lewis's eyebrow. He pressed hard.

"This is a classic way to elicit a pain response," he explained.

Mrs. Lewis twisted her body in pain, and her hand went beneath her buttocks. And quickly she slapped a handful of her own feces all over Rogers's shirt and pressed tie. Then she collapsed back on the bed.

"Dear," Rogers said, turning white.

"That's a shame," Levine said, biting his lip.

"She obviously doesn't know what she's doing," Perkins said, shaking his head.

"Mr. Crichton, see that she's cleaned up. I'm going to try and change. But I don't have a change of clothes at the hospital. I may have to go home."

30

"Yes sir," I said.

So I helped clean up Mrs. Lewis, and I blessed her. And not long after that, I rotated off the neurology service, and went on to psychiatry, where I hoped things would be better.

The Girl Who
Seduced Everybody

Three medical students at a time were assigned a psychiatry
rotation on the wards of the Massachusetts General Hospital. It was a communal-living ward: fifteen psychiatric patients slept and ate in a dormitory setting for six weeks.
After six weeks, the staff made a diagnosis and recom-
mended further therapy for each patient.

The resident explained the whole procedure. As students,
we would each be assigned one patient to interview over six
weeks. We would then make a report to the staff, and
participate in the diagnosis. Other physicians would be interviewing the patients, too, but we would see them more
often than anyone else, and our responsibilities were therefore to be taken seriously.

When we arrived on the floor, the patients were in the
midst of a communal meeting. The resident couldn't inter-
rupt the meeting, but we stood outside the room while he
pointed out our patients. Ellen's patient was a heavyset
woman in her fifties who wore garish clothes and makeup.
This woman had had an affair with a doctor who gave her
amphetamines, and she was now severely depressed. Bob
was assigned a thin, scholarly-looking man of fifty who had
been in Dachau and who now imagined cardiac problems.

I was assigned a tall, strikingly beautiful girl of twenty with short blond hair and a miniskirt. She sat in a rocking chair, her long legs curled under her, looking very calm and composed. She looked like a college student.

"What's her problem?" I said.

"Karen," he said, "has successfully seduced every man she has ever met."

During the psychiatry rotation, you saw your patient three times a week. You also saw a training analyst twice a week, to discuss your case and your feelings about it.

Robert Geller was my training analyst. Dr. Geller was a middle-aged man who had a beard and favored bright striped shirts. His manner was very quick and direct.

Dr. Geller asked me what I hoped to get out of my psychiatry rotation, and I said that I was very interested in psychiatry, that it was something I thought I might end up doing. He said that was fine. He seemed a neutral, balanced person.

"So, do you know anything about your patient?"

Yes, I did. I explained I hadn't had a chance to talk to her yet, that I had only just seen her in the room, a twenty-year-old girl, sitting in the rocking chair.

"And?"

She seemed nice. Pretty. She certainly didn't seem like a psychiatric case.

"Then what's she doing there?"

Well, the resident told me that she had successfully seduced every man she had ever met.

"What did he mean by that?"

I hadn't asked.

"Really? *I* would have asked," Dr. Geller said.

I explained I just hadn't thought to ask; I was trying to absorb everything, just seeing her and so on.

"And how do you feel about seeing her?"

"I don't know," I said.

"You don't know?"

"No."

"You said she was beautiful   "

"Attractive, yes."

"What did you think about having her as your patient?"

"I guess I wondered if I could handle her."

"Handle her . . ."

This was a psychiatrist's trick, repeating your last phrase to keep you talking.

"Yes," I said. "I wondered if I would be able to handle her case."

"Why shouldn't you be able to handle her?"

"I don't know."

"Well, just say whatever comes to mind."

This was another psychiatrist's trick: I was immediately on my guard.

"Nothing comes to mind," I said.

Dr. Geller gave me a funny look.

"Well," he said, "are you afraid you won't be bright enough to deal with her?"

"Oh no."

"No problem there. With brightness."

"No."

"Are you afraid you don't have enough knowledge to help her?"

"No . . ."

"Are you afraid you're so busy you won't be able to devote enough time to her?"

"No, no . . ."

"Then what?"

I shrugged. "I don't know."

There was a pause.

"Are you afraid you're going to fuck her?"

I was profoundly shocked. The statement was so coarse and direct. I didn't know how he could even imagine such a thing. My skull was ringing, as if I had been struck. I shook my head to clear it.

"Oh no, no, no, nothing like that."

"You're sure it's not that?"

"Yes. Sure."

"How do you know it's not that?"

"Well, I mean, I'm married."

"So?"

"And I'm a doctor."

"A lot of doctors fuck their patients. Haven't you heard?"

"I don't believe in that," I said.

"Why not?"

"I believe that when patients come to you, they are in a dependent state, they look up to a doctor, because they want help and they are frightened. And they deserve to be

34

treated, and not have their dependencies exploited by the doctor. They deserve to get what they came for."

I believed all this very strongly.

"Maybe she came to get fucked by her doctor."

"Well," I said.

"Maybe that's what she needs to get better."

I began to feel annoyed. I could see where this was heading. "Are you saying you think that I want to, uh, have sex with her?"

"I don't know. You tell me."

"No," I said. "I don't."

"Then what are you worried about?"

"I'm not worried about anything."

"You just told me you weren't sure you could handle her."

"Well, I meant . . . in general, I wasn't sure."

"Listen, it's okay with me if you want to fuck her. Just don't do it."

"I won't."

"Good. How old are you?"

"Twenty-four."

"How long have you been married?"

"Two years."

"Happy?"

"Sure."

"Sex life okay?"

"Sure. Great."

"So you wouldn't be tempted in the first place."

"How do you mean?"

"I mean, since your marriage is happy and your sex life is good, you wouldn't be tempted by this girl in the first place."

"Well, I mean . . . No, of course not."

"She's pretty?"

"Yes."

"Sexy?"

"I guess."

"I bet she knows how to maneuver men."

"Probably."

"I bet she knows just what to say and do, to wrap men around her little finger."

"Well, I'm sure I can handle it," I said.

"I'm glad to hear that," Dr. Geller said. "Because that's going to be your job."

"How do you mean?"

"The only way this girl knows how to relate to men is sexually. She gets everything—friendship, warmth, comfort, reassurance—from the sexual act. That's not a very good life strategy. She needs to learn there are other ways of relating to men, that she can get the warmth and approval she wants from a man without having sex with him. She's probably never had that experience before. You will be her first experience."

"Yes."

"As long as you don't end up fucking her."

"No. I won't."

"I hope not. Good luck with her. Let me know how things go."

My conversation with Dr. Geller struck me as helpful. Although he obviously had some fixed idea I wanted to have sex with this girl, that didn't worry me in the least. I was quite confident that I wouldn't. I knew that, in becoming a doctor, I was assuming special responsibilities. This was the first of them.

In fact, far from worrying about sexual temptation, I was eager to see Karen, and begin our work together. I went immediately back to the floor and introduced myself to her.

She was very tall. She came up to my shoulder when we stood side by side. She had a lean, athletic body, and clear green eyes that looked at me steadily. "You're my doctor?"

"Yes," I said. "I'm Dr. Crichton."

"You're very tall." She moved closer, until her forehead touched my shoulder.

"Yes."

"I like tall guys."

"That's good." I stepped back a little. That seemed to amuse her.

"Are you *really* my doctor?"

"Yes. Why are you smiling?"

"You look too young to be a doctor. Are you sure you're not just a medical student or something?"

"I'm your doctor, believe me."

"What kind of a name is Crichton?"

"It's Scottish."

"I'm Scottish, too. What's your first name?"

"Michael."

"Is that what they call you? Michael or Mike?"

"Michael."

"Can I call you 'Michael'?"

" 'Dr. Crichton' would be better."

She pouted. "Why? Why are you so formal?"

"We're here to work together, Karen, and I think we should keep that relationship in mind."

"What does that have to do with what I call you? 'Dr. Crichton.' Ugh. I hate 'Dr. Crichton.' "

"I just think it's better, is all."

I found myself nervous, standing next to her this way. Her physical presence was very strong. It left me a little shaky. As part of the workup, I had to begin by drawing bloods for routine chemistries, so I took her into the little examining room. We were alone.

"Aren't you going to close the door?"

"No."

"Why not?"

"It's fine the way it is."

"Afraid to be alone with me?"

"What makes you say that?" I asked. I felt very clever and psychiatric, saying that. Giving her a question back.

"Do I have to take off my clothes?"

"That won't be necessary."

"Really? But don't you have to examine me? My body and everything?"

"Just draw some blood."

She ran her fingers across the examining couch. "Mind if I lie down on this bed?"

"Go ahead."

Having finished my neurology rotation, I was more relaxed about drawing bloods. But right now my hands were shaking. She was sure to notice.

She lay back on the examining table and stretched like a cat. "You want me on my stomach or my back?"

"On your back is fine."

"This couch is too short; I have to put my legs up." Her miniskirt slid around her hips.

"Whatever's comfortable," I said.

"Is it going to hurt?" she asked, wide-eyed.

"No, not at all."

"Why are you shaking, Dr. Crichton?"

"I'm not."

"Yes, you are. Do I make you nervous?"

"No."

"Not even a little?" She was smiling, laughing at me.

"You're a beautiful girl, Karen; you'd make anybody nervous."

She smiled with pleasure. "You think so?"

"Of course."

She seemed reassured by this, and I felt calmer as well. It didn't hurt anything, I thought, to tell her she was attractive.

I started drawing the bloods. She watched the needle, watched the tubes fill. She had a calm gaze, a steady way of looking at things.

"Are you single?"

"No, I'm married."

"You tell your wife everything you do?"

"No."

"Men never do," she said, laughing. It was a sarcastic, knowing laugh.

"My wife is in graduate school," I said. "I sometimes don't see her for days at a time."

"Are you going to tell her about me?"

"What goes on between you and me is confidential," I said.

"So you won't tell her?"

"No."

"*Good.*" She licked her lips.

I lived in an apartment on Maple Avenue in Cambridge. I had known my wife since high school. She was studying child psychology at Brandeis. One block away, my wife's college roommate lived with her husband; they were both graduate students at Harvard. A block beyond that lived another friend and her husband, with whom I used to play basketball in high school. The six of us, all stable, all married, all in school, all connected in the past, spent a lot of time together. The relationships went way back. It was a small, complete world.

My wife liked to cook. She was cooking while we talked. "Is this girl in school?"

"Yes. Junior at BU. Says she wants to be a lawyer."

"Smart?"

"Seems to be."

38

"And she's your patient?"

"Yes."

"What's her problem?"

"She has trouble relating to men."

"And what are you supposed to do?"

"Interview her. Find out what's wrong. Write a paper at the end."

"Long paper?"

"Five pages."

"That's not too bad," my wife said.

The resident told me I could meet with my patient twice a week, or three times a week, if I felt that was necessary. I felt three times a week would be required. There was an interview room that you booked.

I asked Karen how she had come to be admitted to the hospital. She told me she had had a bad trip on LSD in her school dorm; the campus police had brought her in. "But I don't know why they made me stay here. I mean, it was no big deal, just a bad trip."

I made a mental note to check with the BU campus authorities, and then asked her about her background, before college.

Karen spoke freely. She had grown up in a small coastal town in Maine. Her father was a salesman; he fooled around with a lot of women; he had always ignored her. Her father didn't like it when she took up with Ed, just because he was a Hell's Angel. Her father was very angry when she became pregnant by Ed at fourteen. He made her have the baby. She gave the baby up for adoption. Her father never liked her other boyfriends, either. For example, he didn't like Tod, the rich kid who made her pregnant when she was sixteen. He wanted her to have that baby, too, but instead she had a miscarriage. She laughed. "In Puerto Rico," she said.

"You had an abortion?"

"Tod's rich. And he didn't want *his* father to find out." She laughed. "You probably think I'm crazy."

"Not at all."

"You smoke so much when we're together."

"Do I?"

"Yes. You're chain-smoking. Am I making you nervous?"

"Not that I'm aware."

"That's good. I don't want to make you nervous. I appreciate your helping me."

She wore miniskirts all the time. She liked to curl herself in chairs. She would wait for just the right moment, then curl her body and show me her pink underwear. I had to quickly look away, but when my eyes met hers again, I saw that she was laughing at me.

"So? Did you make her pregnant yet?"

"No," I said to Dr. Geller.

"Tell me how it's going."

I told him what I knew so far. Her story sounded terrible. I interpreted it as a cry from a young girl for the attention of her father, a man who obviously wasn't capable of giving her the love and care she required. Instead he was harsh and punitive. Two pregnancies, then dismissed, sent off to various foster homes . . . It was amazing, I felt, that Karen had done as well as she had—had gotten into college and so forth.

"Why are you so protective of her?"

"I'm not."

"Dad's a bastard and she's a victim?"

"Well. Isn't she?"

"How does Karen relate to you?"

"She seems very open."

"Ask about her mother."

Karen didn't have much to say about her mother. Her mother was a retired schoolteacher, crippled in one leg from an automobile accident. Her mother was a weak person who let her father walk all over her, abuse her. And her mother didn't stand up for Karen, even when she knew—

She fell silent and stared out the window.

"Knew what?" I said.

She shook her head, continued to stare out the window.

"Knew what?" I said.

She sighed. "About my father."

"What about your father?"

"My father used to fool around with me."

"How do you mean?"

"He used to, you know, fool around with me. He told me not to tell my mother."

"You mean your father had intercourse with you?"

She smiled. "You're so *formal.*"

We had been talking about her father for a week. "Why didn't you tell me this before?"

"I don't know. I thought you would be mad at me."

She curled in the chair again, in her kittenish way. This time beneath the miniskirt she wore no underwear at all.

"How does she relate to you?" Dr. Geller said.

"I would say, seductive."

"How?"

"Well, she usually doesn't wear underwear under her miniskirts. And one day she wanted to come to our session in her nightgown."

"What did you do?"

"I made her go back to her room and change."

"Why?"

"I thought it was better."

"Why?"

"I'm trying to control her flirtatiousness."

"Why?"

"Well, I still have a lot to find out about her."

"What don't you know?"

After the second pregnancy, her mother found out that Karen had been having sex with her father. Her father then decided that Karen must go to a foster home. Karen lasted only six weeks at the first one.

"Why?"

The guy had a problem. He couldn't keep his hands off her.

"And then?"

Another foster home. This time the woman threw her out, because she saw what was developing between Karen and the husband.

"And then?"

A minister and his family. She lived with them for almost a year. He was a very strict man, a very pure man, and he told her that she should stop it, that he would never be tempted by her.

"And?"

"He lied." She shrugged. "One day his wife came home early and caught us. But by then it was time for me to go to college anyway."

She found college boring, she said. It was so stuffy. She got good grades even though she cut most of her classes. She liked to take trips, to go skiing, or to go to New York. Anywhere, just to get away. School was so boring.

"Did you talk to those people at school?" she said. "The administration people?"

"No, why?"

"Just wondered."

"Should I?"

"I don't care. They don't know anything about me, anyway."

I interviewed the mother, a bland, worn woman of fifty. She had swollen ankles, she kept crossing and uncrossing them. Helen was upset to learn that Karen was in the hospital for a mental problem. She had worried about Karen for a long time. Karen had been such a difficult child to bring up. Helen had hoped that once she was in college she would be all right, but obviously she wasn't.

I asked about Karen's pregnancies. Helen was vague. She couldn't really remember much about them. I asked about trouble between Karen and her father. Helen said they had never gotten along. I asked about improprieties. Helen said, Like what? I asked about sexual activities of any kind.

"Did Karen tell you that?" Helen said. "She is *such a little liar.*"

"It isn't true?"

"I don't know how she could say that."

"It isn't true?"

"Of course it isn't true. Dear God, what kind of people do you think we are?"

"Then why did you send her to foster homes?"

"Because she was still seeing those boys, that's why. We had to get her away from those boys. So she told you that about Henry? And I'll bet you believed her. Men always believe whatever she says."

* * *

"Well, what did you *expect* my mother to say?" Karen said. "You think she'll admit *that?*"

Then she said she wanted a pass to leave the hospital for the following weekend, to go back to school for Saturday and Sunday. There was a party she wanted to attend.

I said no.

"Why shouldn't she get a pass?" Dr. Geller said.

"I just don't think it's a good idea."

"What's wrong? Think she's dangerous? She'll commit suicide?"

"No."

"You think she'll get laid?"

"Probably."

"What's wrong with that?"

"Nothing," I said. "She can do whatever she wants. I don't care."

"So let her leave."

"I'm just concerned about my responsibility."

"Your responsibility is to make a diagnosis, not to run her life."

"I'm not trying to run her life."

"Good. Because you can't, you know."

"I know."

I gave her a pass. All weekend I thought about her. Wondered where she was, wondered what she was doing. I spent some time at my apartment, but my thoughts were elsewhere. Karen's life seemed dangerous; she lived on the edge, in a way that was unfamiliar to me. I had always been so safe, so cautious in my own life. Here was somebody who just did what she wanted to do, said whatever she felt like saying, acted the way she wanted to act.

I was beginning to have dreams about her. Her eyes. Her legs.

"I think I'm a little attracted to her, if you want to know the truth."

"Really?" Dr. Geller said.

"Yeah. I'm a little preoccupied with her and so on."

"Dreams?"

"Sometimes."

"Sexual dreams?"

"Sometimes."

"I imagine I would, too. She must be pretty damn attractive. And she's bright, you say. You like her intelligence."

"Yes, she's bright."

"Nice body, nice young girl, nice legs, and so on."

"Yes."

"So it's natural to be attracted. The thing is, what are you going to do about it?"

"Nothing."

"Perhaps you want to talk to her about your feelings?"

"Why would I do that? She's the patient."

"That's true," Dr. Geller said.

There was a long silence. He waited. I knew from past experience he could wait a long time.

"But what?" I said.

"But if she's behaving seductively toward you, perhaps you could discuss her behavior and how it is making you feel. If you brought it to her awareness, she would have a chance to change it."

"Maybe she wouldn't."

"How do you know?"

I felt suddenly confused. "I don't think that's a good idea. Discussing my feelings."

"Merely a suggestion," he said.

Karen was cheerful and evasive after her weekend off. She had seen some friends. She had gone to some parties. I felt irritable.

"Why?" she said. "Does it matter?"

"To what?"

"To your research paper about me, or whatever you're doing."

"Who said I'm doing a research paper?"

"Ellen told Margie that all the students are doing research papers." Margie was the depressed woman who had been seduced by her doctor. "What are you going to write about *me?*" Karen said.

At home, I had dinner with my wife, our friends. The topic of divorce came up. Somebody Marvin knew was getting a divorce, another couple in graduate school. A little chill passed around the table, a flicker of the candles.

44

I started to think. What if I got divorced? I would be a working doctor. What women would I meet? I would meet my patients, mostly. I would be busy; I wouldn't have much time for a social life outside my work. So the women I met would be my patients.

But even if I was divorced, I couldn't go out with patients. I certainly couldn't have sex with patients. So how would I handle it, exactly? How would I find women to go out with?

And, for that matter, how would I handle my practice, where women might come in whom I found exciting? What was I going to do? The priestly dedication to medicine was fine in the abstract. But when it came to actual limbs, sexy limbs, and beautiful bodies on the examining table, and breasts and necks and girls who didn't wear underwear—

She probably has a disease, I consoled myself. But it wasn't much consolation.

"Yes," I told Dr. Geller. "I am having trouble with my feelings."

"You want her, huh?"

"Sometimes."

"Only sometimes?"

"Listen, I have this thing under control."

"I'm not saying you don't. What about your marriage?"

"My marriage isn't always that great."

"Nobody's is. But sexually?"

"Not that great. Not all the time."

"So you think about Karen?"

"Yeah."

"Listen," Dr. Geller said. "That's fine. In fact, it's normal."

"It is?"

"Sure. Think about her all you want. Just don't fuck her."

"I'm not going to fuck her."

"Great. Glad to hear it."

I diligently assembled facts, dates, information of all sorts. I wrote a twenty-page report, four times as long as required. I presented it to the entire psychiatric staff. My basic picture was of a seriously abused child who had grown

45

up without proper supports and encouragement but who was valiantly struggling to keep her head above water, and who was probably going to make it. Karen had intelligence and strength, and while her obstacles were formidable, I believed she would pull through in the end.

The staff complimented me on my fine and unusually detailed report. But they viewed Karen's case much more seriously. This girl had a prior suicide attempt a year before, while at college. This attempt, unknown to me, had required dialysis at another Boston hospital for barbiturate overdose. Karen had severe problems of self-worth. She had taken a great many psychedelic drugs. She was possibly even borderline schizophrenic. Her intelligence was a hindrance to contacting her true feelings. Her manipulative exterior kept her from feeling her pain. Her prognosis was not good. The chances were better than fifty-fifty that she would commit suicide within the next five years.

I was shocked. I wanted to tell them that they were wrong, that their detachment and their statistics were wrong. I wanted to shake them from their complacency. We were talking about a human life here, a human life. If they really thought Karen was going to die, they should help her. They should prevent her senseless death.

As calmly as I could, I said something to that effect.

The chief of service puffed on his pipe. "The truth is, there's not much we *can* do for her." He paused. "You've seen how she is."

I nodded.

"You've seen how she relates."

I nodded.

"So you are aware of the degree to which she in fact causes the unfortunate events of her life. And the likelihood that she will continue to cause them in the future."

I nodded, and realized. She had seduced me after all.

The chief of service spread his hands. "Well, then. It's hard. But that's the way it is."

She was cheerful, waiting for me in the conference room.

"Did you have the meeting?"

"Yes."

"And what did they say about me?" She was as eager as a child.

"The chief resident will be talking to you."

46

"You tell me now."

"Karen, why didn't you tell me about the drug overdose?"

"What drug overdose?"

"The one last year, when you were at college."

"It wasn't any big deal."

"I think it was."

"I figured you already knew about it. I thought when you called the college they told you about it."

"No," I said, "I didn't call."

"Anyway," she said, shrugging it off, "what did they say about me in the meeting?"

"Well," I said, "they think you need further therapy. They think it's very important that you get it."

"Will you be giving me my therapy?"

"No. I'm afraid my six weeks are up. I'm going on to another rotation starting Monday."

"You are?" She seemed shocked.

"Yes. Remember? I told you last week."

"I don't remember."

"Yes."

"Well, will I at least see you again?"

"Probably not. I don't think so."

"So this is it?" Tears welled in her eyes.

"Yes."

"Really?"

"Yes."

She stood up and looked at me with her steady eyes. The tears, if they had ever been there, were gone. "Okay, good-bye," she said, and marched straight past me, out of the room, and slammed the door.

I never saw her again. I never heard what happened to her. I never tried to find out.

A Day at the BLI

Five teaching hospitals surrounded the Harvard Medical School, but in the eyes of the students, the least interesting was then the Boston Lying In Hospital. Over the years the other hospitals had decided not to do obstetrics, so all deliveries were now done at the BLI: a whole hospital full of babies being born.

Most of my fellow students were unexcited by obstetrics, but I was fascinated at the prospect of seeing a delivery, and even doing one or two.

On my first day at the BLI, I stepped into a world that reminded me of nothing so much as Dante's *Inferno*. Room after room filled with women, all twisting and writhing in rubber-sheeted beds like oversized baby bassinets, all shrieking at the top of their lungs in the most hideous agony. I was appalled. It was like something from the nineteenth century. From the eighteenth century.

"Yeah, well, these women are all on scope," the resident said. "They all insist on it. They come in the door and, the very first thing, they go, Give me the shot. So we scope 'em."

Scopolamine, famed in World War II movies as truth serum, was a soporific drug. But, as the resident explained, it wasn't a painkiller at all.

"That's why they're screaming so much. Scope's not a painkiller."

"Then what's the point?"

"The point is, it's an amnesiac. They're having the pain, but they won't remember any of it when it's over."

And a good thing, I thought, watching them twist and scream and shriek. Many of them had to be tied down to the bed with restraining straps.

"You gotta watch how you tie 'em down, because you don't want 'em waking up with bruises on their wrists. But if you don't tie 'em down, they'll bang around and hurt themselves, pull out their IVs, all sorts of stuff."

I felt embarrassed for these women. Many were wealthy and elegant: carefully applied makeup, coiffed hair, manicured nails. Now they were tied down to a rubber hamper and they were swearing and screaming, utterly out of control. I felt like an intruder, seeing something I should not see.

"Why do you do this?" I asked.

"They insist on it. You tell 'em this is what happens, you show 'em, even—they go, I don't care, give me the shot."

I kept looking at the nurses, trying to see how they felt about it. They were women, too. But the nurses were blank-faced, neutral. As far as they were concerned, this was how it was.

"Isn't there another way?"

"Oh sure," the resident said.

Down the hall were more rooms. No rubber bassinets here, just ordinary hospital beds with women panting and groaning, with the occasional cry of pain. Most of the beds had IV lines hanging from them.

"Now, here, these women get an epidural, a slow spinal drip, for pain. And they maybe get a little Demerol, and they just work with the pain."

It seemed much better here, much more human.

"Yeah. Whatever," the resident said.

There were more rooms down the hall.

"Down there," the resident said, "is where we have the girls from the Home."

"The Home?"

"The unwed mothers," he said, and named the home where they came from.

We walked down there.

"You gotta keep an eye on the nurses here," he said. "If

49

you're not careful, they won't give the girls anything for pain at all. Sometimes they let 'em get all the way to the delivery room with nothing at all. Sort of punishment for their sins."

I expressed disbelief. I was back in Dante's hell.

"Yeah, well, it's Boston," the resident said.

We went into this room. It was incredibly tranquil. Four or five teenage girls, panting and breathing and counting contractions. Only one nurse to attend them, and she was out of the room a lot. Some of the girls were having a great deal of pain, and they looked frightened, to be alone, experiencing this pain. I stayed in the room with them.

One girl, named Debbie, was red-haired and pretty. She was glad for some company and told me all about the Home, and the nuns who ran it. Debbie wasn't Catholic, but her family had been angry when she got pregnant. They had taken her to the Home five months earlier. They hadn't come to see her since. A few friends from school came to visit, though not many. Her sister wrote letters, but said her father wouldn't let anyone from the family visit Debbie until it was over.

Debbie said the nuns were okay if you didn't pay any attention to their lectures about sin. She said the Home was okay. Most of the girls were fifteen or sixteen. They all worried about missing school. Debbie would have to do her sophomore year over.

Debbie had read a lot of books about childbirth, and she told me how the baby developed in the uterus, how at first it was like a pinhead but then a couple of months later there was a beating heart and everything. She told me about breaking water and about contractions and how you had to breathe with the pain; she and the other girls had practiced the breathing. She knew they weren't going to give her painkillers. She had heard that. The nuns had told her.

From time to time as we talked, she would stop to go through the contractions. She asked to hold my hand during the contractions, and she would squeeze it hard. Then she would let go, until the next time.

Debbie explained that the girls talked a lot about keeping their babies, that most of them wanted to keep them, but a lot of the girls wouldn't be fit mothers in Debbie's opinion. She herself wanted to keep her baby, but she knew she couldn't, because her father would never allow it, and anyway she had to go back to school.

50

"Can I have your hand again?"

Another set of contractions. She looked at the wall clock. She told me they were only three minutes apart. It wouldn't be too long now, she said.

I talked to some of the other girls in the room. They were all the same, all right there with the pains, paying attention, going through it. Most of them said they didn't want to see the baby after it was born: they were afraid that it would be too hard if they saw the baby. They were experiencing intense physical pain, and they were talking about intense emotional pain, but they were all right with it. They all had a calmness and a dignity.

Meanwhile, back in the high-class rooms, the private patients, the respectable married women, were strapped down in rubber beds, swearing like sailors, screaming their heads off.

It didn't make any sense to me. The people who were being punished were having the best experience. The people who were being indulged were having the worst experience.

I saw my first delivery. It was, on the one hand, just like what I expected. And, on the other hand, to see the little head appear, and then the little body, immediately transported you to some other reality. It wasn't a medical procedure; it was a miracle. I walked around in a daze. I saw several more deliveries. I couldn't get used to the feeling. I was floating.

I went back to the room with the girls from the Home. It was still peaceful; the girls still panting, alone. Debbie was gone. I checked the other rooms; I couldn't find her.

I found the resident scrubbing outside a delivery room.

"Say, did that girl from the Home deliver?"

"What girl?"

"Debbie."

"Don't know her."

"Sure you do. Cute girl, red hair. Debbie."

"I never look at the faces," the resident said.

I grew to despise the Boston Lying In Hospital. I stopped showing up for my duty hours.

Of course, childbirth has changed greatly since then. You let a husband in the delivery room and he won't permit his wife to be tied down screaming like an animal, even if the doctors and nurses see nothing wrong with it. And the negative consequences of delivering narcotized babies have come to be more clearly acknowledged. Natural childbirth was a rarity in Boston in the late 1960s. The few doctors who did it were considered outlandish kooks. Now natural childbirth is quite unexceptional. In fact, except for the recent enthusiasm for cesarean sections, childbirth practices represent one of the areas where medicine has changed for the better. And the Boston Lying In Hospital has long since been torn down.

Lousy on Admission

Emily was a sixty-six-year-old woman who lived alone in a small apartment. On a routine visit by a social worker, she was found lying unconscious on the floor, and was rushed to the hospital.

In the emergency ward, she was noted to be semicomatose for unknown reasons. Her clothes were filthy and unkempt. She was also infested with lice. She was cleaned up, deloused, and admitted to the medical floor.

When I first saw her, Emily was a tall, gray-haired, sharp-featured woman, sleepy and unresponsive. If you tried to wake her, she would grunt and push you away. Nobody knew what was wrong with her, how long she had been lying on the floor of her apartment, or why she was stuporous, but lab tests showed her chemistries were severely unbalanced.

My resident, Tim, reviewed her chart. "Lousy on admission," he sniffed. "Obviously a lot of neglect here, probably some senility. God knows how long she was lying on the floor."

Emily was given intravenous feedings to correct her body chemistries, but she did not awaken. Meanwhile, nobody was able to find out anything more about her. Apparently

53

she lived alone in a small apartment in an unfashionable part of town. Apparently she had no friends, no living family. No one came to visit her. She was an isolated, neglected old woman, obviously unable to care for herself. She was in our hands.

And we were not able to determine why she was unresponsive. She appeared to be in a deep sleep, but we couldn't tell why.

Abruptly, on the third day, Emily awoke. She looked around at all of us.

"Oh shit," she said.

Her language further distanced her from the resident staff. An old lady who swore: she was obviously senile. We questioned her. What was her name?

"You think I don't know? Scram, Daddy-oh."

Did she know where she was?

"Don't be ridiculous."

Did she know what day it was?

"Do you?"

Did she know who the President was?

"Franklin Delano Roosevelt," she said, and cackled.

A psychiatric consultation was requested. The psychiatrist found Emily to demonstrate "bizarre ideation, strange flow of ideas, and hostile affect." Noting that she had been lousy on admission, he suggested that she might be in the early stages of senile dementia.

We still had no idea why she had been comatose, and we ran more and more tests on her. In the meantime, she seemed to sleep less, to be more generally alert. But she remained distinctly odd: you never knew how she would greet you when you walked in the room.

One day it was "Ah, *Dottore*, how are you today?" in a corny Italian accent. "What news from the Rialto?"

One day it was "All quiet on the Western Front?" and her irritating cackle.

One day it was "Going to stick me full of needles again today? The human guinea pig, huh? You think I don't know what you're doing, Daddy-oh?"

She hated Tim, and the feeling was mutual. But for some reason she liked me. "Ah, the gigantic cherub, *cómo está usted?* Pablo should paint you, dearie."

I talked to her. I was able to confirm that she had no living family, that she had never married, that she had lived alone for many years. I asked her the usual questions you

54

asked old people, like whether she had any hobbies. She would snort contemptuously at the very idea. "Hobbies? *Hobbies?* I'm not an idiot."

"Well, then, how do you spend your time, Emily?"

"None of your fucking business, *Dottore.*"

She puzzled me. She was evasive, but there was a strange strength to her, a kind of imperiousness. I speculated she might be a rich old Boston lady fallen on hard times, and now embarrassed by her condition. I speculated she might be foreign-born. She seemed to know a lot about artists and literature and music, making all sorts of references to Pablo and Ezra and Thelonius and Miles.

These references went right past Tim and the other residents. They just thought she was senile. In fact, Tim became increasingly annoyed with her. He ordered more and more tests on Emily.

We still didn't know what was wrong with her. Emily had lots of minor problems—a slight hypothyroidism, a degree of anemia—but nothing that would explain her stuporous condition on arrival. A condition that was now gone. Yet Tim continued to order tests. Finally he said, "We have to deal with her anemia. I'm going to order a bone-marrow biopsy."

Bone-marrow biopsies were painful. "Why?" I said.

"Just to complete the workup."

"But her anemia is improving, and it's probably iron-deficient," I said. "There's no evidence of any other problem. Why are you putting her through a biopsy?"

"I feel it's required," Tim said.

Actually, I didn't like Tim. I'd had terrific luck in most of the residents I had been assigned to for my year of clinical work, but it was inevitable that sooner or later I'd be paired with someone I didn't get along with.

Many things about Tim troubled me. He wasn't well educated except in narrow scientific matters; he didn't know sports, or politics, or popular culture, like current movies. So he didn't understand what patients were telling him if they alluded to any of these things.

Either because of this or for another reason, Tim was sarcastic about the patients. He made nasty cracks about nearly everyone under his care. He also complained about the patients' families, and the trouble they caused when they visited the hospital.

Finally, his physical manner was rough and harsh. He'd

yank and pull at people in their beds, shoving them around, yelling at them, "No, no, not like *that,* just stay the way I had you!"

In retrospect, Tim was a frightened man trying to hide his own sense of inadequacy behind a façade of bullying sarcasm. But at the time I thought he was outrageous. All of the house staff had witnessed his behavior; more than once, glances were exchanged at the bedside. I felt Tim ought to be taken aside. I felt he needed psychiatric help. But nobody was doing anything about Tim, and it wasn't my position to suggest that a member of the house staff needed a shrink. I was just a medical student, the lowest of the low. And at the end of three months, Tim was going to give me my grade.

But now Tim was planning to do a punch biopsy on Emily's hipbone, a painful and, I believed, unnecessary procedure. I felt he wouldn't dare to do it if Emily weren't an old woman without friends or relatives, a woman no better than an alcoholic bum, a woman who had been lousy on admission.

"I'm doing it at one o'clock," he said. "Want to assist?"

"No," I said.

"I'll let you do it, if you want." A bribe.

"No," I said.

"Why not?"

I'd already registered my protest, so all I said was "I have clinic follow-ups all afternoon."

"Okay," Tim said. "You missed your chance. I'll get the nurse to help me."

I still hoped he wouldn't go through with it, but he did. The test was negative. Emily's marrow was fine.

Still, they kept Emily in the hospital. She had been there two weeks now. There was an unspoken rule about old people, which was that you discharged them from the hospital as soon as possible. Emily had gained strength steadily during the first week, but now she was starting to decline, to drift into a vague passivity.

At rounds the next day, the house staff discussed further tests for Emily. More exotic blood chemistries. Another EEG. A series of brain X-rays, a pneumoencephalogram. These tests would take at least another week.

I was already feeling guilty about the bone-marrow biopsy. Now I felt I had no choice. I spoke up.

I said that, while Emily was clearly a strange person, her

health now seemed basically good. There wasn't any compelling reason to do further tests. If she was senile, as everyone thought, then these tests wouldn't benefit her. There was no advantage to diagnosing an incurable disease. True, we had never found out what had put her in a coma, but we had been trying for two weeks and there was no reason to think we would succeed in a third week. Meanwhile, Emily was in noticeable decline. I argued we should discharge her, and do any further tests on an outpatient basis. And I suggested that if Emily had a family, they would now be pushing us to let her go, and that by keeping her around, we were open to a charge of exploiting her as learning material.

I was sweating by the end of my speech. Everybody stared at me. The chief resident said nothing. He turned to Tim, and asked when the tests would be scheduled.

Tim said the tests would be scheduled all during the coming week.

The chief resident said, Fine. Go ahead.

And that was that.

We went on to the next patient.

"What do you people think is wrong with me?" Emily said later, when she and I were alone.

"We're not sure," I said.

"Nothing is wrong with me," Emily said. "I feel fine. I don't want any more tests."

"I can understand that feeling," I said.

"Well, then, why do I have to have them? He hurt me," she said, pointing to her bandaged hip.

I was on dangerous ground now. I had to choose my words carefully. "If you want to leave the hospital," I said, "no one can stop you."

"You mean I can just walk out of here?"

"No, you have to be discharged. But if you insist on it, they have to discharge you."

"They do?"

"They'll try to talk you out of leaving, but they can't make you stay."

"Good," Emily said. "I'm sick of all you fucking doctors and your fucking tests."

"Guess who checked out?" Tim said that night in the cafeteria. "Emily."

"Oh yes?"

"Yeah. Discharged herself against physicians' advice."

57

"When?"

"Tonight. Screaming and swearing, nobody could talk any sense to her. They had to let her go. I think somebody put the idea into her head."

"Oh, really?"

"Yeah. Somebody talked to her."

"I wonder who?"

"I think somebody from Accounting. They're not sure if she's covered by Medicare, you know, and I think Accounting got nervous about the expense and decided to get her out." He sighed. "But you wait. She'll be back in a few weeks, covered in lice, just like before. Crazy old bitch."

Two months later, I was walking through the lobby of the outpatient department when I felt a pain in the ribs. Somebody had banged into me. I grunted and kept going.

"Hey! Doctor!"

I stopped and turned. A rather elegant woman stood there, wearing a green cape and a beret set at a rakish angle. She smoked a cigarette from a long ivory holder. She carried a cane in one hand. She was staring at me expectantly.

"Don't you say hello, Doctor?"

Patients never understand how many people you see, how many faces pass before you, particularly in the outpatient clinic. You may see fifty in an afternoon. "I'm sorry," I said, "but do I know you?"

She cocked her head, and seemed amused. "Miss Vincent."

I hadn't a clue. "Miss Vincent?"

"Emily."

I stared, still not recognizing her. I tried to dredge up anybody named Emily Vincent. And suddenly it all fell together. Emily! The lady who was lousy on admission!

Seeing her now, her stance, her dress, her manner, I understood. Emily was a bohemian. In the 1920s, she had been one of those rebellious, independent, artsy women. Of course she knew all about artists and writers. Of course she had never married. Of course she swore and smoked and was fiercely independent and advanced. Of course she was contemptuous of the doctors around her. Of course she liked to say shocking and outrageous things. As the years went on, Emily would have been in turn a flapper, then a

58

wartime riveter, then an aging beatnik. Of course she said things like "Daddy-oh." Emily was a hipster.

"Emily," I said, "how are you?"

"Quite well, *Dottore*. You may call me Miss Vincent."

"You're coming to the clinic?"

"They say I have a little something with my thyroid, and I take pills," she said, puffing on her cigarette. "Frankly, I think it's crap, but my doctor is so handsome, I indulge him."

"You look wonderful, Miss Vincent," I said, still trying to adjust to what I was seeing.

"You, too," she said. "Well, I must be off. *Ciao.*"

And, with a dramatic wave, she turned, cape flying, and was gone.

Heart Attack!

A major disaster befell the medical wards of the Beth Israel Hospital. All the interns and residents went around shaking their heads. The disaster was that, by some quirk of fate or statistics, two-thirds of the patients on the ward had the same illness. Heart attack.

The residents acted as if all the theaters in town were playing the same movie, and they'd seen it. Furthermore, most of these patients would be here for two weeks, so the movie wasn't going to change soon. The home staff was gloomy and bored, because, from a medical standpoint, heart attacks aren't terribly interesting. They are dangerous and life-threatening, and you worry about your patients, because they may die suddenly. But the diagnostic procedures were well worked out, and there were clear methods for following the progress of recovery.

By now I was in my final year of medical school, and I had decided I would quit at the end of the year. So my three months at the Beth Israel were going to be all the internal medicine I would ever learn; I had to make the best of this time.

I decided to learn something about the feelings the patients had about their disease. Because, although doctors were bored by myocardial infarcts, the patients certainly weren't. The patients were mostly men in their forties and fifties, and the meaning of this illness was clear to them— they were getting older; this was a reminder of their impending mortality; and they would have to change their lives: work habits, diets, perhaps even their pattern of sexual relations.

So there was plenty of interest for me in these patients. But how to approach them?

Some time earlier, I had read about the experiences of a Swiss physician who, in the 1930s, had taken a medical post in the Alps because it allowed him to ski, which was his great passion. Naturally, this doctor ended up treating many skiing accidents. The cause of the accidents interested him, since he was himself a skier. He asked his patients why they had had their accidents, expecting to hear that they had taken a turn too quickly, or hit a patch of rock, or some other skiing explanation. To his surprise, everyone gave a *psychological* reason for the accident. They were upset about something, they were distracted, and so on. This doctor learned that the bald question "Why did you break your leg?" yielded interesting answers.

So I decided to try that. I went around and asked patients, "Why did you have a heart attack?"

From a medical standpoint, the question was not so nonsensical as it sounded. During the Korean War, post-mortems on young men had shown that the American diet produced advanced arteriosclerosis by the age of seventeen. You had to assume that all these patients had been walking around with severely clogged arteries since they were teenagers. A heart attack could happen any time. Why had they waited twenty or thirty years to develop a heart attack? Why had their heart attack happened this year and not next, this week and not last week?

But, my question "Why did you have a heart attack?" also implied that the patients had some choice in the matter, and therefore some control over their disease. I feared they might respond with anger. So I started with the most easygoing patient on the ward, a man in his forties who had had a mild attack.

"Why did you have a heart attack?"

"You really want to know?"

"Yes, I do."

"I got a promotion. The company wants me to move to

Cincinnati. But my wife doesn't want to go. She has all her family here in Boston, and she doesn't want to go with me. That's why."

He reported this in a completely straightforward manner, without a trace of anger. Encouraged, I asked other patients.

"My wife is talking about leaving me."

"My daughter wants to marry a Negro man."

"My son won't go to law school."

"I didn't get the raise."

"I want to get a divorce and feel guilty."

"My wife wants another baby and I don't think we can afford it."

No one was ever angry that I had asked the question. On the contrary, most nodded and said, "You know, I've been thinking about that. . . ." And no one ever mentioned the standard medical causes of arteriosclerosis, such as smoking or diet or getting too little exercise.

Now, I hesitated to jump to conclusions. I knew all patients tended to review their lives when they got really sick, and to draw some conclusion about why the illness had happened. Sometimes the explanations seemed pretty irrelevant. I'd seen a cancer patient who blamed her disease on a lifelong fondness for Boston cream pie, and an arthritis patient who blamed his mother-in-law.

On the other hand, it was accepted in a vague way that there was a relationship between mental processes and disease. One clue came from timing of certain illnesses. For example, the traditional season for duodenal ulcers was mid-January, just after the Christmas holidays. No one knew why this should be, but a psychological factor in the timing of the disease seemed likely.

Another clue came from the association of some physical illnesses with a characteristic personality. For example, a significant percentage of patients with ulcerative bowel disease had extremely irritating personalities. Since the disease itself was hard to live with, some doctors wondered if the disease caused the personality. But many suspected that it was the other way around: the personality caused the disease. Or at least whatever caused the bowel disease also caused the personality.

Third, there was a small group of physical diseases that could be successfully treated with psychotherapy. Warts, goiter, and parathyroid disease responded to both surgery and psychotherapy, suggesting that these illnesses might have direct mental causes.

And, finally, it was everybody's ordinary experience that the minor illnesses in our own lives—colds, sore throats—occurred at times of stress, times when we felt generally weak. This suggested that the ability of the body to resist infection varied with mental attitude.

All this information interested me enormously, but it was pretty fringe stuff in the 1960s in Boston. Curious, yes. Worthy of note, yes. But nothing to pursue in a serious way. The great march of medicine was headed in another direction entirely.

Now, I was getting these data from the heart attack patients. And what I was seeing was that their explanations made sense from the standpoint of the whole organism, as a kind of physical acting-out. These patients were telling me stories of events that had affected their hearts in a metaphorical sense. They were telling me love stories. Sad love stories, which had pained their hearts. Their wives and families and bosses didn't care for them. Their hearts were attacked.

And pretty soon their hearts were *literally* attacked. And they experienced physical pain. And that pain, that attack, was going to force a change in their lives, and the lives of those around them. These were men in late middle life, all undergoing a transformation that was signaled by this illness event.

It made almost too much sense.

Finally I brought it up with Herman Gardner. Dr. Gardner was then chief of medicine at the hospital, and a remarkable, extremely thoughtful man. As it happened, he was the attending physician who made rounds with us each day. I said to him that I had been talking with the patients, and I told him their stories.

He listened carefully.

"Yes," he said. "You know, once I was admitted to the hospital for a slipped disc, and sitting in bed I began to wonder why this had happened to me. And I realized that I had a paper from a colleague that I had to reject, and I didn't want to face up to it. To postpone it, I got a slipped disc. At the time, I thought it was as good an explanation as any for what had happened to me."

Here was the chief of medicine himself reporting the same kind of experience. And it opened up all sorts of possibilities. Were psychological factors more important than we were acknowledging? Was it even possible that psychological factors were the most important causes of disease? If so, how far could you push that idea? Could you consider myocardial infarctions to be a brain disease? How would medicine be different if we considered all these people, in all these beds, to be manifesting mental processes through their physical bodies?

Because at the moment we were treating their physical bodies. We acted as if the heart was sick and the brain had nothing to do with it. We treated the heart. Were all these people being treated for the wrong organs?

Such errors were known. For example, some patients with severe abdominal pain actually had glaucoma, a disease of the eye. If you operated on their abdomens, you didn't cure the disease. But if you treated their eyes, the abdominal pains disappeared.

But to extend that idea more broadly to the brain suggested something quite alarming. It suggested a new conception of medicine, a whole new view of patients and disease.

To take the simplest example, we all believed implicitly the germ theory of disease. Pasteur proposed it one hundred years before, and it had stood the test of time. There were germs—micro-organisms, viruses, parasites—that got into the body and caused infectious disease. That was how it worked.

We all knew that you were more likely to get infected at some times than others, but the basic cause and effect— germs caused disease—was not questioned. To suggest that germs were always out there, a constant factor in the environment, and that the disease process therefore reflected our mental state, was to say something else.

It was to say mental states caused disease.

And if you accepted that concept for infectious disease, where did you draw the line? Did mental states also cause cancer? Did mental states cause heart attacks? Did mental states cause arthritis? What about diseases of old age? Did mental states cause Alzheimer's? What about children? Did mental states cause leukemia in young children? What about birth defects? Did mental states cause mongolism at birth? If so, whose mental state—the mother's or the child's? Or both?

It became clear that at the farther reaches of this idea,

you came uncomfortably close to medieval notions that a pregnant woman who suffered a fright would later produce a deformed child. And any consideration of mental states automatically raised the idea of blame. If you caused your illness, weren't you also to blame? Much medical attention had been devoted to removing ideas of blame from disease. Only a few illnesses, such as alcoholism and other addictions, still had notions of blame attached.

So this idea that mental processes caused disease seemed to have retrogressive aspects. No wonder doctors hesitated to pursue it. I myself backed away from it for many years.

It was Dr. Gardner's view that both the physical and the mental aspects were important. Even if you imagined the heart attack had a psychological origin, once the cardiac muscle was damaged it needed to be treated as a physical injury. Thus the medical care we were giving was appropriate.

I wasn't so sure about this. Because, if you imagined that the mental process had injured the heart, then couldn't the mental process also heal the heart? Shouldn't we be encouraging people to invoke their inner resources to deal with the injury? We certainly weren't doing that. We were doing the opposite: we were constantly telling people to lie down, to take it easy, to give over their treatment to us. We were reinforcing the idea that they were helpless and weak, that there was nothing they could do, and they'd better be careful even going to the bathroom because the least strain and—poof!—you were dead. That was how weak you were.

This didn't seem like a good instruction from an authority figure to a patient's unconscious mental process. It seemed as if we might actually be delaying the cure by our behavior. But, on the other hand, some patients who refused to listen to their doctors, who jumped out of bed, would die suddenly while having a bowel movement. And who wanted to take responsibility for that?

Many years passed, and I had long since left medicine, before I arrived at a view of disease that seemed to make sense to me. The view is this:

We cause our diseases. We are directly responsible for any illness that happens to us.

In some cases, we understand this perfectly well. We

knew we should have not gotten run-down and caught a cold. In the case of more catastrophic illnesses, the mechanism is not so clear to us. But whether we can see a mechanism or not—whether there *is* a mechanism or not—it is healthier to assume responsibility for our lives, and for everything that happens to us.

Of course it isn't helpful to blame ourselves for an illness. That much is clear. (It's rarely helpful to blame anybody for anything.) But that doesn't mean we should abdicate all responsibility as well. To give up responsibility for our lives is not healthy.

In other words, given the choice of saying to ourselves, "I am sick but it has nothing to do with me," or saying, "I am sick because I caused the sickness," we are better off thinking and behaving as if we did it to ourselves. I believe we are more likely to recover if we take that responsibility.

For one thing, when we take responsibility for a situation, we also take control of it. We are less frightened and more practical. We are better able to focus on what we can do now to ameliorate the illness, and to assist healing.

We also keep the true role of the doctor in better perspective. The doctor is not a miracle worker who can magically save us but, rather, an expert adviser who can assist us in our own recovery. We are better off when we keep that distinction clear.

When I get sick, I go to my doctor like everyone else. A doctor has powerful tools that may help me. Or those tools may hurt me, make me worse. I have to decide. It's my life. It's my responsibility.

Drs. W, X, Y, and Z

Mr. Erwin, a fifty-two-year-old man, was admitted to the hospital because of a spot found on a routine chest X-ray taken by his private physician. Once he was in the hospital, the X-rays were repeated. The spot was there, no doubt about it, in the upper left lobe of his lung.

Mr. Erwin was told that he should have surgery, and he agreed. But when it came to signing the forms, he asked for time to think it over. The next day, he was again advised to have surgery, and again he agreed, only to back out at the last moment. A week passed in this way.

Mr. Erwin never asked what was in his lung that required surgery. He never asked anything at all. And nobody volunteered to tell him. For one thing, the X-ray image was anomalous; it appeared to be some sort of tumor, but it didn't present a classical picture. Mr. Erwin was extremely nervous, and the house staff chose to wait.

On the other hand, a week was a week. It became difficult to justify keeping someone in an expensive bed, but the house staff didn't want to discharge Mr. Erwin because they felt he'd never confront his illness once he left the hospital. So there was an impasse. Mr. Erwin still didn't ask about the operation. And still no one told him.

Finally, at the end of the week, Dr. W, a surgeon from a nearby hospital, came to conduct visiting rounds. Dr. W, a former athlete, was a big blustery man who performed surgery with drama and verve. The house staff presented him with the case of the reluctant Mr. Erwin. Dr. W was outraged at the way the staff had coddled this man, and insisted on seeing him at once.

Dr. W walked into the man's room and said, "Mr. Erwin, I'm Dr. W; you have cancer and I'm going to take it out!"

Mr. Erwin burst into tears, and agreed to surgery.

The following day, the operation was performed. A granulomatous lesion was removed. In the center of the lesion was found some stringy material identified by the pathologists as beef. Apparently Mr. Erwin had, at some earlier time, inhaled a bit of meat while eating. The beef had lodged in his lung, and had been overgrown with a protective coating of tissue.

When Mr. Erwin awoke, he was told the good news by the delighted house staff. Mr. Erwin remained glum. He still cried frequently. As the days went on, he said he knew the house staff was lying to him, that he had cancer; Dr. W had told him so. The residents assured him that Dr. W was wrong, that there was no cancer. They showed him the pathology reports. They offered to let him see his chart. Mr. Erwin believed none of it.

Two days later, Mr. Erwin crawled out the narrow window of his room, and jumped to his death.

Dr. X performed surgery on the leg of a thirty-five-year-old woman. His intention was to tie off the femoral vein. Immediately after surgery, the woman complained of severe pain in the leg, which was noted to be blue and cold, with little pulse. Twenty-four hours after surgery, when there was no improvement in her condition, it was realized that Dr. X had mistakenly tied off the femoral artery, not the vein. The woman's leg would now have to be amputated at the hip.

Dr. X was an elderly Jewish refugee from Nazi Germany. He was known to have made such errors before, and his surgical privileges had been revoked at a suburban hospital. The question was whether Dr. X would now lose his privileges at this hospital as well.

Two things interested me. The first was that nobody told the woman anything was amiss. In those days, before the flood of malpractice litigation, a woman who had been grossly mistreated by a physician known to be negligent was not being told anything by the other doctors around her. The woman was relatively young, and the mother of two; with one leg amputated, she was now going to have a very different life.

The second thing was that there was discussion about whether Dr. X would lose his surgical privileges, as if the question were in doubt. (In fact, the hospital did not revoke his privileges entirely. He was merely forbidden to operate alone any longer.)

Dr. Y was discussing the case of a traveling salesman who had been admitted for gall-bladder surgery. The salesman was a chronic alcoholic, and the staff was afraid that he would go into the DTs while in the hospital, which would complicate his treatment and might even kill him. It was decided that he should be allowed beer while in the hospital; every day the salesman got a case of beer delivered to his bedside.

I asked whether Dr. Y was troubled by the fact that this alcoholic patient was also a traveling salesman. Presumably, once his medical condition was resolved, he would be back on the road, drinking and driving. Did the hospital, knowing the man was an alcoholic, have any greater responsibility to the man, his employers, or the wider society of drivers?

"Well, this is a very difficult problem," Dr. Y said. "For instance, I recently performed an insurance exam on an airline pilot who was a chronic alcoholic."

What did you do in that case? I asked.

Dr. Y shrugged. "I certified him," he said. "What else could I do? I couldn't take away his livelihood."

Dr. Z was a seventy-eight-year-old physician who entered the hospital in a near coma, in end-stage cardiac and renal failure. His son was also a physician, but not on the staff of the hospital, so he could only visit like any other relative, and he had nothing to say about his father's care. He did, however, state that he wanted his father to die peacefully.

The old man was on the critical list for nearly a week. He had a cardiac arrest one night, but he was resuscitated. His son came in the next day and asked, with a certain delicacy, why the staff had resuscitated the old man. Nobody answered him.

Later that day, old Dr. Z suffered sudden massive congestive heart failure. The hospital staff was making rounds; they all rushed to his bedside. In a moment he was entirely surrounded by white-jacketed interns and residents, working on the old man, sticking needles and tubes into his body.

In the midst of all this, he somehow emerged from his coma, sat bolt upright in bed, and shouted clearly and distinctly, "I refuse this therapy! I refuse this therapy!"

The residents pushed him back down. He got the therapy anyway. I turned to the attending physician, and asked how such a thing was possible. This man was, after all, a physician, and he was unquestionably dying—if not today, then tomorrow or the next day. Why had the house staff contradicted his wishes, and those of his family? Why was he not being allowed to die?

There was no good answer.

Dr. Z finally died on the weekend, when hospital staffing was light.

Incidents such as these troubled me throughout my clinical years. Everyone around me seemed to shrug them off, and to go on about their business, but I was unable to do that. My concerns in these areas eventually became one of the major reasons why I decided to quit medicine.

Quitting Medicine

Back in my first year, shortly after I cut open a human head with a hacksaw, I decided to quit medical school. I went to Dr. Lorenzo, the dean of students, and said I wanted to quit, that medicine wasn't for me.

"Okay," he said. "Go see Tom Corman. After that, if you still feel the same, you can quit."

At this time it was the policy of the Harvard Medical School that you had to talk to a shrink before you quit. Dr. Corman was the shrink. He was well known among the students. A lot of us had been to see him.

Dr. Corman was short, intense, and direct. "What's your problem?"

"I want to quit medical school."

"Why?"

"I hate it."

"So?"

This confused me. I explained that I had been at the school for three months, I had given it a try, but I just didn't like it. I didn't like what I was studying, I didn't like the experience, I didn't really like my classmates. I didn't like anything about it.

"So?"

I asked him to explain.

"Why did you come to medical school?" he said.

"I want to be a doctor."

"Meaning what?"

"I want to help people."

"And how many patients have you seen so far?"

"Almost none."

"So you're not doing what you came here to do. You came here to help people and instead you sit in classes all day, right?"

"Right."

"I can understand that you hate it," he said. "Most of your classmates hate it. That doesn't mean anything."

I thought it did mean something. It meant that I hated it.

"The first two years of medical school don't have anything to do with being a doctor, which is what you want to be. I think you owe it to yourself to wait until next year, when you start seeing patients in a clinical setting."

I said that was too long to wait. I wanted to quit now.

"All right," he said, "But consider the academic realities. It's not advisable to quit in the middle of an academic year. It doesn't look good on your record when you apply to graduate school in some other field. You'd be better off finishing this year, and then quitting."

That was true enough. So, in the end, Dr. Corman talked me out of quitting. And after the first year, I felt a little better about medicine. I thought I'd give the second year a try.

The second year was even worse. I was back in Dr. Corman's office.

"I want to quit."

"Still don't like it?"

"I hate it."

"What do you hate?"

"The classes." And I did. For such a famous medical school, the quality of instruction was a disgrace. It was so bad that the students had recently rebelled, and demanded the right to tape the lectures, and to assign one student to each lecture to go over the tape and make decent mimeographed notes for the class. The faculty was up in arms

72

about this, but the students were adamant, and won in the end.

To listen to one of those lectures, again and again, trying to put the speaker's points into some kind of logical order, consulting the textbooks to explain what he forgot to explain, was a startling demonstration of how poor the lectures really were.

I had taught a lecture course at Cambridge University, so I'd had the experience of preparing and delivering lectures. I knew how long it took—in my case, ten to twenty hours to prepare an hour's lecture. I knew how it felt to give a lecture when you were fully prepared; how it felt to be almost prepared; how it felt to be poorly prepared; and how it felt to wing it.

The Harvard lecturers were mostly winging it. One man after another would stand up with a fistful of last year's lecture notes, including a few scribbled changes in the margins, and start to talk. The fact that a few instructors, like Don Fawcett and Bernard Davis, were superb only threw the inept majority into sharper relief.

"And are you seeing any patients?"

"Yes." We were doing some introductory clinical work.

"How is that?"

"I like that."

"Well, the classes you dislike will stop in a few months, and then you'll just be seeing patients. So is it correct to quit now?"

He talked me out of it.

Pretty soon another year had gone by. I was in my third year, doing full-time clinical rotations, more or less living at the hospital. By then I'd concluded I wanted to be either a surgeon or a psychiatrist. But when I did my three-month surgical rotation, I found myself surprisingly bored. I liked the pragmatism of surgeons, I liked their active stance toward the world, I liked the crises and pressures, and I liked telling people what to do. All that appealed to me. But I noticed that surgeons were interested in each case in a way I was not. To a good surgeon, every gall bladder presented new features of interest. But as far as I was concerned, if you'd seen one gall bladder, you'd seen them all.

So I suspected I was not destined to be a surgeon.

This left psychiatry, but I'd had a disturbing experience with a female patient; I'd been uncomfortable as a therapist.

And, worse, as I worked in the clinic, seeing as many patients as possible, I began to feel that psychiatry was not a powerful field. I didn't think psychiatry could really help people much. On the one hand, I had seen severely ill, institutionalized people with dramatic mental disease. But psychiatry didn't seem able to do much for them, and certainly couldn't effect cures. And, on the other hand, there were lots of well-to-do people who didn't strike me as sick but, rather, as self-indulgent. For them, psychiatry appeared to offer a glorified kind of hand-holding that I didn't admire. And I wasn't at all sure that it did them any good, either.

So I was disillusioned with both surgery and psychiatry. Back to Dr. Corman.

"Well," he said, "you haven't finished your clinical rotations. How do you know you won't like pediatrics, orthopedics, or internal medicine?"

"I'm pretty sure I won't."

"This far along, don't you owe it to yourself to find out?" He talked me into staying again.

When I was finally convinced that no clinical specialty appealed to me, I had completed three and a half years of a four-year program. And then it really didn't make sense to quit.

I went back to Dr. Corman and said I was going to get my degree, and then quit. He sighed. "I thought you would quit in the end," he said. "Your fantasies are too strong."

In this he was correct. I was supporting myself in school by writing thrillers, and my imaginative tendencies were overpowering. I often listened to patients, thinking, How can I use this in a book? And sometimes when I heard the symptoms of their disease, I'd think, It's obviously anemia, but can I imagine a new disease that would present with these same symptoms?

Of course, when you go to a doctor, you don't want him to view you as a book chapter, and you don't want him making up fictional diseases to explain your case of anemia. I was clear on that. I understood that I was not behaving like a doctor that *I* would want to consult. So I thought I ought to quit.

* * *

There were other problems, too. Much of medicine, as it was practiced in those days, I simply didn't agree with. I didn't agree that abortion on demand should be illegal. I didn't agree that patients had no rights and should shut up and do whatever the doctors told them to do. I didn't agree that, if a procedure presented a hazard, the patient shouldn't be worried with the facts. I didn't agree that terminally ill people should have treatment forced upon them, even if they wished to die in peace. I didn't agree that, when malpractice occurred, doctors should cover it up.

Beyond these broad issues of ethics, I didn't agree with the style of the new physician-scientist, so popular at that time. I didn't think of people as a sack of biochemical reactions that had somehow gone awry. I thought people were complex creatures who sometimes manifested their problems in biochemical terms. But I thought it wiser to deal primarily with the people, not to deal primarily with the biochemistry. And while there was much lip service given to my view, in practice nobody did anything but treat the enzyme levels. Again and again, I met patients who had been in the hospital for weeks and who had obvious problems that nobody had ever noticed—because they didn't show up in the lab tests. It made you suspect that the doctors weren't really looking at their patients. Not as people.

And the trend toward the physician-scientist had brought to the medical school a kind of student with whom I had little in common. My classmates tended to think that literature, music, and art were irrelevant distractions. They held these "cultural" matters in the same intellectual contempt that a physicist holds astrology. Everything outside medicine was just a waste of time.

In those days Harvard had built a new medical library. One day a pale, ethereal-looking man wandered in and looked around. It took me a moment to realize it was Louis Kahn, who was one of my heroes. I was very excited and reported the news at lunch: "Louis Kahn was in the library today!"

"Who?"

"Louis Kahn."

Frowns. "The new professor of medicine?"

"No, the architect."

"Oh . . ." And the conversation turned away.

Louis Kahn was not only a famous architect, he was

75

arguably the most influential *medical* architect in the world, as a result of the building he had done at the University of Pennsylvania some years before. Harvard was putting up a lot of new hospital buildings at this time, and there was much discussion of their merits and faults. How could you have informed discussions if you had never heard of Louis Kahn?

This single-mindedness led to some bizarre medical episodes. Once I heard a group of residents plan the surgical treatment of a middle-aged businessman. The best thing for his intestinal problems, they agreed, was to schedule five separate surgical procedures. The first would clean up his bowel. The second would cut a hole in his stomach so he could defecate into a bag. The third would do something else. The fourth would repair the hole in his stomach and reconnect his intestines. The fifth would do something else again. All together, the man would be out of the hospital, good as new, in nine months.

The alternative was a two-stage procedure that would require only three weeks and no colostomy bag, but it was obviously inferior to the five-stage treatment.

I suggested that the man might not agree to the five-stage treatment. Everyone listened to this view with astonishment. Why on earth wouldn't he agree?

I said perhaps the man didn't want to spend nine months of his life in a hospital, undergoing one operation after another. I suggested that a busy corporate executive was worried about many things besides his health. He was worried about his family, about his income, about his rank in the company. A nine-month hiatus from daily life was going to give him a lot of problems.

I also said that to live with a colostomy bag was a major body alteration and it would not be lightly accepted by anyone, even temporarily.

No, no, they said. When we explain it to him, he'll certainly agree to the five-stage treatment.

Of course the man didn't agree to it. He wanted the fastest possible treatment, and he thought their elaborate plan was crazy. He reacted to the idea of a colostomy bag with horror. The residents came away shaking their heads: What can you do with somebody who doesn't care about his health?

Yet the fact that the patients were complex human beings

76

with a rich life beyond the hospital never really sank into the consciousness of the residents. Because they had no rich lives beyond the hospital, they assumed no one else did, either. In the end, what they lacked was not medical knowledge but ordinary life experience.

Nor did the attitude of practicing physicians encourage me. I liked them much better as people; they often had a breadth of interest missing from the current crop of students. But, all too often, the senior physicians were dissatisfied with their work. Even if they loved medicine—and most did—they came to dislike the life style. In those days, when group practices were less common and doctors had a more direct one-to-one relationship with their patients, clinical practice was enervating in a way that seemed to catch up with physicians after a decade or two. These men had families they hardly knew, boats they had hardly sailed, and trips they had many times canceled. It seemed their patients took everything in their lives. And not enough came back.

I had assumed the life of a doctor was, without doubt, devoted to helping people, but practicing physicians weren't so sure. They saw many patients who apparently had nothing wrong with them. They saw terminal illnesses, which they could not cure. Again and again, they would say, "I'm not so sure I really help people."

At first I chalked it up to temporary fatigue, or to fashionable self-doubt. Eventually I began to believe it. They were serious. And a lot of them felt that way.

Of course, I wanted to quit to become something else. I wanted to be a writer.

This had been my earliest life ambition. It went back almost to the beginning of my ability to read and write at all. When I was nine, my third-grade class was told to write a puppet show. Most of the students wrote brief skits; I wrote a nine-page epic involving so many characters that I had to get my father to retype it for me with multiple carbon copies before it could be performed. My father said he'd never read anything so cliché-ridden in his life (which probably was true); this hurt me and confirmed a pattern of conflict between us that persisted for many years. But my father unquestionably influenced my interest in writing; he was a born storyteller; at bedtime we insisted he tell us stories, which he would illustrate on the spot with little comic-strip drawings until we slowly drifted off to sleep.

When I was growing up, my father was a journalist and an editor; at the dinner table there was always talk about writing, and correct word use, with frequent pauses to consult Fowler's *Modern English Usage* when arguments arose. Many of his editorial dicta stayed with me. "Be careful about 'obviously.' If it's really obvious you don't need to say it, and if it's not obvious it's insulting to say that it is.")

My father insisted on clarity, and brevity, and he could be a harsh critic. But he was also full of good humor in those days. Journalists hear more jokes than anyone else, and each night he would come home with a new one, often risqué; my mother would say, "Now, John," as he told it, to the glee of the children.

My father considered the ability to type a necessary life skill, and all his children learned at an early age; I learned to type when I was twelve. And it is surely no accident that of his four children, three have published books, and the fourth is working on one.

In any case, I wrote extensively from an early age. It was something I liked to do. I began submitting short stories to magazines when I was thirteen, and I sold a travel article to *The New York Times* when I was fourteen. What happened was that, on a summer trip, my family visited Sunset Crater National Monument, in Arizona. I found this place fascinating, but there was nobody else around that day, and I suspected most tourists bypassed it, not realizing how interesting it really was.

"Why don't you write about it?" my mother said.

"For what?"

"*The New York Times* publishes travel articles from different people." My mother was a great clipper of articles.

"*The New York Times*," I said. "I'm just a kid."

"Nobody needs to know that."

I looked at my father.

"Get all the published information they have at the ranger station," he said, "and interview the ranger."

So my family waited in the hot sun while I interviewed the ranger, trying to think of things to ask him. But I was emboldened by the fact that my parents seemed to think I could do this, even though I was only thirteen.

Back in the car, driving to the next place, my father said, "How many visitors do they have every year?"

"I didn't ask that," I said.

"Is it open all year round?"

"I didn't ask that, either."

"What was the ranger's name?"

"I didn't ask."

"Jesus," my father said. "What published information did you get?"

I showed him the pamphlets and brochures.

"Well, that'll be enough. You can write the story from that."

When I got home, I wrote an article and sent it in. And the *Times* bought it and ran it. I was ecstatic. I was a published writer! Years later I discovered that the travel editor, Paul Friedlander, lived near us and his daughter Becky was in my class at school, so he probably knew a kid had written this article, and he was probably amused to publish it. But at the time I thought I had sneaked past the system, and had done a grown-up thing, and it gave me tremendous encouragement to continue writing. After all, I had been paid sixty dollars, which in those days was a lot of money for a kid.

I began doing other journalistic writing. I covered high-school sports for the town paper; I was both reporter and photographer, and was paid ten dollars a week. And in college I wrote for the Harvard *Crimson,* where I was book-review editor (free books) and sometime movie reviewer (free theater passes). And I covered sports for the *Alumni Bulletin,* which paid about a hundred dollars a month.

So, with this history of writing, it was natural for me to think of writing to pay for the cost of medical school. My father had three other children in college at the time, and he couldn't pay the cost of school. I had to make money in some way.

Clearly I couldn't make enough writing free-lance articles, so I decided to write novels. In those days James Bond spy novels were popular, and I read a lot of them. I decided to write novels like that.

By then I was married, and my father-in-law knew somebody at Doubleday. He sent Doubleday my first novel. Doubleday said that they wouldn't publish it but Signet might. Signet bought it as an original paperback and called to ask who my agent was, to negotiate the deal.

I didn't have an agent, but my father-in-law arranged for me to meet some. I met three. The first agent represented many famous authors and intimidated me. The second told me how I should write and annoyed me. The third was a young girl who had been an agent's secretary and was just starting out on her own. She said she wanted to represent me. Since she was the only one who had said she wanted to represent me, it seemed like I should sign with her, so I did.

For the next three years, while I went to medical school, I wrote paperback thrillers to pay my bills. Of course, there wasn't much time for writing, but I did it on weekends and vacations. And, with practice, I learned to write these spy thrillers quickly. Eventually I wrote one in nine days. But I didn't take any particular interest in this work. It was just a way to pay the tuition bills.

Then, slowly, almost imperceptibly, the writing became more interesting to me than the medicine. And as my writing got more successful, the conflict between writing and medicine became increasingly awkward.

Under a pseudonym I wrote a book called *A Case of Need*. It had many lightly disguised references to people in the Harvard Medical School. When the book was published, there was a lot of talk about this author, Jeffery Hudson, who seemed to know so much about Harvard. I joined right in: Who could this Hudson fellow be, anyway? What a mystery.

That was fun. Then the book was nominated for an Edgar for the Best Mystery of the Year. That was fun, too. Then the book won, which meant somebody had to accept the award.

Suddenly it was not fun any more.

I knew that if anybody found out I had written that book I would be in a lot of trouble. At Harvard, in your clinical years, you were given grades according to the informal opinion of the people you worked with. If these people found out I was writing books, my grades would fall precipitously.

I went to New York and accepted the award with dread. But I needn't have worried. There wasn't much publicity, and I was protected by the prejudices of the physician-

80

scientists, who regarded literary matters as a waste of time. Nobody ever knew.

But then this same troublesome book was bought for the movies, and the movie company wanted me to fly to Hollywood to talk to the screenwriter. I said I couldn't come, I was in medical school. They said, Come for the weekend. They were very insistent. I had to go to the chief of service to get Friday off. Dr. Gardner was a very nice man. I asked if I could take off Friday.

"Is there a death in the family?" he asked.

That was the usual excuse we used. By the third year, each of us had had our grandparents die three or four times.

"No," I said.

"An illness?" he said.

"No," I said.

And I gulped and told him the truth: that I had written this book, and it had been bought for the movies, and now the people in Hollywood wanted me to come out and talk to the screenwriter, and so I needed Friday off to do that, but don't worry, I'll be back on Monday for sure.

He looked at me strangely. What a lunatic excuse! Why didn't I just say my grandmother had died like everybody else?

But all he said was, All right.

So I went to Hollywood, and I rode around in limousines and had dinner with famous people, and then I came back and went to the hospital again. There was a discontinuity in my life, a gap between the parts, and as time passed it grew wider.

I made the decision to quit in the summer of my third year. At that time, medical students apply for an internship. I didn't apply, which meant I'd be dropping out after graduation.

A few weeks after I decided not to continue, I developed numbness in my right hand. Over several days, the numbness extended up my arm to the shoulder. I thought perhaps I'd slept on my arm and had compressed the nerves a little. The numb sensation was mild, and I ignored it.

I had every reason to ignore it. During all the clinical rotations I had developed convincing symptoms of every disease I had studied.

In dermatology, I was sure my moles were growing; I went home each night and used a hand mirror to check my back, where I was convinced melanomas were popping out like beads of sweat.

During surgery, I developed bloody stools, symptomatic of a hemorrhagic ulcer, a true surgical emergency—although one of the residents said disdainfully that I had just developed hemorrhoids, and welcome to the club.

During genitourinary, I developed pain on urination and would spin down my urine in the lab each day, looking for micro-organisms that I felt sure were there, although I could never find them.

In each instance, the day the clinical rotation ended, the symptoms mysteriously vanished—only to be replaced by new symptoms, which developed as I began my new rotation. So, no matter how persuasive these new symptoms seemed to me, I had learned, after a year, not to panic. I certainly wasn't going to panic now over something as peculiar as numbness in my right arm. I chose to avoid thinking about it; I refused even to look up the symptoms in my textbooks.

Then, one day in the cafeteria lunch line, I reached into my pocket for change and realized I could not distinguish the coins I was feeling in my pocket. I had to bring the coins out and look at them in my palm to see which was which. I knew what this was called: asterognosis.

I knew it was definitely abnormal.

Still I ignored my symptoms. Nothing further happened for two weeks, but the numbness did not go away, either. One day I asked a classmate who was a superb diagnostician, "What can give you numbness in your right arm?"

He thought about it for a while, shook his head. "The only things I can think of are spinal-cord tumor and multiple sclerosis."

I thought, What does he know, he's only a medical student. I still did nothing. I expected the symptoms to go away. They didn't. I worried more and more about my arm, until finally I looked up the symptoms of spinal-cord tumor and multiple sclerosis.

It was immediately clear that spinal-cord tumor was highly unlikely. If I had anything wrong with me, it would seem I had multiple sclerosis.

Multiple sclerosis was a progressive degenerative disease

of the nervous system, which tended to afflict young people. It was an autoimmune disease, in which the body's defenses became confused and attacked its own nerve fibers as if they were foreign intruders. The progress of the disease was highly variable. There was no known cause, no effective treatment, and no cure.

According to my reading, MS could first appear in almost any way. The fact that I had numbness without pain in only one extremity, with no prior history of injury, was highly suspicious. But it was impossible to make a diagnosis of MS based on a single set of symptoms. You needed to see a pattern of neurological attack and remission, over time, to confirm a diagnosis.

I stopped reading. I went on to my next rotation, and hoped the symptoms would disappear. They did not. My arm remained numb. By now it had been almost two months.

One day in October, while bending over a patient's bed, I noticed shooting electrical tingles going down both legs. From the reading I had already done, I knew what this was: Lhermitte's sign. Technically, paresthesias on flexion of the neck.

Lhermitte's sign was pathognomonic of multiple sclerosis. I had the disease.

I did more reading—a lot more reading. For a man of twenty-six, the news was not encouraging. Multiple sclerosis was highly variable, but, according to the statistics, I could expect substantial impairment within five years; serious handicaps that interfered with a job within ten years; very severe limitations including loss of bladder and bowel control within fifteen years; and death within twenty years.

I was horrified. The thought of becoming bedridden and incontinent, of undergoing the subtle loss of mental functioning, filled me with dread. But I reminded myself I still had not been examined by a doctor; no objective diagnosis had been made.

Finally I couldn't keep my worries to myself. The internist at the Health Services listened to my story, did an examination, then named a neurologist he wanted me to see. I said I would call.

"No," he said. "I'll call. Maybe he can see you right away."

The neurologist saw me that day. He was young and

83

brisk. I sweated profusely while he examined me. When he finished, he said I could get dressed and come into his office.

I dressed and went to the office.

"Well," he said briskly, "you have had a demyelinative episode."

"Does that mean I have it or not?" I asked. I couldn't bring myself to say the words.

"You mean, do you have multiple sclerosis?"

"Uh-huh," I said.

"Well," he said, "you have had a single attack, yes."

I felt as if a great powerful wave washed over me, knocked me down, spun me around in boiling surf. I felt as if I were drowning in this man's office, sitting in a chair facing his desk.

The neurologist started speaking very quickly. "But let me tell you how to think about this," he said. "I assume you have been reading up on it?"

"Yes."

"Well, the books are wrong. Listen to me, and forget the books."

Sure, I thought. Try and cheer me up.

"The books are based on old and inadequate data. I'll tell you how to look at this disease—or, really, this syndrome, because it's more a syndrome than a disease."

He spoke fast and loud, realizing that my attention was wandering, that I was withdrawing into myself in panic. He said that a large percentage of people had a single episode like mine sometime during their lives. Most people would never consult a doctor about it, and so doctors had no idea how common a single episode might be. But he thought they were very common, perhaps occurring in as much as ninety percent of people. He told me that several of my classmates had had such single episodes. Only one had had subsequent episodes.

So the question in my case was whether I would have no further attacks at all, or whether I would have occasional attacks and experience some loss of function, or whether I would have frequent and severe attacks and serious difficulty in my life.

"Think of this as a heart murmur," he said. "It's a warning of a possible problem, but you can't say now whether a heart murmur will remain asymptomatic all your life, whether it will give you some trouble, or whether you'll die of it. You'll simply have to wait and see."

"How long do I have to wait to find out what sort of case I have?" I said.

"Two to five years," he said. "If you have no further attacks for two years, I think you can relax. And if you have no symptoms for five years, I think you can forget about it completely."

He then discussed what I could do in the meantime. The answer was, basically, nothing. Multiple sclerosis was a disease of unknown cause. There were some helpful treatments during acute episodes, but no cures. Since there wasn't anything to do, he said I should take care of my general health and avoid stress and mental upset, but otherwise try not to think about it.

This neurologist was so straightforward, so matter-of-fact, that I was able to leave his office and go back to the wards to work. Despite the bad news, I was okay.

Two days later the internist called me in. He said he had gotten the report from the neurologist. He asked me how I felt. I abruptly started to cry. I was embarrassed to be crying in this man's office, but I couldn't help myself. The internist said he wanted a second opinion and sent me to Dr. Derek Denny-Brown, who was the most famous neurologist at Harvard at that time. I had had lectures from Dr. Denny-Brown. I was not happy to be seeing him now as a patient.

He told me the same thing. Yes, I had probably had an episode. Yes, I would have to wait and see what would happen in my case. Yes, it would be two to five years of waiting. Yes, I had the disease. Yes.

I cracked completely. I couldn't go back to the wards; I just went AWOL for a few days. I cried constantly. I was terrified and sad and angry. I had just celebrated my twenty-sixth birthday, I was just beginning to be successful as a writer, I was starting to look forward to leaving medicine and beginning a career as a writer, and now . . . *this*. This dreadful shadow.

Each morning I woke up tense, wondering if I was blind, or numb in another part of my body, or paralyzed. And I was going to have to wait years to find out for sure. I could hardly bear to wait a week. How could I wait two to five years? The suspense was intolerable.

But, since there was nothing I could do, eventually I had to go back to work, to resume some normalcy in my life.

My internist said I should see a psychiatrist. Had I ever met Dr. Corman?

Yes, I said. I was well acquainted with Dr. Corman.

Dr. Corman listened to my story and sniffed. "Actually," he said, "there is a third possibility besides spinal-cord tumor and multiple sclerosis."

"What's that?"

"Conversion hysteria."

"Oh, come on," I said. Conversion hysteria was an old psychiatric concept. Back in the nineteenth century, people—usually women—developed all sorts of bizarre symptoms, including seizures, blindness, and paralyses, that had no organic cause. These were considered hysterical symptoms, in which the patient converted some psychological problem into a physical manifestation.

I certainly knew such things happened. In the clinic I had treated a young woman with hysterical blindness. She would just become blind from time to time, then regain her sight. She was obviously screwed up. I had also seen one case of pseudocyesis—hysterical pregnancy. This woman developed all the signs of pregnancy and actually went into labor, though of course she didn't deliver a baby, since she wasn't pregnant.

"That's not me," I said. "I'm not hysterical."

"Really?"

"Of course not," I said, insulted. I pointed out that hysterics were mostly women.

"We're seeing more hysterical men," Dr. Corman said.

I pointed out that in cases of conversion hysteria patients showed a characteristic indifference to their diseases. They weren't really worried. My woman who went blind from time to time complained about it, but she wasn't as upset as you might expect. Whereas I was extremely upset about my case.

"Really?" Dr. Corman said.

He was annoying me. I said so.

"Well," Dr. Corman said, "if I were you, I'd consider the fact that, of all your possible diagnoses, conversion hysteria is actually the most favorable."

I didn't believe that I was hysterical. Later on, other doctors who followed my case mentioned this possibility, too. Although the numbness continued for several years, I never developed further symptoms. And I learned that it was indeed common to have a single neurological episode.

Fortunately, I have never had another. I have learned to knock on wood, and to take good care of my general health.

Almost ten years passed before I could look back and wonder whether the decision to leave medicine was so difficult, so traumatic, that I needed the added boost of a serious illness—or at least a possible illness. Because the immediate effect of the terrifying diagnosis was bracing: I was forced to ask myself what I wanted to do with the rest of my life, how I wanted to spend it.

And it was clear to me that if in fact I had only a few years of unencumbered activity, then I wanted to spend those years writing and not doing medicine, or any of the things that colleagues, friends, parents, or society in general expected me to do. The illness helped me to stand on my own, to make a difficult transition.

In quitting, I was following my instincts; I was doing what I really wanted to do. But most people saw only that I was giving up a lot of prestige. In those days, the prestige of physicians was high. Polls ranked doctors just below justices of the Supreme Court. To quit medicine to become a writer struck most people like quitting the Supreme Court to become a bail bondsman. They admired my determination, but they thought I was pretty unrealistic.

Then, in my last year of school, it became publicized that I had written a book called *The Andromeda Strain* and sold it to the movies for a lot of money. Overnight, I was identified as a successful writer, and it changed everything in my life. All the doctors and residents who had shunned me became suddenly interested in me. I had been eating lunch alone; now I was never alone—everybody wanted to sit with me. I was a celebrity.

The blatant insincerity of the way I was treated troubled me very much. I didn't yet understand that people used celebrities as figures of fantasy; they didn't want to know who you really were, any more than kids at Disneyland want Mickey Mouse to pull off his rubber head and reveal that he's just a local teenager. The kids want to see Mickey. And the doctors in the cafeteria wanted to see Young Dr. Hollywood. And that was what they saw.

I just sat around and watched them do it.

The difficulties I experienced adjusting to my new position barely hinted at the kinds of experiences I would later have. Many of those experiences have been painful and difficult, but most have been, on balance, exciting. I often think back to medicine, and my life as a student. I wouldn't have had to change if I had remained a doctor. Quitting medicine assured me that I would be forced into all sorts of changes I might not otherwise have made.

Travels

1971–1986

Sex and Death in L.A.

In 1971 I was living in Los Angeles and my wife was in La Jolla. We had separated, because, after five years together as students, she wanted to start a family and I wanted to pursue my career in books and movies. That was why I had gone to Los Angeles, to try to work in movies. Los Angeles was a strange city; I didn't know anyone there, and I was lonely and unhappy much of the time.

I moved into an apartment building in West Hollywood that was well known as a place where people went when they got divorced, because you could rent a furnished apartment for only six months. My apartment was furnished in green crushed-velvet couches and chairs with a vaguely Mexican look. The carpet was green with gold flecks. The kitchen was yellow. The view overlooked the Sunset Strip. It was Hollywood, all right, and it was exciting!

In the afternoons I would sit by the swimming pool. The same group of tenants could always be found at the pool. There was a Rams football star and his actress girlfriend (they were always fighting); there was a model who had been Miss Arizona and was extremely beautiful in a bikini (she was always shy and insecure); there was an accountant with a portable radio and a big cigar who read the New

York papers (he never spoke); there was a woman in her thirties reputed to be a madam (she always swam laps, and then read the *Hollywood Reporter*).

I had imagined that living in a Hollywood apartment would be more exciting than it was. The football player and his girlfriend made an attractive couple, but since they were always glaring at each other, I tended to stay away from them. And the lovely Miss Arizona was recuperating from an unhappy marriage to a rock-and-roll star; she never went out at all; she stayed home and watched television and worried about her car payments. There were some movie stars in the building, too, but they always wore dark glasses and never talked to ordinary people.

Later the accountant with the cigar stopped coming to the pool. I asked Miss Arizona if he had moved out. She showed me a newspaper clipping. The man had been found in the trunk of a Cadillac at Kennedy Airport with a bullet in his head.

You never knew what to expect. One night I was getting dressed for dinner when the front doorman knocked on my door.

"Dr. Crichton?"

"Yes?"

"It's Miss Jenkins."

"Miss Jenkins?" An unfamiliar name.

"In the building. You know Miss Jenkins?"

"I don't think I do."

"Well, she lives in the building; I thought you might have seen her."

"What about her?"

"She fell off the commode."

I couldn't see why that was any business of mine, and I said so.

"I think you should see her."

"Why?"

"She fell off the commode."

"Well, did she hurt herself?"

"It is only one floor up, on the eighth floor. . . ."

"But why should I see her?"

"Because she fell off the commode."

This conversation could go on forever. In the end, he led me upstairs and with a grave dignity unlocked the door to Miss Jenkins's room.

Her apartment also contained green crushed-velvet furniture in a Mexican style. I recognized Miss Jenkins as a bespectacled woman of about forty with short blond hair, the younger of a pair of lesbians who had lived together in the building at least as long as I had. Miss Jenkins was now fully dressed, lying on her back on the living-room couch, one arm dangling limply on the floor. Her skin was pale blue. She did not seem to be breathing. Her lover, the other woman, was not there.

"Where is the other woman?" I said.

"Walking the dog."

"Walking the dog? Does she know about Miss Jenkins?"

"Yes. She was the one who told me."

"What did she tell you?"

"That Miss Jenkins fell off the commode."

By now I had quickly checked Miss Jenkins, noting a thready pulse, shallow, intermittent respiration, dilated eyes, an open can of beer, and a half-empty bottle of sleeping pills.

The doorman said, "Is she dead?"

"No," I said.

"No?" He seemed surprised.

"No," I said. "She's taken an overdose."

"I was told," he said, "that she fell off the commode."

"Well, the problem is a drug overdose."

"You can help her?"

"No," I said.

"Aren't you a doctor?"

"Yes, but I can't do anything." And indeed I could not. I was not licensed to practice medicine and I faced serious lawsuits if I did anything at all in this situation. "Call the police," I said.

"I did," he said. "Although at the time I was not sure if she was dead."

"She's not dead," I said. "What did the police say?"

"They said to call the fire department."

"Then call the fire department," I said.

"Why should I call the fire department?" he said. In the end, I called the fire department and they said they would send an emergency vehicle.

Meanwhile, her roommate returned with a yapping Lhasa apso on a rhinestone leash. "What are you doing in my apartment?" she said suspiciously.

"This man is a doctor," the doorman said.

"Why don't you help her?"

"She's taken a drug overdose," I said.

"No, she fell off the commode," the roommate said. She was a tall, slender woman of fifty, graying hair, a stern manner. She looked like a schoolteacher.

"Do you know what drugs she took?" I said.

"Are you really a doctor?" the woman said. "You look too young to be a doctor."

By now the Lhasa was jumping on the comatose woman, licking her face and barking at me. The dog was leaving muddy footprints on Miss Jenkins's blouse. The scene was becoming chaotic.

The roommate turned to me, holding the beer can. "Did you drink this beer?"

"No," I said.

"Are you *sure?*" She was very suspicious.

"I just got here."

She turned to the doorman. "Did *you* drink this beer?"

"No," the doorman said. "I came with him."

"This beer can wasn't here before," she said.

"Maybe Miss Jenkins drank it."

I checked Miss Jenkins's pupils again and the Lhasa apso bit my hand, drawing blood. The roommate saw the blood and began to scream. "What have you done to Buffy?"

She grabbed the barking dog into her arms, and then she began to kick me, shrieking, "You bastard! You bastard! Hurting a poor, innocent dog!"

I was trying to avoid her kicks, and I looked at the doorman. "Can't you do something about this?"

"Shit, man," he said.

There was a loud knock on the door, but nobody could get to the door, because the roommate was kicking and fighting. Now she was shouting, "You robbed me, you robbed me!"

Then we heard a loudspeaker voice say, "All right! You people inside, stand clear of the door, we're coming through!"

"Shit," the doorman said. "Cops!"

"So?"

"I'm carrying!"

"Aha!" the roommate shouted. "I *knew* it!" She flung open the door, and there stood a fireman in a yellow slicker and pointed hat, standing with his ax upraised. He was ready to hack down the door, and he looked disappointed to have it opened instead. "What the hell's going on in here?" he said.

"She fell off the commode," the roommate said.

"Did you put it out already?" the fireman said.

"I was walking the dog, I don't know what happened."

"There isn't any smoke," the fireman said suspiciously. "What are you people up to?"

"This woman's had a drug overdose," I said, pointing to Miss Jenkins on the couch.

"Hell, then we need the paramedics," the fireman said, looking at the woman. He called on a walkie-talkie. "There's no damn fire here," he said. "Who reported a fire?"

"Nobody reported a fire," I said.

"Somebody sure as hell did," the fireman said.

"This man is not a doctor," the roommate said.

"Who are you?" the fireman said.

"I'm a doctor," I said.

"Then I'd like to know what he is doing in my apartment," the roommate said.

"You got some identification?"

"I called him," the doorman said. "Because he's a doctor."

"He is not a doctor."

"All I want to know is, who reported a fire? Because that's against the law."

"Coming through," the paramedics said, arriving at the door with a stretcher.

"Never mind," the fireman said. "We already got a doctor here."

"No, come in," I said to the paramedics.

"You don't want to treat her?" the paramedics said.

"I'm not licensed," I said.

"He's no doctor. He cut Buffy."

"You're not what?"

"I'm not licensed."

"But you're a doctor, is that right?"

"Yes."

"I've never seen him before in my life."

"I live in the building."

"And he drank my beer."

"You drank her beer?"

"No, I never drank any beer."

"I think he took something, too."

"You mean this beer here?"

Meanwhile, the paramedics were working on Miss Jenkins, getting ready to take her to the hospital. They asked what drugs she had taken, but the roommate would only say she had fallen off the commode. The fireman was giving me a hard time about being a doctor until Buffy leaned over and bit him viciously on the hand. "Son of a bitch!" the fireman said, reaching for his ax.

"Don't you dare!" screamed the roommate, clutching her dog.

But all the fireman did was take his ax and head for the door. "Jesus, I hate Hollywood," he said, and he slammed the door behind him.

I was out the door right after him. "Where are you going?" the fireman asked me.

"I have a date," I said. "I'm late."

"Yeah, right," he said. "Only think of yourself. You guys. Shit."

It turned out the manager had listed my name on the lobby board with an "M.D." after it, because he thought it gave the building class. Whenever there was a suicide attempt, the doormen would look at the building directory and call the doctor. I was the only doctor. I got all the calls. It was a large building. There was a suicide attempt nearly every week.

The second time it happened, I told the doorman right away, "I don't have a license, I don't practice, there's nothing I can do."

"Would you just check him? I'm pretty sure he's dead."

"How do you know?"

"He jumped from the twelfth floor. Would you just check him, make sure he's dead?"

"Okay. Where is he?"

"Out front."

I went with him to the lobby. There was a woman crying. I recognized her as a girl from Atlanta who had come to Los Angeles to sell cosmetics but who hoped to get discovered for the movies while she was here. She was always heavily made up. Now she was sobbing, "Oh, Billy, Billy . . ."

I hadn't been aware this girl had a boyfriend. I looked at the doorman.

He nodded sadly. "Billy jumped from her balcony."

"Oh."

We went out to the street.

"Did you call the police?" I said.

"Do I have to?"

"Of course," I said. "If he's dead."

Out on the street, I didn't see a body immediately. I was tense now, steeling myself against what I might see, wondering how bad it would be, how gruesome. We walked around the side of the apartment building. Then the doorman pointed to some low bushes that were planted near the building. "Billy's in there."

"In *there?*"

For an awful moment I thought Billy might be a child. I walked forward to the bushes and saw the body of a yellow cat.

"Billy's a *cat?*" I said.

"Yeah."

"You called me out here for a *cat?*"

"Sure. What'd you think?"

"I thought it was a person."

"No, hell. Person jumps, we always call the police."

Psychiatry

My wife called me in Los Angeles almost every day. She thought we should get back together, but I wasn't so sure.

She suggested I see a psychiatrist. I refused. I didn't think psychiatry did any good for people. It was just a lot of hand-holding.

One day she called to say she had gotten the name of a psychiatrist in Los Angeles for me. This man, Dr. Norton, had worked with a lot of writers and artists and he was very eminent, a professor at UCLA. She said I should go to see him.

I didn't want to.

Then she said, "He probably won't take you anyway, he's so important and busy."

I was immediately offended. Why wouldn't he take me? Wasn't I an interesting person? Wouldn't he find my case interesting? I called his office immediately and scheduled an appointment.

Arthur Norton was a fit, tanned man nearing sixty. He explained he didn't usually take new patients, but he would hear my problem and then refer me to someone else. I said okay.

I now found myself in a peculiar situation. I didn't really

believe in psychiatry, I didn't want to see a psychiatrist, and I didn't think there was anything wrong with me, but I was challenged to present myself to Dr. Norton in a fascinating way. For an hour, I revealed all my most unusual sides. I made jokes. I expressed provocative opinions. I really worked hard to interest him in me. I kept glancing at him out of the corner of my eye, to see how I was doing; he appeared friendly but completely unreadable.

At the end of the hour, he said that he thought I had some life issues to consider, and that during this period I might benefit from talking about them. And he offered to serve as the person I talked to.

Aha! Success!

I left the office elated. I had talked him into it.

But I still wasn't sure psychiatry did any good. And it was expensive, sixty dollars an hour. Anything that cost so much must surely be an indulgence. Rich lazy people went to psychiatrists.

I decided to keep track of how much it was costing me to see Dr. Norton, and I assessed each session when it was over to determine if it had been worth the sixty dollars.

I found Dr. Norton puzzling because he was so normal. I'd tell him my story and he'd say things like "Time will tell" or "You can't make an omelet without breaking eggs."

I thought, Sixty dollars an hour to hear you can't make an omelet without breaking eggs? What good is this?

But I enjoyed going to him and complaining about my life, how I had managed to survive all the people who had abused me. I had a lot of energy for this sort of complaint. And he seemed sympathetic.

Then on the fifth session—three hundred dollars down the drain so far—he said, "Well, now, let's see where we are."

"Okay," I said.

Dr. Norton said, "You've explained that as a child you didn't get any approval from your parents."

"Right."

"If you got a ninety-eight on a test, they wanted to know why it wasn't a hundred."

"Right."

"They never appreciated or complimented you."

"Right."

"They belittled your achievements."

"Right."

"And now, as an adult, when you write a book, you are fearful that you won't be accepted, even though you always seem to be."

"Right."

"And you feel that you have to do whatever other people want; people call you up and ask you to give a speech or to do something, and you can't say no to them."

"Right. People won't leave me alone."

"In general you feel you have to please people or they won't like you."

"Right."

"Okay," he said. "What kind of a person are you describing?"

I suddenly went blank.

I couldn't remember what we had been talking about. My mind was absolutely empty. I was enveloped in a confusing fog.

"I don't understand what you're asking me," I said.

"Well," he said, "you're a doctor. If you were presented with a person who never received praise and encouragement, no matter how hard he worked, who felt that what he did was never enough, and who as an adult was very unsure of himself, and easily manipulated by total strangers, what kind of a person would you say that was?"

"I don't know," I said.

I had no idea at all. I could see Dr. Norton was driving at something—I just didn't know what. I was still in a fog. I couldn't seem to organize my thoughts, or to keep track of things. I was disoriented, dazed. I stared at him. He waited, calmly.

There was a long silence.

"I'm sorry," I said. "What was the question again?"

Dr. Norton tried a few more times to get me to see it, but I couldn't. And finally he said, "Aren't you describing an insecure person?"

I was stunned. He had laid out all the evidence. I couldn't deny the conclusion. And the very fact that I couldn't see where the evidence pointed was itself significant. He was telling me I was insecure, and he was obviously right.

I felt amazed. Just as amazed as if he had shown me that I had a third arm coming out of my chest, an arm I had never noticed before. How could I not have noticed this before? But I never thought I was insecure. If anything, I saw myself as astoundingly confident.

100

Could I really have held such an incorrect view of myself?

Dr. Norton tried to soften the blow, and explained that many things about ourselves were difficult to see without outside help. That was the whole point of a therapist. He was an objective outsider.

This was a new idea to me, that there might be some things about myself that I couldn't see without outside help. But it obviously was true.

I never kept track of how much I was spending again.

It became clear that my marriage was finished and that I was going to remain single in Los Angeles. I was in my late twenties, I had a reputation as a writer, I had a psychiatrist, and I had a Porsche Targa. In short, I was ready for whatever life had to offer.

But my academic past had left me rather sheltered, and I was unrealistic, particularly where women were concerned. I kept imagining that I could do things that I couldn't.

At one point I was going out with a girl who worked in a literary agent's office. Pretty soon I decided I liked another girl in the same office. I wanted to go out with this second girl, but I didn't want the first one to find out.

"Do you think I can keep it secret?" I asked Dr. Norton.

"No," he said.

"Why not?"

"I think two girls in the same office will talk, and they'll discover they're both going out with you."

"Even so," I said, "is that so bad?"

"Well, I think they may both decide not to see you."

That seemed an unpleasant outcome. I didn't like the idea of going from two girls to none. "Oh, I don't think that would happen," I said.

Dr. Norton shrugged. "Time will tell."

Of course, that's exactly what happened. The girls found out, and they were both indignant that I would try such a low trick.

Later I began to get interested in my secretary, a cute blonde with large breasts. I'd never been involved with a large-breasted girl before.

"I think I'm falling for my secretary," I told Dr. Norton.

"Don't," he said.

"Why not?" I said. I couldn't see why it would be a problem.

"It tends to complicate not only your work but your private relationships as well. That seems to be what usually happens. At least, it happens often enough to lead to the rule that it's unwise to get romantically involved with your secretary."

"Well," I said, "maybe that's the rule for most people. But I think I can handle it."

"Time will tell," Dr. Norton said.

Within two weeks, my life was living hell. I quickly learned this cute, large-breasted girl was not for me. I knew it, and she knew it, too. Suddenly nothing worked right in the office: things didn't get done; callers were insulted; appointments were missed; details overlooked. And my cheerful, sunny California secretary now filled the office with glowering rainclouds. Her every word and comment to me was sour and accusing.

I couldn't believe it. Not only had our affair not worked out; now I was going to have to fire her.

"What a mess," I said to Dr. Norton.

"Hell hath no fury like a woman scorned," Dr. Norton said.

By now I saw the point of these homilies. Dr. Norton was trying to get me to understand that certain rules of life had been around for a long time and that life probably wasn't going to make an exception for me. I was having trouble understanding precisely that. I kept thinking that things would be the way I wanted them to be. And I kept learning I was wrong.

I had been going out for several months with a girl I liked when I met a famous movie star. Suddenly I wanted to go out with this movie star, but I figured it would be a short-lived thing that would quickly end, and I didn't want my regular girlfriend to find out.

"If you date a famous movie star, your girlfriend's going to find out," Dr. Norton said.

"How?" I said. "I'm just going to dinner in an out-of-the-way restaurant."

It turned out my out-of-the-way dinner was reported the same night by a television gossip columnist. Not only my girlfriend but all her family and friends found out what I had done. My girlfriend broke up with me. I was considered a rat.

102

I felt pretty bad, too. I couldn't seem to manage my social life. I blamed my sex drive. "I can't help it," I said to Dr. Norton. "I'm going out with some girl, and then I see another girl, and I want her. And then I see another girl, and I want her, too."

"Uh-huh," he said, noncommittal.

"When is it going to stop?" I said to Dr. Norton. "Maybe when I get older. Maybe, in a couple more years, I'll calm down sexually. It'll stop then."

"Well," he said, "I'm almost sixty . . ." He shrugged.

"It never stops?" I said.

I couldn't decide whether to be pleased or appalled by this prospect.

Dr. Norton had a different idea about the nature of my problem. He seemed to think I kept getting into trouble because I wasn't telling women the truth. He thought I should tell them all that this was a time in my life when I was seeing a number of women, and leave it at that. "That way you don't have to be secretive," he said.

But I couldn't do that, because I was afraid none of the women would like me if they knew I was seeing other women.

A year later I got divorced. I bought a house in Hollywood. My life settled down a little. I managed to write some screenplays, and I tried to set up a movie to direct. I liked my life pretty well, but I was moving further and further from the academic existence I had known for so many years. Many things about movies perplexed me. For example, all the people in the movie business lied. They lied all the time. They said they liked your screenplay when they didn't; they said they were going to hire you when they had no intention of hiring you. I couldn't understand why movie people didn't just say what they meant. It was so confusing. Why did everybody lie?

And there seemed to be a different style in movies from the academic style I was used to. In talking over a movie, the studio head said, "What about casting Joe Mason?"

"I don't really think so," I said.

Then, the next week, we had another casting meeting, and the studio head said, "What about Joe Mason?"

"He's not really right," I said. "And I never liked him myself."

Then, at the next meeting, the studio head said, "What about Joe Mason?"

By now I was frustrated, because the movie wasn't getting cast. I stood up and leaned over his desk and shouted, "I *can't stand* Joe Mason! He makes me *vomit* whenever I see him! I *hate* Joe Mason!"

"Hey," the studio head said, raising his hands, "all you have to do is say so."

So I began to learn that the ordinary, everyday style of communication in Hollywood required what was, in academic terms, wretched excess. You were expected to shout and scream and carry on in a way that would never have been acceptable at Harvard. But apparently in Hollywood they didn't listen to you unless you shouted and screamed.

And the Hollywood environment was exotic. There were homosexual and theatrical people, and people who were into drugs and orgies and odd things of all sorts. This had its own fascination, but I often felt uneasy.

Eventually I was going out with a girl who was a famous sex symbol. I was quite pleased that I was going out with a famous sex symbol, although we never really had sex. She wasn't interested in sex, and she bathed infrequently, so she had strong odors, which deflected my enthusiasm. But she was a lively, friendly person, and I enjoyed spending time with her.

One day she called to say she'd be late, because she was going to see a psychic. This didn't surprise me. Hollywood people were into all this loony stuff, psychics and astrology and peculiar diets. Everybody was interested in what your sign was. What's your sign? I used to answer, "Neon." It was a lot of foolishness.

When she showed up, she was very excited. "Michael, you have to see this woman!"

Why? I asked. I didn't believe in psychics.

"Listen," she said, "this woman told me stuff nobody could possibly know!"

Sure, sure, I thought. That's what they always say.

"No," she said. "Listen. I ran out of money and I had to get a job, so I made a low-budget movie in the Philippines. I never told anybody."

I certainly didn't know about this film she had made.

"And while I was there, I met this pilot in the air force, and he used to take me for rides in his jet fighter."

I didn't know about that, either.

"Well, this psychic told me all about it. And there's no way she could have known!"

I wasn't impressed.

"Go and see for yourself."

I didn't want to go. It was a waste of time and money.

Later on in the evening, I was talking about a movie called *Westworld* I wanted to make. The studio, MGM, was behaving in a discouraging fashion. One day they said they were going to make it. The next day they said it was off. I was worried about what would finally happen.

"Go and ask her, Michael."

And she made the appointment for me to see my first psychic.

The psychic was a British woman, about fifty, wearing a quilted housecoat in the middle of the afternoon. She lived in a small frame house in the San Fernando Valley. She kept all the shades drawn, so it was dark and gloomy. She led me into a back room with barbells on the floor and an exercise bicycle to one side. The room smelled of talcum powder. And it was dark with the shades drawn. And she sat me down on a bed and then she sat next to me. She took my hand.

"Just relax, love," she said.

She was silent for a moment. Holding my hand.

I decided that, as long as I was going to a psychic, I'd try to help the process along by making my mind a complete blank. Sitting with her, I tried not to think about anything but just to be blank.

"What are you doing?" she said, after a few moments. "I can't read you, what are you doing?"

"I'm trying to make my mind blank."

"Well, just relax. Don't try to do anything."

"Okay," I said. So I just stared at the barbells and the exercise bicycle. And then she began to talk.

"I see you surrounded by books," she said. "Lots and lots of books."

She said I had a project that was up in the air, but that I shouldn't worry, it was just a little premature. The project would begin in late February.

I found it quite agreeable to be with her, and not at all weird, the way I imagined it would be. She was just a lady who seemed to get things out of the air, and talk about them. I felt as if I was listening to her daydreams about me. That sort of feeling.

But I knew what she was telling me was wrong. This was now November. MGM had set its final decision for December 15. No matter what the studio said at that time, there was no way to begin the picture, either at MGM or elsewhere, by February. So she was definitely wrong.

And she said that I was drawn to psychic and spiritual things. That was wrong, too. I was a scientist. I had no interest in this stuff.

And she said I was psychic myself, which proved to me—if proof were necessary—that neither of us was psychic. Because I knew I wasn't.

She made some other comments about my past and my family, but nothing unambiguous. Sitting there with her, I began to imagine how I would recount this experience for the amusement of my friends. Psychic? Some woman in her bathrobe sitting in a room with barbells? Give me a break!

A few weeks later, on December 15, MGM canceled *Westworld*. As far as I was concerned, that was the final nail in the psychic coffin.

Then, two days later, MGM changed its mind. The studio would make the movie after all, if the producer and I would agree to an absurdly tight production schedule. We didn't like the schedule, but we wanted to make the movie, so we agreed.

The movie began shooting on February 23 of the following year, so I had to admit that she had gotten one thing right. But by then I had lots of other things on my mind. I was finally shooting a movie!

In August of 1973 I was flying back from Chicago, where I had screened *Westworld*. It appeared the picture would be successful. The producer and I had survived an impossible budget and an impossible schedule: to shoot and release a picture in six months. Many people had predicted we couldn't do it; some had even bet their jobs we couldn't. Heads would soon roll at the studio—but not ours! Now, with the intense pressure abruptly ended, the producer and I shared in a mood of almost hysterical self-congratulation. We had done it: not only had we made our dates, but the little low-budget picture actually seemed to work! Sitting on that airplane, we literally felt on top of the world.

Suddenly I broke out in a drenching sweat. My clothes were soaked through within seconds. I was panic-stricken, in the grip of a powerful anxiety attack. But why at this instant of airborne elation? It took a while to figure it out.

All my life I had pursued clear goals: in high school, to get into a good college; in college, to get into medical school; in medical school, to become a writer; as a writer, to make a movie.

I was thirty years old. I had graduated from Harvard, taught at Cambridge University, climbed the Great Pyramid, earned a medical degree, married and divorced, been a postdoctoral fellow at the Salk Institute, published two bestselling novels, and now had made a movie. And I had abruptly run out of goals for myself.

I was stranded within my own life. That was why I broke into a sweat: *what was I going to do now?*

I had no idea.

In the following weeks, I fell into a lethargy, then a full-blown depression. Nothing seemed worthwhile. Needless to say, sympathy for my condition was in short supply. To be depressed by success was not attractive, or even understandable. My friends didn't realize that they might be next in line.

I took to haunting bookstores, buying five hundred dollars' worth of books at a time, carrying them off in cartons. Books on every conceivable subject: dinosaurs, hot-air ballooning, Charles II, saturation diving, Islamic art, weather forecasting, computer graphics, Indonesian cooking, criminology, Benjamin Franklin, the Himalaya, Victorian cities, high-energy physics, tigers, Leonardo da Vinci, the British Raj, witchcraft, vegetarian cooking, the Inca Empire, Winslow Homer. Since nothing interested me, everything was equally uninteresting.

One day I came across a book called *Be Here Now*. It was an esoteric, quasi-religious Eastern-philosophy book of the sort I didn't usually look at, but it had a handmade quality and an odd shape that caught my eye. The author was Ram Dass, formerly Richard Alpert, an expelled professor of psychology at Harvard. I had been a reporter on the Harvard *Crimson* during the sixties when Alpert and his colleague Timothy Leary were thrown off the faculty for giving LSD to undergraduates. I remembered those incidents well. Now here was his book.

I took it home and read it. The book was in three sections. The first section contained straightforward prose; the second section consisted of hand-printed words and pictures, a kind of messy collage; the third section was a guide to meditation.

I read the first section. I expected to find the disorganized ramblings of a poor fellow whose brains had been scrambled by too much acid and too many mystical journeys that went nowhere. But instead I found a lucid history of a driven, successful East Coast intellectual who suddenly found his life, his houses, his cars, his lovers, his vacations, his work, to be unsatisfying.

I knew exactly what he was talking about.

I felt exactly the same way.

Richard Alpert, a Harvard renegade, an obviously unbalanced man who had gone off the deep end of his life, now appeared before me as somebody I identified with strongly. I had a juggling act to do, to make it all right for me to agree with him. Richard Alpert must have something on the ball after all.

But there was a further implication. Alpert, now Ram Dass—the new name stuck in my throat—I didn't even want to say it—Ram Dass had gone to India. And after several years he had come back with answers that seemed to work for him. He seemed to feel better about things, to have found a new perspective.

He had made a pilgrimage to India.

Should I?

I couldn't stand the idea of it. The implications of it. I couldn't see myself as a holy seeker after truth. Wearing white robes, contemplating my navel. I still shopped at Brooks Brothers. I still liked Brooks Brothers.

There had to be another way.

My attitude toward mystical journeys was typified by the joke about the student who seeks the holy man in India, finds him meditating at the top of a mountain, and asks breathlessly, "What is the meaning of life?"

The holy man says, "Life is a flower."

The student is outraged: "Life is a flower?"

To which the holy man replies, "You mean it's not?"

That was my idea: nobody knew any more than I did. Not really. A professor might know more about his particular subject, and the resident of a city might know more about that city, but as far as *reality* was concerned, nobody knew any more than I did. I figured I knew all there was to know.

What I knew was that the history of man demonstrated

the inexorable triumph of reason over superstition, culminating in our acceptance of science as the best method for learning the truth and exploring the universe. That in the past men had believed all sorts of nonsense, but through the fruits of science we were able to roll back the darkness and live in the light of reason.

This meant that, however bad life might be now, it could only have been worse in past ages. The history I envisioned was a history of steady progress. Nothing was lost, only gained. In no way were the people of, say, the Middle Ages better off than I was. That was inconceivable. Medieval people were suffocated by their social structure, impoverished by their economy, and driven by their religion to make those idiotic (if beautiful) cathedrals.

I lived in a fast-paced scientific world, where technical journals were removed from the library after five years. In general, I preferred to look forward. We lived in an exciting time, in which we were learning the nature of reality at the subatomic level, the nature of the universe, and the nature of life. I was living in the most enlightened, the richest, the most advanced, the most liberated period in the history of man.

And I knew that, despite fame, fortune, and psychiatry bills, I was miserable.

And it seemed Ram Dass was not.

I reread his book several times, trying to find another way, my own way, in his story. Each time I read the book, what Alpert was saying seemed to make more sense. It became more straightforward. It became more clearly a better way to behave, a better way to look at things.

But I still wasn't about to give up my life and go to India.

What I did was, I read books. There was a bookstore called the Bodhi Tree that specialized in these esoteric areas. I went there a lot, and pretty soon names like Krishnamurti and Yogananda were as familiar to me as Watson and Crick, or Hubel and Wiesel. And I went a lot to Maui.

In the early seventies, Maui was a wonderful place. You could go diving and listen to the mysterious underwater songs of the humpback whales. You could hike into lush hidden valleys without being shot by dope growers. In two hours, you could go from the beach to the freezing summit of Haleakala, ten thousand feet above sea level. Inside the crater of Haleakala there were at least three distinct environments: cinder-cone desert, alpine meadow, and tropical

109

rain forest. The silence inside the crater, the unworldly appearance of the landscape, made it especially impressive.

In those days, Maui wasn't crowded; they hadn't built those monstrous hotels that appear to have been designed by Walt Disney and Albert Speer. Lahaina was a sleepy, run-down little town populated by hippies; the bookstores were stocked with "spiritual" books. I hadn't seen most of these books before. I first read the Seth books there, and Carlos Castaneda, and Ken Wilbur. I read all sorts of books there for the first time.

The other thing that I did was, I began to travel again.

Bangkok

I had traveled before. I had traveled all my life. My parents were inveterate travelers, and they took their kids with them. They'd cram all of us into the car each June when school was over, and we'd head off for some faraway destination. The Southwest and Mexico, one year. The Pacific Northwest, one year. The Canadian Rockies, one year.

By the time I graduated from high school, I had been to forty-eight states, to Canada and Mexico, and to five countries of Europe.

After college I won a Henry Russell Shaw Fellowship, and for a year traveled in Europe and North Africa. That was in 1965. A year of travel, what an opportunity—and as a student I was obsessively thorough. I entered the museums of Paris and Amsterdam loaded down with guidebooks and commentaries. If I was in a city where an important museum was closed, I stayed an extra day. I saw everything. I ate everything. I experienced everything. In Egypt, I climbed the Great Pyramid of Cheops, went inside it, and then visited every archaeological site of importance between Saqqara and Aswan. Nothing was too small or too distant to escape my inspection; it was never too hot or too buggy; if there was any question about it, I saw it. In Ma-

111

drid, I sought out obscure apartment buildings that represented the early work of Antonio Gaudí; in France, I went down a checklist of buildings by Le Corbusier. I fought the traffic of Naples in search of Caravaggios. In France and Spain, I visited every prehistoric painted cave known. I developed an interest in Romanesque cloisters. In Greece, I spent two weeks in the Peloponnese alone, looking at classical sites outlined by the *Guide Bleu.* I used the *Guide Bleu* because it was the most detailed guide I could find, and I preferred it even though I was obliged to struggle through the site descriptions in my bad French.

So, by the time I started medical school, I could say of all North America, Europe, and North Africa, "I've been there." I knew my way around. I was comfortable with different languages, different currencies. My passport and luggage were suitably battered. I could enter a strange city, find a hotel, speak enough of the language to get along, to be at ease.

I was an accomplished traveler.

The financial pressures of medical school prevented much traveling during those years. And afterward I fell out of the habit. I didn't have much curiosity about other places any more. I was pursuing my career, getting on with my life. Eventually, I realized it had been almost a decade since I'd taken a real trip.

When I hit my doldrums, I decided I had better get moving. I decided to go to Bangkok, where my friend Davis Pike had urged me to visit him. I booked a flight, cabled Davis that I was coming, and set off. My first stop was Hong Kong.

There are few sights as exciting as landing in Kai Tak Airport in Hong Kong at night. The mountains, the water, the lights of the buildings make it magical, like flying into the center of a glowing jewel. I was tremendously excited as I looked out the window. And then to step off the plane and be assailed by the smells—that peculiarly Asian combination of sea water, dried fish, packed humanity—my excitement increased tenfold. And driving in a taxi through the city, past the open, brightly lit stalls, people squatting on the pavement, working, all the street life—fantastic! I had never seen anything like this!

I arrived at the Peninsula Hotel, and it appeared to me

the grandest in the world. There was nothing in Europe like this. Everything was subtly different. There were white-liveried people on every floor to help you. The rooms were sumptuous. And in the elegant marble bathroom there was a carafe of drinking water, and a little sign saying that you shouldn't drink the tap water. Fabulous! Exotic! This combination of expensive marble and the little sign! Europe had nothing like this!

I went to sleep blissfully happy.

I awoke the next day ready to see Asia. Guidebook in hand, I walked the streets of Kowloon, then took the Star Ferry to Victoria. I wandered, enjoying all the street activity. Then I went to the Central Market, thinking markets are always good to look at, a good orientation to how people live. I'd always enjoyed seeing the markets in rural France and North Africa.

The Central Market was a two-story open concrete structure with tiled surfaces. The place smelled like a morgue. They were slaughtering chickens and small animals right on the street. I saw one man slice open a pig's intestines on the sidewalk, and sluice out the ruffled inner surface with a garden hose.

Suddenly I was exhausted. I had to go lie down. It was jet lag, catching up with me. I returned to my hotel and slept several hours.

That afternoon I took a taxi to Aberdeen, on the other side of Victoria. In those days Aberdeen was a spectacular place, a giant boat basin where thousands of people lived. I hired a boat and went for a tour of the basin. It was terrific to see the vignettes of life on the boats. I was excited again. Afterward I went to the onshore market in Aberdeen, where the boat people purchased their food.

The Chinese place great importance on fresh food. I would often see a Chinese woman carrying a plastic bag filled with water, with a live fish swimming inside it; this, I was told, was her family's dinner, kept fresh to the last minute.

The Aberdeen market was under dark-green tents, very extensive, very crowded. I got the kind of stares and jokes that I always get in Asia because of my height, but the Chinese are cheerful; I enjoyed the whole thing. I looked at the freshness and variety of the vegetables; I looked at the clothing and other things for sale. I came, with some trepidation, to the meat section. But I was psychologically prepared; the Aberdeen market did not upset me. I moved through to the section where they sold fish, men shouting the freshness and quality of their wares. One man had filleted his fish, about a dozen of them set in a sloping incline in front of him. Each fish had a red spot on it. The red spot pulsed. I couldn't imagine what that was. I looked more closely.

He had filleted each fish with such skill that he had left the hearts intact. These exposed fish hearts were now beating, as a kind of visual display, and as a proof that his fish were fresh. I was looking at a dozen beating fish hearts.

I had to go lie down.

Soon I fell into a pattern of exploration punctuated by some sight that would leave me unexpectedly exhausted, driving me back to my room to recuperate. But it was humiliating, in a way. I was an accomplished traveler. These little experiences shouldn't bother me. Why was I getting so upset?

I was sure it must be jet lag. But whatever the reason, my symptoms got worse.

Some American girls picked me up and took me to a big Chinese dinner. The dinner was pleasant but extremely strange. The first course was shrimps. Little shrimps. We all peeled the shells with our hands, and ate the shrimps. Then the second course came. We all dumped the shells on the tablecloth next to our plates, to make room for the next course. And that's where the shells stayed, in a little pile next to each diner, for the rest of the evening.

Then there was toasting. The Chinese love to drink healths, and a dinner is continually interrupted by this routine. But I saw that everyone was drinking with one hand holding the glass, and one finger from the other hand touching the bottom of the glass. I asked an Australian woman seated next to me, Why does everyone do this? She said, You have to drink a toast holding the glass with two hands, but a single finger from the other hand suffices.

More courses. They kept coming for hours. You got accustomed to having something put in the center of the table, picking at it for a while, and then getting something else.

At one point, a cooked fish, one of many, was placed in the center of the table. I was talking with someone, and I looked back—the fish was gone! Picked clean. Yet it had only been there a few seconds. What happened to that fish?

I asked. That fish is a great delicacy, I was told. Everyone appreciates that fish. That fish costs four hundred dollars.

Having missed this fish, I was alerted. I immediately made a stab with my chopsticks at each new thing put on the table. Pretty soon there was another fish everyone liked. In a few moments the top was picked clean. Now we were looking at the backbone, and the flesh beneath. It seemed a simple matter to flip the fish over or to remove the backbone, but nobody at the table was doing this. The fish just lay there, half eaten.

Finally I couldn't stand it. I said, "May I turn the fish?"

"I don't know," said the Australian woman next to me.

"I mean," I said, "is it acceptable to turn the fish?"

"Yes, of course."

"Then why isn't anyone doing it?" I asked.

"Well, because of how they came here, I expect."

"How they came here?"

"And how they'll go home, of course."

I didn't understand. We seemed to have drifted from the primary question of the fish. I said, "Then it's all right for me to turn the fish?"

"How will you be going home?" she asked.

"The same way I came here, in a taxi, I imagine."

"But won't you cross over water when you go home?"

"Yes . . ." We had taken a little boat to come to this restaurant.

"Then you can't turn the fish," she said. And she explained that if you were going to cross water after your meal, you couldn't turn the fish.

"Perhaps if I just remove the backbone?" I asked hopefully.

She shook her head. "Sorry."

Then she said something quickly in Chinese, and a waiter came over and flipped the fish. And everyone started to eat again.

"He lives here," the woman explained, nodding to the waiter.

So it went on like that, with all of us sitting next to our piles of shrimp shells, drinking toasts with our fingers on the bottoms of the glasses, and nobody able to flip the fish. You never knew what would happen next. Finally, at the end of the evening, the guest of honor, an elderly man who was a Chinese movie star, gave a martial-arts demonstration. He flung his body around the room, quick, agile, graceful, strong. He was sixty-seven years old.

I thought, There's a lot I don't know about.

When I landed in Bangkok, I was met by my friend Davis, who had lived in Thailand for five years. "What were you doing in Hong Kong? It's so *boring* there, completely Western. Not the real Asia at all. You'll have a *much* more interesting time here."

Driving back from the airport, Davis gave me essential advice for getting along in Bangkok. "There are four rules you must never break while you are in Thailand," he said. "First, if you are in a temple, never climb on a statue of Buddha."

"Okay."

"Second, always keep your head lower than the head of a Buddha statue."

"Okay."

"Third, never touch a Thai person on the head."

"Okay."

"Fourth, if your feet are lifted off the floor, never allow them to point at a Thai person. That's *very* insulting."

"Okay," I said. Personally, I thought that these circumstances were pretty unlikely. I told Davis I thought I could get through my visit to Bangkok without breaking any of his injunctions.

"I doubt it," he said, gloomily. "I just hope you don't break all four."

Next he instructed me in how to say my street address in Thai. I was staying at Davis's house; he explained that I had to be able to tell a taxi driver where to go, and since the driver wouldn't understand English or read Thai writing, there was nothing to do but commit the oral address to memory. I still remember it: *Sip-jet, Sukhumvit soi yee-sip.*

Davis's house was beautiful, all elegant polished hardwood, opening onto a lovely garden in the back, with a swimming pool. I was introduced to the servants, reminded to remove my shoes at the front door, and shown to my bedroom on the second floor.

"Now, the Buddha in your room has been moved," Davis said. "We've put it on top of the armoire, which is the tallest piece of furniture in the room, but in your case I don't know if—ah, no, you see, you're still taller than the Buddha when you stand. That's not good. I'll speak to the servants."

"What about?"

"Well, I think they'll agree to make a special case for you, since you're so tall. But it would help if you would sort of hunch over when you're in the room, so you won't be taller than the Buddha any more than necessary."

I thought, This is a single bedroom. No one is ever going to see me in here. I am all alone in here, and Davis is telling me to stay hunched over because of the Buddha. It seemed a little crazy, but I said I would try.

I thought perhaps Davis was kidding me, but he wasn't. The Thais are wonderful, easygoing people, but they take their religion seriously, and they are not, in these matters, tolerant of foreigners. I later saw a Thai-censored version of a Peter Sellers film, *A Girl in My Soup*. To watch the movie was a bizarre experience: Peter Sellers would stand up from a table, and suddenly the Buddha statue in his wall niche would explode like a black-ink sparkler, which continued until Sellers sat down again. Then you could see the peaceful Buddha once more. The Thai censor had inked out the image of the Buddha, frame by frame, whenever Peter Sellers was higher than the statue.

So the Thais were serious, all right, and the servants were spoken to, and I stooped in the privacy of my bedroom. But, technically, one of the four rules was already broken.

The next day we were walking down a Bangkok street, and we passed some young kids. They were cute and friendly as they clustered around us; I patted one on the head.

"Ah ah ah," Davis said.

Two of four broken.

"Buddhists," Davis explained, "believe the head, the highest part of the body, is sacred and shouldn't be touched. It's barely acceptable with kids, but don't ever touch an adult that way. I'm serious. In fact, it's better not to touch an adult Thai at all."

Chastened, I said all right. That night we were at a dinner party, and I was talking with a Thai cameraman who shot commercials for Australian companies, as well as feature films for the Thai market. He was a very interesting fellow; we talked about crew requirements and methods of working. Then the hostess called us in for dinner. We walked together, and when we came to the door, I gestured for him to go through first, and put my hand on his shoulder, to ease him through. It was a very natural, casual gesture. The cameraman stiffened for a fraction of a second, then went through the door.

I looked over. Davis was shaking his head.

So, this second rule was more difficult than I had imagined. I had to watch my natural tendency to touch people.

After dinner, we sat on pillows, around a low, round table. There was a Thai woman across the table from me. She was rather aloof, talking to someone else. As the night went on, she began to give me dirty looks. Later she'd break off her conversation at intervals to glower at me. I didn't know what her problem was.

"Michael," Davis said. "Ah ah ah."

I looked down at myself. Everything seemed okay.

"Feet," Davis prompted.

I was sitting on a pillow, leaning back on my elbows on the ground. My legs were crossed. My feet were fine. No holes in my socks.

"Michael . . ."

Because my legs were crossed, one foot was off the floor—and pointing at the Thai woman. She was giving me dirty looks because my foot was pointing at her.

I uncrossed my legs, put them flat on the floor. The woman smiled pleasantly.

"Try and keep your feet *on* the floor," Davis advised. "It's really the only way."

Three out of four rules broken.

Meanwhile, I was making all sorts of minor mistakes as well. I could never remember to remove my shoes when entering people's houses. Also, I became enamored of the Thai greeting in which you bow and make a temple of your fingers in front of your face. This is called a *wai.* I liked to do it, and the Thais were amused to see me doing it. One day a little kid in a tailor's shop did it to me. I did it back.

"Never *wai* a kid," Davis said.

"Oh God," I said. By now I was becoming accustomed to my clumsiness. "Why not?"

"To *wai* an adult is a sign of respect. *Wai* a kid, it shortens his life."

"I didn't know."

"Never mind, the parents didn't seem too upset."

At least I didn't break the fourth rule, about climbing on a Buddha in a temple. Tourists are jailed in Thailand for that. The Thai temples are exquisite, beautifully maintained. Often they sit as tranquil, gilded oases amid an ugly expanse of roaring traffic and gray concrete buildings.

Thailand was the first Buddhist country I had ever been in. I was surprised by everything—the gaudiness of the temples, the way people behaved inside them, the flowers and the incense and the yellow-robed priests.

But I also found that I *liked* being in these temples. I wasn't sure what I liked, certainly not the exhausting ornateness, but something. I liked the feeling. I liked the way the people behaved in a temple. I knew absolutely nothing about Buddhism. I didn't know what the religion taught, what its principles were. In one of the temples, a Thai who spoke English told me that Buddhists didn't believe in God. That seemed pretty extreme, a religion that doesn't believe in God.

I found it interesting, that I liked this religion, because for many years I had been vociferously atheistic and anti-religion. But here in the temple it was just . . . peaceful. I went to a bookstore and started to read books on Buddhism.

Other things were happening, too. Davis had a dinner party for Peter Kann, who was then the Asia correspondent for *The Wall Street Journal.* I had known Peter from the Harvard *Crimson* many years before. He was still easygoing, funny, very smart and very competent, but now there was also a tough, worldly quality that I admired. Peter had been a correspondent in Vietnam and had remained in Asia after the war was over. He could wear shirts with epaulets and get away with it.

At the dinner party, I was seated next to an English hairdresser whose hair was dyed red on one side of her head and green on the other. I suspected this might be the latest thing in London, but I wasn't sure. I didn't even know whether I should refer to it or not, so I kept my mouth shut.

Conversation at dinner was desultory until someone casually mentioned that Peter had been to Hunza. Instantly the table became charged with excitement. Hunza, really?

How incredible. How fantastic. Nick Spenser, a neighbor of Davis's, was full of questions. "Did you go to Gilgit, then?"

"Yes," Peter said.

"Fly to Gilgit?"

"Yes."

"How long did that take?"

"A week in 'Pindi."

"Not so bad."

"No," Peter said, "it was all right."

"And Chitral as well, did you?"

"No, not this time," Peter said.

I was trying to figure this out. Hunza, Gilgit, 'Pindi. Hunza was obviously some geographic location. But I was very much at a loss, and I couldn't imagine how everyone at the table could know so much about a place I hadn't even heard of. What was the appeal of Hunza, anyway? Some sort of local resort?

I never found out, because the conversation moved on. "Been to Bhutan as well?"

"No, never," Peter said. "Can one go?"

"Billy's been to Bhutan."

"Has he! Never mentioned it to me. How'd he manage it?"

"Knows a friend of the ruling family. Did it from Darjeeling."

"What about Nagar?"

"Yes, well, see Hunza, might as well go to Nagar."

The conversation continued in this way, affording me no deductive opportunities. I listened in silence for about fifteen minutes. When I couldn't stand it any more, I turned to the hairdresser with the red-and-green hair, and said quietly, "What are they talking about?"

"Countries," she said.

I was ready to collapse. They were talking about *countries* and I hadn't heard of any of them.

"Bhutan and Hunza are countries?"

"Yes. In the Himalaya."

Well, I felt a little better. Who knew what was tucked away in the folds of the Himalaya? I felt my ignorance could be excused. But as the conversation continued, I realized that the world I inhabited was a world where, if I did not know everything, I had at least heard of most of it. My ignorance about Himalayan states, on the one hand so embarrassing, was also in its way enlivening. I'd certainly do some reading when I got home.

Davis's friend Ed Bancroft, a handsome investment banker living in Bangkok, was a rake. He was the only rake I had ever met. As the dinner guests departed, Bancroft announced to Peter and me that he was taking us to see the famous nightlife of Bangkok. Davis begged off, pleading fatigue.

In Patpong, once a Vietnam R & R district, there were clubs with names like "The Playboy" and "The Mayfair." In The Playboy Club we saw Thai girls demonstrate varieties of muscular control with cigarettes and bananas, all done under ultraviolet lights while the crowd shouted and screamed. The spectator appeal of this activity struck me as limited unless you were really drunk, as most of the spectators were.

We visited several more bars, and then went to a massage parlor. It was a gigantic modern place, the size of a hotel. Ed Bancroft suggested that, as out-of-towners, we might like the full-body massage, where the girl slithers all over you in a soapy bathtub.

We were taken to a one-way mirror where we could look into a room full of girls, all wearing starched white uniforms and number tags. The girls were all looking in our direction, because there was a television mounted just beneath the mirror. The idea was, you picked a number and the manager called the girl out to give you your massage.

Because he spoke Thai, Ed talked with the manager at the window and second-guessed our decisions. Apparently certain choices among the girls were not desirable; I never did figure it out.

The whole business of standing at the mirror was very bizarre. It was a little too much like the slave trade or the auction block or outright prostitution for my taste. Yet nobody was treating it that way. There wasn't any sordid, sinful feeling; it was exactly like a massage parlor, sort of healthy and straightforward. I retired with my girl to a fully tiled room that had a low circular tub sunk into the floor. The girl made a bucket of suds, put a little hot water into the tub, and got me to sit in it. She scrubbed me with a rough brush, which was nice in a masochistic way, and gestured for me to lie on my stomach. Then she took off all her clothes, soaped her body, lay down on my back, and writhed with the soap.

I had a few problems with this. For one thing, I didn't fit in the tub: my legs hung over the edge. So when she lay on top of me it was extremely painful on my shins. Also, because my back was arched, we didn't have good contact; she kept giggling and trying to push me into a better position, but there just wasn't room in the tub. Then soap got up my nose and I began to cough.

We decided to call it a day. She rinsed me down, and I dried myself and got dressed and headed back upstairs.

"How was that?" Ed said. "Wasn't that unbelievable?"

"Unforgettable," I agreed.

Peter showed up, and we were off again, Ed with a peculiar gleam in his eye. He was building up to something. "A whorehouse?" he asked.

"I dunno," I said. "It's getting late."

Peter made noncommittal noises.

"Just a look," Ed said. He was showing us the town; he was the resident expert; he didn't want to stop this wild ride.

"Okay, just a look."

But the mood in the car was declining. My shins still hurt from the slippery massage, though I'd never admit to the others that I'd anything but unalloyed delight. Peter was saying nothing at all, smoking cigarettes and staring out the window. We were getting into that funny territory that men can share in A Night on the Town, or Chasing the Broads. A situation that says much more about the men being together than about any broads. What was happening, at 2:00 a.m. on a muggy Bangkok night, was that nobody was willing to be the first to quit.

But Ed, our guide, took the silence to mean we were bored with his itinerary thus far. He perceived us as especially jaded, requiring a special stimulus.

"I know what," he said, snapping his fingers. "A *child* whorehouse!"

"Ed," I said, "wouldn't just a regular whorehouse be adequate?"

"No, no, no. A *child* whorehouse, absolutely. Listen, this place is *incredible,* you *have* to see it."

And off we drove in the steamy night.

I'm thinking of Justine in *The Alexandria Quartet,* exotic episodes in exotic foreign countries.

Peter still stares out the window. I'm noticing the epaulets on his shirt again. I say to him, "Have you ever seen a child whorehouse?"

"Not personally," he says. Very cool.

Bancroft pulls up a back alley into one of the indistinguishable gray concrete structures of Bangkok. There is a guard, and a central courtyard. In the courtyard are parking stalls, with curtains in front of each stall.

"That's for the cars; you pull the curtain so people can't read the license numbers," Ed says. "Politicians, really important people come to this place. Wait here."

He jumps out of the car, is gone. Moments later he is back.

"Okay, it's all right."

We go up a broad flight of stairs from the street. Then into what looks like a single large apartment. A long hallway, with doors opening off each side.

"We'll just see what they have here tonight," Ed says. We are led down the hallway to the first door.

Inside, a room draped with gaudy Indian fabric, pinks and reds. Harsh lighting. Sitting on pillows in the room, watching television, women with crude, heavy makeup. They don't look like children to me.

"Pretty old," Peter says, grinning at Ed. Needling him.

"Old! Christ! *Ancient!*" Ed says something quickly in Thai to the man beside him.

"I wonder how old they actually are?" Peter says. Now he has his reporter's voice, his correspondent's voice. So-and-so many women, such-and-such an average age.

We go down the hall to another door. Another room draped with cheap cloth. Women in negligees, bra and panties, garter belts. The bordello effect is spoiled by the fact that some of them are cooking food in a corner of the room. These girls are somewhat younger.

The man looks at us, questioning.

"I don't know *what* this guy is thinking of," Ed says. "The last time I was here, it was with"—he names a distinguished person—"and they had seven- and eight-year-olds here. Really. Extraordinary."

We go farther down the corridor, to still another room. Every time I move down the corridor, I feel more claustrophobic. There are funny smells here, masked by incense. The corridor is getting narrower all the time. Short women stand in the corridor, clustering around us, trying to get us to choose them instead of the women in the rooms. In their dirty underwear, their garish makeup, they pluck at us, tug at us. When they smile, they have missing teeth.

"Ah, *here's* the room," Ed says.

The door opens. We see a handful of prepubescent girls. They look ten or eleven. Their eyes are dark and smudged. Their postures are coy; they strut and throw glances over their shoulders. One girl walks unsteadily in high heels too big for her.

"What do you say, guys?" Ed says. He's grinning with excitement.

I just want to get out of there. I don't care if they think I'm effeminate, I don't care what they think. I just want to get away from these poor children and these reeking corridors with people pulling at me, touching me, little fingers reaching up for me. "Mister . . . mister . . ."

"I think I'll pass," I say. "I'm a little tired."

"Hey, you don't see what you like, we can keep looking."

"No, I'm tired. Really. I'll wait for you outside."

"Okay. Suit yourself." Ed looks at Peter. "Peter?"

This is another classic moment from Night on the Town. One guy has just crumped out, he's tired or guilty or thinking of the wife or whatever, and now let's see which way the rest of the evening is going to go. Are you in or out?

Peter says, "I want a cigarette. I'll wait outside, too."

"You guys," Ed says, shaking his head, disappointed in us. "You don't know what you're missing here."

"I'll have to take that chance," Peter says.

Peter and I go outside and sit on the bumper of Ed's car and smoke cigarettes and talk about what has happened in our lives in the ten years since we have last seen each other. We suddenly have this camaraderie, because it is the middle of the night and we are tired and we have both decided to pass on the child prostitutes and we want to make sure the other guy doesn't think we're chicken or something. We have a really nice conversation, and then Ed reappears.

"You guys. You really missed it. There was some quite extraordinary material there."

"Yeah. Well."

"Okay, what do you say we stop at a coffee shop? See what girls are around? Huh?"

We plead exhaustion. Ed says he doesn't feel we've had a good enough night. We assure him we have. We manage to get back to Davis's house. I walk into my bedroom with my head down so as not to be higher than the Buddha and I fall immediately asleep.

The next night I went to dinner at the house of a man who ran an advertising agency in Bangkok. He was an Australian known for his cooking; everyone coveted an invitation to his meals.

Before dinner, someone unrolled a Thai stick of marijuana, made a joint, and passed it around. Some guests smoked it; others didn't. I smoked some. How could you go to Thailand and not have Thai grass?

When the joint came around, I had some more.

"Better be careful," Davis said. "That stuff is strong."

"Hey, don't worry," I said. "I'm from L.A."

Davis shrugged. I had a couple of vodkas before dinner, too. I was feeling pretty good, sitting around, talking to people. In fact, I was glad to be feeling so good, because for a couple of days I had been having this undercurrent of feeling that I was *far from home*. Meaning that I was overextended, lonely, stretched a little far, having more anxieties about my new experiences than I was admitting to myself.

But then, when we got up to go to the dinner table, I realized that I had misjudged my consumption. I was very high. I was even having a little trouble coordinating things. Oh well, I thought, I'll be okay when we sit down again. I'll be okay once I eat something.

We sat at the table, and there was an Indian woman, the wife of a diplomat, on my left. A Thai advertising account executive on my right. The food was passed around; the conversation was very pleasant.

And then, suddenly, I began to see gray. The gray got darker. And then I was blind.

It was odd. I could hear the conversation, and the clink of silverware around me, but I was completely blind.

The Indian woman asked me to pass something.

"I'm sorry," I said. "I know this is going to sound funny, but I'm blind."

She laughed delightfully. "You are so amusing."

"No, seriously. I'm blind."

"You mean you can't see?"

"No. I can't."

"How extraordinary. I wonder why?"

I was wondering that myself. "I don't know."

"Do you suppose it was something you ate?"

"I don't think so."

"Can you see me now?"

"No. Still blind."

"I wonder what we should do," she said.

"I don't know," I said.

The host was notified. Plans were made. Everyone seemed to be treating this as a normal occurrence. I thought, Have other people been blind in this house before? Next I felt myself carried by several people upstairs to the second floor, and put on a bed in an air-conditioned bedroom.

Some time went by. I opened my eyes. I couldn't see anything.

For the first time I began to worry. It had been okay to be blind for a while, but it wasn't going away. I wondered what time it was, and felt my watch with my hand. Was this going to be a permanent condition? Was I going to have to get a Braille watch? What kind of room was I in?

Some more time went by. Someone touched my shoulder. I looked over and saw an elderly Thai woman smiling at me. She gave me a glass of water, giggled, and went away. After a while, she came back. By then I could see all right, but I felt terrible. After that I went to sleep. Much later Davis came up, clucked his tongue, and drove me home.

In the morning I told Davis that I wasn't going to go sightseeing, I was just going to take it easy, maybe sit in his garden by the pool. Read a book. Get over the strangeness of things.

"Good idea," he said. "Just keep an eye out. The gardener saw a cobra in the garden last week."

Davis announced that we were going upcountry for a couple of days. He had to check on sales for the pharmaceutical company he worked for. Prescription drugs were legally sold over the counter in Thailand at that time, and all the international drug companies treated Thailand as a major market.

The countryside was flat and green and beautiful. We stayed in Chinese hotels and had a wonderful time. Finally we got to Ayutthaya. Davis said he was going to check his stores, see how they were doing. "But there's a large open market around the corner," he said. "Big upcountry market. Have a look, you'll find it interesting."

I went around the corner.

The market was enormous, almost an acre. It was entirely covered by white sheets to block the sun. A beautiful, vast open space, it was filled with everything from produce to clothing. I wandered around, looking at what people were selling. The sheets were so low I had to duck my head, but it was a fascinating market and I was glad to see it.

Because of my height, I caused a considerable commotion. The upcountry people stopped and stared. And, in common with most Asian people, they laughed. The laughter began in scattered places here and there, but it grew, swelling to fill the entire open market. They were all laughing at me, pointing and laughing. I smiled back, good-naturedly. I knew they didn't mean anything. It was just an expression of embarrassment.

The laughing continued. It became a roar in my ears, like an ocean wave. People were dashing off to get their friends. The whole town was running to get a look at me. The laughter built. Now there were four or five hundred people laughing. I was on display. Everywhere I saw open mouths, laughing. Finally I looked down at the ground and saw, at my feet, an old Thai woman rolling on the ground, clutching her stomach in hysterics, she was laughing so hard. Her body blocked me; I couldn't step over her.

I looked around and thought, What an interesting experience. Here is a chance to see how it feels to have five hundred people laughing at you. How does it feel?

And I suddenly thought, *I hate it.* And I turned and walked quickly away.

I went back to the shop where I had left Davis. He was grinning like a Cheshire cat. "Knew they'd get a kick out of you," he said.

"Jesus Christ."

"They don't mean anything."

"I know," I said. "But still."

The Thais are famously good-natured. They are called the Danes of Asia, because of their easy dispositions. A favorite expression, *Mai pen rai,* means—more or less—"Never mind," and is invoked to resolve all sorts of disappointments and upsets. I frequently remarked on the wonderful quality of the Thai character, so different from what I was accustomed to at home.

One day in Bangkok, in a taxi going back to Davis's house, I saw a Thai woman and a European woman in their separate cars, trying to pass each other in the narrow road. They were both leaning out of their cars, having a screaming argument. Nobody was saying *"Mai pen rai."*

I thought, It's time to go home. I left the next day.

All in all, I considered it a traumatic trip. Then I realized that, although I saw myself as an accomplished traveler, I was in fact terribly culture-bound. I had visited only a small part of the world—North America and Western Europe.

I began to think of all the places I hadn't been. I had never been to Africa. I had never really been to Asia. I had never been to Australia. I had never been to South or Central America. In fact, I had never been to most of the world.

It was time to find out what I had been missing.

Bonaire

The setting sun glowed red off the ocean as we waded clumsily out from the beach with our scuba tanks and lights. We paused, waist-deep in water, to put on our face masks and adjust the straps. Behind us, at the Hotel Bonaire, people were heading for the dining room to eat.

I said to my sister, "Hungry?"

She shook her head. My sister had never been night-diving before, and she was a little apprehensive about it.

We had come to Bonaire for a two-week diving holiday in the summer of 1974. Kim had just finished her second year of law school, and I had completed a draft of my next novel; we both looked forward to a good rest and a lot of superb diving.

Bonaire is a Dutch island fifty miles off the coast of Venezuela. The island is actually a sunken mountain peak with sheer sides; twenty yards from the sandy beach, the crystal-clear water was a hundred feet deep. This made night-diving easy: just walk out from the hotel beach at sunset, and drop on down to a hundred feet. You could make your night dive for an hour and be back at the hotel dining room in time for dinner.

This was our plan.

My sister put her mouthpiece between her teeth, and I heard the hiss as she sucked air. She clutched her shoulders and pantomimed that she was cold; she wanted to get started. I bit my mouthpiece.

We sank beneath the surface.

The landscape is deep blue, small fish flicking like shadows over the sand and heads of coral. I hear the burble of my air bubbles sliding past my cheek. I look over at Kim to see how she is doing; she is fine, her body relaxed. Kim is an accomplished diver, and I have been diving for more than ten years.

We go deeper, down the slope into blackness.

We turn on the lights, and immediately see a world of riotous, outrageous color. The corals and sponges are all vivid greens, yellows, reds.

We move deeper, through black water, seeing only what is illuminated in the glowing cone of light from the flashlights. We find large fish sleeping beneath overhanging shelves of coral. We can touch them, something you can never do during the day. The night animals are active; a black-and-white-spotted moray eel comes out of its hole to flex its powerful jaws and peer at us with beady black eyes. An octopus scurries through my beam, and turns bright red in irritation. In a niche of coral we find a tiny red-striped crab no larger than my little finger.

On this dive I plan to take photographs, and so I have my camera around my neck. I take a few shots, and then my sister taps me on the shoulder and gestures she wants the camera. I take the strap from around my neck and hold it out to her. I'm moving slowly; with a flashlight dangling from my wrist, things seem awkward. Kim pulls the camera away.

Suddenly I feel a sharp yank at my jaw, and my mouthpiece is torn from my lips. My air is gone.

I know at once what has happened. The camera strap has caught on the air hose. My sister, in pulling the camera away, has also pulled out my mouthpiece.

I have no air. I am hanging in ink-black water at night and I have no air.

I remain calm.

Whenever you lose your mouthpiece, it invariably drops down the right side of your body. It can always be found hanging in the water alongside your right hipbone. I reach down for it.

130

The mouthpiece isn't there.

I remain calm.

I keep feeling for it. I know it is down there somewhere near my hip. It has to be. I feel my tank. I feel my weight belt. I feel my backpack. My fingers run over the contours of my equipment moving faster and faster.

The mouthpiece isn't there. I am sure now: it isn't there. The mouthpiece isn't there.

I remain calm.

I know the mouthpiece hasn't been ripped from the air hose, because if it had I would be hearing a great blast of air. Instead, I am in eerie black silence. So the mouthpiece is around me, somewhere. If it hasn't fallen to my right side, it must be behind my neck, near the top of the air tank. This is a little more awkward to reach for, but I put my hand behind my neck and feel around for the air hose. I can feel the top of the tank, the vertical metal valve. I feel a number of hoses. I can't tell which is my air hose. I feel some more.

I can't find it.

I remain calm.

How deep am I? I check my gauges. I am in sixty feet of water now. That's okay. If I can blow out my air in a slow, steady stream and make it to the surface. I am sure I can. At least, I am pretty sure I can.

But it would be better to find the mouthpiece now. Down here.

My sister is hanging in the water five feet above me, her fins kicking gently near my face. I move up alongside her, and she looks at me. I point to my mouth. Look: something's missing. No mouthpiece, Kim.

She waves at me, and gives me the high sign that everything is all right with her. She busies herself with putting the camera around her neck. I realize that in the darkness she probably can't see me very well.

I grab her arm. I point to my mouth. No mouthpiece! *No air!*

She shakes her head, shrugs. She doesn't get it. What is my problem? What am I trying to tell her?

My lungs are starting to burn now. I blow a few air bubbles at her, and point again to my mouth. Look: no mouthpiece. For God's sake!

Kim nods, slowly. I can't see her eyes, because light reflects off her glass face mask. But she understands. At least, I think she understands.

131

My lungs are burning badly now. Soon I am going to have to bolt for the surface.

I am no longer calm.

In the darkness, she swings slowly behind me. Her light is behind my head, casting my shadow on the coral below. She is picking around my air hoses, near my neck. Sorting things out. Now she is over on my left side. Not my left side, Kim! It's got to be somewhere on the right! She moves slowly. She is so deliberate.

My lungs are burning.

I know I am going to have to bolt for the surface. I am telling myself, over and over: remember to breathe out, remember to breathe out. If I forget to exhale on the way up I will burst my lungs. I can't afford to panic.

Kim takes my hand. She gives me something in her slow, deliberate way. This is not the time to be giving me something! My fingers close on rubber: she has put the mouth-piece into my hand! I jam it between my teeth and blow out.

Water gurgles, then I suck cold air. Kim looks at me tentatively. I suck air, and cough a couple of times. Hanging in the water beside me, she watches me. Am I all right?

I suck air. My heart is pounding. I feel dizzy. Now that everything is okay, I feel all the panic I have suppressed. My God, I almost died! Kim is looking at me. Am I all right now?

I give her the high sign. Yes, I am all right. We finish the dive, though I have trouble concentrating. I am glad when it is over. When we get to the beach, I collapse. My whole body is shaking.

"That was weird," she says. She tells me that somehow the air hose has gotten twisted around, so that it was hanging down behind my left shoulder. "I didn't know that could happen," she says. "It took a while to find it. Are you all right?"

"I think so," I say.

"You're shivering."

"I think I'm just cold."

I take a hot shower. Alone in my room, I have a terrible urge for sex, a compulsive desire. I think, This is a cliché— escape death and seek procreation. But it's true. I am feeling it. And here I am with my sister, for Pete's sake.

By the end of dinner, I have calmed down. The next couple of days are more ordinary. We make another night dive. Nothing bad happens. I settle into the novels I have brought. I work on my suntan. For the next week, we have a good time. And we do all of the standard dive spots that every diver does in Bonaire.

But I want to do more.

"I won't tell you where it is," the divemaster said, when I asked about the wreck. I had read there was an interesting wreck somewhere on the north shore of the island.

"Why not?"

"You'll die if you go there," the divemaster said.

"Have you been there?" I asked.

"Sure."

"You didn't die."

"I knew what I was doing. The wreck's deep, the shallowest part is 140 feet. At that depth, no-decompression limits are four minutes."

"Is it really a paddle-wheeler?"

"Yes. Iron-hull. Nobody knows when it was wrecked, maybe around the turn of the century."

I tried to get him talking about it, hoping that he would drop enough clues so I could find my way.

"The ship rolled down the incline?" I had read that, too. Bonaire is surrounded on all sides by a steep drop-off, an incline that goes from the shore almost straight down 2,000 feet in some places.

"Yeah. Apparently the ship originally crashed on the shore—at least there're some fragments from it near shore, in about 30 feet of water—and then sank. When the ship sank, it rolled down the incline. Now it's on its side, 140 feet down."

"Must be something to see."

"Oh yeah. It is. Hell of a big wreck."

"So there're fragments in 30 feet of water, near the shore?"

"Yeah."

"What kind of fragments?"

"Forget it," he said.

Finally I said, "Look, I know what I'm doing; I've been diving with you guys for over a week, so you know I'm okay. You don't have to sanction what I'm doing, but it's unfair of you not to tell me where this famous dive is."

"Yeah?" he said. "You think you're up to this dive?" He got truculent. "Okay, here's how you do it. Drive east five miles until you find a little dock. Then load up, jump in with all your gear on, and swim north from the dock about a hundred yards, until you pass a green house on the shore. When the house gets to be about two o'clock to you, start looking down in the water. You'll see a spar and cables in thirty feet of water, right below you. Swim down to the spar, and then go right over the edge and straight down the incline as fast as you can go. When you get to 90 feet, leave the incline and swim straight out into the open ocean. You think you're swimming straight, but actually you'll be dropping, and you'll hit the wreck about 140 feet down. It's huge. You can't miss it. Okay? Still want to go?"

The directions sounded difficult, but not impossible. "Yes," I said. "Sure."

"Okay. Just remember, if anything happens to you, I'll deny I told you where it is."

"Fine."

"And remember, at that depth you'll be narked, so you have to pay attention to your time; remember, your no-decompression limits only give you four minutes down there. The wreck is so huge there's no way you can see it in four minutes—don't even try. Make sure you observe all the stops on the way up. There isn't a decompression chamber within eight hours' air time of Bonaire, so you don't want to screw up. If you get the bends, there's a good chance you'll die. Got it?"

"Got it," I said.

"Another thing—if you do decide to go, remember to leave your camera. Your Nikonos is only certified to 160 feet, you'll warp the case."

"Okay," I said. "Thanks for your help."

"Take my advice," he said. "Don't go there."

I asked my sister what she thought about it.

"Why not?" she said. "Sounds interesting."

The next day we drove up to have a look at the site.

There was a sort of industrial pier that went a few yards out into the water. It looked broken-down, disused. There were several ratty houses along the shore, none green. Still farther north, there was some sort of refinery or industrial complex, with big ships tied up. The water by the dock was murky and unappealing.

I was all for giving it up. I asked my sister what she thought. She shrugged. "We're here."

"Okay," I said. "At least we can look for the mast."

We put on our gear, inflated our vests, and floated north. It was a fairly strenuous swim; I kept watching the houses on the shore. I had about decided that the divemaster had given us bad instructions when I suddenly saw, at two o'clock as I looked back, a green door. It was not visible from the dock.

I looked down in the water. Directly below us was a heavy mast and spar, some metal cables draped over the coral. It looked almost new.

"Think that's it?" I asked my sister.

She shrugged. "Looks like what he described."

I asked her what she thought we should do.

"We've come this far," she said.

"Okay, let's go," I said. We put in our mouthpieces, deflated our vests, and went down to the spar.

Up close, the spar was big—forty feet long, a foot in diameter. It had very little marine growth on it. We swam along its length, moving out from the shore. Then we ducked over the edge, and plunged down the incline.

That's always an exciting moment, to drop over an undersea ledge, but my heart was pounding now. The landscape was ugly, with heavy pollution from the nearby industrial site. The water was cloudy and visibility was poor; we were swimming in crud. There wasn't a lot of light, and it got quickly darker the farther down we went. And we had to go fast, because we had to conserve our air.

At ninety feet, I looked out at the open ocean and decided the instructions were wrong. Anyway, it was difficult to leave the scummy incline and head straight out into the cloudy murk. I decided to go deeper before heading out. At 120 feet, I headed outward. I couldn't see more than a few feet ahead of me, but once I had left the incline behind, it was difficult to know where to focus my eyes. There was nothing to look at except the milky strands of crud suspended in the ocean.

I was chiefly concerned that we would miss the wreck; at this depth, it was not going to be possible to hunt for it. We would have neither the time nor the air for that.

And then, suddenly, my entire field of vision was filled with flat rusted metal.

I was staring at a vast wall of steel.

The wreck.

The size of it astonished me: it was far bigger than I had imagined. We were at the keel line, running along the bottom of the hull. We were at 160 feet. I started my stopwatch, and swam up to the side of the hull, at 140 feet. The metal surface of the hull was covered with beautiful sponges and wire corals. They made a wonderful pattern, but there wasn't much color this deep; we moved through a black-and-white world. We went over the side of the hull, and onto the deck of the ship, which was almost vertical, with the masts pointing down the incline. The geography was pretty crazy, but you got used to it. I took some pictures, we had a quick look around, and then our four minutes were up. We returned slowly to the surface.

When a diver breathes compressed air, nitrogen enters his bloodstream. Two things then happen. The first is that the nitrogen acts like an anesthetic, and causes an intoxication—nitrogen narcosis, the famous "rapture of the deep"—which becomes more pronounced the deeper you go. That narcosis was dangerous; intoxicated divers had died because they took out their mouthpieces to give air to the fish.

The other thing is that the nitrogen that enters the blood must be allowed to come out of the blood slowly as you return to the surface. If the diver surfaces too quickly, the nitrogen will bubble out of his blood like soda from a bottle when the cap is removed. These bubbles cause painful cramps in the joints; hence the name "bends." They also cause paralysis and death. The time needed to decompress is a function of how long the diver has been down, and how deep.

According to published dive tables, my sister and I were not required to decompress at all, but the need for decompression depends on such variables as temperature, the health of the diver that day, or whether part of his wet suit binds him and prevents the nitrogen from coming out of solution. It's so highly variable we decided to do double decompression stops—two minutes at twenty feet, six minutes at ten feet—just to be safe. We made our decompression stops, and swam back to the dock.

We were both exhilarated; we had dived the wreck, and hadn't died! And the wreck was remarkably beautiful.

We decided to dive there again, and explore it further. Given a four-minute limit, we felt that we would have to make a separate dive to see the stern, and another to see the bow.

A few days later, we swam around the stern of the ship, about 180 feet deep. The dive went smoothly; we had a good look at the steel paddle-wheels. We were starting to feel quite comfortable around this wreck. Our pleasure was considerable. We felt like kids who had broken the rules and were getting away with it, consistently. We were very pleased with ourselves. And we were getting used to the narcosis, too, accustomed to the way we felt drunk the minute we reached the wreck.

A few days after that, we made a third dive, and explored the bow. The bow was 210 feet down, and as we came around it, I felt the narcosis strongly. I gripped my instruments and kept checking my gauges, to be sure my air was all right. I was aware I was having trouble concentrating. We started each dive with 2,200 pounds of air, and I liked to head back with 1,000 pounds remaining, since it took us nearly eleven minutes to reach the surface.

The wreck was incredibly beautiful; this was going to be our last dive on it; I had 1,200 pounds of air remaining, and we still had a little time left, so I decided to show my sister a tiny, delicate sea fan on one of the masts, 180 feet down. We swam out and had a look, and then it was time to go back. I checked my watch; the four minutes were gone, we were moving toward five minutes. I checked my air. I had 600 pounds left.

I felt panic: 600 pounds was not enough air for me to make it back. What had happened? I must have misread the gauges.

I looked again: 500 pounds.

Now I was in trouble. I couldn't go up fast; that would only increase my risk of the bends. I couldn't hold my breath, either; an embolism would kill me for sure. Nor could I breathe less often; the whole point of blowing off the nitrogen was that you had to breathe it out.

I looked up toward the surface I could not see, 180 feet above me. I suddenly felt the weight of all this water over me, and my precariousness. I broke into a cold sweat, even though I was underwater. I didn't know such a thing was possible.

There was no point in wasting time; the deeper you are, the faster your air is consumed. We started up quickly.

The rule is, you ascend at 60 feet a minute, which meant it would take us three minutes to get to the surface. After one minute, at 120 feet, I had 300 pounds of air left. After two minutes, at 60 feet, I had 190 pounds left. But still before me were the decompression stops.

I had never known such a predicament. Of course I could easily reach the surface—but that wouldn't do me any good. I had been under too long, and the surface was dangerous, possibly deadly, to me now. I had to stay away from the surface for as long as possible. But I couldn't stay down seven more minutes with only 190 pounds of air.

We stopped for the first decompression at 20 feet. My sister, who never consumed much air, showed me her gauge. She had 1,000 pounds left. I was down to 150 pounds. She signaled: did I want to share her air?

This is something you practice in diving class. I had practiced it many times. But now I was panicked; I didn't think I could manage the procedure of taking my air out of my mouth, and passing her mouthpiece back and forth. I was much too frightened for that.

So much for diving class.

I shook my head, no.

We went up to 10 feet, and hung in the water just below the surface, holding on to arms of staghorn coral. I tried to tell myself that the decompression stops were doubled, and not really necessary anyway. True, we had exceeded the no-decompression limits, but not by much. Maybe a minute. Maybe less.

I couldn't convince myself that I was fine—all I could think was how damned stupid I had been, to cut it so close, and to put myself in this danger. I thought of all my friends who had been bent, and how it had happened. The stories were always the same. Got a little sloppy one day, got a little careless, got a little lazy. Didn't pay attention.

Exactly my story.

I stared at my air gauge, watching the needle slowly go down. In my mind, the gauge was magnified, as big as a saucer. I saw every scratch, every imperfection. I saw the tiny fluctuations, the tiny pulses in the needle with each breath I took. The gauge was down to 50 pounds. Then 30 pounds. I had never had my air supply go so low. I noticed a tiny screw in the gauge, a stop-screw to keep the needle from going below zero. I continued to breathe, wiggling my arms to make sure nothing was binding. I completed the six minutes of decompression, just barely. The needle hit the stop-screw.

I had sucked the tank dry.

On the surface my sister asked me if I was all right, and I said I was. But I felt very jittery. I figured I was all right, but I wouldn't know for sure for a few hours. I went back to my room, and took a nap. In the afternoon I woke with a crawly sensation on my skin.

Uh-oh.

That was one of the signs of the bends. I lay in the bed and waited.

The tingly, crawly sensation got worse. It was first on my arms and legs, then my chest as well. I felt the tingling creep up my neck, taking over . . . moving toward my face. . . .

I couldn't stand it any more; I jumped out of bed and went into the bathroom. I didn't have any medicines, but I would do something, at least take an aspirin. Something.

I stared at myself in the mirror.

My body was covered with an odd pink rash. It was some sort of contact dermatitis.

I went back to bed and collapsed in a sleep. I never got the bends.

As best I could tell, the dermatitis was caused by the hotel soap.

In more than ten years of living, I had never gotten into trouble. But during my vacation in Bonaire, I experienced serious trouble twice in two weeks.

At the time I just saw these incidents as accidents, bad luck. More than a year passed before I began to reflect on the pattern behind my own behavior, the fact that I had repeatedly taken ever-more-daring risks until I finally got myself into trouble. I was startled when I finally recognized what I was really doing. The conclusion was inescapable: on some level, for some reason, I was trying to kill myself.

Why would I want to kill myself? I could find no explanation in the events of my life at that time. My work was going well. I had ended an unhappy love affair, but that was months in the past, and no longer on my mind. All in all, I felt cheerful and optimistic.

And yet the pattern was there. I had engaged in repetitive, daredevil behavior without ever being consciously aware of the underlying pattern.

But was I really unaware? Because when I thought back, I remembered some odd and uncharacteristic worries during my stay in Bonaire. For a man on vacation, I had been unusually fretful. I worried that the dive shop would fill my tanks with bad air. I worried that the restaurants would give me food poisoning. I worried that I would have a fatal car accident on the road. Yet the roads were nearly deserted; the restaurants were spotless; the dive shop was scrupulously managed. At the time, I had commented to myself that these fears were particularly unfounded. Now I had to recognize that they were not fears at all, but disguised wishes.

In any case, I hadn't put the pieces all together during the time I was in Bonaire, and the entire episode left me with a renewed respect for the power of the unconscious mind. What I had demonstrated, to myself at least, was that my ordinary assumption that in some casual and automatic way I know what I am doing, and why, is simply wrong.

The acceptance of unconscious motivation obliged me to assess my behavior by methods other than ordinary introspective awareness, because what I think I am doing at the time is almost certainly not what I am doing. In some way, I had to get a perspective on myself.

One time-honored way is to listen to the perceptions of an outsider—a friend, associate, or therapist. There are also ways to get perspective by shifting consciousness, changing to what is sometimes called "the witness state." Those meditative states didn't interest me in those days. But I stumbled on another useful technique for entirely different reasons.

Starting around 1974, there was a lot of attention paid to so-called circadian rhythms, the daily rhythms of the human body and its hormones. It had been found that most human beings didn't follow a precise twenty-four-hour cycle, but that the usual cycle was slightly longer or shorter, which meant that we were sometimes in synchronization with the day, and sometimes not.

In addition, the psychological effects of the female menstrual cycle were receiving new consideration. In England, there were rumors of legal acceptance of a condition called PMS, premenstrual syndrome. And it was commonly accepted that many women experienced some monthly fluctuation in mood and behavior.

I began to wonder if there might be a male menstrual cycle as well. Or something equivalent. After all, there are physical analogues between the sexes—the male scrotum to the female labia, the testicles to the ovaries, the penis to the clitoris, and so on. It seemed to me unlikely that women would develop a complex monthly cycle of hormones and that there would be no trace of such a cycle in men.

That was a job for an endocrinologist, but I wasn't interested in the hormones. I was interested in seeing if there were patterns in my own moods that I wasn't aware of. How to keep track of this?

I asked my friend Arnold Mandell, a neurobiologist, how to keep an objective record of subjective mood. Because the danger, of course, is that you will inadvertently create a pattern in your own data. Arnold said the best way was each day to put a mark at the edge of an unmarked diary page, using the top of the page as the best mood, and the bottom as the worst mood. So I began to do this.

Since I was keeping a daily diary mark, I started to record little thoughts for the day, too. I had always thought keeping a diary was a belabored, Franklin-esque thing to do. But since I was doing it for another purpose, it was all right.

After a few weeks, I looked back over my notes with astonishment. Every day, I was so critical! One nasty comment after another, about something or somebody.

I didn't regard myself as particularly critical, but evidently I was. I began to observe my state more carefully during each day. It did indeed seem that I was frequently judgmental and snappish, even when I didn't mean to be. So I decided to watch for that behavior and modify it. It was surprisingly difficult to do.

I never was able to detect a monthly cycle of my own mood changes, though from time to time I tried again. In later years, I wrote a computer program to record my responses on a blank screen. I still suspect there is such a cycle, perhaps bimonthly, running seven or eight weeks. But I have never demonstrated it.

However, I demonstrated a great value to keeping a

diary, and have kept one even since. I reread Franklin's *Autobiography,* and noted that he kept a record of himself, as I did, for exactly the same reasons. This most practical and observant of men had decided that careful record-keeping was the only way to find out what he was really doing.

Pahang

I became interested in the Sultan of Pahang, ruler of the largest and richest state in Malaysia. I had some notion of writing about him, and I had heard that his birthday celebrations were worth witnessing—horse races on his palace grounds, native dances, and a ceremony in which his subjects ritually poison fish in the river and collect them for a special dinner. It all sounded suitably exotic. From the Malaysian consulate in Los Angeles I learned the Sultan celebrated his birthday in late May, and a week before the date I flew to Singapore with the idea of finding someone there who would assist me in attending the party as a journalist. Failing that, I would crash it.

I was delighted at the idea of crashing the birthday of the Sultan of Pahang. I told everyone that was what I was doing. It sounded so eccentric and dashing.

Unfortunately, when I arrived in Singapore I learned that the Sultan's birthday was not in May. The *old* Sultan's birthday was in May, but he had been dead several years. His son, the present Sultan of Pahang, celebrated his birthday on October 22. I was five months early.

I felt like a fool. And in the meantime, there was the question of what to do, now that I was in Singapore. I decided to see something of the province of Pahang—birthday party or not—and learned that there was a national park in the middle of the jungle called Taman Negara. I arranged to visit it in a week's time. The Malaysian government required a week to process my application to visit the park, because there was still fighting with Communist guerrillas in that region.

My friend Don, with whom I was staying, instructed me about guerrillas. Don was an international lawyer, but he had been in Vietnam during the war. "Now," he said, "in case there's an ambush, you know what to do."

No, I said, actually I didn't.

"If they ambush your vehicle, you want to run in the direction of fire."

"Really?" That didn't seem logical.

"Yes," Don said. "Get out of the car, and run toward the fire."

"Why?"

"Because what they do is, they put two guys on one side of the road, who open fire. They put everybody else on the other side of the road, expecting you to get out on the opposite side of the vehicle. So when you get out you're exposed: that's when they let you have it."

I made a mental note to remember that. Run toward the fire.

"Probably won't come up, but it's good to know these things," Don said. "Now, you have your compass?"

No, I said. I was going to have a guide.

"Jesus, never go into the jungle without a compass," Don said. "And try and get a decent map. It won't be easy, but try and pick one up in KL."

Okay, I said. I would do that.

"Now, you know what to do about leeches?"

Don had lots of information. He instructed me long into the night. In no time at all, I felt dashing again. I bought a compass and a map, and I flew to Kuala Lumpur to meet my guide. He was a young Chinese biologist named Dennis Yong. We set off the same day.

Here is how you go to Taman Negara:

In Kuala Lumpur, the modern capital of Malaysia, you get into a Land Cruiser and start driving. For the first three hours, the road is a two-lane paved highway in mountainous jungle. Then it is a one-lane paved road, then a dirt road, then a mud track. After half a day of driving, the mud

144

track stops at a river, at a place called Kuala Tembeling. Kuala means "mouth of the river," and most villages are at the juncture of rivers.

At Kuala Tembeling, you get into a long, slender boat powered by an outboard motor, and you head up the Tembeling River. The river is incredibly tranquil; you pass small villages interspersed with regions of jungle. As the hours go by, there are fewer villages, more jungle. Finally there are no villages at all. There is only jungle.

After three hours on the river, the boat pulls over at a place called Kuala Tahan. Here I find several plain, concrete buildings—a restaurant pavilion, and four or five guest cottages. This is Taman Negara, formerly the private retreat of the Sultan of Pahang, now donated to the nation as a park.

I have never been in a jungle before. Certainly I have never been so far from civilization. The place is quite comfortable, and Dennis radiates competence. Yet I feel so *far* from anything I know. I would never admit I am frightened, but I am.

We go at once to the nearest hide, not far from the cottages. Dennis tells me there are tigers, rhinos, and elephants in Taman Negara, but the animals are shy and rarely seen. We must not make any noise or the animals will not come.

On the path through the jungle, Dennis gestures for me to be silent, and we do not speak after that. We climb a flight of wooden steps and sit in the hide: an elevated wooden hut, with narrow windows looking out onto a clearing. In the clearing is a cake of salt, surrounded by the muddy prints of many animals. At the moment, I see no animals.

We wait, not speaking.

It's comfortable for me not to talk. I have spent years writing, never speaking. Silence doesn't bother me. We stare out at a clearing of grass with a salt lick, and wait for animals to come.

Pretty soon an English couple arrive. They sit in the hide with us, but they speak. I put my finger to my lips. They whisper, "Oh, sorry," and don't say anything for about thirty seconds. Then they begin to whisper. I think it must be something urgent, but it's not. Just random chatter. I don't like to be pushy, but I ask them to please be quiet. Dennis explains to them that no animals will come unless the hide is entirely silent. They say irritably that there aren't

145

any animals out there anyway. They are silent for a couple of minutes. Then one of them drums his fingers on the bench, and the other begins plucking at the thatching of the hide. Then they smoke cigarettes, and pretty soon they are whispering, and then speaking in low voices, and then talking in ordinary tones.

When I catch their eye, they fall silent again, and the cycle begins all over. I realize that these people *can't* be quiet. They are incapable of silence. They want to see animals, but they can't be still long enough to let the animals come. It amazes me to watch them: they seem to have a kind of incontinence. They would be embarrassed not to be toilet-trained, yet they show no embarrassment at their inability to sit silently for more than a few seconds.

Eventually they leave. Dennis and I remain alone in the hide for another hour. No animals come.

We return to the hide after dinner. The night is dramatic, because the overcast sky glows with silent bursts of heat lightning, casting flickering bluish light on the field before us.

The surrounding jungle is noisy. Crickets make a shrill sound, toads and frogs a low rumble. An owl gives a kind of abrupt, cut-off hoot, which is answered across the valley.

Around ten the sounds begin to die. By midnight it is quiet. No animals come. We go to bed.

I am staying in cottage number 5. Dennis tells me that this was the Sultan's own cottage, when he was in residence. I think, At least that's something. I am sleeping in the Sultan's cottage. At least that.

The next day we hike in the jungle. Paths in the national park are more than ten feet wide. Dennis explains they must be cut wide because the jungle grows back so quickly. We pass flowering red ginger, spiky rattan, and the occasional small orchid, but for the most part the landscape is monotonous green, very dark, and hot.

Dennis has promised I will see gibbons, and we hear them hooting everywhere in the canopy of trees above us, a distinctive "cow-wow" sound. I also hear them crashing through the branches, but I don't really see them. Finally, with binoculars, I glimpse four black shapes, far off, silhou-

146

etted against the sky. They shake the branches and are gone. I have seen my gibbons; I never see them better.

In trying to get a clear look at them, we have wandered a few yards off the trail. I turn and see I am surrounded by ferns and plants as tall as I am. I can only see a few feet in any direction. I am utterly lost.

Dennis laughs and leads me back to the trail.

As we walk, he tells me that the *orang asli,* the aboriginal tribesmen of the Malay forest, can walk in the jungle for weeks and not get lost. Dennis has gone with aborigines on long expeditions, several hundred miles of walking, and on the route back, weeks later, the aborigines unerringly return to precisely the same campsites each night.

I ask how they are able to do it. Dennis shakes his head. He doesn't know. He has spent a lot of time in the jungle, but he can't fathom it, he says. You must be raised here, he says. It must be your city, the way we grow up in a city. You have to know your way around.

He points out some tiny hazards—a small scorpion in a rotting tree, and leeches wiggling like thin worms along the trail. Dennis himself walks barefooted on the trail. The leeches never bother the first man in a party, he says. They respond to vibration; as the first man passes, the second and the third man get the leeches. I look down, and see one crawling through my boot laces. Dennis tells me not to worry; if it's still there later, he will show me what to do. I think, If it's still there later?

The air is hot and humid beneath the trees. I am soaked in sweat. Occasionally on the trail the views open out to a wider vista of the jungle. The trees are all faintly dusted with color—red and yellow and white and pink; a hillside here looks like an autumn hillside in Vermont, but paler, washed out. Dennis explains this is the dry season and the trees are blossoming. That is why they display those dusted colors. I am seeing thousands of tiny blossoms.

We walk for an hour and finally reach the view we have been seeking. I'm out of breath, extremely tired, and glad for a rest. We stop, and I immediately learn a consequence of all the flowering trees.

Bees.

This entire vast jungle is in bloom, and there are thousands and thousands of bees. I have not noticed them while walking, but now that I have stopped they descend upon me. They crawl all over my camera and my hands as I take pictures. Looking down, I see they are on my arms, and crawling over my tee shirt.

Dennis says to be calm, that the bees are only attracted to my salty sweat, and will not sting if I remain calm and move slowly. That's all I need to hear, and I immediately relax. I am not particularly afraid of bees anyway, nor am I allergic to them. A few bees won't bother me. It's kind of an interesting experience.

The bees continue to land.

I feel them crawling over my cheeks and forehead. I feel them in my ears, and hear the hum of their many wings. I see them crawling on the frames of my glasses. I feel them tickling as they walk on my eyelids. I feel them clustered on my lips. I am no longer relaxed.

I want to scream.

It is all I can do to keep from screaming. The bees are now so thick on the lenses of my glasses that I can hardly see Dennis. He has quite a few bees on him, and he is smiling at me.

"They prefer you," he says. "Nice and salty."

I am trying to control my breathing, to avoid jagged, short, panicky gasps. I am doing okay, I am holding my own, but, even so, at any moment I may begin to scream.

"Do the bees bother you?" Dennis asks.

A little, I say.

"If you are bothered," Dennis says, "we can start walking again, and the bees will fly away." But I am too tired to walk right now. I must endure the bees for a few moments longer. And as they crawl over me, down my shirt and up toward my armpits and around the back of my neck and between my fingers, as I feel them everywhere, I realize that I am waiting to be stung. If I could really believe they wouldn't sting me, I would be able to relax.

"They won't sting you," Dennis says again. "They just want to lick you. They are very gentle."

It seems inconceivable that they will not sting me. By now I am encrusted with bees; I have so many on me that I feel their added weight on my body.

And I haven't been stung yet. I look down and see my chest, carpeted with bees, rising and falling. I don't want to take any more pictures—I can't see well enough to do it anyway, through all the bees.

Finally Dennis says, "Ready to go back?"

"Yes," I say.

148

We start to walk, slowly. The bees slip away, one by one. In a few moments I am free of them, back on the trail.

I was never stung.

That afternoon I meet some *orang asli* of the Semai tribe. They are short, stocky Negroid men with curly hair, very different in appearance from the Malays and Chinese who constitute the majority of the population. They find me funny because I am so tall.

One man appears to be cooking nails in a pot. I am told he is making poison. The Semai take sap from the Ipoh tree and then boil it with nails and snake heads (although Dennis says the snake heads are a ritual ingredient, not necessary for efficacy). The resulting poison on a blowdart produces convulsions and death in animals as large as monkeys.

Nearby, another man is stir-frying Chinese tobacco with sugar. The Semai prefer to smoke it that way.

The men seem jittery. Dennis says that they are always a little paranoid, because, even well into the twentieth century, the Malays shot them for sport. There are stories of Malay sultans riding on the bonnets of their Bentleys and firing into the jungle at the little forest men.

Dennis tells me aboriginal shamans are highly respected, and often consulted by prominent Malays when they become sick. The Semai call their shamans *berhalak*, meaning someone who can go into a trance. The Semai believe everyone in their tribe can go into a trance, and therefore everyone is a shaman to some extent, but certain individuals are especially good at trances and therefore become accomplished shamans who combat evil spirits and heal people. A person is generally called to become *berhalak* by a dream of a tiger, and the most powerful shamans are believed to be were-tigers.

Dreams are important to the Semai, and even the dreams of a young child will be exhaustively discussed, and further dreams directed and encouraged. The Semai believe they can control their dreams.

That night we sleep in a hide a half-mile from Kuala Tahan. The distance from even that much civilization is exciting. I am certain I will see a tiger tonight. I feel it. I stay awake

149

for hours, watching the heat lightning flash over the landscape. I never see a tiger.

In the morning I wake stiff and cold in the hide. Dennis is gone. I look out the window at the salt lick. He is bent low, inspecting hoofprints in the mud.

"Tracks of a wild pig," he says. "We missed him."

A wild pig does not sound exciting. Privately I am glad I slept instead of waiting all night to see a pig. "No tigers?"

"Not last night."

On a boat, we go up rapids to Kuala Trengganu, where we see a monitor lizard near the river edge, and a hornbill flying overhead. Then we see tiger tracks in the wet riverbank. Everyone is enthusiastic about the tiger tracks, but if anything, they make me feel more frustrated: I am seeing the signs of everything, never the thing itself.

From Kuala Trengganu we had planned to go up a smaller stream, but the boatmen tell me that, this late in the dry season, the streams are low and we cannot make it up.

Still frustrated about the tiger, I suggest we try.

They shrug, warn me it will not be possible to get up very far.

I *insist* we try.

They shrug and smile, and we start up the river. Almost immediately, we strike a dry rapid. The boat must be ported upstream past it. We get out, the boat is dragged, we climb back in, scrape along the rocky bottom, manage another hundred yards, until the next dry rapid. Again we get out and carry the boat. We do this three more times, until I suggest there is no point in continuing, the river is too low.

They shrug and smile, and we head back. Nobody says anything.

On the way back, I find myself newly interested in the tiger tracks and want to stop to inspect them. But the wake of our passing boat has washed the shore clean. The tracks are gone.

That night after dinner I am walking back in the darkness toward my cottage with Dennis. He shines his light around the woods and says, "Mat is here."

"Mat?" A pair of gleaming eyes, a heavy, dark shape on the ground.

"Yes. And one of her children."

I see a second pair of eyes.

Dennis sets out, and I follow. Pretty soon I see that Mat is a pregnant deer, sitting calmly on the ground. As we approach, Mat stands. She is six feet high, and beautiful, and she remains calm even when we come close.

Dennis explains that "Mat" is the Malay word for "Friday," which is the day, many years ago, that this deer wandered out of the jungle and into the settlement. The villagers fed her, she stayed, and when she had offspring some of them came into the settlement, too.

"Mat is why they don't have goats here," Dennis says. "In every village, the Malay people like to raise goats and eat them, but once Mat arrived here, they found she did not like the goats and would kick them to death."

"So what did the villagers do?"

"They didn't keep goats any more."

"But if they are so fond of goats . . ."

"I know. But Mat came, so they didn't have goats any more."

In the end, the story of Mat and the villagers came to symbolize the trip to me. The village people had encountered a deer, and the deer stayed, and so they didn't eat their favorite food any more. That's all.

I could think of a dozen alternatives. I would have built an enclosure for goats. I would have tried to train Mat to tolerate goats. I would have raised goats at a nearby village and brought them here at the last minute. I would have gotten a freezer and kept frozen goat meat. Maybe I would have discouraged Mat from coming any more.

In short, where I would have struggled, the villagers simply accepted the situation and went on with their lives.

I began to realize how many times the trip had repeated that lesson for me.

The bees—I didn't like them, but I had to tolerate them, there was nothing I could do.

The low water on the river—I wanted to go upstream, but there was nothing I could do.

The absent animals—I didn't like not seeing them, but there was nothing I could do.

I couldn't make it rain; I couldn't fill up the rivers, or stop the jungle from flowering, or make wild animals appear.

These things were beyond my control, and I was forced to accept that. Just as I was forced to accept the couple that wouldn't stop talking.

In fact, I began to realize that, although they couldn't stop talking, I had a much greater problem. I couldn't stop trying to control everything around me—including the couple. I couldn't leave things alone. I was an urban, technological man accustomed to making things happen. I had been taught countless times that you were supposed to make things happen, that anything less implied shameful passivity. I lived all my life in cities, struggling shoulder to shoulder with other struggling people. We all were struggling to make something happen: a marriage, a job, a raise, an acceptance, a child, a new car, new life, new status, the next thing.

I'd lived in that frantic, active way for more than thirty years, and when I finally began to crack, when I tried to control everything about my life and my work and the people around me, I somehow ended up in the Malaysian jungle and experienced a solid week of events over which I had absolutely no control. And never would. Events that reminded me that I had my limits—rather severe limits, in the greater scheme of things—and I had no business trying to control as much as I did, even if I could.

When I went home, I noticed I felt much better. Not rested, the way a certain kind of vacation rests you, but literally better. I couldn't figure out why for a long time.

Back in Los Angeles, nobody even knew where Malaysia was, and people asked why I had gone there. I kept telling them about the deer named Mat and how the villagers stopped eating goat. This wasn't a very dramatic story, nobody responded to it, and I wondered why I kept repeating it. "What is it about that deer and the villagers?" I wondered. And then one day I got it.

Ten years after my trip to Pahang, I wrote these notes in Los Angeles. Then I changed clothes and went to an exercise class.

In class I noticed I had put on the same blue tee shirt that I had worn in the jungle a decade before, when the bees had covered me. I had always been fond of this tee shirt, now much faded. It was one of the oldest articles of clothing I owned.

When I got home, I threw it out.

Enough is enough. One way I control myself is to hang on to things too long. My past is too present in my life. So I threw the tee shirt out. It seemed a step in the right direction.

An Elephant Attacks

In 1975, Loren and I were staying at the Craig Farm, a sixty-square-mile preserve in northern Kenya. She and I had met the year before, and we were now in the middle of a passionate romance. A trip to Africa seemed a fine idea. We had gone to the Craig Farm because I wanted to walk among the animals, which is illegal in the government game preserves.

I'd studied anthropology in college, and, after so many years of academic work, I hoped to have firsthand experience, however brief, of what it must have been like to be a primitive hunter on the African savanna. I imagined myself stalking wild beasts, getting dangerously close to them, until I could see the muscles quiver beneath the skin, and could observe their behavior intimately. Then, at some unknown signal—perhaps my own error, the snap of a dry twig—skittish heads would jerk up in alarm, they would look around in fright, and they would thunder away.

Well, it wasn't like that at all.

The animals saw me from a quarter of a mile away, and calmly moved off. If I stalked them, they moved a little farther. I was never able to get within a quarter mile from them. I was never able to see them worried, let alone

154

alarmed. Their heads never jerked up. Instead, they would glance over from time to time in a bored way, notice my pathetic stalking, and move off.

William Craig, who walked with me, explained that each animal maintained a characteristic distance from man. It was a kind of invisible perimeter; if you came within it, the animal simply moved until the distance was re-established. For most animals it was a fraction of a mile.

We spent the day hiking on open plains, among zebras and giraffes and antelopes, with the snowy peak of Mount Kenya rising in the background. It was quite exciting, but frustrating, too.

Clearly, to sneak up on a giraffe (as I had seen pygmies do, in movies) was far more difficult than I had imagined. Giraffes were not as dumb as they looked; they had excellent eyesight, and they tended to cluster with zebras, animals that had an excellent sense of smell.

I began to realize that stalking animals was a skill rather like pole vaulting—it looked easy when others did it, but if you tried it yourself you were in for a surprise.

Nothing turned out the way I expected it to be that day. I found that zebras gallop like horses, but bark like dogs: that bark is their characteristic sound. And we didn't see a great variety of game. No elephants or lions or really exciting animals.

And all the animals seemed maddeningly indifferent to my presence. I didn't frighten them; I bored them. Actually, it was a little insulting. I took everything that happened that day personally, and the animals in their natural setting seemed so impersonal—so fundamentally *uninterested* in me.

It was in this frame of mind that I returned to Lamu Downs Camp in the evening, to spend my first night under the African stars. I had never camped before, except one night at the age of eleven in the Nassau County Boy Scout Camp on Long Island. That was a far cry from Africa.

The Craigs showed Loren and me how everything was set up, the camp beds, the hissing gas lanterns, the open-air shower attached to the back of the tent, and so forth. It was all quite luxurious. I felt very comfortable.

Then we had dinner in the mess tent, and the Craigs talked about their ranch and the animals found there. They were concerned because, although this was the dry season, the drought had gone on for a long time and the elephants

155

had disappeared. They usually had quite a few elephants on the ranch, they said, but the elephants hadn't been seen for weeks now. We talked and ate as darkness fell.

When dinner was finished, Loren and I headed back toward our tent. It was now very dark. I found that a few more questions had occurred to me. One was about wild animals. The same wild animals I had been unable to approach during the day might, I suspected, come and visit me in the night.

The Craigs laughed. No, no, they said, animals never entered the campground at night. Of course, there *was* the time they woke up in the morning and found a big rhino asleep in the embers of the fire from the night before, but that was unusual.

How unusual? I wanted to know.

I hadn't yet noticed the easy way these people simultaneously gave reassurance and took it away.

Very unusual, they said. You were almost never bothered by animals. Of course, you had the occasional monkey screeching in the trees, keeping you awake, that sort of thing. But not animals on the ground, no.

By now my concerns had shifted. The fabric of my tent looked flimsy as I imagined a sleeping rhino just outside. Would an animal ever enter the tent?

Oh no, they said. Of course, there *was* the time that leopard clawed right through the tent fabric, scaring the hell out of the lady inside. She woke up shrieking, frightened the cat off. But there had been something peculiar about that incident. They couldn't remember what, exactly. People had food in the tent, or the woman was having her period—anyway, something peculiar. It wasn't as if a leopard would just come up and claw your tent for no reason.

Really? I asked.

Really, the Craigs said, wearying of their own game. Really, there aren't animals around the camp at night. Animals don't like to be around people and they won't come near. Anyway, see these lanterns?

They pointed to three hurricane lanterns spaced around the tents. The lanterns were lit all night, they explained, and the light kept the animals away. Count on it. Never any animals around the tents. Now, you see the stream over there? Sometimes you find the odd animal on the far side of the stream. But never over on this side, where the tents and the lanterns and the people were.

156

Have a good sleep, they said cheerfully, and said good night.

Loren and I zipped up our tent and went to bed.

Loren had camped a lot in her childhood and was relaxed about sleeping in the woods in a tent. I, on the other hand, was far too nervous to sleep. I read for a while, hoping to become sleepy.

I remained wide awake, listening for sounds outside.

There weren't any sounds outside. It was completely quiet. A cicada, a gust of wind blowing lightly through the acacia trees. Otherwise silence.

On the cot across the tent, Loren rolled away from the light. I watched her shoulder rise and fall rhythmically. I thought, She can't really be going to sleep, just like that.

"Hey!" I whispered. "Are you going to sleep?"

"It's night, isn't it?"

"Are you tired?"

"Just go to sleep, Michael."

"I'm not tired!" I whispered.

"Just close your eyes and pretend you are."

I heard something outside, a sound of some kind.

"Hey! Did you hear that?"

"It's nothing. I'm going to sleep, Michael."

Pretty soon Loren was snoring. I envied her effortless drift to unconsciousness.

I, on the other hand, had to urinate.

I ignored the urge. There was no way I was going outside the tent at night. Anyway, the latrine tent was all the way across the camp.

As time went on, I found I couldn't ignore the urge. I was going to have to do something. I looked under the bed to see if there was a chamber pot. These people were British, you never knew. No chamber pot. I inspected the zippered flaps to see if there was any way I could do it without leaving the tent. There wasn't any way.

By now I had a voice saying, Oh, for God's sake, Michael, pull yourself together. What are you afraid of? The dark? What do you think is out there? You're being ridiculous. It's a good thing Loren is asleep or she would really lose respect for you, a grown man afraid to go out of his tent at night to pee!

And another voice was saying, Look, you don't have to go far. Just about three feet outside, and you can do it right there. And think how much better you'll feel afterward!

157

Because by now the urge was intense. So I pulled on my sneakers, unzipped the tent, held my breath, and stuck my head out.

The night was pitch black. The lanterns they had promised to keep on all night had gone out. And it wasn't even midnight!

I felt like a cartoon character, with my head sticking out of the tent, neck muscles straining with tension, waiting, listening, looking. . . .

At nothing. There was nothing out there. No sounds, no animals, no nothing. My eyes became accustomed to the darkness and I still saw nothing at all. I realized I had been holding my breath. I leapt out, moved just beyond the tent ropes, relieved myself, dashed back inside, and zipped up the flap behind me.

Safe!

I looked around the tent. Loren was sleeping, breathing softly. It amazed me that she could do this. She was sleeping as easily as if she were in a nice secure hotel room somewhere.

I envied her, but, on the other hand, it was important for *somebody* to stay alert, out here in the bush. I turned out the light and lay on my back, wide awake, listening to the sounds. There still were none.

It was absolutely quiet. And it was almost midnight.

Despite myself, I was beginning to feel drowsy when suddenly I heard a distinct dry *crack*. It was the sound of a branch breaking underfoot. Then I heard a crashing sound. Something large moving through dry brush.

It sounded to me like an elephant.

Very near.

Loren still slept peacefully.

I listened some more. There was silence for a while, and then I heard the crashing again. The crashing sound had a lazy rhythm, exactly like an elephant moving. Anyway, whatever it was, it was damned big, and damned close.

I listened a while longer, and when I couldn't stand it any more, I whispered, "Hey! Are you asleep?"

"Uhhhh," she said sleepily, rolling onto her back.

"Hey," I said, "listen! *There's something out there!*"

She was instantly awake, sitting up on one elbow in alarm. "Where?"

"Out there! Outside! Something big! It sounds like an elephant."

She collapsed back on the bed. "Oh, Michael. You heard what they said. They haven't seen any elephants for weeks."

"Well, *listen!*"

We listened together, for a long time.

"I don't hear anything." She sounded annoyed. "Why are we whispering?" she said, now speaking in a normal voice.

"I swear to you," I said in a normal voice. "I heard something."

Just then the crashing sound came again. Very distinct and loud.

Loren sat bolt upright, whispered, "What do you think it is?"

I whispered, "An elephant!"

"Have you seen it?"

"No." Actually, trying to see the source of the sounds had not occurred to me before. "I don't think we can. The lanterns have all blown out. It's pitch black out there."

"Use the flashlight." We had a powerful flashlight in the tent.

"Okay. Where is it?"

"Right by the bed."

"Okay."

More crashing sounds. Unless my ears were playing tricks on me, the source of those sounds was now very close, only a few feet away.

I crept up to the zipper with the flashlight. I opened a little air ventilation flap that was covered with mesh mosquito netting and shone the light out. But the light reflected off the netting. I could see nothing.

"What do you see?"

"Nothing."

"You have to open the zipper!"

"Not a chance."

"What are you, afraid?"

"Yes!"

"Okay," she sighed. "I'll do it."

She got out of bed, took the flashlight, and crawled to the front flap. She unzipped the tent from the bottom about six inches.

More crashing outside.

"Sounds close," she whispered, hesitating.

I waited.

She unzipped it six more inches, and shone the light

outside for a few seconds, then zipped the tent shut and clicked the light off.

"Well?" I asked.

"I didn't see anything. I don't think there's anything out there."

"Then what's making the noise?"

The crashing noise, the branches cracking, still continued. Still close.

"I don't think it's anything," Loren said. "It's the wind."

"It's not the wind," I said.

"Okay, then, you look."

I took the flashlight. I approached the zipper. I listened again to the intermittent crashing sounds.

"What do you think it is?" she said, listening.

"I think it's an elephant," I said.

"But you heard what they said, it can't be an elephant. It must be something else, a big bird in the trees or something."

I unzipped the tent a full three feet, and shone the light out. The round beam shot into blackness. I swung it around. I saw the branches of trees. Then I saw some kind of round brown shape in the beam, with furry things hanging down in front of the round thing. I couldn't make it out at first.

Then I realized: *I was looking at an enormous eye.* The furry things were eyelashes. The elephant was so close his eye filled the flashlight beam. He was just ten feet away from me. He was huge. He was eating brush and grasses.

"It's a goddamn elephant," I whispered, snapping off the beam. I felt strangely calm.

"You're kidding!" she whispered. "An elephant? You saw it?"

"Yes."

"Why'd you turn off the light?"

"I don't want to upset him."

I was thinking the elephant might not like having a light shone in his eye. I didn't want him angry, or confused, and trampling the tent. I didn't know anything about elephant emotions, but this one seemed calm right now, and there was no point in changing that.

Loren jumped out of bed and took the flashlight. "Let me see. Where is he?"

"Don't worry, you can't miss him."

She shone the light out the tent. Her body went rigid. "He's *right here.*"

160

"I told you." I couldn't help it; I had been right all along; there had been an elephant.

"But what about how they never cross the river and all that?"

"I don't know, but I know there's a huge elephant right outside our tent."

"What're we going to do?"

"I don't know."

"You think he'll hurt us? I don't think he'll hurt us." Loren had a habit of raising a question and resolving it for herself without waiting for assistance or disagreement.

"I have no idea what he'll do."

"Should we try to get away?"

"I don't think so," I said. "I don't think we should leave the tent."

"Maybe out the back, where the shower is?"

"I don't think so."

"We could shout for help—the other tents are just across the way."

"Shouting might upset him," I said. "Anyway, what would we say?"

"We'd say, There's an elephant outside our tent!"

"And what would they do?"

"I don't know, but they must know what to do when there's an elephant outside the tourists' tent."

"I think shouting could make him nervous."

"Maybe we can scare him away."

"He's a lot bigger than we are."

"Then what can we do?" she asked.

All the time we were discussing plans, the elephant was peacefully crashing around in the underbrush outside the tent, eating and moving around in his slow, ponderous way. The elephant didn't seem upset. And all our options for action seemed unworkable.

I got into bed.

"What're you doing?" she said.

"Going to bed." I was calm.

"Just like that? With a dangerous elephant right outside?"

"There's nothing we can do about him," I said, "so we might as well go to sleep."

And I did. I fell asleep almost immediately, listening to the elephant crashing around in the brush outside.

The next morning, after breakfast, I said, "By the way, I noticed an elephant outside my tent last night."

Oh no, they told me. That couldn't be. Elephants haven't been seen for some time because of the drought, and, anyway, animals never cross to this side of the river.

"Well, he was right outside my tent."

There was an awkward silence. The tenderfoot explorer, however misinformed, is still paying the bills, and politeness must be maintained. Someone coughed, asked if I might have been mistaken.

"No," I said. "It was an elephant all right. A big one."

"Well," my courier, Mark Warwick, a brilliant twenty-three-year-old naturalist, said, "let's have a look, shall we?"

We all went over and inspected the ground outside my tent. There were plenty of elephant droppings, which are hard to miss, and there were circular footprints in the soft earth. Each print was the size of a large serving platter.

"What do you know," they said. "There was an elephant here last night!"

"Damned big one, too," someone else said.

"Came right up to the tent, too. Didn't give you any trouble, did he?"

Oh no, I said. No trouble.

"Sleep all right and so forth?"

Oh yes, slept fine, I said. Didn't bother me at all.

And the truth was, I *had* slept well, when I finally stopped worrying. I was impressed with the instantaneous flip in my own emotional state, from a barely controlled hysteria to a detached calm once I saw the giant eye. How had that happened?

For a long time I felt it was because I am a practical person who, faced with an elephant outside his tent, examines all the possibilities—to run away, to call for help, to scare the elephant off—and, having rejected them all, sensibly decides to go to sleep.

But later I realized that we are all like that. We all can work ourselves into a hysterical panic over possibilities that we won't look at. What if I have cancer? What if my job is at risk? What if my kids are on drugs? What if I'm getting bald? What if an elephant is outside my tent?

What if I am faced with some terrible thing that I don't know how to deal with?

And that hysteria always goes away the instant we are willing to hear the answer. Even if the answer is what we feared all along. Yes, you have cancer. Yes, your kids are on drugs. Yes, there is an elephant outside your tent.

Now the question becomes, What are you going to do about it? Subsequent emotions may not be pleasant, but the hysteria stops. Hysteria accompanies an unwillingness to look at what is really going on; it promotes an unwillingness to look. We feel we are afraid to look, when actually it is not-looking that makes us afraid. The minute we look, we cease being afraid.

Knowing in advance what you are going to do about something is not so easy. I remember in 1968 I was getting ready to dive off a boat in the Virgin Islands, and some man was putting on all this equipment. I was interested, because the man was a diving instructor, and instructors don't usually carry a lot of equipment. Finally he strapped a knife on his calf. All my life I had been seeing divers strapping on knives, and I never understood why.

I said, "Excuse me, but why do you carry a knife?"

"Oh," he said, "you know. Just in case."

"Just in case what?"

"You know. In case something happens."

"Like what?"

"Like you get your lines fouled, and have to cut yourself free."

"How would that happen?"

"Oh, like in a wreck. Diving in a wreck, you get your lines fouled."

"But there aren't any wrecks here."

"I know, but a knife is still good to have. You see something nice, a piece of coral or whatever, you cut it free and bring it back."

"This is a protected undersea park; you can't take anything."

"I know, but there're other reasons, too."

"Like what?"

"Defense."

"Defense against what?"

"Whatever's down there. Say, sharks."

This was a little knife with a nine-inch blade. I tried to imagine the undersea battle. "This knife would help you fight off a shark?"

"Damn right."

"You think it would cut the skin? Sharks have pretty tough skin."

"Oh yeah, sure. It would cut the skin."

"So you figure you'd kill the shark with that knife."

"Pretty much, yeah."

"Of course, to stab the shark you'd have to be awfully close to it, wouldn't you? The shark would really have to be close."

"Well, they do that, you know."

"I know. But the thing is, when you first see the shark, instead of backing away to safety, you would have to move forward, because you have to get close to attack the shark with your knife."

"Oh, I wouldn't do that."

"You wouldn't."

"Oh no. I'd back away. Sure. See, the knife is *just in case.* In case he *comes after* me."

"If he comes after you, then you'd try and stab him?"

"Well, no, what I'd probably do is, I'd hit him on the nose with the handle. You know, sharks have very sensitive noses; you pop them on the nose and they generally turn and run."

"But why wouldn't you hit him on the nose with your movie camera?" I said, pointing to a big piece of equipment at his feet. "That'd be in your hands anyway, and it's a lot easier to hit a shark with a big movie camera than a little knife handle."

"Yeah, that's probably what I'd do," he said.

"So why are you carrying the knife?"

"You never know," he said. And he plunged into the water.

I couldn't argue with that.

Later, when the dive was over and we were back in the boat, he unstrapped the knife he hadn't used and said, "You know, I was thinking about what you asked me, why I carry a knife. You know why?"

"Why?" I said.

"Because I just feel safer with it."

164

I couldn't argue with that, either.

"I just feel ready for anything when I have the knife strapped on."

"Gee," I said, "every shark I've seen has seemed so big and powerful and fast, I don't think I would've felt any better to know I had a little knife with me."

He looked up suddenly. "You've seen sharks?" he asked.

Once, on Bora-Bora, I was diving with my brother. There were two other divers in the boat, a man and his ten-year-old son. Because the boy was so young, we were diving in the lagoon and not on the outer reef.

The boy's father could talk about nothing but sharks. He kept saying, "Are there any sharks around here?"

We kept saying, "Nothing dangerous, nothing to worry about." Actually the lagoon was full of white-tip reef sharks. You saw them all the time; you saw them while you were snorkeling twenty feet from the hotel beach.

And the man was saying, "Now, don't worry, son, about any sharks." The man was nervous, speaking rapidly, his hands shaking. Meanwhile, the kid wasn't worried about sharks at all. He was just going diving.

They plunged into the water first. My brother said, "I hope that guy is going to be okay." Because the guy was almost certainly going to see sharks down there.

We dropped over the side and went our own way, exploring the coral heads. A little while later we saw the man take his son to the surface. The kid had run out of air. Then the man came back down and poked among the coral, taking photos with his Nikonos and flash.

Pretty soon a white-tip came cruising by. I held my breath, waiting for the guy to freak out. But the guy didn't see it at all. He was busy with his pictures.

Other sharks appeared. Sharks passed to his left. Sharks passed to his right. Sharks glided over him; sharks slipped beneath him. He must have had a dozen encounters with sharks in the space of ten minutes.

Back on the boat, he said, "Beautiful dive, wasn't it?"

"Beautiful," we agreed.

"Thank God I didn't see any sharks," he said. "I don't know what I would have done if I had."

Kilimanjaro

"The odds are seven to one against," the courier said.

"Against what?" I said.

"Against your making it to the top of Kilimanjaro. I polled the men, and they are seven to one you'll never make it."

It was late afternoon in my camp in Ngorongoro Crater in Tanzania; I was approaching the end of a two-week safari in Africa with my courier, Mark Warwick. Next I was scheduled to climb Kilimanjaro. I hadn't really thought much about Kilimanjaro until now.

Curious, I said to Mark, "How did *you* vote?"

"I voted no."

"You don't think I'll make it, either?"

"No."

"Have you climbed Kilimanjaro?"

He shook his head. "I'm not that crazy. I've heard the stories from the people who came back."

"I heard it was pretty easy," I said. "Just a walk to the top."

"Well, a lot of people don't finish the walk," he said. "Don't kid yourself. It's bloody difficult, trekking above eighteen thousand feet."

166

That wasn't how it had seemed months before, when I had read the African guidebooks, planning my trip. The books merely said that the famous Mount Kilimanjaro was an extinct equatorial volcano, with a broad sloping cinder cone, which meant that, although it was the highest mountain in Africa, you simply walked to the top, with no need for technical gear or specialized mountaineering knowledge. Since Kilimanjaro was on the equator, the weather was milder than comparably high mountains elsewhere. The climb was routine; thousands of people did it every year. The standard ascent took five days, and was easily arranged by any travel agency. It sounded like fun.

Sitting on the floor of my house in Los Angeles with guidebooks opened all around me, I had said to Loren, "Hey, look at this, we can climb Kilimanjaro. Want to do it?"

"Sure," she said. "Why not?"

So I had called my travel agent and said I wanted to climb Kilimanjaro, and the agent said no problem; she'd set it up to follow the safari; we should remember to pack boots and a parka, and that was that.

I had never done any climbing, but I owned a pair of hiking boots I'd gotten to shoot a movie a few years back. I'd worn the boots for a week in the desert, and I remembered them as fitting okay—not great, but okay. I had an old parka from my Boston days. I packed a sweater and an extra pair of jeans; the travel agent said everything else would be provided.

If it was just walking, I figured I could do it. I played tennis once a week or so, and I didn't get too tired. But, just to be safe, I cut back on my cigarettes and beer during the final two days of the safari. Just to be safe.

But now here was my courier, my guide and leader, the white hunter who had taken Loren and me around Africa for two weeks, telling me in the pleasant African twilight, as the air cooled and the sun set and a line of wildebeest moved in stately procession across the floor of Ngorongoro Crater, here he was telling me that he and the men who ran the camp had concluded I'd never make it to the top of Kilimanjaro.

I just looked at him oddly, as if he were misinformed. "I don't think it'll be a problem," I said.

"You ever been at altitude before?"

"Sure," I said, thinking back. When I was a kid, I'd been

167

on glaciers in Canada. I had visited some relatives in Boulder, Colorado. Sure, I'd been at altitude.

I didn't think it was such a big deal.

"Eighteen thousand feet's pretty high," Mark said, shaking his head. "That kind of altitude changes everything."

"Uh-huh," I said vaguely. I continued to feel that he was misinformed, or at any rate that there was something he didn't understand. Mark mistook my vagueness for concern.

"Look here, don't worry about it," he said, laughing and slapping me on the shoulder. "I was just joking."

"You weren't."

"I promise you, I was."

"What do you want to bet I make it?" I said.

"Look here, Michael," he said. "It was just a joke. You're taking this entirely too seriously."

I persisted. "I'll bet you a dinner, when I get back to Nairobi," I said, and named a French restaurant that he had mentioned as expensive and good.

Mark agreed to the bet. "Right," he said. "Now: how will we verify that you actually get to the top?"

"Do you think I'd lie?"

He raised his hands. "I'm just asking how I'll know. A bet's a bet. How'll you prove it?"

"Well, there'll be pictures," I said. "I'll have pictures."

"They won't be developed yet."

"I'll develop them in Nairobi for you."

It turned out that you couldn't get color processing done in Nairobi; the film was all sent to England and took weeks.

"I'll get a statement from the guide or whoever."

"Could be forged."

"Well, Loren will tell you whether I made it or not."

"That's true," he said, nodding, "she'll tell me whether you got up there."

So we agreed that, once back in Nairobi, if Loren said I had climbed Kilimanjaro, he would buy the dinner.

Then a thought occurred to me. "What if Loren doesn't make it?"

Mark shook his head. "The boys are six to two that she'll make it to the top. We're not worried about her. We're worried about *you.*"

"Great," I said.

* * *

168

The Marangu Hotel stood at the foot of the mountain. It was run by a charming elderly German woman. The hotel had once been a farm; it was Spartan and efficient, and seemed to exist only as a staging place for tourists to climb the mountain. I was told there were several such hotels in the area.

Loren took a bath, remarking on how plentiful the hot water was.

"Yeah," I said, "I guess they have to have it. When people come down off the mountain, they must want hot water and no fooling."

While she took her bath, I walked out into the garden behind the hotel. It was early evening. Although we had been driving near Kilimanjaro for the last two days, I still hadn't seen the mountain because of haze. I could not see it now, but among the roses in the garden there was a little shellacked photo on a wooden pedestal showing the mountain and the route up, so I suspected, as I looked at the photo, that Kilimanjaro was probably directly in front of me.

I went back into my hotel room, and mentioned to Loren that I felt a certain frustration about not being able to see the mountain I would be climbing tomorrow. Loren didn't seem to mind; it didn't matter to her, this abstract quality of the whole adventure.

That night in the dining room with its dark polished floors there was only one other party, a family of Americans at a nearby table—a husband and wife and their teenage son. They didn't say much, and had a dazed look on their faces, but their movements, even the way they spooned their soup, conveyed an unusual economy of gesture; they were people who had been through something.

I was sure they had come down from the mountain.

"Well," Loren said, "why don't you ask them how it was?" On the eve of our departure, the question was much on our minds. We felt a little giddy with anticipation. Our giddiness didn't seem to accord with the flat, dull quality of the returning American family. I waited until they were leaving, and walking past our table, to ask them if they had climbed the mountain.

Yes, they said. They had just come down that afternoon.

"You all made it to the top?" Loren asked.

Yes, they all made it to the top.

"Anybody in your group not make it?"

They weren't sure, but they had heard about a group of English students from another hotel who had been climbing at the same time. Several of the English students had not made it, and had turned back. Some of them had gotten sick from the altitude.

As they spoke, the dull look never left their eyes. I couldn't tell if they were tired, or disappointed, or if something odd had happened that they weren't talking about.

"Well," I said brightly, "how was it? The climb?"

They paused. Nobody seemed to want to answer this question. They looked at one another. Finally the wife said, It was good. It was a good climb.

"Hard?"

In some places. The fourth day was not easy. The rest of the time it was okay.

I was disturbed by the flat intonation, the inward manner. We were curious about them, but they showed no curiosity about us at all. They didn't ask where we were from; they didn't ask if we were climbing; they didn't offer any tips or hints or reassurances. They just answered our questions, volunteering nothing, then let the conversation trail into silence, said good night, and left.

"Huh," Loren said, watching them go.

"What are we letting ourselves in for?" I asked.

"I think they were just tired," she said.

I slept uneasily, and woke shortly after dawn. I went out into the chilly garden. The atmospheric haze had thinned, and for the first time I saw, hanging suspended above the roses, the broad white sloping cone of Kilimanjaro. Its profile was so wide I felt disappointed; I had imagined a view more like the dramatic cone of Fuji than the bland arc of snow now before me. I almost didn't take a photograph, it looked so unspectacular.

On the other hand, Kilimanjaro looked safe, matronly. More like a breast than a mountain. And that encouraged me.

How bad could it really be?

The German woman gave the orientation lecture. We were surprised to find we were not the only people climbing: there were six others. We were instructed to divide ourselves into groups of four, since four people shared each overnight hut. Loren and I joined a California lawyer named Paul Myers, and a Swiss surgeon named Jan Newmeyer. Both were experienced climbers, but both were a decade older than I. I felt I would be able to keep up with them. Loren was not worried: she was only twenty-two and in good shape.

The German woman had charts and photos and maps; she had given this lecture countless times before, and she did it smoothly and well. Today, the first day, we would hike through rain forest to nine thousand feet. The second day we would hike in meadowlands to twelve thousand feet. The third day we would cross the high, cold, windswept saddle between the two peaks of Kilimanjaro, and spend the night in a tin hut at fifteen thousand feet, at the base of the cinder cone. At two the next morning, our guides would awaken us and we would begin climbing, in darkness, to reach the summit in early morning, when the weather and the views were best. Everyone would reach the summit if we took our time; not long ago, she said, a sixty-year-old man had reached the summit—arriving a bit later than most, but reaching it without difficulty, nevertheless. Remember, at the summit there was only half the oxygen as at sea level. The key thing at altitude, she told us, was to take your time. And she added, rather peculiarly, that we should not let the guides push us—they sometimes offered to push you, but we would not find pushing helpful. We were warned about the dangers of altitude sickness, and told to turn back immediately if we developed a dry cough.

From the summit we would descend to sleep in the huts at twelve thousand feet. The following day we would return to the hotel. All together we would be gone five nights. All together we would walk seventy-two miles. The guides and porters were highly skilled; if we needed extra clothing, it would be brought to our rooms while we packed; she was sure we would have an enjoyable trip and she wished us luck.

The group starts from the hotel at a brisk pace. Little children from nearby villages walk with us, chatter in broken English, beg. The sun is shining; the warm morning carries an air of expectation, of adventure. I am terrifically

171

excited. I have never done anything like this in my life and I am sure it will be rewarding.

In less than an hour my enthusiasm is gone. The begging children have become reminders that we are not trailblazers, but more like commuters en route to a well-established tourist destination. I find their cuteness irritating, because it has been honed on my predecessors and thus reminds me that thousands have gone before me.

The atmospheric haze has closed in; we can no longer see the mountain that is our destination. We are walking up a dusty road through poor farming villages, the views are not attractive, and the day has turned from warm to hot. I am sweating profusely. My clothing chafes at waist and crotch and armpits. What's worse, I feel blisters on my feet, though I have not been walking for an hour.

I stop by the side of the road, pull off my boots, and inspect my feet. Loren tells me I should have worn two pairs of socks, a thin inner one and a heavy outer one; I dismiss this double-sock camping lore with a wave. My feet will be all right; I'll put Band-Aids on them in the evening. Paul walks by, mentions he has some moleskin if I need it; I say no thanks, wondering to myself what moleskin is. I have never heard of moleskin.

I keep walking.

We enter the rain forest on the lower slopes of Kilimanjaro. It is a beautiful and lush setting, gurgling streams and hanging moss on huge trees that arch overhead and block the sun. It is cooler here, and the trail follows a fresh stream. Monkeys chatter in the trees. I feel renewed enthusiasm. However, before long the humidity, the moisture trapped beneath the canopy of the trees, the dripping of water like a constant rain, gets on my nerves. My clothes are now entirely soaked. I no longer appreciate the beauty, no longer enjoy the clear water tumbling over the smooth rocks. And my feet hurt more and more.

It was a relief to enter the rain forest, and it is a relief to leave it in early afternoon, emerging into an open meadow of grass six feet high. However, by now I am very tired—astonishingly tired—and the path up the meadow is steep. I am wondering how much farther I must go. There are no signposts to tell me how I am doing, how far before we reach the huts. Unable to plan, unable to pace myself, I find my fatigue feels extreme. Do I have an hour still to go? Two hours? Then I see, on a ridge above the high grass, the brown geometric A-frames of the Mandara huts. They are very close. It is only four o'clock in the afternoon. I am not really so tired after all.

We have afternoon tea. Paul and Jan have been here for an hour, so much faster was their pace. The Mandara huts are at nine thousand feet, so I have a chance to feel the altitude. It doesn't seem to make much difference. My spirits are good as I walk around the huts, looking around.

The only problem is my feet. They hurt considerably, and when I remove my boots I find that I have large blisters on the heels and on the small toes of both feet. I put Band-Aids on them, eat an early dinner of bread and canned beef stew, and go to sleep. Paul says he never sleeps well at altitude. I sleep badly.

I'm nervous about the coming day.

The second day is strikingly different. On the first day, the landscape was varied—from desert savanna to rain forest to mountain meadow—but there was never any wider view, never any orientation, any sense of where you were on the mountain. You were just climbing.

On the second day, the landscape is unchanging alpine meadows. An hour from the huts, we suddenly see the peak of Kilimanjaro with perfect clarity, the sides of the volcano streaked with snow. I am excited. We stop for pictures. Here, in a field of low grass, with open topography, I can see where I am—moving on the flank of an enormous wide cone. But so wide is this volcano, and so gentle its slopes, that soon we cannot see the peak any more; it is somewhere ahead, hidden behind deceptively gentle ridges. Once again, deprived of a view of my destination, I am discouraged, and ask the guides when we will be able to see Kilimanjaro.

They invariably point to the ground beneath my feet and say, "*This* Kilimanjaro." When I make myself clear, they shrug. They don't seem to understand my anxiety about seeing the mountain when I am walking on it. Finally our guide, Julius, says, "You see the top with snow tomorrow, all day tomorrow. Not today, but from tomorrow."

I walk on. It is never really hot today, and the walking is pleasant, the ground dark and spongy underfoot. Occasionally the trail is a knee-deep trench dug by all the feet that have passed before. And we are seeing more people on the trails, too: apparently climbers from other hotels. All

173

sorts of people, all sorts of ages. I am encouraged by the diversity.

All in all it is a pleasant day. My only concern is my feet, which are painful. Today I am wearing sneakers instead of boots, but the damage is already done. And I am often winded; I stop to rest every fifteen or twenty minutes. Loren never seems to tire, but I am thirty-three, she is twenty-two. Even so, as the day goes on, I notice she appreciates my frequent stops.

In the absence of the peak, I am looking for the lobelia trees, which I have been told characteristically appear at the eleven-thousand-foot level. I don't know what lobelia trees look like, and since we are above the tree line, every kind of odd plant receives my scrutiny. I ask the guides, "Lobelia? Lobelia?" and they just shake their heads.

Finally, when we break for a late lunch, we find ourselves sitting next to a light-green plant about four feet high with puffy, bulbous leaves. Julius points it out as lobelia.

At every break, the guides and porters sit and smoke cigarettes. I can't believe they are doing this. I am gasping and wheezing and stopping for breath every fifteen minutes. The lobelias at eleven thousand feet mean, I remind myself, that I am barely halfway up.

I begin to wonder if I can make it to the top, after all.

During the rest of the day, I have nothing left to look for except the Horomba huts where we will stay the night. When we reach them, I am extremely tired, and my feet are very painful.

The location of the huts is spectacular, A-frames set on a ledge of black lava at 12,300 feet, looking down on a bank of clouds. At sunset, the air is pink and purple. I feel I am walking around at an altitude normally reached only by airplanes; it is exhilarating. It's also making me light-headed. Now that I am just strolling around the camp and not pushing along the trail, I realize how severely the altitude affects me. I can't breathe comfortably, even sitting down. A term comes back from medical school: "resting dyspnea," shortness of breath while sitting down. I never appreciated how panicky it feels not to be able to catch your breath.

I wonder about altitude sickness, which starts to be a problem at this height. Altitude sickness makes your lungs fill up with water. The cause is unknown, but if you have a dry cough or a headache, you must head back down at once or you may die. I give an experimental cough. I don't have altitude sickness.

My feet are my real concern. I am reluctant to take my sneakers off and see the extent of the damage. When I finally do, I find that the Band-Aids have shifted and done little to protect me; the blisters are larger than yesterday and they have burst, exposing red, inflamed, exquisitely tender skin.

It's sufficiently bad that I abandon my pride and ask Paul for help. He takes one look and calls Jan, who is, after all, a surgeon. Jan gets out his moleskin—moleskin turns out to be a thin, padded cotton sheet with adhesive on one side—and cuts pieces to fit my blisters. We use all his moleskin fixing me up. He stands back and pronounces himself satisfied with the dressing.

I thank him.

"Yes," he says sadly, "but it is too bad."

"Why?"

"Well," he says, looking at my feet, "now you must go back."

"No," I say.

"I think," he says judiciously, "that you cannot go on with your feet this way. You must go down the mountain tomorrow."

"No," I say. "I'll continue." I am surprised at the strength of my own conviction, sitting there with my feet bandaged and my breathing labored. But it doesn't really feel like conviction, it just feels like logic. I've already walked two days. If I go back, it will take two days. That's four days. Whereas, if I push on an extra day, in a total of five days I will have reached the summit and returned.

I've gone too far to turn back, at least in my own mind.

Jan leaves. Pretty soon Loren comes over. "I talked to Jan. He's very worried about your feet."

"Uh-huh."

"Jan says you could get a bad infection. He says the dirt from the trail gets ground into your open skin and you could get a serious infection."

I wonder where she is leading with this.

"I've already talked to the guide," she says, "and it's no problem. They do it all the time. They'll send one porter back down with you, so you don't need to worry about getting lost. And don't worry about me; Paul and Jan will keep an eye on me, and I'll be fine."

Her whole attitude is so casual. Climbing this mountain

just doesn't mean that much to her. I wonder why it means so much to me.

"I'm not going back," I say. Even as I say it, I realize I am being unrealistic. We are at 12,300 feet on the side of a mountain. I have very bad blisters. She's right: I should go back.

"Your feet look so awful. Are you sure?"

"I'm sure."

"Okay," she says. "I guess you know what you're doing."

"I do."

"They say tomorrow is the worst day," she says.

"That's fine," I say. "I'll be ready."

We start early on the third day. The terrain turns abruptly vertical; for an hour we scramble hand over foot up lava ledges. The air becomes much colder; we start out in sweaters but soon we are wearing parkas; then gloves, then hoods.

After two hours, we break out of the narrow lava ledges onto the saddle. It is an abrupt and startling view; at last I can see the geography.

Mount Kilimanjaro is actually two major peaks. Kibo is a broad cinder cone with snow on its southern flanks. A few miles to the east, an older volcanic peak, Mawenzi, presents a different appearance—jagged, harsh vertical lines and streaks of snow over crumbling, rocky pinnacles. Mawenzi is about 16,900 feet high, and Kibo 19,340. The two peaks are separated by a distance of seven miles, and between them lies a sloping desert plateau averaging about thirteen thousand feet in altitude, called the "saddle."

It is here that we have emerged, at the base of Mawenzi, looking across the windswept saddle toward Kibo, its blunt summit cloudless in early morning. The view is spectacular in a bleak way. For the first time on the trip, I appreciate my vulnerability in a hostile environment. I am standing on a desert plateau two and a half miles high. There are no trees, no plants, no life at all, just red rocks and sand and freezing wind. Ahead of me, at the base of Kibo, I see a sparkling dot—the tin roof of tiny Kibo Hut, where we will spend the night before making the ascent in darkness up the cinder cone the following day.

The clothing that was once too hot, that clung and chafed, is now flimsy as paper before the wind. I am chilled;
176

I put on everything I am carrying in my day pack, and Loren and I set out across the saddle.

Even walking on flat terrain is difficult at this altitude, and Loren calls for a rest—the first time on the trip she has done so. After midday, clouds appear around the peaks, and cast swift-moving shadows on the desert floor. We are now on a gentle rise up to the hut at 15,500 feet. Distances are deceptive here; the hut looks only about an hour distant, but after an hour it still seems no closer.

We walk slower and slower, and when we finally come up to Kibo Hut to greet Paul and Jan, who have been here for a while, we feel as if we are moving in slow motion. Paradoxically, the thin air makes us behave as if we were underwater, in a dense medium.

Paul and Jan have lost their usual good spirits. In fact, everyone is distinctly irritable as they trudge up to the hut. People complain—about the wind, the bunks, the food, the weather. The general mood is grim. Paul says, "I've seen it before. It's the altitude. Makes you irritable. And, of course, everyone's wondering."

"Wondering?"

"Whether they'll make it to the top."

That's certainly what I am wondering, but Paul is an experienced climber who's been on several trekking expeditions in Nepal. "*You're* worried about it?"

"Not really. But it crosses your mind. It has to."

The accommodations at Kibo Hut are reminiscent of a Siberian prison camp. Triple-decker bunks line all four tin walls; in the middle of the room, a central pit for eating. The wind whines through the cracks in the walls; nobody removes any clothing indoors. We have dinner at 5:00 p.m., porridge and tea. Nobody can eat much. We are all thinking about the ascent. We must reach the top before ten the next morning, because after that the weather is likely to sock in, closing off the views and making the summit dangerous. If we climb too slowly, we risk being turned back from the summit because of the weather.

One of the guides tells us the plan: we will be awakened with tea (no coffee at these altitudes) at 2:00 a.m., and we will begin our ascent in darkness. One lantern for every two people. We will stay together, so as not to get lost in the darkness. It is six hours from here to the summit; after three hours, there is a cave where we can stop and rest, but otherwise there is no shelter until we reach the summit, and come back down to Kibo. It will be very cold. We should wear all the clothing we have.

I'm already wearing all the clothing I have. I'm wearing long johns and three pairs of pants, two tee shirts, two shirts, a sweater, and a parka. I wear a wool balaclava on my head. I wear all these clothes to bed, removing only my boots before climbing into my sleeping bag. Everyone else wears their clothes to bed, too. We're in bed by 7:00 p.m., silent, listening to the wind whine.

Sleep is impossible. Every time I begin to drift off, I snap awake, suddenly fearful, convinced I am suffocating, only to realize that it is simply the altitude.

I am not the only one with this problem. Inside the darkened hut, I hear groans and curses in a half-dozen languages throughout the night. It is almost a relief when the guide shakes me, and hands me a plastic cup filled with smoky hot tea, and tells me to dress.

All around me, people are pulling on boots and gloves. Nobody speaks. The atmosphere is, if anything, even more grim than before. Paul stops by to wish us good luck on our ascent; he hopes we make it. I wonder if it's some sort of mountaineering tradition, this last-minute wishing of luck. After all, we've come so far, there is so little left, who would turn back now? Nobody in his right mind. After all, I think, how bad can it be?

We take our lanterns and leave the tin hut, and climb the mountain in darkness.

Very quickly it becomes a nightmare. The lantern is useless; the wind blows it out; the darkness is total. I cannot see anything and continually stumble over rocks and small obstacles. I am sure this would be painful if I could feel anything in my feet at all, but they are numb with cold. Even when I wiggle my toes in the boots, I feel nothing. As I stumble up the mountain, the numb cold creeps up my legs, first to the shins, then the knees, then the mid-thigh. The trail upward is steep and exhausting, but the cold is so penetrating we stop for only a few moments at a time, just enough to catch our breath in the blackness, and stumble on. I feel rather than see the presence of the guides, the porters, the other hikers. Occasionally I hear a grunt or a voice, but for the most part everyone trudges along silently;

I hear only the wind and my own labored breathing. As I walk along, I have plenty of time to wonder whether I am getting frostbite in my numb feet. It's my own fault—I was completely unprepared for this trip, I didn't bring the right equipment, including the right boots; it was a serious oversight; I may be penalized now. Anyway, frostbite or not, I am having real trouble. I frankly don't think I'll be able to make it. I can go on for a while, but I doubt I can last much longer.

Somewhere around me, I hear Loren. "Is that you?"

"Yes," I say. "Can you feel your feet?"

"I haven't been able to feel them for an hour," she says. There is a pause. *"Listen: what are we doing here?"*

The question takes me by surprise. I don't really have an answer. "We're having an adventure," I say, and laugh cheerfully.

She doesn't laugh back.

"This is crazy," she says. "Climbing this mountain is crazy."

Her words enter my consciousness directly. I have no doubt in my mind she is right. It is crazy to be doing this. Yet I feel protective toward the decision to make the climb, as if it were a friend I don't want criticized.

I am trudging onward in the darkness, tired, numb, gasping for air, freezing cold, a prisoner on a forced march. I put one foot in front of the other. One foot in front of the other. I try to set a rhythm, to keep moving forward in that rhythm.

To consider whether or not this is crazy does not help my rhythm right now. I ignore her statement and concentrate on walking in my rhythm. How long I continue in this way I am not sure; it is too much trouble to look at my watch: clumsily peeling away layers of clothing to expose a glowing green dial that is hard to read through chilled, tearing eyes. After a while the time doesn't matter any more; I just keep walking.

The arrival at the cave at the halfway point is a surprise. The cave isn't warm, but it's out of the wind and so seems warmer. We are all able to light our lanterns, so we have light. We can look at one another. People huddle together, talking quietly. I see the shock on many faces. I am not the only one who finds this climb a nightmare.

Loren sits next to me, whispers, "I hear the English couple is going back."

"Oh?"

"She's sick. She's throwing up from the altitude."

"Oh." I don't know who she is talking about. I don't really care.

"How do you feel?" she says.

"Terrible."

"How're your feet?"

"Blocks of ice."

A pause, and then she says, "Listen, let's go back."

I am shocked. This woman who has so much energy, is so much in control of her body, now wants to quit. She's had it. She wants to quit.

"Listen," she says, "I'm not embarrassed to say we got to seventeen thousand feet and then quit. We're not in shape. Seventeen thousand is damned good."

I don't know what to say. She's right. I think it over.

Loren continues quickly, "It's insane to be doing this. There's no reason to be doing this. It's some kind of crazy proving of ourselves—for what? Who cares? Really. Let's go back. We'll tell everyone we climbed it. Who will know? It won't matter. Nobody will ever know."

All I can think is: *I'll know.*

And I think a lot of other things, about not being a quitter, and how I think that quitting is contagious, that once you start to quit it spreads through your life—but that's sports talk, coaching talk, I'm not sure I believe it.

What I believe is, *I'll know.* I feel trapped by an inner honesty I didn't know I had.

"I want to keep going," I say.

"Why?" she says. "Why is it so important to you to get to the top of some stupid mountain?"

"I'm here now, I might as well do it," I say. It sounds evasive. The fact is, I have no better answer. I have put up with a lot of pain and a lot of anxiety to get this far, and now I am in a cave in predawn darkness within a few hours of the summit, and there is no way I am going to quit now.

"Michael, this is crazy," she says.

The others are filing out of the cave, resuming their ascent. I get to my feet.

"Just go one more hour," I say. "You can make it another hour. Then, if you still want to go back, we will." I figure in another hour it will be dawn, and everything will seem better to her, and she will be encouraged to go on. I figure she'll never quit if she knows that I am continuing.

And I am continuing. I surprise myself with my own strength and conviction.

Dawn is a beautiful prismatic band that throws the jagged peak of Mawenzi into relief. I tell myself I should pause for a moment to enjoy it. I can't. I tell myself I should pause and take a picture of it, so I can enjoy the picture later. I can't even take a picture. I have lost the ability to do anything that some animal part of my brain judges to be nonessential energetic movement. It is not necessary to take a picture. I don't take one.

A few thoughts enter my awareness anyway. I have never seen a sky so indigo-black. It looks like the sky from space pictures—and I realize that it should, that I am now more than three miles above the surface of the earth, and the normal blue sky, created by atmosphere and suspended dust, is gone.

The other thing is that the horizon is curved. There is no doubt about it. Sunrise is an arc that bends down at the sides. I can see with my own eyes that I am standing on a spherical planet. But the actual sensation is uncomfortable, as if I am viewing the world through one of those curving wide-angle lenses. I look away.

I put one foot in front of the other, one foot in front of the other. I lean on my walking stick and breathe and keep my rhythm. I wait for the air to warm; eventually it does, a little. At least I can see where I am walking. But when I look up, the summit seems far away. Most of the other climbers are farther along, and their bright jackets contrast with the beige scree of the volcano.

"Scree" is a geological term for small cinders of volcanic origin. We are walking up, ankle-deep in scree. It is like walking on a vertical beach. You take two steps up, and slide one step back. Two steps up, one back. The destination never comes any nearer.

Two hours after sunrise is the worst time for me. I am utterly exhausted, and I am suddenly aware, looking at the climbers farther up the slopes, that they are walking like mountaineers in a *National Geographic* special. One of those movies where the intrepid climbers plod through the snow, heads down, with a dogged, deliberate rhythm. Step, breathe, breathe. Step, breathe, breathe.

The hikers above me are moving like that. And so am I.

I have become a character in a television special. I am totally out of my element. Loren is right—I never expected it would be this hard. I'm not cut out for this. I'm not in shape for this. I'm not interested in doing this, now or ever again. Who cares about this climbing business anyway? A million people have already climbed Kilimanjaro, there's nothing special to it. There's no real accomplishment. It's no big deal.

My guide, Julius, sees that I am fatigued. He offers to push me. I tell him no. He offers to push Loren, and she agrees, and he stands behind her with his arms on her waist and pushes her up the slope. But it doesn't seem to me that he helps Loren. It seems to me that you have to do this one alone.

Pretty soon Loren tells Julius to stop pushing her, and she continues by herself. She doesn't seem to be aware of me any more, although we are only a few feet apart. She is lost in some private world of focused effort.

I am trying to figure out what is going on inside my head. I have begun to understand that climbing at altitude is a mental process, an exercise in concentration and will. I notice that some thoughts sap my energy, but others allow me to continue for five or ten minutes without stopping. I am trying to figure out which thoughts work best.

To my surprise, the mental pep talks ("You can do it, you're doing great, keep up the good work") don't help. They just provoke the counterthought that I am kidding myself and will ultimately fail.

Nor does focusing on my rhythm, my pace, counting my steps or my breathing, going for a kind of mindlessness. That just puts everything into mental neutrality, which is not bad, but not particularly good, either.

Equally surprising, to focus on my exhaustion is not deleterious. I can think, God, my legs ache, I don't think I can lift them another step, and it doesn't slow me down. It's the truth, and my legs don't feel worse just because I think the truth.

In the end, what seems to work is to think of a nice warm swimming pool in California. Or the nice beer and curry dinner I will have when I get back to civilization. Hawaiian palm trees and surf. Scuba diving. Something far from my present surroundings. A pleasant fantasy or daydream.

So I think about swimming pools and palm trees as I plod up the gritty scree. Around 8:00 a.m. Julius begins to show concern. Already people are coming down from the summit—I resent them deeply—and Julius wants to make sure we reach the top before any bad weather closes in. I ask him how far away the summit is. He says forty-five minutes.

He has been saying forty-five minutes for the last two hours.

In a way, it's not his fault. The higher slopes of Kilimanjaro provide a bizarrely undramatic perspective. It's like the view an ant would have on the outside of an overturned salad bowl—all you see is a curved surface that gets narrower as you approach the top, but otherwise looks pretty much the same all the time.

It's very dramatic to *be* there, because your body can feel the steepness of the ascent, and it is dizzying to look up to climbers above you. But it doesn't *look* like much at all.

Julius begins to urge us onward, bribing us with chocolate bars, threatening us with clouds. He needn't bother. We are going as fast as we possibly can, and finally, around 9:00 a.m., we arrive at Gillman's Point, marked by a small concrete plaque at 18,700 feet. Although the actual summit, Uhuru Point, is at 19,340 feet, most hikers stop at Gillman's Point and consider honor satisfied. I certainly do.

I stand on the summit, pose for pictures, read the plaque, and look at the flags and mementos left by previous climbing groups. I stare indifferently at the views. I'm not elated, I'm not self-satisfied, I'm not anything. I'm just here at the summit. I have gotten here after all, and now I'm here.

Loren tells me I have gotten her to the top, and I tell her she did it herself. We take pictures of each other. And all the while I keep thinking one thing: I am here. I got here.

I am at the summit of Kilimanjaro.

Shrieking at the top of our lungs, we ski down the scree in our boots, sometimes falling, laughing, then sliding on the scat of our pants. It has taken us seven hours to make the ascent from Kibo Hut; we're back down in an hour. From Kibo, we walk another ten miles across the saddle. The threatened bad weather finally arrives, with intermittent snow and sleet. Finally we reach Horombo Hut, where we spend the night. All together we have walked eighteen miles since 2:00 a.m. that morning.

That night, at the huts, I inspect my feet. When I pull my boots off, my socks are stained red. I quickly pull the boots back on. My injuries don't matter now anyway. Tomorrow night we will be back at the hotel. Loren comes up with a small mirror, laughs, asks if I want to see how I look; I say sure. I have not seen myself in four days. I stare at a dirty face with a scraggly beard, red skin, bloodshot eyes. In the tiny mirror, it is the face of a stranger.

Some local entrepreneur at Horombo Hut is selling Tusker beer for five dollars a bottle, and he has plenty of takers. Paul and Jan have one, and so do I. I go almost immediately to sleep, around 5:00 p.m.

The following day I discover that climbing down a mountain calls upon a whole other set of muscles; my legs are trembling before lunch. I also discover that, while my heel blisters are rested by the descent, my toe blisters now hurt fiercely. So coming down is not easier on my feet.

Although we retrace our route exactly, I am surprised by how different the views appear on the way back. In part, this is a standard trekker's discovery: any route looks different going and coming. But in part it is my own sense of having succeeded in climbing the mountain. I feel different.

In the hotel, the bathwater turns opaque black. We each take two baths, trying to get clean. Sitting on the hotel bed, I peel off my socks and moleskin and finally take a good look at my feet. The blisters are open, exposing great patches of bleeding, raw, dirty skin around the heels up to the anklebone. My feet are so bad I make Loren take pictures of them, but they turn out like pictures in medical textbooks and I later throw them away.

For a couple of years afterward, the skin of my feet remained discolored, and if I was at the beach, or had my shoes off, people would say, "What's the matter with your heels? They're funny-colored," and I then would start to explain about climbing the mountain, and they would get an odd look in their eyes, and I would stop talking. Eventually I never talked about climbing the mountain.

What I learned was this: that I had defined myself as a person who didn't like heights or cold, a person who didn't like to be dirty, a person who didn't like physical exertion or discomfort. And here I had spent five days cold, dirty, and exhausted; I had lost twenty pounds; and I had had a wonderful experience.

I realized then that I had defined myself too narrowly.

The experience of climbing Kilimanjaro affected me so powerfully that, for a long time afterward, if I caught myself saying, "I'm not a person who likes to do that activity, eat that food, listen to that music," I would automatically go out and do what I imagined I didn't like. Generally I found I was wrong about myself—I liked what I thought I wouldn't like. And even if I didn't like the particular experience, I learned I liked *having* new experiences.

Second, although I am tall, I had always secretly defined myself as a physically weak and somewhat sickly person. After climbing Kilimanjaro, I had to acknowledge that I was mentally and physically tough. I was forced to redefine myself. Climbing the mountain was the hardest thing I had ever done, physically, in my life, but I had done it.

Of course, part of the reason it was hard was that I had approached it like a damned fool. I was not in shape and not prepared, and I refused to listen to anybody.

Now it seems inconceivable to me that I had no inkling what was in store for me, no idea what exertion was implied by an eighteen-thousand-foot summit, no idea about proper conditioning and equipment. So much of my behavior looks to be deliberately unconscious, designed to give me a shocking, hard experience. It certainly was that. And it was an experience that I didn't fully appreciate for years afterward.

But at the time it just left me flat. After we had taken our baths, and Loren had photographed my heels for posterity, we got dressed and walked to the polished dining room. Paul and Jan were eating silently at one table; other climbers at others. We felt a camaraderie as we sat down to eat. We were very tired, far more tired than hungry, but we were also away in some special world reserved for exhausted athletes, a world in which triumph is muted, the gains countered by the costs.

At another table, a family stared at us curiously. I knew they were going to climb tomorrow morning, and they wanted to know what it was like.

I thought, What can I tell them? I can't tell them what it's really like. What would be the point of that? I found myself looking away, hoping they wouldn't ask.

The father: "Did you climb the mountain?"

"Uh-huh," I said.

"You make it to the top, both of you?"

"Uh-huh."

A silence. "How is it up there?"

It's good, I said to them. It's hard but it's good. Some days are very hard, but it's good. Just do a day at a time. It's good.

They stared at me. I knew that stare. They were trying to figure out why I was so flat. I didn't care. Tomorrow they would find out for themselves, and the climb would mean whatever it meant to them.

When we walked back to our room after dinner, the sun was just fading. Kilimanjaro hung above the garden like a pale, reddish, disembodied ghost. Unearthly. Unreal. Already unreal.

The next day we flew to Nairobi.

Pyramid of the Magician

Dawn appears as a yellow band over the Yucatán jungle horizon, as I climb the steep Pyramid of the Magician and look out over the extensive Mayan ruins of Uxmal.

It is an extraordinary sight to watch the rising sun illuminate the pale buildings of that ancient city. Guidebook in hand, I pick out the sights. Directly before me stands the white courtyard structure known as the Nunnery. To the west, the great tiered House of the Governor, which has been called the single most magnificent building ever erected in the Americas. Near it, the House of the Turtles and the House of the Pigeons. And beyond, the humped green shapes of more ruins still to be uncovered in the surrounding jungle.

At dawn, Uxmal is deserted. The tourists still sleep; an occasional parrot cries, but for the most part the jungle landscape is silent. The city before me is serene, yet I feel anxious.

Looking straight down the Pyramid of the Magician, with its nearly vertical incline of steps, is dizzying. But even more disorienting is the recognition of where you really are, for Uxmal is a great mystery.

The pyramid on which I stand is an oval structure, 125

feet high. It is called either the Pyramid of the Magician or sometimes the Pyramid of the Dwarf, for reasons that are unclear. The Nunnery and the House of the Governor are names applied by convention; the ruins already bore those names when archaeologist John Lloyd Stephens stayed in them, in 1841.

The House of the Turtles is named for a row of turtles on its façade. The House of the Pigeons is so named because its roof suggests a dovecote. But no one knows what those buildings were really called, or what went on in them. No one has any idea at all.

It is easy to become anxious atop the pyramid, for I am looking at extensive ruins that no one understands. Uxmal is a city fifty miles from the ocean and a hundred miles from Chichén Itzá. Why was it built here? How does it relate to other Mayan cities? How many people lived in this great complex, which records date to A.D. 987? What was this city for?

The night before, I had watched the sound-and-light show at Uxmal, similar to sound-and-light productions elsewhere in the world, only here the narration artfully concealed from the audience exactly how little was known. Uxmal was not a French château or an Egyptian pyramid. There was no clear chronology, no well-understood purpose. Rulers could not be named, their edicts could not be quoted, histories of construction could not be cited. Uxmal was an utterly mysterious ruin. Sitting there watching the colorful play of lights on the buildings, I felt a sort of conspiracy among the audience, a conspiracy not to acknowledge the depth of the ignorance. It was almost intolerable to look at this vast complex and to admit that we didn't know about it. We *had* to know. It was too large for us not to know. Uxmal is not a detail, not a footnote to history. It's a big, impressive city.

How can we not know all about it?

I watched the sun rise over the buildings. The jungle grew warm. An hour later the first tourists begin to arrive, walking through the ruins, guidebooks in hand. They read confidently about the rules of the ball games that were played in the ball courts, and the meaning of various ceremonies and human sacrifices. They read the date of founding of Uxmal and they read that its Late Classic architectural style is termed decadent. Sources of information are never cited.

Visitors are not reminded that scholars cannot easily read the hieroglyphs the guidebooks so glibly summarize. Nor are they reminded that scholars do not know how this ancient temple-building civilization of the Mayas arose, why it flourished, or why it died. Such reminders would be unnerving. Nobody on vacation wants to walk through a great ruined city and be told, "We know nothing about this place."

But the truth is, we don't know.

The closer one looks at history, the less coherent it becomes. From a distance, from the chapter headings of a textbook, history looks very tidy indeed. But on closer inspection it all breaks down. The Dark Ages weren't dark; it is hard to be sure what the Middle Ages stood in the middle of; the Renaissance is as much a birth as a rebirth. Anyway, these headings only apply to European history, a small fragment of world history. Things were different in other parts of the globe, and in other cultural traditions.

For the most part, the constructions we make of our own past are invisible to us. The interpretations themselves become real. Nowhere is this clearer than in the interpretations we place on the artifacts of prehistory and early history. When we look at ancient ruins, our beliefs are manufactured whole. At Knossos, on Crete, Arthur Evans found a ruin he called the Palace of King Minos. Tourists have dutifully tramped through it ever since. Yet there is no clear evidence that Knossos was a palace, or that King Minos—if he was a historical figure—had anything to do with its construction or its habitation. Similarly, the story of Heinrich Schliemann's discovery of Troy is endlessly retold. But Schliemann merely found a previously unknown city in Asia Minor. There is no evidence that Schliemann found Troy. There is no compelling evidence that Troy ever existed, except in the imagination of a poet.

Schliemann went on to excavate at Mycenae, a known historical site in Greece. Schliemann decided he had found the grave of Agamemnon. There is no evidence that he did. He found a grave, and he called it Agamemnon's grave. But there is no evidence that Agamemnon was a real person, either.

The internal psychological pressure to make up a story,

to explain the ruins before one's eyes, is powerful indeed. That was the shock that I felt atop the Pyramid of the Magician, as I watched the morning sun spread across the face of the ancient city. Soon enough I, too, clutched my guidebook and walked through the ruins of Uxmal, pretending that I understood far more than I did.

My Father's Death

When I was in high school, my mother used to wait up for me until I came home from dates. This is, of course, a time-honored form of parental harassment of young people of dating age. If I asked why she stayed up, she said, "I was worried something might happen to you."

There was no reasoning with her, no asking why she thought staying up would help in the unlikely event that something *had* happened to me. It was not polite to question a mother's love, or her logic.

But I was bizarrely reminded of this on December 27, 1977, when, as I climbed back into the boat after a ninety-foot-deep dive on a paddle-wheel wreck called the *Rhone* in the British Virgin Islands, the divemaster Bert Kilbride looked at me and said significantly, "Call home."

"What is it?" I said. My first thought was that my house had burned down. That's what usually happened in California. And I had known Bert for many years. He'd tell me if he knew.

"I don't know," Bert said. "The hotel just radioed to find out if you were on the boat. They said you had a call from home."

That didn't sound like a fire.

"Can I call from the boat?"

"No. Better wait until you get back."

"Won't the radiophone let me connect through to the mainland?"

"Radiophone isn't working so good. Better wait until you get back."

That definitely didn't sound like a fire.

I tried to think what it could be. It was two days after Christmas, and I was spending the holidays on Virgin Gorda in the British Virgin Islands. Most of my family was at my parents' home in Connecticut.

When I got to the hotel, I called. My younger sister answered the phone. She said, "Oh, Michael, when are you coming back?"

"What happened?"

"Didn't they tell you?"

"Nobody's told me anything."

"Dad died."

I started to feel very stupid. Slow and tired and stupid. "Dad died?"

My father was fifty-seven. He was young. He was in good health.

"In his office," my sister was saying. "He had a heart attack this morning. Kimmy and Dougie have gone to identify the body. When are you coming home?"

I said I'd be home as soon as I could make connections. I would check the airlines. I'd try to be there tomorrow. I said I would call back.

I got off the phone. Løren said, "What happened?"

"My father died."

"Oh, Michael, I'm sorry."

"Yeah," I said, looking around at the hotel, the palm trees. "He screwed up my vacation pretty good."

Because I was suddenly angry, really angry with him, for having done this thing. Leaving me at such an inconvenient time.

Loren said she'd call the airlines for me. I sat at the bar. I didn't feel sad, I didn't feel anything. I just stared around the hotel, at the people coming up from the beach, and the bartender washing his glasses and setting out the bowls of nuts for the afternoon, and I felt annoyed. I wanted to stay here and now I had to leave.

And I thought, *Be careful. It's harder to feel grief when you're not on good terms.* Because my father and I had not

192

had an easy time together. We had never been the classic boy and his dad. And it hadn't gotten better as we got older. It was no accident that I was down here in the Caribbean, and not at home with my brother and sisters. As far as I was concerned, he was a first-rate son of a bitch. And now he was dead and everything was up in the air. No more conversations, no more irritations, no more hopes for resolutions. Just—bang!—dead. Haven't got anything more to say to you, Nicko. The end.

Except I had to go back to attend the son of a bitch's funeral and mess up my much-needed vacation. And all his goddamned friends were going to be there, telling me what a great guy he was. . . .

Be careful.

I was really angry. I woke up the next day very early, four in the morning, unable to sleep. I was still angry. I stayed angry on the flights home. I got to Connecticut late the next night in a state of fatigue and high irritation. I was really annoyed to have to be here. I wouldn't say that to the others in my family, because they were all grieving. But I was just plain angry.

I woke up the next morning at four, too. I couldn't sleep. By now I was so tired it was hard to be angry. There was a terrible exhaustion about the house. People were calling continuously, from all around the country. Everyone was being very nice. And there was a lot to do, a lot of details, flowers and food and so on, and relatives were flying into town. The situation seemed to have all the disadvantages of a huge party with none of the benefits.

I decided I ought to keep busy and do the errands, especially since I was the only one who wasn't crying all the time. My brother had noticed that, and had said to me, "Listen, I know you didn't like him, but he was still your father, you know, he was Dad, he did the best he could."

"Yeah? Fuck him," I said. That pretty much summed up my feelings. My brother was understanding, which made it worse. But I said that somebody had to remember, in the midst of all these maudlin carryings-on, that the guy had had a really nasty streak in him. And not just with me. Dad couldn't have been my brother's favorite, not after some of the incidents I could remember. And what about the time he beat up my sister so badly the doctor was going to call the—

"Yeah, well, whatever," my brother said, and walked away. He turned back. "Listen, Mike. He's *dead* now."

I understood that my brother had always had a soft spot for everyone. My brother had a sweetness I'd never had. He had forgiveness in him. I didn't. It'd been hammered out of me years before, as far as this particular subject was concerned.

So I did the errands. It was okay. The only thing was, I was so *tired*. I could hardly get around. When I pulled up at the florist, it was a huge effort to open the car door, to get out of the car, to close the car door, to walk inside, to remember what I had come for, to talk to the florist in normal declarative sentences, to answer when he asked me how I wanted to pay for this. It was like it was all happening underwater. Or like I had a bad heart and couldn't get my breath. Slow; painfully, exhaustingly slow.

After I did all the errands, I was really exhausted, and I found myself in the kitchen peeling vegetables with Kim, my older sister, and I said with annoyance, "Listen, I don't see why I have to be the one who does everything around here, why I have to be the one who holds himself together while you all collapse."

"Nobody's asking you to," she said.

When she said that, I realized she was right—I had imposed this role on myself. So I went to my room and cried.

I cried with complicated feelings, because I was still angry but I was also sad. I was sad for what had happened to my father and me, sad that nothing would ever be resolved, sad that he had lived his life as he had, with the unhappiness that he had felt and concealed.

I was having all these feelings simultaneously on several levels; it was quite peculiar, but it was a distinct relief. I was still angry, but I wasn't so pent up. And I was able to accept things a little better. There were plenty of trials ahead: the arrival of the relatives, the viewing of the body tomorrow, and the funeral the day after.

I took a sleeping pill, but I still woke at four in the morning, with the feeling that there was something I had to do, something I had to solve. Then I remembered: I couldn't do anything. He was dead. There was nothing to solve. I couldn't do anything to make it better for my mother, or anyone else. The whole thing was out of my hands.

There was nothing to do.

It was strange to feel that. There was nothing to do. Just somehow get through it and get yourself back together and keep going. I was crying a lot now, whenever I felt like it, and that was very good. I thought: We have this wired into us, the way we have the ability to give birth. We already know how to grieve. We only screw it up when we get in the way of the natural process.

So, I thought, I was doing the natural thing now. But I was not looking forward to that most awful of rituals, going to the funeral home and viewing the remains.

Even making the arrangements seemed gruesome. I called the funeral home in the morning and they said my father wasn't ready yet, they were having some problems, and they were a little behind schedule. They were sorry, but would two-thirty be all right?

I said yes.

My mother said, "What did they say?"

I wondered what to tell her. A little late finishing up the body? "Uh, they said they're very busy and . . . uh . . . they won't be ready until two-thirty."

She nodded. "They're having trouble with his mouth," she said, very matter-of-factly. Apparently my father had died in his chair with his mouth open, and rigor mortis had set in. She seemed so calm about it.

At two-thirty everybody put on coats and grabbed Klee-nexes and went to the funeral parlor. I was afraid to go. I had never seen the dead body of anybody in my family, anybody I was really close to. I didn't know how I would feel. I would have preferred to stay home, but I was the elder son and I had to accompany my mother. So I went.

The funeral parlor was a Connecticut frame house. There was ice on the steps; you had to be careful going up. The sun was shining but it was cold outside.

My mother met her sister in the hallway, and we watched to see if they would be all right together. They were. We all went in to view the remains.

Immediately, as I walked into the room, I had the crazy and unexpected thought, *He's here. He's still alive.*

Meanwhile, my mother had run forward and flung her arms around my father's body, and was crying and talking to him and kissing him. I was embarrassed, as if I shouldn't be witnessing this scene between them. At one point she turned to me and said, "He's so cold." But she was really

195

in her own world, her own way of handling things, and it was remarkable for its force and directness. She cried, she talked to him, she wiped her tears from his cheek. She was really dealing with it.

I tried to figure out why I had thought he was still here. I checked again: yes, I felt it. *He's here. He's hanging around this room. He's confused.*

I knew that people had reported these impressions, but I was not one of those who believed that a soul stayed around a dead body, particularly following a sudden death.

So where did the feeling come from? A sensation that the room was warm. A feeling that he was hovering near the ceiling, looking down on all of us, wondering why we were here. Or was it the projection of my own difficulty accepting that my father was really dead? Because certainly I was having trouble accepting it. I kept staring at his chest, waiting for him to take a breath. I was sure he was still alive. I knew he was in this room. I just couldn't figure out how I knew.

Then I cried some more. Finally my mother kissed my father goodbye, said she was done. On the way out she told the undertaker that they had done a good job, that my father looked very nice. Then we all went outside.

Tomorrow was the funeral.

The next day my mother announced that she wanted to view the remains a final time, before the funeral. Nobody had much enthusiasm for this, because the previous day's viewing had been very emotional. But I wanted to confirm my reaction of the previous day, so I said I would go with her.

We went back to the viewing room. As soon as I entered the room, I wondered how I could ever have thought my father was here. He was gone. The room was cold and empty except for a body that once had belonged to my father. My mother looked at it, walked up to it, cried a little, looked at it some more. But she didn't hug it or kiss it. She just stood there for a while. Then we left and went to the funeral.

My father was an important man, and he had many business friends who came to the funeral. The funeral was very impressive and a nice gesture to his memory. By now

I was so confused about my feelings about his being present or absent that I sat in the church service and wondered, Is he here? He wasn't there. The church service had very little meaning to me.

I noticed that, even though I was on an emotional fast track, being taken for a rough ride by my feelings, I was clear about what made sense and what did not. For example, visitors coming to the house made sense. You just seemed to keep going if you were forced to chat with people for a while. Small talk made sense. It was fine: let's talk about basketball for a while, or what Jimmy is doing in school. And it wasn't necessary to say anything about how sorry they were about my father. People always say, "I don't know what to say." There isn't anything to say. Just coming over to the house said everything.

But visitors who cried a lot or who stayed longer than half an hour did not make sense. They were draining.

And food being brought over made sense, but only if it was very easy to prepare, because anything more than heating a dish was an impossibly difficult job.

Viewing the remains made sense. Telegrams and phone calls made sense, even at late hours, since nobody was asleep anyway.

But the religious service in the church didn't make much sense to me. The church itself seemed dead, full of old rituals and old ways of doing things that had been worn out centuries ago and no longer provided comfort, at least not to me. My emotions were overwhelming; they demanded some genuine response, not this stately ceremony of artifice, the most recent components of which reached back to the nineteenth century. It was nobody's fault. It was just how it was, for me. Mother was comforted, and important social functions were served by the church service.

Afterward we went out to the cemetery and had the burial service. It was a sunny day, a nice day but cold. Everybody was tired. I looked at the tombstone and wondered if my father was here. By now I was looking for him everywhere. But he wasn't here in the cemetery. The tombstone seemed small. We got back in the cars, and drove away.

I asked my brother whether he had felt anything unusual in the viewing room that first day.

"Like what?"

"Like Dad being there. Hanging around the room."

"Oh, you felt that, huh?" he said.

"Yes. Did you, too?"

"No," he said, "I didn't. I was just sorry he was dead."

The next day I went back to California.

Ireland

I am the director of a film called *The Great Train Robbery*, loosely based on an actual train robbery that occurred in Victorian England. We are shooting in England and Ireland. The cast includes Sean Connery, Donald Sutherland, and Lesley-Anne Down.

A secret, lifelong desire is fulfilled. I am an international film director, shooting in foreign locations with big movie stars! What a thrill! Put on the safari jacket and hang the director's finder around your neck!

But I am also secretly terrified. This is only my third movie, and I'm not really an experienced director. I've never shot in a foreign location. I've never made a period picture. I've never worked with a foreign crew. And although I've worked with good actors, I've never directed such big stars.

To direct a movie you must be authoritative, and I don't feel authoritative at all. On the contrary, I feel isolated and under intense pressure. I am alone in Dublin; Loren is back in America finishing law school. There are only three Americans on the show: myself; the producer, John Foreman; and the stunt coordinator, Dick Ziker. John is experienced in foreign filming and I rely on his judgment, but in the end I am the director and I must do the job myself. And I'm afraid.

I've never known what to do with these fears of new undertakings. There doesn't seem to be anything to do but live through them, get past them. At least some of the terror of new undertakings is justified; at least some degree of anxiety will actually improve performance. But here in Dublin, I am not exerting my authority well. It just isn't working. John Foreman has told me the English film crews call the director "governor" or "guv." Nobody calls me "guv." Nobody calls me "sir." They don't call me anything.

Even though I am thirty-five years old, the crew thinks I am too young to know what I am doing. The company tries to second-guess me, to do things behind my back. I ask for something to be done a certain way, and they go off and do something else. We have lots of arguments.

Then, too, there are many differences between British and American filming procedures. In America, the director plans shots with the cameraman; in England, with the camera operator. Scenes are numbered differently. Technical terminology is different. English crews take four food breaks in a day, but Americans break only for lunch. If you want to work overtime, the British crew has to meet and vote.

Even the most basic signals seem to get crossed. In America, I am considered a laconic director, but the English find my energy level bizarrely high. My assistant director, who is openly critical of me to the point of insolence, finally asks if I am taking something. He means drugs, speed. I am astonished and ask him why he should think so. He says the whole crew thinks so, because I do everything so fast. I assure him I am not on drugs.

The first few days of shooting go badly. We have a split crew, half English and half Irish, and the two halves dislike one another, reflecting an ancient antagonism. Whenever something goes wrong, each side blames the other. Our progress is slow. Nobody listens to me. I set up the camera in a certain place and the crew moves it. They always move it, even if it's just six inches. I move it back to where I want it. The weather is terrible. It seems we are always on a food break. We fall behind schedule.

Each night I drag myself home to my Dublin hotel room. It looks like the anteroom to a tuberculosis sanatorium. The floors are uneven, the wallpaper stodgy Victorian. I'd like to call home, but there is a telephone strike. Then a mail strike. I am entirely isolated.

I ask John Foreman what to do. He says, "Talk with Geoff. Geoff likes you."

Geoffrey Unsworth is the lighting cameraman. He's very courtly and distinguished. Everyone adores him. Each day Geoff and I drive to the location together, so there's plenty of time to talk. Geoff seems to understand my difficulties, but it's not easy to discuss the matter frankly. He has his British reserve, and I feel awkward. How can I ask him why I'm not getting any respect? That's a Rodney Dangerfield line. So we talk about technical things: why we're not making more setups, how to get things to run more smoothly.

Geoff keeps saying, "I'd like to see one of your films." I think he's just being polite. My last film, *Coma,* is still in release in America, and it will be difficult to have a print shipped to Ireland.

Meanwhile, the problems continue. After a week or so, Geoff says, "You know, I think the crew would enjoy seeing one of your films." I tell him again of the difficulties of getting a print. But I manage to telex MGM in Los Angeles and order one.

Our problems get worse. The situation is deteriorating. Sometimes there are shouting arguments between the Irish and English crew members. As a group we have no cohesion, and I know it is because we have no leader. We are painfully slow. The work is good, but it is taking far too much time. The film is a negative pickup deal, which means that when the money runs out we will have to shut down production, whether we have completed the film or not. The pressures on me are enormous. Get more setups. Finish more scenes. Pick up the pace.

But the pace never picks up.

Geoff says, "I wish we could see one of your films."

Finally the print comes, and we run it for the crew on Friday night after work. Most of the crew attends.

On Monday morning, I come to work, ready to fight my usual uphill battle. I come onto the set, picking my way among the cables and light stands. One of the electricians smiles at me.

"Morning, guv," he says.

What happened was that the crew decided *Coma* was a

pretty good movie, and I must know what I am doing after all. Thanks to Geoff, from then on the atmosphere is entirely different, and our progress much better.

The crew stretches a white bed sheet in the middle of a field so the helicopter will know where to land. A crowd of local people line the fences around the field. They stare at the sheet, waiting for something to happen. Their attention turns the sheet into a work of art, a Christo. *Wrapped Irish Farm Field, 1978.* I would find it funny if we weren't behind schedule.

It is eight in the morning and bitterly cold. We are in a provincial train station outside Mullingar, Ireland, about to start a week of filming on top of a speeding train. Sean Connery has agreed to do his own stunts on top of the train. The little 1863 locomotive is hissing steam in front of the station, with our specially constructed coaches trailing behind. It's time to start filming, but the camera helicopter has not arrived yet from England. I suggest a test ride on the train. We climb up a ladder onto the roof of the cars, and set off.

Within minutes Connery is grinning like a kid on a carnival ride. He's a superb athlete who could have been a professional footballer. Now he hops lightly from car to car, thoroughly enjoying himself. We approach a bridge, and must lie flat on the deck. The bridge whips over us, inches from our faces. Connery laughs uproariously. "Bloody fantastic!"

We return to the station and begin shooting. The exhilaration fades, and the work becomes work. Constant vigilance is required. The Irish Railways have permitted us to use twenty miles of track in the most beautiful part of the country, but since this is Ireland, the twenty bridges that span the rails are all of different heights. Some are very low. We have previously mapped and measured each bridge, but no one is willing to trust a map. Before each shot, we creep slowly beneath the bridge, to check our clearance.

Even more dangerous are the telephone and electrical wires that sometimes span the track; these are unmarked and difficult to see until the last moment.

Then, too, our authentic period locomotive spews a stream of glowing cinders and ash back at us. We literally set the countryside on fire wherever we go. Each night, when we return home, I take a shower and wash my hair. The water hits the tub inky black.

Connery throws himself into his work with abandon. He is one of the most remarkable people I have ever met, lighthearted and serious at the same moment. I have learned a great deal from being around him. He is at ease with himself, and is direct and frank. "I like to eat with my fingers," he says, eating with his fingers in a fancy restaurant, not giving a damn. You cannot embarrass him with trivialities. Eating is what's important. People come over for an autograph and he glowers at them. "I'm *eating,*" he says sternly. "Come back later." They come back later, and he politely signs their menus. He doesn't hold grudges unless he intends to. "I spent a lot of my life being miserable," he says. "Then one day I thought, I'm here for the day, I can enjoy the day or not. I decided I might as well enjoy it." There is that quality about him, that sense of choice and control over himself and his moods. It makes him integrated, self-assured. The most common remark about him is "That's a *real man.*"

Once, on an airplane, a woman sighs, "Oh, you're so *masculine.*" Connery laughs. "But I'm very feminine," he insists. And he means it; he delights in that side of himself. A gifted mimic, he likes to rehearse alone, playing all the parts himself. He does startlingly accurate imitations of everyone in the cast, including Donald and Lesley-Anne, his leading lady. He always seems to enjoy himself. He takes pleasure in all his aspects, all his appetites.

I am not equally open, and he teases me. Once, after a shot, I feel his hand gestures were a little effeminate. I call for a retake, but I'm not sure how to tell Sean what needs to be changed. How do you tell 007 that he's effeminate?

"Sean, on that last shot, you had a hand gesture. . . ."

"Yes, what about it? I thought it was good."

"Well, uh, it was a little, uh, loose. Limp."

His eyes narrow. "What are you trying to say?"

"Well, it could be a bit crisper. Stronger, you know."

"Stronger . . ."

"Yes. Stronger."

"You're saying I look like a poof?" Now he's grinning, amused at my discomfort.

"Yes. A little."

"Well, just say so, ducky!" he roars. "Just say what you

want! We haven't got all day!" And he shoots the scene again, with a different gesture.

Later he takes me aside. "You know," he says, "you don't do any favors beating about the bush. Making us try and deduce what you mean. You think you're being polite, but you're actually just difficult. Say what you mean and get on with it."

I promise to try. And I do better, but I never manage to be as direct as he is. He says, "You should always tell the truth, because if you tell the truth you make it the other person's problem."

He follows his own dictum; he always tells the truth. Sean seems to live in a kind of present moment, responding to events with an unaffected immediacy that disregards the past and future. He is always genuine. Sometimes he compliments people I know he doesn't like. Sometimes he blows up angrily at his close friends. He always tells the truth as he sees it at the moment, and if somebody doesn't like it, it's their problem.

The days of shooting on the train continue. The crew is extremely careful; no one is hurt. By now we have shot the most hazardous sequences, the ones that require Sean to not see the bridges as they rush up behind him, and to duck down at the last moment, his head missing the bridges by inches. Those shots were carefully arranged and timed, but we are all relieved they are behind us.

Finally we are shooting a long take where Sean comes running up the length of the train, jumping from car to car. Because we are shooting in all directions, the camera operator and I are hanging out on a side platform, and everyone else is inside the train. I am trying to watch the scene and also to remember to duck down at the right time so the camera lens can swing over my head.

Filming begins. Sean runs up the length of the train. I smell a harsh, acrid odor. I feel a sharp pain on top of my scalp. I realize that my hair has been set on fire by the cinders from the locomotive. I am frantically brushing at my hair, trying to put the fire out, because I don't want smoke coming from my head when the camera swings over me.

While I am doing that, Sean jumps to the nearest car, stumbles, and falls. I think, Jeez, Sean, don't overdo making

204

it look dangerous. He is carrying a bundle of clothes, a story point. He drops the clothes as he falls and I realize Sean would never do that, that he must have really fallen. Meanwhile, I am still trying to put the fire out on my head. Sean scrambles to his feet, retrieves the clothes, and moves on, wincing in genuine pain. I get the cinders out of my head as the camera swings over. We make the shot.

Afterward we stop the train; everybody gets off. He has a bad cut on his shin that is being attended to.

"Are you all right, Sean?"

He looks at me. "Did you know," he says, "that your hair was on fire? You ought to be more careful up there."

And he laughs.

His fresh view allows him to reach some surprising conclusions. On the fourth day of filming, we put everybody inside the train except Sean, because we are filming with the helicopter, and the camera will see the entire length of the train. So I am inside, wearing a top hat, with a walkie-talkie in my lap. As the train starts, I hear the engineer call out the speed, "Twenty-five miles an hour . . . thirty . . . thirty-five miles an hour . . ."

We have previously arranged for this speed. The helicopter radios that it is in position. I call for action on the radio, and the shot begins. I sit there, listening to the thump of the helicopter as it moves overhead, trying to imagine the shot, trying to figure out by the sound how it is going.

The pilot announces the shot is good. We stop the train, and Sean comes down from the top. He is furious, stamping and complaining. "It's bloody dangerous up there! This bloody train is not going bloody thirty-five miles an hour!"

"Sean," I say, "it is."

After so many days of shooting, the control of speed has been well worked out. This is essential, because in making a film you must travel at different speeds depending on which way the camera is pointing. If you are shooting sideways to the direction of travel, your apparent speed is faster, and so you must make the train go slower. If you are shooting in the direction of travel, you must go faster than usual. If you do not vary the speed in this way, in the final film the train will appear to go faster in some shots than in others.

So we have long since worked this out. One of the assistant directors is in the open cab of our locomotive, with a walkie-talkie. As we start each shot, he calls out the speeds. When we hit the prearranged speed, we begin filming. This is the procedure we have used throughout.

I click the walkie-talkie. "Chris, how fast was the train going on that last shot?"

From the locomotive, the voice says, "Thirty-five miles an hour."

I look at Sean, shrug.

Sean grabs the walkie-talkie and says, *"How do you know it was thirty-five miles per hour?"*

There is a long pause.

"We count telegraph poles," the voice says.

Sean hands the walkie-talkie back to me.

Slowly the pertinent facts emerge. The engine is an actual 1863 locomotive, and it has no speed instrumentation at all. To estimate speed, the men in the cab time telegraph poles as they go by. But this is obviously a terribly inaccurate method. Suddenly we wonder: how fast was the train really going?

The helicopter was flying parallel to the train for most of the shot. We radio the pilot. "How fast was the train going on the last shot?"

"Fifty-five miles an hour," comes the reply. "We thought Mr. Connery was bloody crazy to be up there!"

Vindicated, Sean folds his arms across his chest. "You see?" he says.

In the end, that episode represented to me all the power of a fresh perspective. We had been filming for days, we had fallen into a comfortable routine, and not one of us had bothered to look at what the cab of the locomotive was like. For days no one had thought to ask, How do you know the speed? The question was always there to be asked. It was just that no one had asked it, until Sean did.

One day, after lunch, Sean says, "I'm through at the end of the day."

"What?"

"I'm through on the train," he says evenly. "Finished. Going back to Dublin, have a kip."

We have three more days of filming scheduled. I don't think we'll need all three days, but I feel there is at least one more full day of work. Why is he quitting?

"I've had it with this bloody train," he says.

It has been such fun, such exhilarating fun, I can't understand why his mood has changed so suddenly. Of course, he has seen all the dailies, and he knows how much good footage we already have. I have already shot about six hours of film to make what will eventually be a fifteen-minute sequence. So I am just being overcautious, as directors tend to be. Is he calling my bluff?

"I'm done," he says. "I'm done." And that is all he will say. He leaves at the end of the day, driving back to Dublin.

The next morning we shoot some final bits and pieces, points of view, establishing shots, and so on. I am on top of the train, with a stunt man and a camera operator. We are going very fast. At high speeds, the train rocks and jerks erratically; it is nerve-racking.

And suddenly, in an instant, I am done with the train, too. The tunnels aren't fun any more, the overhanging wires aren't a challenge any more, the jolts from the track and the freezing wind aren't bracing any more. It is just dangerous and exhausting and I want to stop at once and get off the train. And I realize that is what happened to Sean the day before. He'd had enough, and he knew when to stop. The sequence is finished. It is time to go back to the studio, and do something else.

London Psychics

It was called the Spiritualist Association of Great Britain;
I called it the psychic smorgasbord. They had all kinds of
psychics, and you could consult them for only ten dollars
an hour.

The association used its psychics to attract people to the
religion of spiritualism. I had no interest in that, but I was
very interested in the possibility of psychic phenomena, and
the range of psychics was wonderful.

There were psychics who worked by psychometry, holding an object while they read; there were psychics who just
started reading as you walked in the door; there were psychics who read tea leaves, others who read tarot cards, others
who read flowers; there was one who did something with
sand; there were psychics who told you about your family,
your dead relatives, and your past lives; there were psychics
who were psychological, and others who were very pragmatic. All together there were forty psychics associated
with the association, and for anyone who had an interest in
the general phenomenon of psychic behavior, it was almost
too good to be true.

I went nearly every day, on my way home from work.

Coming in the door, you passed the chair of Sir Arthur

Conan Doyle, the association's most famous and influential member. That chair was always a sobering reminder to me. Anyone with a scientific background who becomes interested in metaphysical things must find the example of Sir Arthur Conan Doyle disturbing.

The creator of Sherlock Holmes was a Scottish physician, a lapsed Catholic, a vigorous athlete, and a Victorian gentleman. Although he is most closely associated with the cool, deductive mind of his fictional detective, Conan Doyle showed an interest in spiritualism, mysticism, and metaphysics even in medical school. His stories frequently contained a strong element of the supernatural; in such works as *The Hound of the Baskervilles* there is a continuous tension between a supernatural and a mundane explanation for events.

In 1893 Conan Doyle joined the Society for Psychical Research, a highly respectable organization: the politician Arthur Balfour was its president, and its vice-presidents included such eminent scientists as the American psychologist William James and the evolutionary naturalist Alfred Russel Wallace. Yet there was controversy as well, as exemplified by the scandal of the physicist William Crookes and the medium Florrie Cook.

In the nineteenth century, séances were popular. A group of paying customers would sit together in a dark room, and a medium would attempt to call up spirits from the Other Side. A good deal of paraphernalia was involved: silver trumpets through which the dead spoke, cabinets in which the mediums were locked, flying tambourines and other luminous objects that whipped through the air above the sitters. In the most spectacular displays, the medium would manifest ectoplasm, the face or form of a dead person. This was the specialty of Florrie Cook.

During her séances, Florrie would be locked in a cabinet, where she would go into a trance. Soon an extremely attractive young woman, wearing phosphorescent gowns, would step out. This beautiful apparition, supposedly a murderess named Katie King, would walk around the room. Naked beneath her diaphanous veils, she caused a sensation in Victorian England.

After attending a séance, William Crookes became so fascinated by mediumship that he moved Florrie Cook into his house for a period of months. In due time, Crookes pronounced Florrie genuine.

But it seemed obvious to most people that Florrie Cook and Katie King were the same person. Crookes claimed on two occasions to have seen both Florrie Cook and Katie King appear simultaneously, but his own objectivity was considered compromised, and in any case he was famous for his bad eyesight.

Eventually the controversial ghost Katie King ceased to appear, and Florrie Cook materialized a new ghost named Marie. One night Sir George Sitwell grabbed Marie, who screamed and ran from the room. The sitters opened the locked cabinet and found it empty, with Florrie Cook's clothes lying on the floor. Fraud was finally confirmed.

The episode of William Crookes and Florrie Cook seems an object lesson in the gullibility of a scientist. Yet Conan Doyle behaved much like Crookes; all his life he evinced a surprising willingness to accept all sorts of unlikely events. Although he said "the unmasking of false mediums is our urgent duty," and although he exposed several instances of fraud himself, he was generally trusting to an extraordinary degree. This culminated in the episode of the fairy photographs, which bears all the characteristics of an incautious Conan Doyle adventure into the spiritual world.

In 1920 two Yorkshire children, Elsie and Frances Wright, claimed they had photographed fairies in a country garden. The girls' father was an amateur photographer who kept his own darkroom. For this and for other reasons, the photographs immediately aroused suspicion. A spokesman for Eastman Kodak claimed they were "visibly fake." An expert for the New York *Herald Tribune* said the fairies were dolls. Many people asked why the fairies were dressed in contemporary Paris fashions.

Conan Doyle sent a friend to interview the girls—he himself never met them. Then he examined the photographs, and published, in *The Coming of the Fairies,* his belief that the pictures of little winged people were genuine and proved fairies were real.

This was my concern: that an otherwise sensible physician-turned-author could go so far as to persuade himself, by degrees, of the existence of fairies. I had in the past strongly identified with Conan Doyle, and now I appeared to be following in his footsteps rather closely. I determined to proceed with caution.

It seemed as if the first thing was to get a sense of whether "psychic" behavior really occurred at all. Because I certainly knew, from my own medical experience, that you could learn an enormous amount just by observing somebody. And I had once spent a memorable hour watching a pair of Turkish street vendors in the Istanbul bazaar accost passing customers in a dozen different languages, always correctly. Plenty of ordinary, nonpsychic insight was possible, and I wanted to minimize that. So I set the following rules for myself:

1. I never gave my own name.
2. I never gave verbal cues during the reading. In practice, this meant I tried to say nothing at all, so that the psychic wouldn't even know if I was English or not. If I was pressed to speak, I would make a nondescript murmur like "Ummm" or "Hmmm." However I first said this murmur, I would try to repeat it exactly the same way, with no change in inflection, for the rest of the interview. If the psychic pushed me to speak, I would say "Maybe" or "I'm not sure." And then stick to that phrase throughout the reading.
3. I never gave visual cues during the reading. No extraneous body movements, no shifting in the chair as the reading was given. Take a position and hold it.
4. I tried to keep my mind blank. Just in case somebody could read my mind. You never know.
5. I tried to keep track of everything said, the hits and misses. There is a tendency to be impressed by the hits in psychic readings and to ignore the misses. I wanted to retain the balance. I took constant notes.

I was satisfied with this plan, but I knew it would be extremely difficult to carry out in practice. Although it was my intention not to give the psychics anything to "read" about me through ordinary channels, the fact is that we all present a huge amount of information to one another—clothing, posture, skin tone, body position, body movement, body smell, breathing rates, and so on—all the time. There isn't any way to prevent that except by doing an interview by phone. Our physical presence is inescapably informative.

And although I did not intend to permit any body movements or voice inflections that would give feedback, I felt it unlikely that I would be able to follow my plan as perfectly as I would have liked. Nevertheless, I intended to make it as tough as possible.

As luck would have it, the first psychic I saw was wonderfully suited to my plans. She was past sixty, and nearly blind. She couldn't hear very well, either, because she thought I was from London. I didn't disagree with her. I just sat there. To make my mind blank, I concentrated on her swollen ankles.

She talked about this and that, making a few psychological comments, but nothing particularly specific. After about half an hour of rambling, she suddenly said, "What on earth do you do for work?," with a sort of alarm in her voice.

Immediately she said, "Don't tell me, don't tell me. It's just that I can't put it together. I've never seen anything like this before." Then she told me what she was seeing.

She saw me working in a room like a laundry, with huge white baskets, and there were black snakes coiling in the baskets, except that they weren't snakes. And she heard this terrible sound, repeated over and over again, a kind of *Whaaaa-whoooo, whoooo-whaaaa,* and she saw pictures going forward and backward, forward and backward. And something about hats, or high hats, or old-style fashion.

This was what she couldn't put together. And she found it unpleasant, these sounds and snakes and things. She said, "You are the most peculiar person."

I, of course, knew exactly what she was seeing. She was seeing the place I had been virtually living in for the last two weeks, the editing room where we ran the film back and forth to the accompaniment of those hideous sounds. The film was *The Great Train Robbery* and the actors all wore high hats.

There was absolutely no way this little blind lady with swollen ankles could have known about that.

I left the interview feeling odd. All my careful plans now seemed irrelevant. No matter how I might have failed to control my body movement, my verbalizations and grunts, no matter how much she might have feigned blindness as she did a "cold reading" on me, I knew damned well I couldn't have conveyed to her images of what an editing room looked like—images she would misconstrue as a laundry with snakes. I hadn't tipped her off about that. It wasn't possible. And not many people in the world had ever seen an editing room: it wasn't common knowledge.

So where had she gotten the information?

I could think of two possibilities. One was that she had been informed. I had made my appointment by phone under a different name, but when I walked in the building, I might conceivably have been recognized by someone at the desk, and this person might have somehow told the woman who I was, that I had something to do with movies. There wasn't any phone in the psychic's room that I could see, but you never knew. Being informed would explain everything.

The other possibility was that she was psychic, and the phenomenon was real.

I returned to the Spiritualist Association a couple of days later. This time I saw a small, precise man with a snippy manner. He held out his hand, snapped his fingers, and said, "Well? Give me something."

"Like what?"

"Your watch will do."

I gave him my watch.

"Don't worry, I'll give it back. Sit down over there."

He held the watch in his hand, rubbed it between his fingers, toyed with it. He sat in a rocking chair. I was starting to get a headache. I didn't like being around him.

"Do you believe in spiritualism?" he said.

"I don't know."

"Was your grandfather a soldier?"

"I don't know."

"I see, you're one of those who say the same thing all the time, are you? Don't want to give me any help, is that it?"

"I don't know," I said. I was following my plan, but it seemed stupid.

"It doesn't matter," he said. "Please yourself. I see your grandfather riding on a horse; he looks like a soldier. I see your grandfather working with stone. I see chips of stone on the ground; he works with stone."

My grandfather died in the army, in the influenza epidemic of 1919, before my father was born. My grandfather had worked as a gravestone cutter. I had seen photographs.

"Your father is dead," the psychic said. "Recently passed over?"

My father had died eight months before. "Yes," I said.

"He's all right. Your mother is grieving too much. You should tell her that your father is all right and he wants her to stop grieving so much. Will you tell your mother that?"

"Yes." Thinking, Oh brother, sure. I'm going to call my mother up and say, Some obnoxious little creep held my watch and said that Dad is on the Other Side and everything is fine, Mom. Sure I am.

And also thinking this was a stock situation. Once this guy had guessed that my father had recently died, then he could say, without much fear of contradiction, that my mother was grieving too much and that I should tell her Dad was okay. It was a stock situation and it didn't mean anything.

The man rubbed the watch in his hands.

"Your father did some good things and some bad things."

Another stock comment. Applicable to any dead person. I was unimpressed.

"Your father feels bad about what he did to you."

I said nothing.

"Your father did the best he could with you, but you see, he had no father of his own to teach him."

That was true. And not easy to guess.

"Your father didn't know how to behave around you, and you of course intimidated him. So you and he had difficulties. But he knows he injured you, and now he feels bad about it. He wants you to know that. He wants to help you now."

I said nothing.

"Often at night you walk in the city. At those times your father is close to you, and he wishes to help you."

In London, I had been seeing a woman who lived near my hotel. I would often walk home at night, enjoying the cool air and the light London fog, and during those times I would think of my father.

"I get that your sister is a lawyer," he said suddenly. "But she is American. Why is she in England?"

My sister and her husband were at that moment on vacation in England. Somewhere—I hadn't seen them yet, and

214

wouldn't until they arrived in London at the end of the month.

And so it went, for the rest of the hour. The little man might be annoying, but he was pretty accurate.

I was back a couple of days later. I saw a middle-aged woman who wore a Scottish tweed suit and who looked like a tall version of Miss Marple. In tones of great authority, she informed me that I was from Malta, that I was an only child, and that I was in a business that had to do with food or restaurants and I had better watch out, because I was being cheated.

I left stunned. This woman had been entirely wrong. It had seemed that by chance alone she would stumble onto something about me that was true. But this reading had been wrong in every detail.

Because I was directing a movie, I had a car and a driver. My driver, John King, became interested in why I was going so often to this association.

"What is it they do there exactly, Michael?"

"Well, they have people who do readings, psychic readings."

"They tell you the future?"

"Sometimes. Or sometimes they just tell about you, what kind of person you are."

"You don't already know what kind of person you are?" John had this practical side.

"Well, it's interesting if someone who doesn't know you tells you."

"And they're right?"

"Usually, yes."

John was silent for a while. Then he said, "You believe a person can tell the future?"

"I think something is happening here," I said.

That was as far as I had gotten at that point. It would have been absurd to insist that all of my readings could be explained in some ordinary way. One psychic had told me the names of my friends in California. Another had described my house and the modifications I had made to it. A third had recalled a traumatic incident in the third grade when I had released Miss Fromkin's pet canary and the bird

215

had flown into the ceiling air vent and hadn't come back for an hour.

A network of the most diligent informants couldn't explain that one. Nor had I inadvertently conveyed the information to the psychic by any normal channel. I couldn't have "leaked" anything about Miss Fromkin's canary. I hadn't even remembered the incident until I was reminded of it.

I was quite clear about all that. I was clear about what *hadn't* happened.

But I was less clear about what *had* happened, and what it all meant. In particular, I was reluctant to jump from accepting these accurate depictions of my past to the idea that somebody could see the future. Seeing the future appeared quite a different proposition from seeing the past.

For one thing, we can all communicate the past. I can tell you about my life and you will know something about it. There's nothing mysterious about this. The ability of somebody to do the same thing without speaking, the ability to "read my mind" without words, could be seen as merely a refinement of a pre-existing skill, just as a jet plane is a refinement of a biplane. I didn't have any real problem with it, even though I didn't understand how it was done.

On the other hand, I felt there were theoretical objections to seeing the future. Similar to the theoretical objections to traveling faster than the speed of light. I couldn't really understand how it *might* be done, and that interfered with my ability to consider whether it *was* being done. After all, the past existed, in the sense that the past was a prior present, now retired. But the future did not yet exist. So how could it be perceived?

Anyway, I wasn't sure how much future information I was actually getting. As far as I could tell, I was being told accurate information about the past and the present. Not much about the future.

These thoughts made me hesitant as I talked to John.

"What do you like about it," John asked, "going to see these people?"

"Just . . . I don't know. I'm interested." That was the best explanation I could give. In a way, it still is.

Then, because he still looked puzzled, I said, "Tell you what. The next time I go, I'll make an appointment for you, too."

I came out from my next session to find him already in the car. He was pale and frightened.

"Cor, that bloke. Know what he said to me?"

"No. What?"

But John didn't say. "How do they know those things, then?"

"What things?"

"Oh, I couldn't believe it, how he knew those things. Gives me shivers up and down me spine."

"What did he say, John?"

"Oh. Well. I don't mind telling you, I didn't care for that. Never going back there, I don't mind telling you."

He would only talk about his responses to the experience, not the experience itself.

"I don't know why you like it," he said later. "I don't know why you like going there."

"I don't know why you don't," I said.

I couldn't work out his reaction. I could understand skepticism, or indifference. But fear?

Days later he gave me a clue. We were driving out to the studio and he said, "To tell the truth, I don't want to know that much about myself. And I don't want somebody *else* knowing."

So that was the fear. A fear of exposure. A fear of invasion of privacy. A fear of secrets or weaknesses that will be discovered. A fear of what the future holds.

I could understand that. I remembered the first time I had ever seen an actual psychiatrist. He was the father of a girl I knew in college, and I was seated next to him at dinner. I didn't want to open my mouth all night, because I thought, If I say *anything at all* he will see through me, and he will realize I am a shallow, sex-crazed, deeply disturbed fraud of a young man. So I kept my mouth shut.

After a while this psychiatrist said to me, "You're very quiet."

"Uh-huh," I said.

He asked me some questions about what I was studying in college, to draw me out. I answered tersely; I wouldn't be drawn out.

Finally he said, "Do I make you nervous?"

"A little," I said. And then I told him my fear, that he would be able to analyze me from my chance comments.

He laughed. "I'm off duty," he said. "You learn to turn it off."

But that wasn't really satisfying. I guess he knew it, because he said, "You know, psychiatry isn't all that powerful. If you don't want me to know something, I doubt I'll find out over a dinner conversation."

That was more like it. I relaxed a little. And eventually we had a pleasant conversation.

But I still remembered the unreasoning fear of another person's power, and the terrifying feeling of the unexplored psyche. Who knows what was in there? Better not look. Better not let anyone else look, either. You could be in for a nasty shock.

Fear wasn't a problem for me any more, and in London I pursued my psychics enthusiastically. As time went on, I began to notice patterns in the way the psychics behaved.

For example, the psychics tended to circle around things. They were like blind people touching a statue on all sides, trying to figure out what it represented. They got bits and pieces of the whole. And they tended to repeat themselves. Just as if they were going around and around something, trying to feel it, to give their impressions.

I also noticed that they tended to speak as if they were translating. Trying to shift from one language, or one system of representation, to another. Sometimes this led them to speak very vaguely. A movie producer was "a person who is responsible for other people." A film editor was "a person who is given things previously made that he assembles into a new whole." A sabotaging secretary was "a person who thinks she is doing the right thing but who is angry and makes errors she is not aware she makes."

At other times they seemed overconcrete. They wouldn't say I was a writer; they'd say, "I see you surrounded by books." They wouldn't say I had a modern house; they'd say, "Your house is very open, with lots of glass and green trees outside." And so on.

I also noticed there seemed to be a groove or a track they followed. They would be on the track for a while, and then they'd go off the track—abruptly becoming irrelevant, or just plain wrong. Once they started to make incorrect statements, I learned that they might remain incorrect for a while, until they got back on the track.

I tried to notice what was associated with their going off and coming back. It seemed that they went off whenever they paid too much attention to me. If they really looked at me, they might make some ordinary observation such as "You look very young" or "You're very tall" or "You're not English, are you?" And then they would go off the track. So it seemed as if they had to ignore me to do a good reading. When they were most accurate, it was as if they were talking to themselves, behaving as if I weren't even in the room. In this sense, what they were doing was the opposite of cold-reading techniques that required close scrutiny of the person before you. Here it seemed that close scrutiny caused errors.

Also, I noticed that psychic information was disorderly, an odd and sometimes irritating mixture of the significant and the trivial, as if everything counted the same. It was as if our usual procedures for weighing information were bypassed in psychic readings.

Finally, I noticed psychics seemed to have specific, reproducible areas of confusion. One had to do with similarities. They would confuse Colorado with Switzerland, or a beach with a desert, or medical books with law books. They were likely to confuse time—they were much more likely to get the season of the year correct than the year itself. They often got the order of things and the amounts of things wrong. It seemed that you couldn't really expect psychics to be accurate about quantities and timing; they simply couldn't do it.

The psychics I saw all appeared to be distinct personalities. They had little in common as people. But in the way they obtained and handled information, they seemed more alike.

This increased my conviction that there was indeed something going on, that these people had access to some information source that ordinary people did not. I didn't know why they had access and the rest of us did not, but there didn't seem to be any hocus-pocus about it. On the contrary, they seemed as a group to be remarkably straightforward. No séances. No phosphorescent ectoplasm. Just sit there while I give you my impressions.

Two of the psychics said that I was psychic. One said that I would be writing about the psychic world. I thought, Sure, sure.

After three months of visiting psychics, the movie was finished, and it was time to leave London.

"Well?" John King said to me. "What have you decided?"

I hadn't decided anything. I didn't know what to think. I was certain that some people, whether by an accident of birth or by some peculiarity of training, could tune in to another source of information and could know things about people we didn't think were possible to know.

I was less sure that the future could be foretold. Maybe, maybe not, was my opinion. And I was mindful of the reckless example of Conan Doyle. I promised myself I wouldn't make his mistake.

All this was symbolized for me by the plane flight home from London. After I checked in, British Air announced the flight was delayed, and the passengers were held in the lounge for several hours.

Finally BA decided that the flight would leave after repairs were completed, so they boarded everyone and served drinks. By now it was dark outside. Sitting in my seat with a drink in my hand, reading a book and glancing out the window at the blackness, I felt as if I were actually flying. Then a forklift truck drove past my window, and the illusion was shattered. If I didn't see any ground vehicles, the illusion crept back.

I felt a little like that about psychic experiences. It seemed as if we were flying, but I felt I'd better wait a while, and make sure I was not still on the ground.

Baltistan

A trek into Baltistan followed the mountaineer's route toward Masherbrum Peak, at 25,660 feet a major climbing peak in a remote area of Pakistan's Karakoram Mountains.

There was much I did not know about the Karakoram Mountains. On the map, they are a part of that great crumpled range of mountains that runs from Afghanistan to Burma, a range pushed up as the Indian continent drifts north into Russia—a range I always called the Himalaya. But it turns out that "the Himalaya" refers only to the eastern section of the range. To the west, the mountains are called the Karakoram, and, still farther west, the Hindu Kush.

I had also thought the Himalaya was the highest range in the world, but it is not. The Himalaya boasts Everest, the single highest mountain, but the Karakoram is the highest mountain *range,* claiming the second highest peak, K-2, as well as three other peaks above twenty-six thousand feet. All together, ten of the thirty highest mountains in the world are strung along the small Karakoram Range, which extends barely two hundred miles, little more than a tenth the length of the Himalaya.

Finally, I imagined the Karakoram to be green and forested, like the American Rockies. I did not understand that the major Karakoram summits were an average of two miles higher than those of the Rockies, and that they were in essence desert peaks rising above a high desert floor— possessing a remarkable windswept, bleak grandeur, but desert peaks nonetheless.

All this I could see from the PIA airplane, flying from the capital city of Rawalpindi north to Skardu. These jagged, sharp peaks had no counterpart in the New World; they made the American Rockies look like tired old foothills, while the greatest of the mountains, like Nanga Parbat, were positively stupefying.

And when we landed at the airfield in Skardu, we stepped out into a desert setting: suffocating heat, convection waves shimmering off the tarmac, distorting the rugged, bare peaks in a bowl all around us. Skardu was our staging place for the trek; we collected some final supplies from the bazaar, and met our military liaison, a handsome twenty-eight-year-old Pathan major named Shan Affridi. Every tourist party in Pakistan had to be accompanied by a military liaison.

We drove all the next day in jeeps, following the Indus River on a road cut into the cliffs, and camped for the night at Khapulu, a large village of four hundred houses, which is how villages are sized in this part of the world. Our leader, Dick Irvin, hired porters for the coming trek. This was an elaborate negotiation that continued into the evening. It was complicated by the fact that we did not have good maps for the area we were entering. Accurate maps of Pakistan are difficult to obtain in any case; Dick carried Xeroxed notes from someone who had made the trek a couple of years earlier. That was all we had. Thus we weren't very clear about the order in which we would pass villages; some of the Khapulu porters intended to quit at one village or another, and so there were arguments, still more negotiations. The porters insisted we didn't know where we were going. It was obvious to me they were right.

Major Shan maintained a discreet silence throughout the negotiations. I felt he was sure we didn't know where we were going, either.

I talked to Loren about it. Loren and I had married the previous winter; this trip was to be a deferred honeymoon. Loren had just finished law school, and her attitude was especially carefree.

222

The next morning we cross the Shyok River on a *zak*—a raft of inflated goat intestines tied under a platform of wooden poles, pushed by local boatmen. The morning sunlight reaches down into the river canyon, and the temperature soars above a hundred degrees, although it is only eight o'clock. We open umbrellas, and start to walk. Our destination for the first night is Mishoke, a small village we believe lies between the villages of Kande and Micholu.

We are now in the region called Baltistan. High, rocky gray mountain peaks and, in the valley where we walk, terraced yellow wheat fields and small villages with clumps of apricot trees. The landscape is starkly beautiful and filled with contradictions. In this region, Muslim women are instructed to cover their faces and flee if they see a strange man. All day long, as I walk on the road, I see women running from me in the yellow fields. It makes me feel strange, as if I were some kind of leper. But then I hear the women giggling as they run away, and the whole business becomes a cultural game, a sort of formality, like shaking hands but in reverse.

You could not photograph the women, and of course, as a man, you could not talk to them. In Muslim Baltistan the sexes are strictly separated. Sometimes in the evenings, the women in our party would go off to sit with the village women. Loren's blond hair invariably provoked astonishment. Women clustered around her, touching her hair. Often they assumed she was ill. Young children hid from her, thinking her a ghost. The women were also interested in Loren's clothing, since she wore trousers. Sometimes they squeezed her breasts, to verify her sex.

Balti customs concerning the separation of sexes produced unexpected difficulties. When we arrived at a village in the evening, we would have to wait to go to the well for water, because if strange men were seen at the well the women would stay away for the next hour or so, fearing that the men might come back unexpectedly. This would delay their evening dinner and upset village life, so we waited until all the villagers had drawn their water before we went to get our own.

After several days on the trail, Loren went upstream to take a bath near a village. She went alone, since to be accompanied by me would insult local custom; she was advised to bathe as quickly as she could, an unnecessary injunction in an icy mountain stream. Soon after, she came running back to camp, clutching her clothes, her hair foamy with shampoo. While she had been bathing in her underwear, a group of village women had come upon her, and stoned her until she fled.

In another village, the women grew angry when Loren refused to nurse their infants; even when Major Shan (standing a discreet distance away) called out to explain Loren had no milk, the women remained surly. They could not believe that a woman of Loren's age did not have a child, and was not nursing.

During the day, temperatures reached 120 degrees. Sweating beneath our umbrellas, we developed a new obsession: water. I had never had any particular interest in water before. It was something that came out of a tap, always available, always plentiful. Water was not something you thought about. But here, each morning before we set out, Dick Irvin would consult his notes and tell us where, during the day, we could expect to find water. There was always water in the villages, of course, but the villages were several miles apart. We had to watch for streams and irrigation ditches in between. We each carried two quart bottles, and whenever we saw water, we filled our bottles.

The water was always polluted, and so we purified it with iodine crystals, which turned the water reddish brown and made it taste medicinal. The purification process required time and was a function of the coldness of the water. We had to keep track of how long the iodine had been in the water before we drank it. Because the consequences of drinking polluted water were too dire to contemplate.

In this, and in other ways, we were always made aware of our isolation. Isolation brought its own reality. Even mundane events became worrisome.

For example, we had to ford some rivers—not raging torrents, but ordinary, slippery, icy, fast-moving rivers. Normally I wouldn't have thought twice about crossing these streams, but here you were forced to recognize a new reality. If you slipped and broke your leg while crossing the river—and if you suffered a compound fracture—the chances were that you would die before you could get out to civilization. If you slipped and just twisted your ankle,

224

then a couple of porters would have to carry you back, and you'd have a painful time, and your trip would be ruined.

So: Faced with a simple river to cross, you felt a lot of pressure not to injure yourself in any way. Faced with polluted drinking water, you felt a lot of pressure to make sure you treated it properly, because you didn't want incapacitating diarrhea. And so on.

That was one aspect of the isolation. Another was the nature of the villages themselves. Balti villages were sometimes just a couple of dozen wooden houses clustered along the main road. The villages were about five miles apart, and we were walking about twelve miles a day, so we would generally leave one village, pass another around midday, and camp for the night near a third. Considering how close the villages were, they varied sharply. Even my untrained ears could hear the difference in speech patterns from one village to the next, and I could see the variations in the architecture of each village's wooden houses. Each village had its own distinctive style. This degree of variation was astonishing to me; but these were mountain villages, and for most of the year they were isolated from one another by deep snow—as isolated as if they were hundreds of miles apart.

As the days of trekking continued, it became known that there were *ferengi* walking on the road. At each village there would be shouts announcing our arrival, and people would turn out to see us. Parents would take their children by the hand and lead them to the road to show them the foreigners; people would stand on the roofs of buildings and look down on us as we passed by below. This open curiosity was entirely friendly, but it was odd, too.

Only a handful of tourists ever came up this way; there had been a party of Japanese climbers making the ascent to Masherbrum the month before, but since then, nobody much.

Again and again we were confronted by the facts of isolation. We were eating freeze-dried camper's food, but it was hard to boil water at altitude, and our dinners frequently tasted like soup with colored bits of cardboard. Someone asked Dick Irvin to bargain for fresh food from a village.

"I don't think we should," he said. He explained that in these remote villages the Baltis grew wheat and apricots and a little livestock, and that whatever they grew they would need to get through the hard winter. They had no extra food to sell visitors.

"Even if we paid them?"

"Well," he said, "they don't really have much use for money."

"What do you mean?" someone asked. How could people have no use for money?

"Well, there isn't a bank or a bazaar anywhere around here except in Skardu, and that's a hundred miles away. Most of these people have never been to the next village, five miles away, let alone to Skardu. If you pay them money, they just keep it somewhere in the house, and never do anything with it."

He explained that, when the government changed the currency a few years ago, it had sent word to all the villages to bring in their old money before it was declared valueless. Years later the old money was still turning up, and village men were enraged to be told it was no longer worth anything.

After two days of walking, we could see good views of Masherbrum Peak before us. I walked ahead of the rest of the party, enjoying being alone on the trail. Around four o'clock, I arrived at a village, drowsy in the hot sunlight. I suspected this was Kande, where we would camp for the night.

A gang of children came running out to greet me. They clustered around me, touching me, my backpack, my camera. They were asking me something, over and over, but I didn't pay much attention, since I spoke no Urdu and wouldn't have been able to understand.

I pointed to their village and said the name I thought it was, Kande. I pronounced it "Candy," and hoped it was right. They paid no attention to me, I suppose for the same reason—they assumed that whatever I was saying would be unintelligible to them. I tried to get them to understand I was asking the name of their village, but I didn't have much success. I gave up, frustrated.

I sat down, opened my pack, and ate a handful of trail mix. The children watched everything I did, and discussed my every move.

By now they had stopped touching my clothes and my shoes, but they were still pointing to my Nikon. They kept

226

up about the camera, saying something, pointing to me, and then to the camera. They were asking me something. Finally I got it—it wasn't an Urdu word at all. They were saying "Nippon? Nippon?" over and over. First pointing to the camera, then to me.

"Nippon? Nippon?"

They were asking me if I was Japanese.

I was too astonished to laugh. I am nearly seven feet tall and distinctly Western. I could not imagine that even a child would mistake me for Japanese. Couldn't they see the obvious differences between a Westerner and a Japanese?

The answer was no, they couldn't.

Thinking it over, I realized that, in their eyes, the similarities between me and the previous Japanese climbers must far outweigh any differences. We were both exotic foreigners wearing heavy boots and synthetic clothing in bright, unnatural colors, carrying backpacks, umbrellas, and cameras, eating exotic snack food that we carried in little plastic bags—in all these ways, the Japanese and I were the same. We were overwhelmingly the same, and overwhelmingly different from the village children. What did it matter that our skin color wasn't quite the same, or that our heights were a little different? Those differences were obviously irrelevant.

I looked at it from their point of view, and decided they were right.

I couldn't be critical of these children, because I had made some similar perceptual errors. Three years earlier, driving in East Africa, Loren and I came upon a Samburu *manyatta* that was in the process of moving. The Samburu are a seminomadic tribe, and there was a drought in northern Kenya that was forcing them to move in search of grass for their cattle.

The women were driving donkeys laden with all their worldly possessions; we stopped the Land Rover to talk to two of them, a mother and her daughter. These women had shaved heads, and wore elaborate beaded jewelry that encircled their foreheads and looped down their noses. Their ears were pierced and stretched, so the lobes hung in long loops; they had a lot of hand-tooled metal, bracelets and necklaces, as well. Flies buzzed around their faces, and crawled over their skin; they didn't bother to swat them away.

227

Alongside them were their donkeys, carrying wicker and woven things, articles made of hide. Everything they possessed was simple, made by hand from natural substances.

They chatted happily with the courier in Swahili, we shared chewing gum, and I found myself working to make some kind of human contact with them. I looked again at their shaved heads and the jewelry, and tried to see them as women, as sexual creatures, but I had unexpected difficulty; I worked hard to admire the workmanship of the articles in their possession; I became, in truth, a little panicky as I watched the flies crawling over their faces and recognized that in a moment we would get back into the Land Rover and drive away, and we would leave them here, in this hot, desolate landscape, driving their donkeys with their handful of simple possessions, and suddenly the gulf between them and me became too much, and I found myself thinking, *These aren't people. These aren't human beings.*

I was horrified at my own thoughts. After all, I had studied anthropology in college; I was better prepared than most to perceive the humanity behind the mask of cultural artifacts. But here I was, struggling to see two tribal women as human, as "the same as you and me." And I was failing. I saw them as animals, creatures who possessed some simple, rather pitiful stuff.

Ordinarily when I think something alarming like this, I worry that other people will somehow pick up on it. I fear they will know that I don't like them, or that I think they're stupid, or whatever it is I am thinking. But now I watched these women with complete equanimity. Because I knew: *They'll never figure out what I am thinking.*

And so I stared, and took a couple of pictures, and we got in the car and drove away, and pretty soon the women had disappeared behind us in a cloud of dust from the Land Rover. And pretty soon after that, I had forgotten my inability to see the women as people. It all drifted away, and I began to wonder whether the pictures would turn out well, and what my friends would say when I showed them pictures of the Samburu women.

A few days later we were driving in Masai territory, on the way to Lake Baringo. All day we had been seeing Masai people, the men standing in the fields with cattle, the children playing by the side of the road.

Around midday we passed a row of young girls wearing frilly white dresses. The girls had white paint on their faces, too, and they were giggling and laughing, in a festive mood. "Oh, look," Loren said, "they're going to first communion." We stopped the car. The girls clustered around it, smiling and waving to us happily. "Isn't that sweet?" Loren said. "I remember my first communion."

Our courier cleared his throat. "It's not, uh, communion," he said.

"Really? What is it?" Loren said.

He explained that these girls were going to their ritual clitoridectomy. Masai young women underwent surgical removal of the clitoris in adolescence. Loren listened in shocked silence, staring at the smiling girls. "Why are they so *happy?*" she said.

Then she wanted to know the rationale for such a mutilation, but of course the rationale made no sense. Masai men said they removed the clitoris to diminish the excessive sexual appetites of the women, but Masai women were known to have excessive sexual appetites anyway; after bearing her first child, a Masai woman was not expected to be sexually faithful at all.

"Then why is it done in the first place?" Loren asked.

"It's like graduation," the courier said.

"Some graduation," she said.

In the early afternoon the Land Rover overheated, so we stopped for a while to top up the radiator and let the engine cool. We broke out our box lunches and had sandwiches. Pretty soon a young Masai boy came over from a nearby field, where he had been tending cattle. I gave him a sandwich, which he accepted gravely.

Then another young boy came running up. I said to Loren, "Brother, now I've started something. I'm going to have to feed the whole damned neighborhood." I started poking around in my box for a piece of sandwich I didn't want. Where were the cheese sandwiches? I hated those.

But when the newcomer arrived, the first boy tore his sandwich in half and gave a piece to the other boy. He did this immediately, without any reluctance to share. Both children stared at me, each holding half a sandwich. I felt ashamed.

Pretty soon we had a group of kids clustered around the

car, and we gave away the rest of the food. The kids were sweet and shy, and mostly just stared in silence. They watched everything we did—how we handled the cameras, how we loaded film, how we kept our sunglasses in a tray on the dash, how we drank our soft drinks from metal containers.

They watched all this with the polite solemnity that I had learned to expect from Africans, and after a while we got used to one another. I sat on the seat of the car with the door open, facing out, and I stared at the kids, and they stared back. And it was like that for a while, and I daydreamed, and when my attention returned I noticed that they were behaving oddly. One after another, they would bend over, and twist their heads, and look at me sideways.

At first I thought it was a game. I smiled.

They didn't smile back; they just did this odd sideways looking. And they chattered among themselves.

And then I got it: they were trying to look up my shorts. They had seen I was very tall and they were curious about whether everything was in proportion.

Yet they would never have behaved in that open way unless they were thinking, *He'll never figure out what we are doing.*

And I knew only too well what that thought implied. It implied that they were seeing me, and the other occupants of the metal Land Rover, as somehow not quite people, not quite human beings. *These aren't really people; they don't have the same thoughts and feelings we do, and they won't understand what we are doing.*

Nearing the end of the trek to Baltistan, we returned to Mishoke, the large village nearest the Shyok River. There, in the evening twilight, the people were celebrating an annual ritual in which the women placed lighted candles on the graves of the dead in the village cemetery. It was a beautiful ceremony to watch, even though the men refused to participate, sitting to one side jeering at the women. At Mishoke we also heard that the ferrymen had gone on strike, and now there was no way to cross the river and get back home.

I turned to Loren. She just shrugged and smiled. Loren refused to be worried; she believed that somehow everything would work out. But I was definitely worried. As far as I could tell, our situation was not good.

In less than twenty-four hours, the jeeps were coming out from Skardu to pick us up at Khapulu. If we were not at Khapulu to meet them, no one was sure what would happen. The jeeps might wait for us, or they might not. There was no radio in Khapulu to call them back if they departed. All in all, it seemed best to somehow get to Khapulu.

Only we could not cross the river.

Could the boatmen be convinced to end their strike? No, they were gone. We offered exorbitant bribes. No, the boatmen had left the river and no one knew where they had gone. Could anyone else pole the rafts? No, that was not possible, either. Was there any other way across the river?

Yes, there was a bridge west of Khapulu. It was twenty-five miles from Mishoke, where we were now. However, some people felt the bridge had washed out the previous winter. More inquiries were made. The village people agreed that the bridge had been damaged, but was probably still standing and serviceable.

In any case, we could not walk twenty-five miles in a single morning. More inquiries were made, while we ate our cardboard dinner. It developed that someone in the village owned a gasoline-powered tractor, and this tractor had a sort of cart attached to it. Perhaps we could hire the tractor, and ride to the bridge?

Yes, we could hire the tractor. Unfortunately, there was no gasoline for it. That stumped us for a while. More bribes were offered. Eventually people began to show up with small liter bottles of gasoline, like bottles of beer. We purchased them. We inspected the tractor and hired it for the following morning.

So we had a plan, but for my taste there were too many uncertainties ahead. I fretted that night in the tent. Loren was serene. It bothered me that she was so calm; I felt a split between us, a split in our realities. I was worried and thought it correct to worry. She was not worried and saw no reason to be worried. We were out of step with each other in a way that troubled me.

The next day we bounced and jolted on this tractor cart over rugged terrain and several broad rivers. By the end of the journey, we were exhausted, caked in dirt. But we reached the bridge, which was in excellent shape. We

231

crossed it, and on the other side most people pulled off their boots and stuck their feet in the cold river. I was feeling annoyed with Loren, distanced from her, so I went up into the hills with Major Shan to look for the jeeps. Major Shan and I sat in the shadow of some rocks, and waited in the blazing midday heat for the jeeps. From our high vantage point, we could see several miles of the road twisting through the beautiful and desolate landscape. We smoked cigarettes. Shan squinted at the road, which shimmered in the heat. Finally he said, "Good place for an ambush."

"What?" I said.

"Good place for an ambush," he repeated. He pointed out that from our high position we commanded the road; a handful of men here could stop a large number of vehicles. The men in the vehicles would have nowhere to go; we could kill them all.

I stared at him. He was completely serious. He was thinking about the best way to kill people. I was surprised that his perceptions of this landscape could be so different from mine.

"We are close to the Indian border," he said. "As a military man, you cannot afford to deceive yourself. You must see things as they are."

Then he changed the subject, and asked me how long I had been married.

"Ten months," I said.

"This is not your first marriage?"

"No. My second."

"You have children?"

"No. No children."

"You will have children with Loren?"

"Yes, we plan to."

"She is a lawyer," he said.

"Yes. She just finished her training."

"Ah." He shook his pack of cigarettes, offered me another. It seemed to end the conversation.

The jeeps finally came, and we rode back to Skardu that night. In the rest house, Loren collapsed on the bed: "Thank God!"

"What's the matter?" I said.

"I was so worried!"

"I thought you weren't," I said.

"Are you kidding? No boats? No way to get back across the river?"

232

"Why didn't you tell me?" I said.

"Because," she said, "you were freaking out, and there was no point in both of us being upset, that would have just made things worse."

"I wish you had told me, anyway," I said.

"Why? It wouldn't have done any good."

I knew what she was saying, but now I was feeling another kind of isolation, not the isolation of geography, of being in a remote place, but the isolation that existed between people, even between Loren and me. Something unstated, something unclear and perhaps inevitable.

And that was how we left Baltistan.

Shangri-La

Five years after hearing my friend Peter Kann talk about his visit to the fabled place, I, too, was going to Hunza. The tiny mountain state, known as the original Shangri-La and traditionally closed to foreigners, had been opened the year before. It was the place where the people were beautiful, intelligent, and immune to disease; where they lived to be 140 years old on a diet of apricots; where they existed in harmony in a spectacular mountain setting, cut off from everything that was bad and corrupting in the civilized world.

That was Hunza. I was excited to go.

In Islamabad, our group waited two days for a plane to Gilgit, the staging area for trips to Hunza. Two days was nothing to wait; Peter had waited much longer than that, and mountaineering parties had sometimes waited a month for a flight. But we were on a schedule; besides, there was now another way to get from Islamabad, north to Gilgit— the Karakorum Highway.

This extraordinary feat of engineering was a road two hundred miles long, traversing the most rugged mountain range in the world. For most of its length it followed the gorge of the Indus River, one of the great canyons of the world. In fact, the road had been built by the Chinese, and hundreds of workers had died during its construction.

We hired a bus, loaded it with our stuff, and set out. The trip was thought to take fifteen hours, perhaps longer; nobody seemed quite sure. The bus was a typical brightly decorated Pakistani bus, which looked, to the casual glance, like a 1960s psychedelic fantasy. Every exposed surface, inside and out, was covered with signs, woven fabric, bits of mirror, hammered tin, and the whole thing was painted a swirling design in garish Day-Glo colors. It was horrible in a way, but it had the virtues of exoticism—and there was certainly plenty to look at if you tired of the passing view.

Our Pakistani driver had been hired specifically because he knew the road. He brought with him a teenage boy, who sat at his feet, on the steps leading down to the exit door. Every bus driver brought a boy, who received a small wage and did odd jobs for the driver, bringing him his meals and looking after the baggage for the passengers.

For the first few hours, we passed flat wheat fields; neat villages; camels on the road. We stopped for lunch in Abbottabad, a town with many old British colonial buildings, which had once been the farthest outpost of the British Empire in this part of the world. From Abbottabad, the British in the nineteenth century had twice tried to conquer Afghanistan, and twice had failed. This area of West Pakistan, bordering Afghanistan, is populated by Pathan and other tribes. Like the Afghans, they are fiercely war-like fighters; their lives are structured around militance in a way that Westerners do not readily understand.

From Abbottabad, the land became more desolate and more rugged, and we entered the gorge of the Indus River. For the next several hours, we twisted and turned along the river, seeing spectacular views of the plunging river, and the twenty-five-thousand-foot peak of Nanga Parbat on the east.

All morning the driver had smoked cigarettes with the unmistakable odor of hashish, and now, in the warmth of midday, he began to fall asleep. The boy at his side would nudge him awake when his head drooped, but often the bus took the hairpin turns too widely for comfort.

Finally we confronted the driver, who denied anything was wrong. We asked him what would make him feel more alert. He said music. Soon we were listening to Pakistani music blasting through this psychedelic bus as we careened along the Karakorum Highway, along the Indus River Gorge, on our way to fabled Hunza.

After ten hours of driving, we stopped at a little roadside spot for *chapatties* and a chance to stretch our legs. There we met a British hippie, who told us that the highway to the north was closed because of a landslide. Passage to Hunza was impossible; we would have to turn back. After ten hours, we received this news with disbelief, and many comments on what a dirty little bugger he was, obviously on drugs, obviously wrong.

At the next stop, we asked again. Yes, it was true, a landslide blocked the road. Vehicles were not able to cross to Hunza.

I looked at Major Shan. He didn't seem concerned: "Perhaps it will be cleared," he said, shrugging.

I could imagine it would be cleared, for we had been passing landslides all day. They were usually small piles of stone, bulldozed out of the roadway; they did not seem to have presented any great problem. The rock of the river gorge was friable, and it seemed that the Karakorum Highway was destined to suffer these small landslides as long as the road existed.

Anyway, after a dozen hours bouncing on the bus, nobody seriously considered turning back. We pressed on, north toward the landslide.

I said, "When did this landslide happen?"

"Two days ago," Major Shan said. "Perhaps three days ago."

One of the others on the bus shook his head. "Imagine. The road's blocked two days ago, and they still haven't got it cleared. What a country!"

The landscape became flatter, a desert plain. It was extremely desolate, with low hills in the distance. On the maps it was marked "Tribal Territory."

The light turned softer as the sun descended in the sky. We stopped for gas at a roadside station: a small shack, some pumps, and, for miles in every direction, desert. It was beautiful and desolate.

Major Shan took me aside, and we went to the back of the bus. He kicked the tire with his foot, and seemed reluctant to speak. Behind his dark aviator sunglasses, I could not read his eyes.

236

Finally he said, "I did not bring a gun."

"Oh yes?" I said.

"I could have brought one. I thought of it. But I did not wish to alarm any of the tourists, so I did not bring a gun."

"Is it a problem?"

"Well, now I have no way to get a gun."

"Why would we need a gun?"

"Soon it will be dark," he said, looking around. "The landslide is still one hour ahead on the road. It will be too dark to cross when we get there. We will have to camp for the night."

We all suspected that this might be so, but we were carrying full camping equipment on the bus: food, tents, sleeping bags, the works. It wouldn't be a problem. Would it?

Major Shan looked around. "This area," he said, "is not reliable at night."

The words shot into my brain: *This area is not reliable at night.*

I tried to control my growing sense of disbelief at what he was telling me. It felt like a scene from a bad movie, the busload of tourists suddenly in trouble. I had a hard time working my jaw, making words come out properly. When I spoke, my voice seemed too thin. "What do you mean?"

"This area is not reliable at night," he repeated.

"But what does that mean? Are there bandits or what?"

"I cannot say what might happen. This area is not reliable. We cannot camp out. I am sorry I did not bring a gun."

"What should we do?" I was looking around at the landscape, trying to see it as menacing. It still looked exactly the same to me. I was having a conversation behind our bus with a military man, and it bore no relation to any reality that I could see. He was telling me we were at risk, and I couldn't see why.

"Well," I said, "don't you think, if we pulled way off the road somewhere, pulled a few miles off the road, we could camp out and it would be all right?"

"We cannot camp out." His voice was flat. He pointed to the cars rushing by on the highway. "None of these cars will camp out. By the time the road is dark, they will all be in safety."

"What can we do?"

"I do not want to alarm your friends. There is a military

237

base about fifteen kilometers back, at Chilas," he said. "We can try there."

Now I was beginning to understand. He needed someone to inform the others of this plan. "We can *try* there?"

He shrugged. "It will be very full tonight. Perhaps they will turn us away, but I don't think so, because you are foreigners."

"Okay," I said. I went and told the others that Major Shan suggested that we would be more comfortable spending the night at the army base, fifteen kilometers back, than we would be camping out.

No one argued. It turned out the army base at Chilas was a hundred kilometers back, and by the time we got there the night was inky dark. As the major had predicted, the base was packed, barracks and dormitories filled to overflowing; in our bus headlights we saw travelers sleeping on porches, in their cars, everywhere. By the time we found the headquarters and roused someone, and by the time they sent us to an unused visiting-commandant's cottage, it was nearly 11:00 p.m. Exhausted, we pulled our sleeping bags off the bus and slept on the floor. Later on another busload of foreigners showed up. They slept upstairs; I didn't wake to see them.

We departed at six the next morning. The landscape now seemed cheerfully sunny and empty; we were certain to reach Hunza today, landslide or not. Retracing our steps, we passed the gas station, and once more rejoined the Indus River Gorge. We felt, if anything, disappointed in the adventure just concluded. We had imagined ourselves at risk from bandits or robbers, and saved at the last moment; there was excitement in the fantasy, and obviously there would be no further excitement on the trip.

Then we arrived at the landslide.

I was completely unprepared for its scale. It was a half-mile wide and three-quarters of a mile long, a single sheer, sloping incline of loose sand that ran from the top of the mountains, far above the road, down to the river far below. Millions of tons of loose sand.

"No wonder they didn't clear this in two days," somebody said.

"They are usually very good," Major Shan said, "but this, I think, will be a week. You see how the people deal

238

with it: the trucks and buses from Hunza come as far as the other side, and the trucks from Islamabad come this far, and the people walk across and take another truck or bus on the other side."

I could hardly see to the other side, it was so far away. We were going to have to walk across.

I saw people walking, tiny dwarfed figures on the great sandy incline. They were walking in both directions, on little footpaths hacked into the incline. It was proper terrain for a mountain goat.

I watched this and had a sudden sinking feeling. It was going to be immensely dangerous to cross this landslide, as treacherous as crossing an ice field. I had not signed up for danger on this trip and had just survived what I considered a pleasurable fantasy—bandits, in an area not reliable at night. I was not ready for a real danger, particularly such a mundane one.

Died in a landslide in Pakistan. What a dreary, embarrassing end to my life. And it wouldn't even be understandable to people back home.

You mean he was buried under a landslide?

Oh no, nothing like that. This landslide had already occurred a few days before, and he was walking over it, and he fell down into the river and drowned.

Drowned?

Well, he was swept away. Never found the body.

He was tall. Didn't have good balance, if I recall.

No. I guess not.

I didn't like the sound of any of this.

Meanwhile, on the landslide itself, there was a great deal of activity on the slopes. A couple of hundred yards above the walkers, bulldozers, which looked like little yellow toys, worked to clear the slide. Then, too, every few minutes the army would detonate an explosion, and the ground would shake, and a plume of rock and dust would puff into the air. Through all this chaos, the people agilely stepped across the great steep, shifting, sandy pile. Every so often a big boulder or a small landslide would rush down the incline at the people, but they moved aside and let it crash on down to the river.

I watched, and I knew I could not make it across.

Cut his trip short, I hear.

Oh, really?

Yeah, he got way the hell out in Pakistan and there was

some sort of little mudslide, or I don't know what, and he
panicked. Freaked out. Had to go home.

I was watching the landslide with Major Shan. I offered him a cigarette. I said, "Will we be able to get across?"

"Oh yes," he said. "You see how all the people cross."

"I know," I said, "but we have some older people in our party. . . ."

"I will help the old ones."

"And there may be some who are afraid."

"I will help them, too."

"Yes, good . . . Uh . . . ."

He looked at me expectantly. There wasn't much I could do but tell the truth.

"I don't know if I can make it."

The words seemed to hang in the air, an awkward confession.

Major Shan stared at me for a long time.

He finished the cigarette in silence, then ground it out on the road.

"You can make it," he said.

He was right. There was nothing to do but get across, and I did. It was hair-raising, my heart was pounding, I was terrified, but I managed it.

While I was crossing, one of the others in our party took pictures. But the pictures didn't really show anything. In the pictures it doesn't look dangerous, or even very interesting. But it was the most dangerous thing I had ever done.

Two days later I was approaching Baltit, the capital city of Hunza. Even though I did not believe the stories about Hunzakuts, as the local people are called, now that I was here, it was impossible not to wonder: the claims for the place were so extravagant.

In fable, the mountain kingdom of Hunza had been populated by the descendants of Persian soldiers in the army of Alexander the Great, who conquered India in 327 B.C. This was cited to explain the beauty of the tall, fair-skinned Hunzakuts, as well as their excellent physiques and military prowess. The Hunzakuts were far more intelligent than the neighboring bandit tribes; they enjoyed extraordinarily robust health, whether from life at high altitude, from their simple healthy diet of apricots and wheat, from their unhurried life, or for some other reason. Their social life is healthy as well; the Mir settled the rare disputes that arose in his kingdom.

A group of children came running to greet us. I was struck by how scraggly and unattractive they were. Here a mixture of ethnic origins—Chinese, Persian, Afghani, Mongol—led not to a beautiful blending, but to a stunted, deformed pack of mongrels. In this fabled land of self-sufficiency, the children clutched at our clothing, begging to sell us locally mined garnets. I inspected a few dirty fists; they held gems of poor quality.

In the villages themselves, I looked for the fabulously old people, but saw none. There was disease and poverty, and signs of a harsh mountain life on all sides: genetic defects, evidence of inbreeding, cataracts, rashes, infections, running sores.

However, Hunza's physical setting was captivating, a little principality of green terraced fields nestled in a bowl of high, snow-streaked mountains, with the Hunza River running through the center. Above the town rose a white-washed fortress, its siting spectacular. But the fortress was disused, its windows broken, its white façade peeling.

Hunza was once an autonomous mountain state, one of a string of feudal nations across the Himalaya that included Swat, Ladakh, Nagir, Nepal, Sikkim, and Bhutan. In the nineteenth century, the British supported these states as a buffer between India and powerful neighbors to the north—Russia and China. For centuries, these little nations remained cut off from the world, inaccessible in the mountains, and forbidden to foreigners. Elaborate myths grew up around them.

The British briefly conquered Hunza in 1891, after the Hunza bandit attacks on caravans began to get out of hand, even by the standards of that lawless corner of the world. But the British allowed Hunza to retain her independence. Now the Pakistani government wanted to take over these independent mountain states. Their procedure was simple: they waited until the Mir died, and then did not allow him to be succeeded. The last Mir of Hunza had died two years before; the Pakistani government took over the country and opened it to tourism.

So we were seeing the shell of a former state, the remnants of what once had been. We stayed in Hunza two nights. It was peaceful and beautiful, particularly at sunset, when the valleys, already in shadow, glowed in the light reflected from the mountain peaks. But it was not the Shangri-La of imagination.

From Hunza we went to the Hopar Valley in the adjacent kingdom of Nagir. In fable, the Nagyri have been as much despised as the Hunzakuts have been idealized. The Nagyri are said to be darker, weaker, frailer, and more depraved than the Hunzakuts. The Nagyri are unsanitary, ungracious, and unpleasant. You know you are in Nagir, say the Hunzakuts, because there are so many flies.

As is often the case with neighboring states, the people and ways of life appear virtually identical to an outsider. It is proximity that causes competition, and a natural human tendency to consider all bad traits as located on the other side of the valley.

At Nagir, we camped in a beautiful valley alongside the Bualtar Glacier. I had never seen a glacier before, and I found it quite remarkable, a frozen river of stone. To the naked eye, there appeared to be no ice at all. There were simply two vertical canyon walls of dried mud, and in the middle, between them, this flowing, riverine shape of gray rock. Nagir has many glaciers, including the Hispar—forty miles long, the second-largest in the world outside the polar caps. But the Bualtar was a small, rather tame-looking glacier.

One day our trip leader, Dick Irvin, Loren, and I decided to hike on the glacier. Loren and I were both glad for the excursion; during our stay at this lovely campsite, some unspoken tension had increased between us, which was incongruous in the beautiful setting. I felt there was something on Loren's mind, but I was reluctant to ask her. When I finally did, she just shook her head and insisted she was fine. Yet the tension remained.

So it was good to spend a day on the glacier; I found it a fascinating environment—a little slippery in places, windy, and very cold, which seemed peculiar after the stifling heat of camp. But, following the initial surprise, the glacier proved rather featureless, just a great frozen river covered with rock, and after an hour we grew tired of hiking. Dick, a much stronger hiker, decided to walk on. Loren and I headed back to camp.

We had climbed down onto the glacier on a gentle, sloping trail, but it was a circuitous route and added an extra mile of walking. If we were willing to climb the earthen cliffs, we could go directly back to camp. There were trails going up the cliffs, and we had seen shepherds driving goats up these cliffs, so we knew the trails were passable.

We picked a suitable trail and started climbing. The cliffs were fairly sheer, crumbling dirt. But the trail was easily three feet wide; it wasn't difficult to climb for the first hundred feet of ascent. I often stopped to look back at the glacier as we rose higher and higher above it.

Then the trail became a little steeper, the path a little narrower. I was uncomfortable, and I stopped looking back, but fixed my attention on the trail. Still, we were already halfway up, and it seemed sensible to keep going.

The trail deteriorated. Pretty soon it was less than a foot wide, a mere track in the crumbly earth, and occasionally it gave way underfoot. There weren't many handholds in the sheer dirt walls of the cliffs; and no vegetation to grab on to, so these little collapses were frightening. There were many gaps in the trail, where the ground had broken away before.

As we ascended, the gaps grew wider. They were occasionally two feet wide, then three feet wide. They were difficult to step across—especially since you had no assurance that the earth on the far side of the gap would hold and not give way.

We were now two hundred feet up. Another hundred feet and we would reach the upper surface, and camp. We kept going.

The trail was now very narrow. In most places we had to hug the rock wall, pushing our bodies against the warm dirt, as we moved up the trail. It was more and more difficult to proceed.

And then the trail stopped.

At some time in the past, it had broken away, and there was now a gap of at least six feet between where I stood and where the trail resumed. I was standing with my body flat against the wall. There was hardly any room to stand. There was no room for me to turn around. I was two hundred feet in the air on a narrow trail on an earthen cliff and I was stuck.

I am afraid of heights. I wanted to scream.

"Why have you stopped?" Loren asked. She was behind me, on the trail. She couldn't see anything; my body blocked her view.

"There's no trail."

"What do you mean, there's no trail?"

"I mean, there's an open gap ahead of me, about six feet wide."

"Can you get across it?"

"No, I can't get across it!" I was becoming panicky.

"Let me see," Loren said. "Maybe I can do it."

"I can't move," I said. "And anyway, I'm telling you, you can't do it, either."

"Just move your body a little; let me see."

I moved my chest away from the rock a few inches, so she could peer through to the gap in the trail ahead. I was starting to sweat.

"It's wide," she said. "Too wide for me."

"Can we go back down?" I asked. I couldn't see; her body blocked the trail down.

"Too steep," she said. It is much easier to go up a steep, narrow trail than down it.

"Then we can't go up and we can't go down."

"Yeah."

I was seriously fighting panic now. I had one of those momentary visions—like a near miss in a traffic accident. This is how it's going to happen. Nothing dramatic, no great incident, nothing so big as the landslide. *Just a little day hike from camp in Nagir, they somehow took the wrong route back, got nervous, fell off the trail. We first suspected something when they failed to turn up for lunch. . . .*

"Somehow we have to get across it," she said.

"I can't get across it," I said to her. "We have to go back down."

"I can't go down," she said, "and I know you can't."

And there we were, and there we stayed, frozen for the next few minutes. I don't know how it would have turned out if we hadn't heard a voice say, "What seems to be the trouble?"

It was Dick Irvin. He'd already crossed the glacier, and was on his way back. He'd noticed us climbing the cliffs and had decided to follow.

I was never so glad to see anyone in my life.

"There's no trail, Dick," I told him, trying not to whine.

"No problem," he said. And somehow—I am not clear on the details—he managed to move past us, and I watched him kick a toehold in the dirt halfway across the gap, and he leapt lightly across, and from the other side he held out

244

his walking stick, and he got first me and then Loren across the six-foot gap. Then Dick led us on up the trail. My body was shaking. I was soaked in sweat. My vision seemed greenish and too bright. There were several more gaps in the trail, but Dick got us past them all, somehow.

When we reached the top, I felt dizzy and had to sit down. Dick went on to camp to check on lunch. I sat on the ground and thought I might throw up. Loren kept asking me if I was all right. I said I was, but I wasn't. I didn't eat lunch; I wasn't hungry.

In the late afternoon, when it was cooler, Loren suggested we go for a walk. We moved along the rim of the valley, looking over the town and the terraced fields. In this remote pastoral setting, we found ourselves talking about our plans for the future, our hopes for our lives when we returned home. Standing here in a grove of apricot trees above the Hopar Valley, we talked about having a family and working and about our plans, which were, it became increasingly clear, not shared plans but individual plans. The seriousness of this conversation made us both very calm and polite. Neither of us was willing yet to say the marriage was over, but that prospect hung in the cool afternoon air. Finally we began talking about dinner, and how hungry we were, and we went back to the camp.

The next morning we got back into the jeeps, and started the long trip back to Islamabad. When we got to the landslide, the road had been cleared.

Sharks

"Have you dived in the pass yet?" the proprietor of the hotel asked the first evening, when we told him that we liked the diving.

"No," we said, "not yet."

"Ah," he said. "You must dive the pass. It is the most exciting dive on Rangiroa."

"Why is that?"

"The swiftness of the current, and also there are many fish."

"Sharks?" someone asked.

"Yes," he said, smiling, "usually some sharks."

I was in Tahiti for Christmas with my family—my brother and sister, and assorted husbands, wives, girlfriends, friends. We were visiting several islands, and we had begun with the most remote.

Rangiroa was more than an hour from Papeete, one of the Tuamotu chain of atolls. The highest point on Rangiroa was about ten feet above sea level. From the air, it looked like a pale, sandy ring in the middle of the ocean.

The Tuamotus were old islands; their volcanic peaks had been eroded until they finally disappeared, and nothing remained but the coral reef that had originally surrounded the island, but now merely enclosed a lagoon.

On Rangiroa, the lagoon was enormous—some twenty miles in diameter. There were only two breaks in the enclosing reef, through which the tides came and went twice a day. So much water, moving through just two passes, meant that tidal currents were strong indeed. It also meant that lots of fish were attracted to the pass, because of the great nutrient flow in the water.

"It is very exciting," the proprietor said. "You must do it."

We went to Michel, the divemaster, and said we wanted to dive the pass. He consulted a tide table, and said we would do it at ten the following morning. (You can only dive the pass when the tide is running into the lagoon. Otherwise you risk being swept out to sea.)

The next morning, with everyone out on the dock ready to go, my sister asked Michel, "Are there really sharks in the pass?" We were all experienced divers; she was the only one who hadn't seen sharks.

"Yes," Michel said. "You will see sharks."

"A lot?"

He smiled. "Sometimes many."

"How many?"

He saw she was getting nervous and said, "Sometimes you see none at all. Are we ready to leave?"

We got in the boat and set out. The pass was a quarter-mile-wide gap in the atoll. Inside was the calm lagoon, outside the swells of the ocean, which crashed continually against the outer reef. We took the boat to the outside, and Michel got out a float and a spool of thread. Then he gave us a lecture.

"You must stay together," he said. "Everyone get your equipment on, and everyone go into the water as close together as possible. Go right down; do not stay at the surface. When you are down, try to stay within sight of each other. I will be in front of you, with this float"—he gestured to the float in his hands—"so the boat can follow us. The current is very strong. Partway along the pass there is a valley where we can get out of the current for a rest; keep an eye out for that. From there we will continue, and we will be swept into the lagoon; you will feel the current slow; you can look around the coral at your leisure until you run

247

out of air, and come up to the boat. In the pass, do not go below seventy feet. Okay?"

We got our equipment on, waited until everyone was ready, feeling the swells, the rocking of the boat. Finally everybody was ready, and we went over the side in a mass of back-ended flippered splashes.

In diving there is always an initial moment of adjusting, clearing the mask, feeling the temperature of the water, seeing the clarity, looking around, going down. The water here was clear, and I saw the side of the pass, an irregular rocky wall to my left, that went down from the surface to about seventy or eighty feet, where it became bluish sandy bottom.

We went down. It wasn't until we got near the bottom that I realized how fast we were moving. The current was really ripping. It was tremendously exciting—if you didn't mind being out of control.

It didn't matter whether you were facing forward, backward, or sideways: the current moved you at the same swift pace. You couldn't stop yourself, you couldn't hold on to anything. If you grabbed a piece of coral, you'd either rip it off or rip your arm off. You were just swept along by the current, in the grip of a force orders of magnitude greater than you could possibly fight. There was nothing to do but relax and enjoy it.

After the first few minutes, after getting used to seeing the others perpendicular to the current, or looking up, clearing their masks, or facing backward, but always carried along at the same pace, it became fun. It was a kind of amusement park ride, and our powerlessness became pleasant.

Then I saw the sharks.

At first they were moving at the limit of my vision, the way I am used to seeing sharks, gray shadows where the water turns deep blue-gray, far from you. Then, as I came closer, the shadows gained definition, I could see details, and I could see more sharks. Lots more.

The current was carrying us into the middle of a school of gray sharks, so numerous that it felt as if we were entering a cloud of animals. There were easily a hundred sharks circling in a large cluster.

I thought, *Oh my God.*

I didn't want to go right through the middle. I preferred to go to one side, but the current was uncontrollable and indifferent to my preferences. *We were going right through the middle of them.* In an effort to control my panic, I decided to take a picture. I stared down at the exposure settings on the Nikonos around my neck, feeling slightly idiotic: *Here you are in the middle of a hundred sharks and you are worrying about whether the f-stop is f8 or f11. Who cares!* But it was one of those situations; there was nothing I could do about it, so I might as well think about something else, and I took a picture. (It came out very blurred.)

By now the sharks were all around us, above and below and to all sides. We were being swept along by the current, like passengers riding a train, but they did not seem affected by it; they swam easily, flicking their powerful bodies with that peculiar lateral twisting that makes their movements so reminiscent of snakes.

The sharks turned away, came back, spiraled around us, but I noticed that they never came close. And already we were moving clear of the cluster, swept onward by the current, drifting away from the compact cloud of sharks. And then gone.

My breathing had not returned to normal when Michel jerked his thumb, gestured to me that we were to go down into the crevasse he had mentioned. He was twenty yards ahead of me. I saw him swept across the bottom, and then he ducked down headfirst and disappeared into a trench. I saw a cloud of his bubbles rise as I was swept toward the trench. I also swung over, had a quick glimpse of a shallow little canyon perhaps ten feet deep, and twenty feet long.

I was much relieved to be out of the current, but unexpectedly found myself in a black cloud of surgeonfish. These plate-sized fish, moving in dense, impenetrable schools, seemed agitated. I presumed it was because of the arrival of divers into the trench.

Then the black cloud cleared, and I realized it was because of the sharks in the trench. A dozen gray sharks swam in the far end of the cul-de-sac. They were each about nine feet long, dull-snouted, beady-eyed. They swam irritably, within a couple of feet of me and Michel. I was vaguely aware of Michel, ever calm, looking at me to see how I was taking this. I was only looking at the sharks.

I had never been so close to so many sharks at one time, and a dozen impressions assailed me. The gritty texture of their gray skin (sharkskin). The occasional injuries, white scars, and imperfections. The clean gill lines. The unblinking eye, menacing and stupid, like the eye of a thug. The eye was almost the most terrifying thing about a shark, that and the slashing curve of the mouth. And I saw the way one shark, hemmed in by us, arched his back in what I had recently read was typical gray-shark threat behavior that often presaged an attack—

The other divers came swinging over the lip, blowing bubbles.

The sharks fled. The last of them threaded his way between us as if we were pylons on an obstacle course. Or perhaps he was just showing off.

Now we all looked at one another. Behind the masks, lots of wide eyes. Michel let us wait in the trench for a few minutes; he checked everyone's air; we stared at the large surgeonfish and tried to get our bearings.

Pretty soon Michel gestured for us to go back over the lip, into the current. Again we felt it catch us, and we were swept forward into the lagoon. The current slackened and the water became murkier, the coral more scattered, separated in small heads by an expanse of brown muddy bottom. The coral heads were inhabited by small fish; they were familiar; the best part of the dive was over. We finished our air, and headed for the boat.

One measure of a good dive is the amount of adrenaline still pumping through you afterward, and how much you talk when you get back to the surface.

"Oh my God, *did you see that?*"

"I *thought* I was *going to die!*"

"Wasn't that *amazing?*"

"I was *terrified,* I really was. I *didn't* like it." My sister, seriously. But the conversation swirled past her.

"*What* a *dive!*"

"It was fan*tas*tic."

"Unbelievable! I admit it, *I* was scared."

"Scared! I saw you shaking."

"That was just cold."

"Yeah, right."

"What an *incredible* dive!"

Through all this, Michel just sat patiently, smiling and nodding, letting us burn off the tension, signaling to the boatman to wait a few moments, until we calmed down, before he started the engine and we ran back to the hotel.

At the hotel, we showered and changed and drifted to the bar. We could talk of nothing but the dive, our reactions, what we saw, how close the sharks came, how they looked to us, how we felt, whether the pictures would come out, whether the pictures would do the experience justice.

Implicitly, our attitude was that we had survived a brush with death. Deadly dangerous, but we survived. It was so dangerous we never would have done it if we had known what it would be like. We were lucky to have survived. Sure, it was fun, but it was also terrifying.

Then at dinner my brother said casually, "Anybody want to do it again?"

A silence fell over the table, because he was contradicting our implicit assumptions. If it was really so dangerous, we shouldn't do it again.

"I'm going to," he said.

One by one, we admitted that we *might* do it again.

By the following morning, we were irritable when Michel told us that the tides were not right and we would have to wait until tomorrow to dive in the pass. Wait until tomorrow! We were quite put out.

When we dived a second time, we saw hardly any sharks. Now we were *really* put out. What a waste of time: no sharks. So we were obliged to dive the pass a third time, when we at last saw lots of sharks, and had a delightfully frightening time.

I think the only true expression of one's beliefs lies in action. Like the way my family decided to dive the pass again. Whatever we said about sharks at dinner—then or later—we knew they weren't dangerous.

In 1973 I was shooting a movie that called for an actor to be struck by a rattlesnake. We needed shots of a snake crawling in the desert, then striking, then sinking its fangs into the actor, and so on.

To do this film work, particular rattlesnakes were cast as if they were actors. We had four "crawlers" to perform the crawling scenes, and six "strikers" to do the strikes. These snakes were brought to the location in big plywood boxes.

Immediately one of my first concerns about snakes was answered. Whenever I was in the woods, if I heard a rustling sound, I always wondered· *Is that a rattlesnake?* I was always concerned that I would get bitten by something I had wrongly decided was a cricket.

When the snake wrangler pulled the plywood boxes out of the station wagon, everybody for a hundred yards snapped his head around at the sound. There was no question about the sound. You *knew*. That dry, hissing rattle could not be mistaken for anything else.

Then the wrangler pulled out the snakes. They were each six feet long and as big around as a human forearm, and hissing mean. The crew was impressed.

We set up for the first shot. The camera was placed on a tripod with a telephoto lens, about thirty feet from the snake. A blanket was hung to protect the solitary operator from the dreaded snake; the rest of the crew was even farther away. We all watched as the first mean six-foot rattlesnake was released to crawl menacingly toward the lens.

The snake took one look at all of us, turned around, and wriggled away toward the hills. The wrangler had to go catch him.

We set up again. And again. And again.

Each time the poor rattlesnake just tried to get away. Eventually we had to form two rows of people, standing just outside camera range, and herd the frightened snake between us toward the lens.

Once we had the crawling footage, we set up for the shot where the snake coils and strikes. For this we used our "strikers." They were supposedly mean and angry. The wrangler explained that they had not been milked, which would have made them passive.

For the next hour, we tried to get the strikers to strike. We had a variety of sticks, balloons, rubber hands, and cowboy hats, with which we waved, prodded, and generally irritated the snakes.

Occasionally one struck. But you could smack them around quite a lot before they would do so. It was easy to see why. A rattlesnake's strike is rather pitiful. A snake can strike only a fraction of its body length; these six-foot snakes couldn't lunge more than a foot and a half, or less.

What that means is that, at a dinner party, if the person sitting next to you had a big rattler on his plate, the snake probably couldn't strike you. In fact, it probably would have trouble striking the person whose plate it was on.

And the snakes weren't aggressive. After a strike, these big, ferocious rattlers would get their fangs tangled up in the equivalent of a snake's lower lip. They'd look silly, and they seemed to know it. In any case, they would generally back away rather than strike.

252

Between takes, the snakes were placed under a little yellow-polka-dotted parasol. As the day progressed and I didn't get the shots I wanted, I complained about this coddling of the snakes. Let them feel the sun! The wrangler protested, but I was adamant—and I nearly cooked one in a matter of minutes. The snake became extremely sluggish and had to be exchanged for a fresh one. These fearsome reptiles are unable to control their body temperature, and on exposed ground they will fry like eggs. Rattlesnakes are, in truth, rather frail creatures.

The outcome of all this was that, although we started out with blankets and telephoto lenses and a nervous operator by himself, by the middle of the day all the crew were standing within a few feet of these giant rattlesnakes, turning their backs to them, flicking cigarette ash on them, talking of other things. Nobody worried about snakes any more. We had quickly and unconsciously adjusted to the reality of what we had seen.

The rattlesnakes couldn't hurt us.

In most situations, wild animals are encountered so rarely that it's more appropriate to feel privileged than afraid.

Of course that depends on the situation, and the animal. White-tip sharks are relatively benign; other species of shark may not be. There's no point pretending that African lions are tame and therefore you can get out of the Land Cruiser and go over and say hello. But, by the same token, you should realize that if you did get out, and if there were no cubs around, the chances are that the lions would just move off.

For some reason it seems difficult for people to get an appropriate perspective on animals. In American national parks a certain number of people are killed or injured each year because they approach wild animals, such as bison, to get a better picture, or to feed them. For many urban dwellers it may be that the concept of "wild animals" is itself extinct; the only animals they encounter are pets or animals in zoos, so why not send your four-year-old daughter over to pose next to the buffalo in Yellowstone? It'll make a cute picture.

This kind of blind trust is the reverse of the blind fear that so many people feel. Sometimes I think that man needs to feel a special position within nature, and this leads him to

253

believe that he is either specially hated by other animals or specially cherished.

Instead of the truth, which is that he's just another animal on the plain. A smart one, but just another animal.

I found it difficult to give up my fear of animals. I had to, because my experience was forcing me to stop seeing animals as fearsome; I couldn't pretend I wasn't seeing what I was seeing. But it was still difficult to give it up.

For one thing, a certain thrill is gone. We don't like to give up our thrills. I have told people about the fact that certain sharks and moray eels and barracuda are not dangerous and watched their faces fall, then tighten, grow pinched. They disagree with me. They tell me I am reporting special cases. They remind me of the limits of my own experience. Sharks not dangerous? Morays not dangerous? Snakes not dangerous? Please.

They don't like to hear it. Telling them facts and statistics only makes them more irritable. Yet the chances are almost vanishingly small that any Western person will have a dangerous encounter with an animal. In America, every year, sixty thousand people die of auto accidents, a possibility no one fears. Some seven people die of snakebite every year, and everyone is terrified of snakes.

Then, too, fear of animals is a part of popular culture, a theme of books and movies and TV. If you drop it, it gives you the same feeling of loss as not watching the latest hit TV show, or not knowing about this year's intellectual pinup, or not following professional sports. You lose something in common with other people.

The other thing that happens is that, since fear of animals is a part of popular culture, it reminds you that one of the deep, unquestioned beliefs of popular culture is wrong. This is a little unsettling, because you are obliged to wonder what else is wrong, too.

Fear of animals is also a pleasantly childish feeling, and to give it up is to exchange some of the magical feelings of childhood for some of the more practical feelings of adulthood. At first it's not comfortable. Later you wonder why everyone doesn't do it.

In the end, how does anyone benefit from being afraid? Maybe it's bolstering of the values of civilization, by making nature the bogeyman. Here I am sitting in this traffic jam,

254

breathing carbon monoxide and pollutants, staring at a hideous manmade landscape, but I really am better off because, if all this were gone, lions and bears would attack and eat me.

If wild animals—and wild nature—were less frightening, perhaps civilization would be less palatable. But the truth is that civilization does not protect us from wild animals. It attempts, however imperfectly, to protect us from ourselves.

Gorillas

"I wouldn't study gorillas," Nicole said.

"Why not?" I asked.

"They are men."

Nicole was Belgian and spoke English with occasional unintended meanings; I assumed this was one startling instance.

"Gorillas are men?"

"Yes, of course."

My French was bad, but, between her English and my French, we straightened things out. *"Vraiment? Des gorilles sont des hommes?"*

"Oui. The same as men."

"Do you think so?" I asked. Nicole was a zoologist, with a special interest in an antelope called the topi. After years of studying the topi, no doubt gorillas appeared indistinguishable from men. I said nothing.

"You do not believe me," she said, "but I have seen them in Virunga. Gorillas are not animals. They are men."

Now we were flying west to Virunga. I was wedged into the cockpit of the small plane, next to the pilot. "There, you can see the volcanoes," he said, pointing.

Ahead, emerging from the mist of Rwanda, were three

shadowy mountain cones. It didn't look very spectacular: not the way I had imagined it.

"On the left, Karisimbi; in the middle, Visoke; on the right, Sabinyo," the pilot said. "And there's the town."

Turning away from the line of volcanoes, he circled Ruhengeri, a shantytown built along a single muddy street. It looked incredibly romantic.

We landed, and checked into the Muhrabura hotel. In the bar, I ran into Don Fawcett, my professor of anatomy who had lectured me, that first day so many years ago, about cadavers. Dr. Fawcett had left Harvard to work at the International Laboratory for Animal Diseases in Nairobi; he had been to see the gorillas that day with a group of scientists; they had had an exciting time. Everybody in the hotel was excited about visiting the gorillas. In the bar people talked of nothing else.

I walked through Ruhengeri in the afternoon, a little town ringed by five volcanoes. A single paved street, ramshackle shops in bright colors. A taxi, filled to standing with women singing African songs, rumbled past. Young kids tried to sell me Impala cigarettes in plastic sacks.

Nicole explained about the gorillas of Rwanda. Her husband, Alain, worked with the Park Service and had been instrumental in setting up the program. The story was this:

The Parc des Volcans, on the border of Rwanda and Zaire, represented a large land area for that tiny country. The rich green mountain slopes were increasingly coveted by Rwanda's expanding population, which had grown five hundred percent since World War II. Some years ago, under this pressure, a large section of the park had indeed been turned over to farmland. There were incessant calls to release the rest, but conservationists inside Rwanda had three reasons to resist the pressure.

The first was that making parkland available would do little to ease the population pressure in the long run. After all, each year twenty-three thousand additional families required farmland. If all the land in the park were released, it would provide farmland for only thirty-six weeks of population growth.

The second was that the land on the mountain slopes served as a water catchment area. The spongy volcanic soil held rainwater and released it gradually during Rwanda's two dry seasons. If the slopes were cultivated, the runoff

257

would be immediate, and surrounding farms would suffer immeasurably.

The third reason was that the park, and the adjacent parkland in Zaire, provided the only remaining habitat for the magnificent mountain gorilla. If that land was taken away, the mountain gorilla was doomed to extinction.

To keep the Parc des Volcans intact, conservationists in 1979 decided to make it self-supporting and even profitable. To do that, they habituated three groups of gorillas to human contact. Over a period of years, they made these gorillas, in essence, tourist attractions.

Some years before, the American researcher Dian Fossey had learned that it was possible to approach wild gorilla troops closely. Fossey was able, after many years of patient work, actually to sit amid a troop, watching behavior and taking notes.

Now Fossey was gone, expelled from the country by the government. (This was some years before she returned, and was murdered.) Her original troop, group 5, was reserved for ongoing research by scientists living at Karisimbi Research Station, located between the volcanoes. But other workers employed her techniques over a period of years to habituate three troops, designated 13, 11, and 8, to daily visits by human beings.

The procedure had become routine. If you wanted to see gorillas, you made arrangements well in advance (now several years in advance), and then joined one of the groups of four or six people who would be taken that day to see a gorilla troop.

In the morning, we went to the park station at nine thousand feet on the slopes of Mount Sabinyo. From here we would begin to look for gorillas. Each tourist group had a guide and a tracker; we would be taken first to where the gorillas had last been seen the day before; the tracker would follow the gorillas' trail on the volcanic slopes until we caught up with the troop. We would then follow the gorilla troop until they paused for their midday rest, when they were quiet and usually allowed people to approach closely.

Sometimes tourists found the gorillas in a few minutes; sometimes it took as long as five hours to find them. We were told to be prepared for several hours' hard climbing; that we should wear gloves to protect against the stinging nettles; and that, once among the gorillas, we should stay silent and low, always being sure to keep our heads below the level of the dominant male. We were also told that if the gorillas charged we were to stand our ground, be silent, and *not move*.

With that we set off.

A gorilla trail is fairly easy to follow. There is not only the characteristic three-lobed spoor, but also a great many broken-down branches. In places, it looked as if a jeep convoy had recently passed through.

This should have given me a clue of what was to come. Yet my first view of a gorilla—a silverback male, glimpsed through a stand of bamboo—was shocking. The animal was huge. He appeared so large, I thought I was experiencing an optical illusion caused by the intervening bamboo. He didn't look like a gorilla, he looked like a hippopotamus.

Mountain gorillas are *big*.

Mark, our guide, nodded. By now we were speaking in whispers. "Yes, they are big," he said. "In zoos you see lowland gorillas, the other subspecies. Mountain gorillas are substantially larger. That fellow there is four hundred pounds."

That fellow there was now moving away, through the bamboo. For a hippopotamus-sized creature he was quick. We humans gasped and panted to keep him in sight. Gorillas move with a characteristic loping gait, balancing on stiff forearms, with their hands curled under so they rest on their knuckles. That is genetically determined behavior, but, looking around, I saw we humans were moving exactly the same way. The low bamboo forest forces you to bend to hands and knees, and the stinging nettles on the ground make you close your sensitive palms, and absorb the pain on your knuckles.

It was odd to see: the gorillas moving like gorillas, and the people in pursuit, also moving like gorillas. Except, of course, the people were awkward, particularly when we moved fast. It's hard to jog on your hands and knees.

Soon we observed more animals, in brief, tantalizing glimpses. An adult female, then a juvenile male. This particular troop, group 13, was wary; Mark, who studied the troop, explained there was an elephant in its territory, and the silverback male was jumpy.

For an hour we followed the gorillas at a near trot through the bamboo. Most of the time we could not see them, but we could hear them crashing through the underbrush. Sometimes they were very close, but we were never able to see them well.

Finally the gorillas stopped for their midday rest. The big male rolled over on his back and lazily chomped bamboo. He was perhaps ten yards away. I was frustrated: I wanted to take his picture, but he was low in the brush. For a while, all we saw was a huge hand rising up, grabbing the bamboo, and descending again out of sight. Occasionally he would raise his massive head, look at us, and then lie back again. I busied myself with cameras and lenses, trying to get ready for a coming opportunity to film him. Changing lenses, adjusting f-stop . . .

What happened next was extraordinarily fast. There was a deafening roar, a sound as loud as a subway rushing into a station. I looked up to see the huge male charging directly at me. He was moving incredibly swiftly, bellowing with rage. He was coming right at me.

I moaned and ducked down, pushing my face into the underbrush, backing off. A strong arm gripped my shirt at the shoulders. *This is it.* There had been cases where the gorillas attacked people. Picked them up and bit them and threw them around like a dishrag. Months in the hospital. Now the gorilla was grabbing me. . . .

But it was Mark, holding me down. Keeping me from running away. He whispered fiercely, *"Don't move!"*

My face was buried in the grass. My heart was pounding. I didn't dare look up. The gorilla was right in front of me. I could hear him snorting, feel the earth shake as he stomped around. I felt him back away. I heard a rhythmic ripping sound, off to the right.

Mark whispered, "You can look up slowly. He's tearing grass."

I didn't look up. I didn't move. And a good thing, because the gorilla roared again. He beat his chest, a hollow sound.

"You can look up," Mark whispered. "It's okay."

I didn't look up. I didn't move. I waited, and finally I heard the crashing sound as the gorilla moved away. Then I looked up.

I saw the big male drop down into the grass again. I saw the big hand reach up for bamboo and pull it down.

"He was just reminding us who's boss," Mark said.

I understood that. No question.

"Why did he attack?"

He shrugged. "Something about you he didn't like. Probably too much movement with the camera."

Then he proceeded to give me a lecture about not moving when a gorilla attacked.

The thing was, I knew all about how to behave during a gorilla attack. I had studied gorillas, read all the books. But somehow I hadn't understood, from the books, how fearsome a gorilla charge could be. The noise, the speed of the charge, and the size of the animal were incredibly intimidating. To stand your ground in the face of a gorilla charge was like standing your ground in the face of an onrushing express train, somehow trusting that it would stop before it hit you. It required incredible courage.

Or perhaps just experience. We were charged a couple of other times in the course of the two days, and it was never as terrifying as that first time.

On the second day, I went with Nicole and Rosalind Aveling, a naturalist at the park, to see group II. When we arrived, we found the gorillas in a kind of cul-de-sac of foliage. There were fourteen animals in the immediate area, juveniles here and there, young ones crashing through the branches overhead, and the big male in the center.

We approached cautiously. The big male watched us come. Finally he moved. We all froze.

The male went up to the guide. He raised his massive hand to deliver a blow and swung it down at the guide, who did not move a muscle. At the last moment, the gorilla checked his swing, and lightly tapped the guide on the side of the head. A little tap. Playful.

Then he went over to the tracker, who was wearing a baseball cap. He took the cap, inspected it, sniffed it, and carefully put it back on the tracker's head. Then he moved back a few paces

I whispered to Rosalind, "That's amazing."

"Oh," she said, "he always does that. That's his greeting. You see, he knows them."

Rosalind explained then that the gorillas quickly learned

to recognize people. That was why the park officials didn't let tourists visit the same troop two days running. On the second day, the gorillas would recognize the visitors and allow them to approach more closely than before. And the park officials didn't want the gorillas to catch visitors' colds.

They recognize you in one day?

Oh sure, Rosalind said. They're very bright. You'll learn to recognize them, too.

I doubted I would learn to recognize them. The gorillas looked pretty much the same to me, except that they were different sizes. As one or another popped out of the underbrush, I couldn't tell if I had seen them before or not.

Meanwhile, the guide and the big male stared at each other, nose to nose. The silverback grunted. The guide grunted back. I had already been advised about this grunting. We were all supposed to grunt, *uh-huh,* from time to time, or in response to the male's grunt. The grunt apparently meant something like "I'm here and everything is fine." In any case, grunting was said to have a calming effect on the gorillas.

I was all for that. Because we were very close to them. Never in my life had I been so close to large wild animals without intervening bars. But nobody had a gun or a weapon of any sort. Our safety lay in the assumption that the gorillas would be friendly. And they seemed to be friendly.

But the point was, we were in their hands. We were in their territory, guests in their house. And apparently it was going to be all right.

I relaxed, and drifted into a feeling of extraordinary enchantment. Never in my life had I experienced anything like this. To be so close to a wild creature of another species, and yet to feel no threat. And slowly I began to recognize the different animals, just as Rosalind had said. The female with the big incisor. The older juvenile male who strutted about, being manly. The young ones, hardly larger than human infants, who charged us and beat their chests and then dashed up into the trees.

I never wanted to leave.

The guide led the other tourists back, and I stayed with Rosalind and Nicole. And as time passed, I began to have an uncanny sense that I understood what was going on. A female began to move toward us, and I thought, *You're getting too close, he won't like that.* And, sure enough, the male looked over and roared, and the female backed off hastily. Overhead, some of the young juveniles played roughly. The silverback grunted loudly; they modified their play. But when the older male came up and glowered at us, the silverback let him do it.

It all made a kind of sense. There were spatial arrangements, invisible but nonetheless distinct boundaries, and the silverback was keeping everybody in his or her place. After a while, he went to sleep. He had one of the infants in his huge palm; the baby fitted entirely in his hand.

I was still trying to deal with my feeling that I understood the troop. We have a tendency to anthropomorphize animals, but in this case it was hard not to do it. In a relaxed setting, the gorillas seemed very akin to us. Nicole was right: they seemed like men. I hadn't expected that. I had been around other great apes, and I had never had such a feeling. A chimpanzee, for instance, presents a visual parody of a human being, but it is a distinctly different animal, and in many ways a vicious, unpleasant one. Orangutans appear gentle and morose, but they don't really seem like human beings. Yet here, among a group of gorillas, creatures that did not look or smell like human beings, I had the distinct sense that we all understood one another. It was overpowering, and sad. When I left them, it was like awakening from a dream.

In 1958, when George Schaller studied mountain gorillas, he estimated their numbers at 525. When I visited Virunga in 1981, it was thought there were about 275. Now it is thought there are 200. No one is sure what the minimum breeding population is, or whether the gorilla numbers have already fallen below it. In any case, their prospects are not good.

When I left the mountain, I said to Nicole, "I understand now what you mean about not wanting to study gorillas because they are like men."

"Yes," she said. "I could not." She paused. "And also because it is too sad."

An Extinct Turtle

It didn't seem like much of an adventure: walking past the McDonald's stand in the Singapore airport, going to the Hertz counter to pick up my rented Datsun for the drive north to a resort hotel in Kuantan, on the east coast of Malaysia.

Nor did it get better driving through Singapore itself, a city that has systematically destroyed every vestige of its own exoticism in a period of ten years. When I first went there, in 1973, Singapore was magical—part modern business center, part sleepy British colony, and everywhere beautiful, hot, green. Wherever you turned, it revealed tantalizing glimpses of its own history, like the barbed wire around the balconies of the colonial houses, reminders of the Japanese occupation. It was a city of distinct quarters: the Indian quarter, the Chinese quarter around the river, the Malay quarter, each with its own feeling, faces, architecture, and smells.

But all that is gone now. Even its innocent pleasures, the vast chili-crab palaces along the coast, have disappeared. Whatever its modern virtues, and they are many, Singapore has chosen to destroy its unique face, and replace it with skyscrapers and giant shopping malls so it looks like everywhere else.

It took an hour to drive north, across the bridge into Malaysia, and then to find the road to the east coast. My feeling of adventure did not increase as I crept behind a long line of diesel-belching trucks. Waiting for the light to change: nothing so ruins a sense of exotic adventure as a traffic light.

Driving up the east coast of Malaysia, I had the feeling of visiting someplace that had once been remote but was no longer. A succession of drab little towns on the water, a mangrove-swampy coast, a potted but serviceable highway.

The weather turned cold, and rainy, one of the drenching Malaysian rains that you always expect to be tropical but are somehow chilling and cold. I rolled up the windows, turned the wipers up full, and felt isolated in my car, slowly beginning to feel I didn't know where I was. Even after the rain stopped, I felt disoriented.

Kuantan was a big, ugly town—cement factories and Honda truck dealerships. It seemed an unlikely place for a resort hotel, and I didn't see any signs for the Hyatt Kuantan. I drove on.

Night approached. The features of the countryside began to recede into grayness. The road was badly marked, and I did not want to be driving at night. I missed the road for the Hyatt, asked directions at a little roadside restaurant, doubled back, missed it again. This wasn't high adventure, it was mundane frustration. When I finally arrived at the hotel, I saw immediately it was the kind of place that gives Hyatt a bad name. I wished I hadn't come.

But charming guesthouses on the east coast are not easily telexed at short notice, and I had come here in the spring of 1982 for a particular reason—to see the seasonal egg-laying of the giant Malaysian leatherback turtles.

For several months beginning in May, the turtles emerge from the ocean to lay their eggs on the isolated beaches of the east coast. In fact, so remote are the beaches that the turtles were presumed extinct until the 1950s, when they were observed still laying their eggs.

This was all I really knew, but I assumed I would find out more at the location. So as I checked into the hotel, I asked the receptionist.

"I've come to see the turtles."

"Yes? We have no turtles at the hotel."

"The giant turtles that lay their eggs?"

"Yes. They are not here."

"But on the coast?"

"I don't know. Perhaps farther north. You will have to ask."

"Whom should I ask?"

"Ask the tourist desk in the morning. But I think it is the wrong time."

"It does not begin in May?"

"I don't know. I think there are no turtles, it is the wrong time."

A negative person, I thought, and uninformed as well. The hotel should think twice about having such a person behind the reception desk. After all, the turtles must be a great attraction in this region; a hotel person would logically be expected to know about them.

But in subsequent days I became discouraged. Nobody seemed to know about the turtles. They knew about the windsurfers. They knew about the jungle tours. They knew about the native dance excursions. But no one knew about the turtles. I went into Kuantan town and found the local tourist office. It was closed. They said the woman who ran it was in Kuala Lumpur and would be back in a week.

Finally, one day, as I was arranging for a windsurfer, one of the men who worked at the beach shack said casually, "They saw turtles yesterday."

"Who did?"

"Chinese people."

"Where did they see them?"

He named a hotel.

"Where is that?"

"Up the coast. Fifty kilometers."

"And they saw turtles last night?"

"About two a.m. Three turtles," he said, nodding. "Big ones. Two hundred kilos."

I told him I wanted to see these turtles.

"Yes, why not? It is the season."

"Well, I haven't been able to arrange it."

"No one can arrange it. The turtles do as they please."

"What do I do to see them?"

"Go up to the hotel. They have turtles there."

"Every night?"

266

"No, not every night. You can call first before you drive up."

I called the hotel. Yes, they had seen turtles. They had seen them three of the last four nights. Yes, I could call later on and they would tell me if they were seeing turtles.

I called around ten that night. The woman said they had not seen turtles yet; it was too early in the season.

I called at midnight. No one answered the phone.

I drove up anyway.

On the way, it started to rain. Fifty kilometers to the north, I pulled into a modern hotel, gray concrete structures, grassy lawns. The rain was coming down hard. There was a beach directly ahead. I got out of the car and walked to the beach. There was no one there, and nothing to see. The rain slashed down heavily.

A man came up in the darkness. "Why are you here?"

"I came to see turtles."

"No turtles tonight."

"But I thought—"

"No turtles."

I went home.

I called the following night. The hotel said they had seen many turtles last night, but none so far tonight.

At midnight, I called again. A man said they had seen a turtle. It was on the beach nearby. How long would it be there? I asked. Many hours, he said.

I drove up.

There was again nobody around the hotel. The lobby was deserted. I pushed the buzzer for the manager. Nobody came. I walked out onto the beach. It was a beautiful night, a full moon, fleecy clouds, warm air. I saw nobody on the beach, which extended away for miles in every direction.

Pretty soon a young boy on a motor scooter buzzed down the beach, near the water. I watched him go, the sound fading. About ten minutes later he came back.

"Turtles?" he called to me softly in the darkness. He might have been a drug dealer.

"Yes," I said.

"I am looking for them. I find them, I take you there."

"Good. Thank you."

"You have seen them?"

"No, never."

"You have not seen the one?"

"Where?"

"Close. By the tree." He pointed.

There were trees at the edge of the beach, casting shadows in the moonlight. Beneath one I saw a shape in the sand. I went over and clicked on my flashlight.

The turtle was enormous, the size of a desk. She was facing the ocean. With her flippers she had dug a pit of sand perhaps three feet deep. Now she was laying her translucent, slippery, soft eggs in the pit. Her magnificent head moved slowly back and forth. A tear came to her eyes.

The turtle must have weighed three hundred pounds, perhaps more. To crawl a hundred yards up the beach, dig a pit with her clumsy flippers, and lay her eggs had required an enormous effort. She had an exhausted, dazed look on her face. There were more tears, but these were apparently excretions from the eyes and not true tears. I watched the turtle with astonishment, amazed by the effort, the ancient ritual that led her to do this each year. I was quite content to stay there all night.

There was a commotion to one side. A dozen people, Chinese and Malays, came up the beach. They had heard about the turtle. They brought powerful lights, which they shone on the animal. I began to feel uncomfortable. There were now a lot of people standing around this turtle while she laid her eggs.

The others began to fire flashbulbs, taking pictures of the turtle. They got very close to her face and fired flash after flash. Finally the father of the Chinese family said something to his son, and the boy climbed on the turtle's back while his father flashed another picture. Pretty soon his whole family was posed astride the turtle, as she moved her hind flippers ineffectually.

Finally she managed to flick sand into the face of one of the young children standing nearby. The child began to cry in the darkness. The Malays yelled at the turtle and cursed it. The Chinese took more flash pictures in rapid succession. One of the Chinese men posed near the turtle's head, holding a bottle of beer to the turtle, as if to offer it a drink. Flash. Laughter.

The boy on the motor scooter zoomed up, parked his bike. The other people fell silent. I wondered if he was an official of some sort, but when he stepped into the light I saw he was only ten or eleven. He spoke quietly, apparently telling them about the turtle. From his gestures, it seemed he was explaining what the turtle was doing. He pointed out her tracks, all the way up the beach. How she had laboriously turned around to face back to the ocean. How long she had worked to dig her pit. How much effort it was costing her to lay her eggs. And, after she laid her eggs, how many hours she would lie here, exhausted, trying to find the strength to struggle back toward the water, to return to the surf by daybreak.

They listened in silence. The young Chinese boy got off the turtle's back. The child stopped crying, and was encouraged to touch the turtle's shell, to make peace with the great creature. The entire atmosphere became more respectful. They stepped back from the pit. I thought, They only needed to understand what was happening to this creature. They could not imagine without being told, but once they were told, they became sympathetic and understanding.

Finally they drifted away. I sat there. The boy sat near me in the darkness.

"English?"

"American."

"Ah, American. Rono Reagan."

"Yes."

He pointed to the departing people. "They go now. They see the turtle and they go."

"What did you tell them?" I asked.

"They say, want to buy eggs," he said. "I tell them where to buy eggs, they leave now."

"They will go and buy eggs?"

"No."

"Why?"

"I tell them about the turtle, about the eggs. They listen."

"Ah."

"And I tell them the cost for eggs. The woman say too much. I think they will not buy."

"No?"

He shook his head. "No."

The turtle remained in the pit, moving a flipper occasionally. After an hour, another group of people arrived. There were more flashbulbs, more poses. I went home.

Cactus Teachings

In the fall of 1982 I attended Brugh Joy's conference in the Lucerne Valley desert, in California. Brugh Joy was an eminent Los Angeles physician who had, through intensive meditation, moved progressively away from medicine into areas of personal growth, psychic healing, and so on. For several years he had run two-week conferences in which he shared his findings.

To me this seemed like the first appropriate opportunity to do something in an area of interest which I had had since 1973. After all, when you read a book by Ram Dass, you could see he was always doing something new: living in a Zen monastery, doing breathing exercises, fasting, staying with his guru in India. You had the impression that he was trying many different kinds of experiences.

I had only read about such experiences; I hadn't actually had any of my own. For ten years I had done nothing except read. And ten years is a long time to maintain an interest at arm's length. I was beginning to wonder if my interest was genuine, or if I was just making excuses.

It was with relief that I learned that Brugh Joy, a somber medical man, trained at Johns Hopkins and the Mayo Clinic, had taken his own spiritual journey and now was helping others. His conference seemed the ideal starting place for me.

The conference was held at the Institute of Mentalphysics, in Lucerne Valley. The institute buildings, designed by Frank Lloyd Wright, must have been advanced for their time but now looked distinctly eccentric. The science of mentalphysics ("The Faultless Philosophy of Life") was founded by Edwin J. Dingle, who had been to Tibet in the 1920s. There were faded photos of Tibetan holy men, and Art Deco posters showing the right way to avoid constipation and other health problems. Thus the institute displayed all the hallmarks of California-oddball spiritualism, with the added disadvantage of being out of date.

Brugh Joy turned out to be a pale, slender man in his forties. He drove an old Cadillac, wore jeans and a casual sport shirt. He was gentle, softspoken, and noticeably reserved.

Forty other people attended the seminar. I was reassured to see a large number of buttoned-down professional types, including many physicians and psychologists.

At our first dinner, on Sunday, Brugh announced the rules for the next two weeks. No telephone calls in or out. No leaving the grounds: if we needed anything, someone would go into town and get it for us. No sex, and no drugs. There would be daily group sessions, but he didn't care if we attended them; we would get the benefit of the sessions whether we attended or not.

He said we could either sleep in our rooms or in the desert. He talked about rattlesnakes, and said that nobody had ever been bitten by a snake during his conferences but that if we insisted on being the first, this is how we should behave. . . .

Implicit in his talk was the idea that soon we would all be wandering around in different states of consciousness. I wasn't sure what that meant, but it sounded interesting.

The conference followed a daily routine. There was silence every morning from six-thirty until eight, when we met for breakfast. Meditation during this time was encouraged but not required.

At nine we met in a large conference room. We began by

271

lying on the floor on pillows. Brugh would play loud music from huge speakers for about half an hour. The intensity and vibration made the experience very powerful; people would have waking dreams, and often cry. Afterward we would sit in a circle, hold hands for a moment, and discuss our dreams. Then Brugh would give an informal lecture, and we would break for lunch at twelve-thirty.

In the afternoons we met in small groups, or hiked, or sat around the swimming pool, or slept.

Dinner was at six, followed by an evening session, which again started with music. The evening session continued until ten o'clock, and then we broke for the night.

Brugh played all sorts of music—classical music, electronic music, popular music. Brahms's First Symphony, the soundtrack from *Chariots of Fire,* the *William Tell* Overture, the music from *West Side Story.* You never knew what you were going to hear.

Meals tended to be light and nearly vegetarian. Just when you got used to that, you'd get Southern fried chicken and corn on the cob, or roast beef and mashed potatoes.

Brugh generally lectured, but sometimes he broke up the group to do exercises. One day he passed out notebooks and boxes of colored pens, and said we should draw pictures or write—whichever we were least comfortable doing.

Then, in the middle of the conference, he announced we would have two days of fasting and silence.

Soon it became clear to me that the sense of routine was illusory. Brugh was carefully orchestrating events so that, in a gentle way, you were constantly kept off balance. You didn't know what to expect. You didn't know what was going to happen next.

Early on, he said he wanted us to walk in the desert until we found a rock or a tree or a plant that seemed to have a special relationship to us, and then to spend time with this "teacher," and talk with the teacher, and learn what the teacher had to teach us.

I had read about such practices, using an inanimate object as a meditative or spiritual teacher. Why not? I was here, I might as well go along with the program.

So I set out to find my teacher.

Brugh had said the teacher would make itself known; all you had to do was be receptive. I looked at every rock and bush and Joshua tree in the desert, wondering if it was the teacher.

I had a romantic view of all this. I imagined myself sitting out in the desert for hours, communing with my teacher in splendid solitude. But nothing in the desert seemed compelling to me. Instead I had the persistent feeling that my teacher wasn't out in the desert at all, but within the institute. I didn't like this idea. I wanted a teacher far off. A teacher near these Frank Lloyd Wright buildings just didn't suit me at all.

There was a small meditation room located in one corner of the institute grounds. In front of this meditation room was a rock garden of boulders and many kinds of cacti. And one particular cactus, right at the edge of the pavement, where the rock garden began, caught my eye whenever I passed by.

And kept catching my eye.

This made me unhappy. The rock garden was artificial, a contrived version of nature. It was bad enough that my teacher might be on the institute grounds—but to be in this artificial garden was adding insult to injury. Furthermore, I didn't like this cactus. It was common, a sort of phallic cactus shape with lots of thorns. It was rather battered, with scars on one side. It was not in any way an attractive cactus.

But I kept staring at it. And meanwhile the days were going by, other people were finding their teachers, and I still hadn't settled on mine. I was feeling some pressure. I was feeling like a lazy student. I was falling behind.

One morning I was walking to the meditation room and I passed the cactus and I thought, Well, if this cactus is really my teacher, it'll speak to me.

And the cactus said, "When are you going to stop running around and talk?" Irritably. Like a grouchy old man.

I didn't hear it as an actual voice, I just felt it like an impression. The way you can see someone and get an impression of what is going on with him or her. But I was startled to get a sense of personality coming from a cactus.

It was early in the morning. Nobody else was around. So I said out loud, "Are you my teacher?"

No answer.

"Will you talk to me?" I said. I was really looking around now, making sure nobody could see me standing there talking to a cactus.

The cactus did not answer.

273

"Why won't you talk to me?"

No answer.

It was just a cactus, sitting there. Of course it didn't answer—it was a cactus. I thought, I am talking out loud to a cactus, which is bad enough. But, worse, I am feeling annoyed that it won't answer. This is definitely crazy behavior. They lock people up for this.

Yet at the same time I had the feeling that the cactus was sulking. Its feelings were hurt, or else it was just being hard to get along with.

"I'll come back and talk to you later."

No answer.

I came back and talked to the cactus later. Again there was no one around. I sat for an hour with the cactus, and talked to it. The cactus never said a single word in reply. I felt self-conscious and foolish. Of course, it would have been pretty alarming if the cactus had actually spoken. But from the standpoint of a person engaged in a spiritual exercise that involved projecting one's thoughts onto an inanimate object, I wasn't doing very well if I couldn't imagine any responses from the inanimate object. I was a poor student of metaphysics, with poor concentration, poor ability to imagine. I berated myself. I suspected other people were having wonderful, informative chats with their rocks and shrubs.

However, I felt increasingly convinced that this cactus was my teacher. Challenging and annoying and silent, but my teacher.

I decided to draw the cactus, because drawing something makes you pay close attention to it. Also, I wouldn't feel so self-conscious if someone came across me while I was sitting there drawing the cactus. I drew the cactus a dozen times. It was very revealing.

The cactus was at the edge of civilization. The cactus was positioned where the pavement stopped, like a sort of sentry. The cactus had been transplanted from a natural setting to a manmade garden, making it somewhat on display its entire life. A kind of showpiece, despite its own personal preferences. The cactus had a crew cut of thorns, giving it a military appearance. This cactus had had a rough life, and had been injured when young; one side of it was scarred and atrophied. You could see where the injury had occurred in earlier growth, and had twisted the growing cactus permanently. The thorns were especially dense and protective over the injured area. The only part of the cactus that was growing was the green tip. The rest was just supporting history. The cactus had equanimity; ants ran over its surface, and it didn't seem to mind. It was certainly attractive, with red thorns and a green body; bees were attracted to it. The cactus had a formal aspect; its pattern of thorns gave it almost a herringbone look. This was an Ivy League cactus. I saw it as dignified, silent, stoic, and out of place.

I drew it again and again.

One day, as I arrived with my notebook and pens, the cactus said, "Where have you been?" In that same irritable, resentful tone.

I was surprised. It hadn't spoken since the first day. And this time I really felt as if it had spoken aloud.

I said to the cactus, "What do you care? You haven't said one word to me; why should I hang around all day in the hot sun waiting for you to say something?" Because I was defensive. I felt I had been criticized.

The cactus didn't reply.

Immediately I regretted my words. Boy, I thought, now I've blown it. After days and days of waiting, the cactus finally speaks and I immediately attack it because I feel defensive, and now it won't talk any more. My one chance, and I blew it.

"I'm sorry I yelled at you."

No answer from the cactus.

I wasn't going to ask it to forgive me. That was too much, for a grown man to ask a cactus for forgiveness. On the other hand, maybe if I did it would speak again. I really wanted to know what it had to say.

"Will you forgive me?"

No answer. Hardball from the cactus.

Well, maybe it would reveal something more in drawings. So I drew it again. And today I seemed able to see the injury to the cactus particularly clearly. I felt that the injury had been caused by a person who had scraped the cactus in passing—a preoccupied person who wasn't watching where he was going. A person who had cursed the cactus when he got a few thorns for his mistake. But the cactus had been hurt far more than the passer-by.

I noticed that the cactus had experienced a twisted development for several years following this injury, but that afterward it had grown straight above the injury, and perhaps a little stronger for its tribulation. I thought the injury had toughened the cactus. Made it a better cactus.

I also thought that, although the cactus had recovered physically, it was still psychologically defensive and guarded. I thought the cactus tended to be judgmental. The fact that the cactus would attract me and then refuse to speak suggested that he might be a little hysterical. The cactus had not allowed his mental development to catch up to his physical development.

A roadrunner came by and hung around me while I was drawing the cactus. He was a comical bird, and his presence made me feel good. Even if the cactus still refused to talk.

From then on, whenever I visited the cactus, I had a funny dissociated attitude. On the one hand, I could not escape the sense that I was projecting onto the cactus. An Ivy League cactus! Who was I kidding? But, on the other hand, I was having an interesting time seeing this cactus as separate from me. And certainly I was attracted to it again and again.

Brugh had warned us that a great deal of projection would take place among members of the group, since we didn't know one another. We should be alert to what we felt about other people, what we liked and didn't like, because those feelings were likely to be our own projection and we should "own" them.

Often, in the afternoons, a group of us would walk in the desert. On the first day, we were walking along and a woman said to me, "Are you angry?"

"No," I said.

"I feel you're very angry."

"Well, I'm not." I was actually having a really nice time and was in the best of moods. I thought, Projection. Interesting. She's evidently an angry woman; I'll have to keep an eye on her.

Brugh was particularly interested in what he termed "energy work." He had discovered, by meditation and medical experience, that there was a kind of energy in the human body, unknown to medical science. This energy tended to be focused in spots located on the body. He had mapped these spots, and later discovered that they corresponded roughly to the chakras of Indian Yogic belief.

I knew something about chakras. In Tantric Yoga, for example, it was thought that the vital force, or prana, was distributed through the body along seven junction points, or chakras. These chakras located in the midline of the body. The first two chakras were located in the groin; the third, in the solar plexus, beneath the ribs; the fourth, over the heart; the fifth, on the throat; the sixth, at the forehead; and the seventh, at the top of the head.

The chakras were thought to bridge the everyday physical body and the astral body of emotions and feelings. Each chakra had a characteristic color, and a characteristic function. The first two chakras were concerned with primitive survival and sexuality. The third chakra involved the sense of worldly self—a very highly developed chakra in the West. The fourth, or heart, chakra was the source of unconditional love; the fifth, or throat, chakra was concerned with creativity; the sixth, or "third eye," with bodily secretions, intellect, and the higher self; and the seventh, or crown, chakra with cosmic consciousness.

Sensitive people were said to be able to see these chakras, generally perceiving them as swirling spots of colored light. Each of these chakras could be "awakened." The energy flowing between the chakras could be "balanced." And there was a very dramatic form of energy, called Kundalini energy, that sometimes aroused and alarmed people when they awakened their chakras.

All this, and a great deal more, was believed about the chakras.

Of course, the Yogic concept of a body energy following specific pathways over the body was not so different from the Chinese concept of *qui* energy in being distributed along acupuncture meridians. And I was aware that acupuncture worked. But I did not believe that because acupuncture worked its theoretical framework was therefore correct.

And I had always regarded chakras as a sort of metaphysical delusion. Of course, it might be helpful to think of the breath as drawing in the life force, which was then distributed through the body along a series of energy points. That might make metaphorical sense, as an aid to meditation, a way to visualize what was going on. But I didn't consider chakras real in the same way as the heart and arteries and nerves were real.

Yet here was a physician saying that chakras were absolutely real, and that there were many other energy points on the body as well—over the spleen, the nipples, the knees and toes, and so on. That this energy could be felt by anybody, easily. That it could be seen as well. That disturbances in health could appear as disturbances of this body energy. That body energy was a tremendous force for healing. That the energy could be transferred from one person to another, by touching, or laying on hands.

Brugh believed all this.

I was unconvinced, to say the least.

To begin, Brugh announced that he would do energy work on each of us. He did the seminar in two groups. Since I was in the afternoon group, I could watch what happened to the morning group.

Soft music played. The people receiving energy lay on massage tables. Brugh's assistants, who had been to the conference before, touched the people on the tables in ways that were supposed to activate their chakras and balance their body energy. Then Brugh walked from table to table, spending about five minutes at each. He held his hands over different parts of people's bodies, and then moved on. After he had finished, the people lay on the tables for a while, covered with blankets. Eventually they would get up and leave the room.

That was all there was to it.

It was incredibly undramatic.

I had anticipated some violence, some tension and shaking and wrenching, the way faith healers worked on television. But Brugh just quietly moved from one person to the next. And the individuals receiving the energy didn't gasp or jump. They just lay there on the tables. So there wasn't much to see, to observe, about this energy work.

The only thing I noticed was that the atmosphere in the room got thick. Sitting in that room was like sitting at the bottom of a jar of honey. You felt immersed in something dense and thick. It was very peaceful and pleasant to be there.

Nobody was supposed to talk about his or her experience, so I didn't know what happened to the first group. They walked around and smiled, and I noticed that they tended to disappear from the group after the energy work. But I couldn't tell anything in particular.

My turn came in the afternoon.

I lay on the table while the assistants worked on my body. What I noticed was that they would touch a limb at, say, the knee and the ankle, and for a while it just felt like somebody had placed a hand on your knee and your ankle. Then, after a minute or two, a sensation of warmth would suddenly spread up and down my lower leg. As soon as that happened, the assistants would go on to another part of the body—say, the knee and the hip—and wait until the warmth occurred again. Sometimes this spreading warmth was accompanied by a little twitch in the limb, but usually not. In any case, the assistants seemed able to tell when the warmth began, because they immediately moved to another part of my body. As more and more of my body was treated in this way, I drifted into a deep relaxation close to sleep.

I was vaguely aware of Brugh standing over me. He held his hands a few inches from my body, and they were noticeably hot. It was exactly as if somebody were holding a hot iron over my body. I was surprised at first by the intensity of it, but in my relaxed condition, I couldn't really pay attention. It was all as if I were dreaming. I drifted off to sleep.

After a while someone touched my shoulder and whispered that I was finished, and I could leave if I wanted to. It was dinnertime. I got off the table and walked outside.

There were oleanders in bloom, explosions of oleanders along the path. The sun was setting on the red mountains. Everything was glowing and alive and vivid. I wandered through the oleanders and came upon a little playground. I'd been at the institute for nearly a week, and this playground was right by the path, but I'd never noticed it before. I sat on a swing and rocked back and forth. I felt incredibly benign.

I got lost on my way to the dining room. When I arrived, I discovered I was not hungry, but it was nice to look at the food. Everything looked nice. I could stare at a cut strawberry for an hour, noticing the patterns, the colors. Or bread—a slice of bread was fascinating to look at. Everybody looked wonderful, too, even though I didn't want to talk. My sensations were too immediate, too compelling, to be reduced to conversation.

I became aware of my glasses, artificial frames that stood between me and the world, so I took my glasses off. I could see all right without them, and I was much happier to be rid of this barrier.

Then it began to dawn on me, what all this was: *Bothered by his glasses. Doesn't want to talk. Not hungry but likes to look at food. Gets lost in familiar surroundings. Discovers new things under his nose. Finds the world extremely vivid.*

I was demonstrating all the characteristics of a psychedelic experience, but I hadn't taken any drug. This vivid feeling lasted for two days, and slowly faded.

A few people began to have mystical experiences. The news flashed around the dining-room table. So-and-so had had a vision. So-and-so had heard voices. Inevitably, all this took on a competitive aspect. Brugh himself had said that we were all on our own paths, and that we should not compare our experiences. But we did. At least, I did.

How could I help it? I had come here to have some mystical experiences, and all around me other people were having very dramatic experiences—Joan of Arc–type experiences—and I wasn't. I was just pretending to have an occasional line of dialogue with a cactus. That was the extent of it.

I was jealous. Let's face it, to have a mystical experience is a sign of favor from God. Everybody knows that. And I wasn't getting any favors. It really made me feel bad.

One night, during a coffee break in the cafeteria, when we were having coffee and fig newtons, a psychiatrist named Judith said, "During the session tonight, I could see everybody's aura."

"Is that right?" I said, backing away from her slightly. One more person having a mystical experience. A psychiatrist seeing auras.

"Yes," Judith said. She was smiling and happy. "Have you seen anything like that?"

"No," I said, miserable. "What did they look like?"

"All different colors. Mostly yellow and white. I can still see them."

"Now?" I said. "Here in the cafeteria?"

"Yes. I see everybody's aura. Sarah's is yellow and pink," she said, nodding to a woman next to us.

"Yellow and pink. How far out does it go?" I said.

"About a foot from her head."

I held my hand over Sarah's head. "This far out?"

"No, not so far."

I moved my hand down toward Sarah's head, slowly.
And suddenly I felt warmth. Surprised, I stopped my hand.

"There," Judith said. "Right there."

I could feel it.

I ran my hand over Sarah's head. I could feel a distinct
contour of warmth. It was as if she had an invisible warm
Afro that extended out about a foot beyond her hair. I ran
my hand along this contour. I felt a sort of lump on the left
side.

"The aura goes out further on the left side," Judith said,
nodding. "Like a bump. Yes."

I went around the room, feeling above people's heads.
The minute my hand felt the invisible warm contour, Judith
would say, "There." We repeated it again and again, with
different people.

I was terrifically excited, like a kid with a new toy, a new
discovery. I didn't think about it, I just kept doing it.

Then I began to wonder: what does this mean? What am
I feeling when I lower my hand? Am I actually feeling an
aura? Is there such a thing as an aura? Because I thought
auras were metaphysical delusions, too.

I got a little paranoid. Perhaps Judith was taking a visual
cue from me, saying "there" when she saw my hand stop.
So the next time I stopped my hand above the warmth.

"Come on," Judith said. "It's not out there."

I lowered my hand until I felt the warmth.

"There."

And suddenly I was panicked. I thought, This can't be
happening. I have no explanation for this.

It was impossible, but it was happening anyway. I didn't
know what to do with my experience. I didn't think I was
crazy. I could feel this warm contour, just as distinctly as
you can feel hot bathwater when you put your hand into it.
You know when your hand is in bathwater and when it's
not. There's no mistaking it. It's a physical phenomenon.
Your hand will get warm and wet, even if you don't believe
in bathwater.

What I felt now was every bit as clear and unambiguous.
But I had no idea what it was. I was frantic to explain
it. Yet I knew I couldn't explain it. So I just gave up. It was
a reproducible phenomenon that I couldn't explain; as far
as I knew, *nobody* could explain it; but it was real, anyway.
And if I had had a psychotic break sometime after dinner,

did I believe that Judith had had one, too, so that we now agreed on phenomena that weren't really there?

No, no. It was real, all right.

Something cracked in my way of looking at things. I had to accept this experience, so I did. I thought, Maybe I'll figure it out later. Meantime, I just would have to live with it.

Walking in the desert during the afternoons, two more people, on two separate occasions, asked me if I was angry or upset. I couldn't understand why. Nobody ever asked me if I was angry at other times, just walking in the desert. So if these people were projecting onto me, they were doing it in a pretty odd way. What was going on?

The conference continued. We were assigned meditative exercises. One was to send unconditional love and forgiveness to everyone in your life whom you hadn't forgiven. We were to envision the people standing before us, and then send love and forgiveness, and release them.

I discovered I had a long list of people to forgive. It was startling, how long the list was. I was also startled to see who I could envision and forgive quickly, and who was hard to visualize, hard to forgive. My mind would wander when I tried to forgive these difficult cases.

I took days to work through my list. Everybody else had gone on to other things, and I was still forgiving people. I thought, What a cluttered life I have, carrying all these grudges around with me. It was a relief to get rid of my old animosities, but it was often accompanied by deep sadness.

After I discovered I could feel auras, I relaxed a little about having mystical experiences. And then I had more experiences, although none turned out the way I imagined.

For example, I heard voices.

One hot afternoon I was sitting in the meditation room. There were a couple of experienced meditators there, people who immediately dropped into the lotus position and looked peaceful and serene. I hadn't meditated much before, and I found the positions uncomfortable. I kept shifting around. It was hard for me.

282

Suddenly I heard a booming voice. It seemed to be inside my head, vibrating the bones of my skull, and also inside the room, like a great loudspeaker. The voice was full and resonant and echoing like the voice of God.

The voice said, "Jill St. John!"

I snapped my eyes open. I was sure everybody else in the room must have heard it, too. But the others were all sitting in the lotus position, peaceful, not moving.

Nobody had heard the voice but me.

What could the voice mean? I had met Jill St. John once but I didn't know her, and hearing her name didn't suggest anything in particular to me. It wasn't as if the voice had said, "Go west, young man!" or "Write your congressman!" or something that you could do anything about.

So I thought, Boy, I heard a voice, but now I can't tell anybody, because it said this mundane thing, it said "Jill St. John!" But I was so excited to have heard a voice at all, I told people anyway.

"You know, I heard a voice today."

"Really?"

"Yes. It was big and booming and seemed to fill the universe."

"That's great. What did it say?"

"Uh, it's personal."

I wanted a vision, too. I mean, why not have the whole thing of a desert retreat, voices and visions? I was greedy for spiritual experiences. I wanted more.

But no vision came to me. I sat out in the desert and observed a lot of heat-convection waves and mirages, but no vision.

One day, at lunch, we were talking about the fact that, whenever we did energy work, Brugh always insisted that we begin by imagining a protective cocoon or shield around ourselves, to protect us from any harmful aspects of the work. I wondered if this ritual shielding was really important.

Eileen, a woman from Alaska who had done a lot of energy work, said, "Sure, it's important."

"It is?"

"Sure. All that stuff is important. It's just like fluffing your aura."

"What do you mean, fluffing your aura?"

283

"Haven't you ever fluffed your aura?" Eileen said, surprised.

"No."

"But you know how it's done. . . ."

"I can't begin to imagine."

"Well, you know, you get all the accumulated stuff out of the aura that shouldn't be there, and once it's clean you sort of fluff it up, you know, make it fluffy and nice."

"Oh." I thought this was about as ridiculous as anything could be. I imagined beauty parlors of the future—get your hair and nails done and an aura fluff all for one price. New Age maintenance!

Eileen had to be pulling my leg.

"Here, stand up, I'll do it for you."

"Do I need it?"

She eyed me critically. "Well, it wouldn't hurt."

Just what they always say in beauty parlors!

I stood up in the middle of the cafeteria, and Eileen formed her fingers into claws and raked her hands down my body, about a foot away from my skin. Just as if she were combing invisible fur. At the end of each combing motion, she'd quickly shake her hands clean and comb again. Finally she held her hands palms upward, and made little pushing motions, exactly as if I were covered in cotton wool and she wanted to fluff it up. I watched, fascinated. But already I could feel a difference. It was almost like taking a bath. I felt cleaned up, spruced up . . . fluffed up.

The other people watched and tried to suppress giggles. At the end they said, "Well, Michael, how does it feel to have your aura fluffed?"

"I hate to tell you," I said, "but I notice a difference."

"You don't!"

"I do," I said.

"Of course you do," Eileen said. "Somebody fluffs your aura, of course you'll feel it."

So then all the people in the cafeteria began fluffing their auras. And eventually we stopped making any kind of jokes about body energy.

Midway through the conference, Brugh announced we would have two days of fasting and silence. I had never fasted before, and I was looking forward to the experience. Also, I wanted to stay out in the desert for a while, and I knew if there were meals I would come back for them. I just would.

So two days of fasting and silence sounded liberating to me. And it was: I slept in the desert and stayed out there, and drew pictures. I had a fine time, but I made some surprising discoveries.

The first was that I talked to myself in the desert. I walked along with a constant stream of grunts and curses as I stubbed my toe or scrambled over a rock. No wonder people thought I was angry! Just listen to me swear and groan! I had been entirely unaware that I was doing it. In fact, I found it difficult to stop, and to walk through the desert in silence.

On the second night of fasting, I woke up in the desert in the middle of the night. I looked up at the sky and I saw that all the stars of the Milky Way had been rearranged like skywriting into a single giant word, followed by an exclamation point, that filled the bowl of the sky:

"HI!"

I was finally seeing a vision.

I was excited. I thought, This is great. This means that the universe is looking down at me and saying, HI! It means I am integrated with the universe and All Is One. Fabulous.

I waited for the vision to go away, but it didn't. I looked down at my sleeping bag, then looked back. The sky still said "HI!" I was very pleased with myself. A really nice, stable vision.

Then I thought, The sky only looks like this because of the way I am sleeping. If I were turned around, it wouldn't say that at all. It would say, ¡IH, with an upside-down exclamation point, as in Spanish. That ¡IH seemed to convey indifference, like EH? Who cares? So maybe I was really seeing a vision of cosmic indifference.

With that, I went back to sleep.

The next morning, I left my camp and went off to sketch in the desert. After a few hours, I headed back to camp. I couldn't find the camp. The desert had become absolutely unfamiliar to me. And then I realized I couldn't find the institute, either. I was lost.

I am never lost. My inner sense of geography is good. Yet here I was, alone in the desert, and unable to find my camp or the institute. It took a while for me to realize that with the high mountains at my left shoulder, the institute had to be on my right. I climbed the hills to the right, and saw the institute.

Then where was my camp? I spent another hour looking for my camp. When I finally found it, I saw from my footprints that I had walked all around it for an hour, but hadn't seen it.

Perhaps the fasting was affecting me more than I realized.

Toward the evening, I began to feel filled with tremendous energy. It was almost overwhelming, this tingling, rushing sense of energy. I was restless. I drew pictures in my book and made notes long into the night. Finally, around midnight, I got into bed and lay there for a while, wide awake. I thought, This is ridiculous, I'll never get to sleep. So I got up again and drew for several more hours.

What I recorded while in the grip of this energy seemed terrifically silly. I was preoccupied with cacti, and I recorded all kinds of giddy foolishness in my notebook. I wrote poetry from the viewpoint of a cactus. I wrote cactus philosophy. I also drew designer cactus fashions, a history of cactus religion, Cactus Comics, the Sayings of Chairman Cactus. All profusely illustrated. Page after page of silly stuff. Long into the night.

The next day, I mentioned to somebody that I had experienced all this energy. He questioned me closely about it. Then he said, "I think that was Kundalini energy."

I knew about Kundalini energy. It was a serious, powerful energy occasionally experienced by Yogic adepts, after years of preparatory meditation.

"No, no," I said. "It wasn't the Kundalini energy."

"How do you know?"

"Because I spent all my time drawing Cactus Comics."

People were having a great variety of psychological experiences during the conference. You'd run into people in the desert, or on the paths going to and from the dining room, and sometimes they were happy, but sometimes they were upset or crying about something.

A few people were always the same. One guy was always mad. I began to avoid him, taking another route if I saw him coming down the path, because he was always the same. He was stuck. It wasn't interesting to be around him.

One night Brugh played some music I hated. *Hated.* I thought it was stupid music. I was enraged that I had to

286

listen to it. This music was ridiculous and banal. This music was beneath me. I was steaming when the music was over. I was in a fury.

I complained loudly about the music. I wasn't the only one who thought it was stupid. Other heads in the group were nodding as I spoke. I was right. Idiotic music.

Brugh pointed out to me that the music was simply there, a sequence of sounds, and I had the choice of finding something interesting about it or being annoyed about it, but that I should know I had a choice.

And the group conversation moved on to other areas.

But I was still mad. Brugh hadn't dealt with my objections. He hadn't really responded to my feelings at all, he'd just mentioned them and moved on. Leaving me behind. I couldn't get out of my rage. I was stuck. At the break, when everyone went for coffee, I went off by myself and cried. I was having a tantrum, like a child.

I remained angry for a couple of days. During this time, I complained to everybody who would listen. I was convinced of the rightness of my rage. They all seemed to be sympathetic.

And then I noticed that people were avoiding me. They would see me on the path and take another route. I thought, No kidding. They're avoiding *me*. I've become a bore.

So then I had to deal with some ideas I had about being special and unique, ideas about status and education and "the right things." And finally I could drop my anger and be in a good mood again. And people stopped avoiding me.

But you never knew when the emotional storms would strike. Some people found they were terrified of the desert, and couldn't set foot in it. Some people couldn't be alone. Some people couldn't talk in front of the whole group. Some people couldn't stand their roommates. Some people couldn't stop thinking about the outside world, and the news they weren't hearing. Some people couldn't be part of a group—they had to be leaders. Some people cried during the two days of fasting. Some people couldn't handle two days of silence. Some people always needed to sit next to Brugh.

It was ultimately reassuring, to see all the different things that snagged people. It made you less harsh with yourself. We were all in this together. What difference did it make that I cried because I didn't like the music, and someone else cried because he couldn't eat during the fast? Neither thing was better or worse. These were all just examples of getting stuck, making yourself miserable by your opinions and beliefs.

As if protecting your opinions was more important than having a fresh experience and rolling with the punches.

Brugh continued his energy work. He had developed a series of exercises to teach us to feel the chakras, to identify the different ways that energy could feel, to give energy to other people, and to receive it ourselves. This turned out to be quite easy to do.

If you stand beside a person who lies on his back, and move the palm of your hand slowly down the midline of his body about a foot above the skin, you will feel some distinct warm spots. These are the chakras. Sometimes the chakras don't feel warm, but tingly and breezy instead—as if the body had little fans that blew breezes up against your hand.

You need to be relaxed to feel the chakras, but it isn't a special or spiritual kind of relaxation. It isn't a difficult state to hit. You just need to calm down for a few seconds before you begin. It requires about as much calming as you would need to thread a needle.

Most people discover that one hand is more sensitive to energy than the other. And most people find, after a while, they can't feel anything in their hand any more. They need to snap their wrist a few times, as you would to shake off water droplets; then sensitivity returns. And since metal interrupts the energy, you don't want your subject wearing a big metal belt buckle over the second chakra, or a metal pendant lying right over the heart chakra. (In fact, it's odd how we have designed jewelry to cover our chakras: crowns, tiaras, chokers, necklaces, pendants, and belt buckles are all located at chakra positions.)

Again I noticed that when energy work is done the air gets thick. It's a very agreeable sensation, like sitting in a kitchen where bread is baking. Pleasant in that way.

And it turns out that energy findings are objective. Two people can scan a third, and they will agree on the findings: third chakra hot, fourth displaced, fifth cool, and so on. You can do your investigations separately, write down your findings separately, and then compare notes, if you want to. There isn't any delusion. It is absolutely clear that this body energy is a genuine phenomenon of some kind.

You didn't have to be in the mood to feel it, you didn't have to be a meditating saint, you didn't have to believe in it. You just had to calm down and then hold your hand out over somebody's body. In fact, the body energy was so clearly genuine, so stable and straightforward, that the most common reaction of people in our group was "Why hasn't anybody told us about this before?"

It was easy to feel the energy. Brugh said that you could see it as well. One day he called for the windows to be darkened, and we pulled out dark-blue cloths, set them on the ground, held our hands over the cloth, and squinted; we could see the energy. It was odd. I realized I had seen it as a child, but had dismissed it as some sort of optical illusion. You can see the energy most easily against a dark surface under low illumination. The level of illumination is critical, which seems to be why squinting helps.

The energy looks like streaks of yellow mist extending beyond your fingertips. The mist is strongest close to the fingertips, and dissipates farther out. It looks like yellow fuzz around your fingers.

You need to relax to see the energy, as you need to relax to feel it. If you are panicky, you may not get it right away. It's subtle. But, then, as with so many perceptual things, once you see it you know what to look for. It's much easier after that.

At first I still thought that I was seeing some kind of illusion. But other people can see your energy and talk about it, so it can't be an illusion.

After I could see the energy, I was fooling around—cupping my hands together to make a ball of yellow energy between them, that sort of thing. Trying different things. I was sitting opposite another person, and I thought, I'll try to send energy to him.

Immediately I saw the yellow mist shoot out in long streaks from my fingertips to the chest of the other person. And a third person nearby said, "Look—it's going right into his chest!"

So in the end I had to accept the energy as real.

Brugh gave us tarot decks. I had a great resistance to these medieval fortunetelling cards. I couldn't believe a physician, a scientifically trained person, would waste our time with such foolish superstition. But Brugh had already demonstrated the validity of body energy, so I decided to go along with him on the cards. He said, "Shuffle through the pack and pick out the card you like best and the card you like least."

I liked the Three of Swords least, and the Magician best. My choices seemed straightforward. Some of the cards were clearly more attractive than others, and some were clearly unattractive. There was a range of personal choice, but it wasn't limitless. You'd have to be a pretty strange person to choose Death, or the Hanged Man, as your favorite card. Or a pretty odd person to dislike the Lovers or the Ten of Cups. So I didn't perceive much real choice.

Brugh said, "Now imagine that the card you like least is the card you like best. Say what is good in the card you like least, and what is bad in the card you like best."

I found this reversal impossible to do.

The Three of Swords depicted a red heart pierced by three swords, against a background of storm clouds and gray rain. I couldn't see anything in it but pain, suffering, and heartbreak. I couldn't perceive it as a good card in any way.

People sitting next to me helped. Someone suggested there wasn't any blood, so it was a clean cut. Someone else said it was a decisive card, cutting to the heart of the matter. The rain was cleansing. The three swords were balanced, each penetrating the center. The swords formed a stable tripod. The card had a finality to it, a sense of termination. The storm would pass. The card could be seen as intellect taking charge of emotion, which could be good.

And so on.

I thought I was beginning to get the hang of it. Now I looked at the Magician, my favorite card, and tried to see it as bad. The Magician showed a young man in a white robe standing before a variety of articles, confidently holding a wand high. He had an infinity sign like a halo over his head. I thought he was a powerful, good, white-robed person.

But I couldn't see the card differently. I couldn't see it as bad. Again, people had to help me. The Magician looked young and frivolous. He was a show-off, a trickster. He did not seem serious. He appeared self-involved and showy, insincere. His spotless white robe indicated he didn't do any honest hard work; he just did magic. His wand was actually a candle being burned at both ends, proof of a dissolute life. His infinity sign meant he could never get down to business. All in all, the Magician was a hopeless case of form over substance, appearances over reality.

Hearing this, I wondered why I had ever seen the Magician as a positive card. It had so many evident negative features.

Brugh talked about the value of being able to see a card, or a life situation, from all sides. To see the good and the bad, and not to consider the thing itself as possessing either goodness or badness. He talked about how people became rigid when they assigned fixed values to things.

Then he suggested that the purpose of the tarot was to allow our unconscious free play as we inspected these ancient images. Since the cards themselves were neither good nor bad, how we saw them told us a great deal about the state of our unconscious minds. And in that lay their value.

This made a lot of sense to me, since I had already concluded that most of our actions were determined by our unconscious, not our conscious, minds. Now, by viewing the cards as a window into your unconscious, you were obliged to give them as much power as you gave the unconscious. If you thought your unconscious could see into the future—and certainly *some* people could see into the future—then the tarot cards could help your unconscious do that. If you thought the unconscious was primarily of psychological importance, then the tarot was a valuable tool for psychological insight.

Since the tarot worked by interacting with the unconscious, it also followed that it didn't make any difference what layout you used, or whether you made your own layout. If you said, "The next card I draw will represent my feelings about the future," then by definition the next card would, because the unconscious would interpret it that way.

So I accepted the tarot, and dutifully worked with the cards, but I never really liked them. Tarot cards always felt to me like somebody else's dream.

Next Brugh introduced the *I Ching,* a Chinese method of divination in which you toss three coins six times, do a calculation, then look up the answer in a text.

The procedure seemed mathematical and needlessly

complicated. And when you got to the text, it was often not helpful: "Someone does indeed increase him; even ten tortoises cannot oppose." Or "The well must be repaired before drawing water." It was hard to make sense of that!

Yet, despite these drawbacks, I was attracted to the *I Ching*. At first I thought I liked the *I Ching* because the mathematical aspects appealed to me more than other kinds of divination. Later I thought it was because I was verbally oriented and the *I Ching*'s interpretation was textual. Later I thought that I simply enjoyed reading the book, browsing through it. Eventually I decided that all these things were true.

Of course, the basic mechanism of the *I Ching* had to be the same as the mechanism of the tarot—to provide an ambiguous stimulus to the unconscious mind. The text answers of the *I Ching* are as ambiguous as the visual images of the tarot.

In fact, the traditional scientific complaint about the *I Ching*—that the line readings "could mean anything"—started to make sense to me. Of course the line readings could mean anything! That was exactly what was desired: a neutral Rorschach for the unconscious to interpret. If the line readings were unambiguous, then there would be no unconscious involvement. The interpretation would be entirely conscious. And then there really *would* be a credibility problem: how could a twenty-five-hundred-year-old Chinese book tell you the answer to your modern, Western question? The very idea is absurd.

Because, of course, the book can't tell you the answer. The book doesn't have that power. You do. You can answer your own question. You already know the answer, if you can just gain access to it. And in the end your unconscious mind does answer your own question, and that is why many people, including Carl Jung and the Chinese scholar John Blofeld, have been struck by the specific, personal quality of the answer that is provided.

The purpose of the *I Ching*, or the tarot, then, is to help you get access to yourself, by providing ambiguity for you to interpret. And this quality of ambiguity is shared with nearly all other forms of divination—cast artifacts, or entrails, or weather formations, or events, such as the flight of birds, that one could choose either to see as "omens" or to ignore.

The very thing that makes these divination techniques

292

seem so unscientific is what makes it possible for them to work.

Toward the end of the second week, I began to think of leaving. I wasn't the only one. Several of us talked about what we would do when we finally went home.

Personally, I longed for a Big Mac. As soon as this conference was over, I was driving down the road and buying a big, disgusting, unhealthy, unspiritual hamburger.

I couldn't wait.

On the final day of the conference, I visited the cactus to say goodbye. The cactus was just sitting there. It wouldn't speak to me. I said I appreciated what it had shown me and I had enjoyed spending time with it, which wasn't exactly true because I had felt frustrated a lot of the time, but I thought it was more or less true. The cactus made no reply.

Then I realized that from its position in the garden the cactus could never see the sun set. The cactus had been years in that position and had been deprived of seeing sunsets. I burst into tears.

The cactus said, "It's been good having you here with me."

Then I *really* cried.

On the drive home, I couldn't find a McDonald's anywhere. Finally I passed a Marie Callender's. I went inside and ordered a chili burger and french fries and a Coke and a piece of pie. But when the food came, it seemed rich and heavy. I didn't finish it. It wasn't what I wanted, after all.

Back home, I was shocked to see how beautiful my house was. I lived on the beach at Malibu, but I had long ago stopped looking at the view, and complained about the traffic instead. Now I was astonished that I lived in such a breathtakingly beautiful place.

At the office, I turned on my word processor, and the letters on the screen flashed on and off, like a neon sign. At first I thought the computer was broken. Then I realized I was seeing the screen refresh itself. That happens all the time, but normally we're not aware of it, as we're not aware that light bulbs blink on and off sixty times each second. I looked at the screen and thought, This is a remarkable perception, but I don't know if I can work with a screen that blinks like this.

Later I learned this perception was a commonly reported consequence of meditation. In a few days it faded away.

For a while, after I returned home, I felt wonderfully alive. But then the emotional high of the two weeks faded. It all just drifted away, the way any vacation decays from consciousness. I felt discouraged. I hadn't really made any real progress, any substantial gains. The energy work was real, the meditations were real, but what good was it if you couldn't maintain the high and apply it to your daily life? What had it all amounted to in the end? Just another illusion. Summer camp for adults. A lot of New Age mumbo-jumbo.

Meanwhile, I had practical matters to occupy me. A relationship of two years came to an end. My work was not satisfying. I needed to move my office. My secretary was begging to be fired; I fired her.

It wasn't until much later that I looked back and saw that, within eight months of returning from the desert, I had changed my relationships, my residence, my work, my diet, my habits, my interests, my exercise, my goals—in fact, just about everything in my life that could be changed. These changes were so sweeping that I couldn't see what was happening while I was in the midst of them.

And there was another change, too. I've become very fond of cacti, and I always have some around, wherever I live.

Jamaica

In 1982 I ended my two-year relationship with Terry, a securities lawyer who worked for the SEC in New York and Los Angeles. But after a few months of separation, we drifted back together in a vague and tentative way, and since Christmas was coming up, we decided to take a trip to Jamaica together, with some other friends.

We rented a beautiful house in Ocho Rios, on the north shore. The house was idyllic—set on a hilltop, surrounded by flowers and hummingbirds—but, despite the warm weather and the pleasant surroundings, Terry and I felt even further estranged as the days went on. Terry was angry at me for leaving her in the first place, and here in Jamaica she was even more angry, because she could see that our reunion was not working out and that eventually I would leave again.

This became an unspoken issue between us. We conducted our days, going on excursions, taking rafting trips and boat rides and so on, without reference to what would happen after the vacation was over and we returned home.

Part of the time we were visited by my friend Kurt and Terry's friend Ellen, so the pressure was reduced for a while. But finally we were alone again, the vacation was drawing to a close, and the inevitable separation was at hand.

Before we left Jamaica, I wanted to go to Spanish Town in the south, where I had learned there was a new museum of early Jamaican artifacts. For many years I had been working on a book about seventeenth-century Jamaica, and now I wanted to visit this museum. Terry said she would like to come, too.

On a clear, sunny day, we set off to drive over the Blue Mountains, heading south. Jamaica is one of the most beautiful countries in the world, and it looked especially lovely that morning. The mountain road was spectacular and twisting, and I had to pay attention to the driving, but I felt wonderful. Pretty soon Terry said she wanted to talk about "us," and about our future together. I didn't. I felt that would only provoke an argument. But when I demurred, Terry pressed—why didn't I want to talk about it? what was the problem with talking about it?—and pretty soon we had the argument anyway, and were both angry.

The core issue was that Terry didn't want to break up and I did.

I have never understood this particular romantic impasse—in which one person is dissatisfied while the other person claims not to be dissatisfied at all. I just don't get it. I always thought that if one person is dissatisfied the other person must also be dissatisfied. It didn't seem possible to me that the other person could honestly feel satisfied.

For example, hubby is stomping around the house, irritated all the time, and wifey is saying, "Isn't everything *great?* I think everything's just great." But how can she say that? Why is it great? Who wants to live with a permanently irritated hubby? What is he irritated about in the first place? Why isn't she reacting to this irritation? What's really going on here?

Nothing good, as far as I can tell. Nothing healthy.

I finally decided that people handled the pain of breaking up by adopting stereotypic roles. There was the role of the Leaver, and the role of the Left; the role of the Complainer, and the role of the Sufferer; the role of the Accuser, and the role of the Accused, and so on. These roles weren't adopted with any particular reference to what was really going on. They were just accepted and familiar social roles, like the roles you saw on soap operas. Sort of the psychological equivalent of the cheap plastic costumes they sell kids on Halloween. Ready-made roles, not individually tailored to the people, or created by them for themselves.

Now, Terry and I were having precisely this sort of stereotypic interaction, driving over the mountains toward Spanish Town that morning. I was cast in the role of the Dissatisfied Man, and she was playing the role of Placating Woman in the Face of the Dissatisfied Man.

There were long silences in the car while we drove. The landscape, which was previously lush, now seemed overgrown and thick; Terry, sitting beside me, was sullen and withdrawn.

After quaint Ocho Rios, Spanish Town was startling in its sprawl and squalor. A shantytown west of Kingston, it was poor, colorful, and charged with menace. There were no tourists here; indeed, there were no whites at all; the black faces that stared at us were dull and hostile.

I had been in Jamaica in 1973 and had experienced an uncomfortable hostility toward tourists. Now I had that same sensation once again. I stopped at a petrol station to have the tank filled. The attendant came over to the car. He had a sour expression.

"Nice watch," he said, looking at my wristwatch.

"Thanks," I said, immediately pulling my arm inside the car. My watch was an old plastic Casio; I didn't know what the big deal was, or why he seemed to like it.

"Full up?"

"Please."

The attendant reached through the window, stuck his hand in front of my face, and snapped his fingers.

"Keys."

The gas-tank lock. I gave him the keys, and he went away.

"Jesus," I said, controlling my temper.

"Very nice," Terry said, nodding. "An ambassador for his country."

While the attendant filled the tank, several loitering black men came over and stood around the car, peering in at me, and at Terry. Their expressions were sullen and angry. They didn't speak; they just walked around the car and looked.

"What are they looking at?" Terry said, growing agitated.

297

"Who knows?"

One of the men kicked a tire in front of the car. The others looked to see what we would do. We didn't do anything.

After a moment, Terry said, "You don't think anything would happen here?"

"No, I don't think so." And I didn't think so. These men no doubt enjoyed frightening us, but I doubted very much that anything would happen.

Still, the tension was unmistakably there, and I was glad when the attendant returned, I paid him for the gas, and we drove off.

"This better be good, the reason you wanted to come here," Terry says, as I pull out.

"I told you, it's research."

"Well, it's certainly *that.*"

Now, Terry can, if she wants to, slip into her traveling investigator's mode and accept all sorts of difficulties with good-natured humor. But right now she is annoyed at me, and so she's just sitting back, not helping me at all, letting me squirm.

Within Spanish Town there are few street signs, and the map I have gotten from the tourist office is sketchy, listing only the main thoroughfares. Sometimes as I drive I see a green sign, "Museum" with an arrow pointing, but as I follow streets they loop back on themselves; there are no further signs; eventually I see another sign pointing toward the museum in the opposite direction to the way I am now going. Everywhere the streets were crowded with people, traffic, belching buses, crying kids.

According to the map, the museum I am trying to get to is near a cluster of formal government buildings: the court-house, the archives, the post office.

Eventually I drive past a high white colonial building. I feel I am getting close.

There is a large crowd of black men in front of this building. One street is blocked off; a policewoman directs traffic. I pull over to ask her help.

"Move along! Move along!"

"But—"

"Move along, I say!"

298

I pull my car over to the side of the road, get out, and walk back to her.

"Excuse me, I'm lost. . . ."

"Yes, that's clear." In a singsong voice, very irritating.

I grind my teeth. "Can you help me? I'm looking for the museum."

"No museum here."

"Yes, there is a museum. The Historical Society Museum."

"Not finished yet."

"But where *is* it?"

"I don't know. Not here. That's obvious."

All this time she is directing traffic, not looking at me. I am ready to kill her now. I have been driving in difficult traffic for almost an hour, trying to find my way around this city, and I finally come upon a policewoman and she won't tell me anything. I know she is lying. The guidebook says the Historical Society Museum was finished the year before. I will have to find my own way.

At least, I think, I can get her to help me orient myself now.

"What's the building right here?" I say, pointing to the large white colonial building.

"What does it *look* like? It's the courthouse, of course."

"Courthouse?" I am suspicious. "Then why is it blocked off?"

"These men are here for their court appearances; they are waiting for their appearances, but there is no room inside to house them. Now, get back in your car and move along."

I go back to the car. Terry is waiting for me. I get in the car and slam the door.

"Goddamn it!" I say.

"Never mind," Terry says. "Lester can help us."

I turn.

There is a black man in the back seat of the car.

"Hello," he says. He looks about twenty-five years old, tall, muscular, and strong. He extends his hand for me to shake.

"This is Lester," Terry says.

I twist around in the car to shake Lester's hand. I am very uncomfortable to have this stranger in my car.

"Lester's a guide," Terry says. "At least, he says he is."

"That's right, I can guide you," Lester says. "Anywhere you want to go."

Lester doesn't look like a guide to me. A large knife scar runs down the side of his neck from his ear, disappearing beneath the collar of his shirt. His clothes are dirty. He smells of liquor.

"Where did you meet Lester, Terry?"

"He walked by the car while you were talking to the policewoman, and I asked him where the museum was, and he said he would guide us."

I think: If he walked by the car, then he is part of this crowd of men outside the courthouse. He is waiting for a court appearance. This man is just what he looks like: a criminal.

"It's nice of Lester to help," I say, "but I think we can do this by ourselves."

"Really?" she says. "So far you've just driven in circles for an hour. Or did the policewoman tell you what you wanted to know?"

"No," I admitted.

"I think we need a guide if we're ever going to get out of this godforsaken town," Terry says. "Or were you planning on spending the night?"

"I will guide you, I will," Lester says. He is saying other things, too, in a clipped Caribbean argot that is incomprehensible to me. Lester seems cheerful and friendly, but I don't like him. I don't like the knife scar on his neck, I don't like his manner, and I don't like the fact that he is ensconced in the back seat before I have had a chance to discuss it with Terry.

But he's there, all right. Waiting.

"Okay, Lester," I say. "Great. We want to go to the museum."

"Yes. I will guide."

"Where's the museum?"

"Museum?" He looks completely blank. "Museum?" He shakes his head.

"Terry. I don't think Lester's a full-time guide, Terry."

"Well, he said he was."

I am thinking, *Jesus Christ, will you look at this guy you let into our car? Now what are we going to do about—*

"Stetodengine," Lester says, in a sudden burst of words.

"What?"

"Stetyoudengine," he repeats.

"Start your engine," Terry translates.

"Why?" I say.

"You cannot park here, mon," Lester says. "The police book you if you stay here."

In the mirror I see a policeman approaching our parked car. Lester has already spotted him, and that is why he is nervous. *Good,* I think. A policeman coming. We'll be rid of this Lester in no time at all.

I sit back, do nothing.

"Well, for God's sake, Michael," Terry says. "Start the car."

"No, I—"

"What are you going to do, just *sit* here?"

"I'm thinking."

"About what? Let's get going."

"Terry, I'd like to have a word with you in private about this whole situation—"

"You wanted to go to the museum; that's why we came here. Fine. Lester will take you to the museum."

"Lester doesn't seem to know where—"

"—I know where, I know where," Lester says, suddenly very agitated. "Start your engine, go left at the next turning."

"And where is the museum?" I say, still hesitating.

"Go left, and I will guide you. The museum is very near. Very near."

I think, That's right; according to the map, the museum must be very near here.

"Only two blocks," Lester says.

Terry is looking at me, expectantly.

I think, The policeman can come over and I can get this convict Lester out of the car. But I still have my original problem, which is to find the museum—with Terry glaring at me all the time—and meanwhile Lester seems suddenly to have developed confidence about the location of the museum. What the hell. I'll drive a couple of blocks.

I start the car, and we drive a short distance. Many streets in this area are blocked off, but Lester seems to know where he is going, directing me deftly. Whenever pedestrians block the street, he leans out the side window and shouts at them to get out of the way, and they look at him and then move quickly. Lester has a definite menace about him.

"Stop the engine. Stop the engine. Park here."

I see we have made a loop, and have returned very near

the courthouse. We're on an odd side street, but I see no museum.

"Lester, where is the museum?" I ask suspiciously.

"There, mon," Lester says, pointing across the street.

"Where?"

"*There.* Right there, mon, you see the door."

And then I see a small sign that says "Museum" and the hours. As we watch, a sunburned Scandinavian family in sun clothes, socks, and sandals emerges and sits on the steps.

It's the museum, all right.

"Thank *God,*" Terry says, getting out of the car. She looks at me accusingly. "I'd say Lester did very well, wouldn't you?"

Her whole manner implies that I am a suspicious, prejudiced son of a bitch—and that I have furthermore failed to acknowledge properly that it is only through *her* efforts that we have finally found this damned museum.

And I am, in truth, a bit chagrined. I am relieved finally to be at the museum. And I may well have been mistaken about Lester.

But as I get out of the driver's seat and move the seat so Lester can climb out from the back, as he stands up alongside me, I realize that I am not wrong at all. Lester is six feet four inches tall and powerfully built; he has another scar on the other side of his throat, and he has a strange tattoo on the back of his left hand, a box with an "X" in it. And although he is smiling and friendly at the moment, I have the distinct sense that Lester is *mean.*

We head toward the museum. There is a two-shilling entrance fee. "Well, Lester," I say, "thanks for guiding us." And I give him a ten-shilling note.

"No, no," he says, holding up his hands.

"Yes, yes," I say. "We appreciate your help, but now we're at the museum, and—"

"No, no, I am coming with you. Inside."

"No, thank you, Lester—"

"Yes, yes—"

Terry says, "Will you pay his two shillings and be done with it?"

So Lester comes inside with us.

Once we are inside, it is clear Lester is no guide. The first exhibit displays some horse-drawn coaches from the nineteenth century. I ask Lester, "What're these?"

302

"Old carts," he says. "Wooden carts."

I shoot Terry a look; she shrugs and moves off. She thinks Lester is fine. I can tell by her face, her gestures. She is rejecting my point of view on this.

I would like to get Terry off alone, even for a few seconds, to whisper in her ear, but Lester has a way of positioning his body between me and Terry so I can never grab her by the arm and get her away alone. It's all unspoken, but he's very skillful. And this part of the museum is deserted; no one around, not even a guard.

We see several more exhibits, and Lester makes obvious, or incorrect, comments at each one. Terry still doesn't appear to notice. Next we come to exhibits of ceramics and china. Terry is interested in these. "Lester, were these originally English china?"

"Old plates," Lester says, pointing to the display.

"Yes, I know that, but are they English?"

"No. Not English. Jamaican. Found here."

And he gives Terry an irritable glance, as if he is losing patience with her. This is not the thing to do to Terry. We come to another room, and there are some people there, other tourists. We are no longer alone. Terry says, "I don't think Lester is a guide."

"Really? I'll tell you what he is, he's a convict."

"Oh, for God's sake, Michael. You and your imagination."

"Yes? You see his scars? And what was he doing there by the courthouse today? Did you ask yourself that?"

"He's not a convict," Terry says, "but he's not a very good guide, and I think you should get rid of him."

"Well, I tried to—"

"Let's not argue about it; let's just get rid of him, okay?"

We look over. Lester has been standing across the room, looking at a display case, but from the way his body is positioned I can tell he has overheard us.

Lester turns and smiles.

"Ready to go?"

"Yes," Terry says.

As we move through the other exhibit rooms, there are always other people around, other tourists, and we feel better. But not much better.

"Jesus, aren't there any guards in this place?" Terry says finally.

"No," I say. We haven't seen a guard since we entered.

"No money for guards," Lester says. "Same as in prison."

"In *prison?*" Terry says.

She's spooked. Lester decides to talk to her, ignoring me; he moves directly between Terry and me. He focuses all his attention on her.

"Yes, in prison there is no money for guards, so they have no guards. Prison is very bad in Jamaica."

"I see," Terry says. She is pale. White.

I say, "Were you in prison, Lester?"

"Yes."

"For a long time?"

"No. The last time, only six years."

Six years seems like a long time to me. "What were you in for?" I say.

"For nothing," Lester says.

"You were in prison for nothing?"

Terry glances at me. The legal investigator doesn't think I should continue this line of questioning, whereas I think we might as well get the facts and find out what we're dealing with.

"You were in prison for nothing?"

Lester spins on me and curls his lip, grips my elbow. "I tell you *the truth,*" he snarls. I feel spittle on my face. "I tell you, mon, *the truth. I don't kill no one!*"

Six years, I think. Homicide.

Great.

I look at Terry. Her eyes are very wide. She understands the implications perfectly well.

But Lester is still talking, still defending himself. If anything, he is even more excited. "The last time, yes," Lester says. "Last time, I kill him, yes! I admit it, yes! But this time, no!"

"I see," I say. I am suddenly calm. I understand the problem, and I understand what I must do. I must get rid of Lester as soon as possible. In order to do that, I must find either a policeman or a crowd of some kind. I look at the other tourists in the print room. They are elderly, British, feeble.

"How did you kill this man, Lester?" I say, in as conversational a tone as I can manage. I am hoping he will say a gun, since I can see he doesn't have a gun with him.

"With a knife," he says, as we leave the print room.

"A knife?"

"Yes. Like *this*." And he reaches in the waistband of his trousers in front of his crotch and pulls out a huge switchblade. He flicks it open, stabs the air. "Like *so*."

Terry says, "Put that away, Lester."

Lester puts the knife back in his crotch, leering at her.

I think, Just stay cool and get rid of him. But it is difficult to stay cool now that I have seen the knife. My heart is pounding. And now that I know the facts, of course there is not another person to be seen anywhere. The museum is suddenly entirely empty. We are in a garden now, with some artifacts from old sugar mills, some big stone wheels.

"Big stone wheel," Lester says.

"I think it's time to go, Lester," I say. I remember there was a guard at the entrance, who sold us the tickets. He was elderly, but he was at least a guard. And there are likely to be other tourists at the entrance.

"Yes, we go. This way."

"That's not the way to the entrance," I say.

"No, we go a different way now."

"I would rather go the same way, Lester."

"This way is better," Lester says.

"No," I say. "I want to go the way we came."

There is a moment of frozen tension, neither of us moving, a silent standoff. I don't think Lester will pull his knife in the middle of the museum. I think I can force the issue right now. I can break free of Lester right here in the garden, in the sunlight, beside the stone sugar-cane wheel.

"Oh, for God's sake, Michael," Terry says. "Let's go the way Lester wants to go."

Shit!

Doesn't she realize what she's doing?

"Terry—"

"Well, he's led us so far—"

"Terry, do you mind if I handle this my—"

"I'm just trying to be helpful—"

I don't want to argue with her in front of Lester. I can see she's frightened, and I can see that her way of handling the fear is to be conciliatory, but I think that we could be out of the frying pan and into the fire with Lester; I think that if he gets us alone somewhere we could have a very difficult time with him and his big knife, and that we should therefore make a stand. Whereas her impulse is to play along.

"When we get back to the car," she says, as we start

walking, "you can give Lester a nice tip." So her idea is to ditch him back at the car. But that may not be so easy.

We go through some back areas of the museum, and come out on a deserted street. Our car is at the end of the block; we walk back to it.

"Well, this has been great; thank you, Lester," I say, getting out my wallet. I figure I will give him a pound. Maybe two pounds.

Terry gets in the car. "Thank you, Lester, very much," she says.

Lester looks around nervously. "I will come with you," he says.

"No, Lester—"

"Yes I will come—" He is pushing into the car.

"No, Lester—"

"Yes," he says. "I will guide you to other things."

"We're going home now."

"Then I will show you the road home," he says.

"Lester, we can find the road ourselves. Get out of the car."

And Terry says, very calmly, "I think we could use some help finding the road, Michael."

After I get past wanting to kill her, I realize she doesn't really believe our predicament. Somehow, in the tension of all this, Terry has decided in her own mind that Lester is not really dangerous, that nothing bad can really happen to us, that we are two happy tourists on vacation in Jamaica. She does not see us as two people in great jeopardy.

I assess my choices. I am on a deserted street with a convicted murderer who has a knife and my girlfriend in the car with him. It does not seem wise to pick a fight with Lester in this setting, and since Terry won't get out of the car, since she seems intent on appeasing him, my next-best hope is to try to do something that does not depend on Terry's help in any way—in other words, to start driving, to play for time, and to hope to find a policeman, a traffic accident, an event of some kind that will let us break free of Lester.

I get in the car, and start driving.

Lester, behind me, grins. He's won. He sits to the side, far behind me, so I cannot see him in the mirror. We begin to drive through the crowded streets of Spanish Town.

This is a nightmare.

Terry is close to hysteria; she is chattering away to Lester about our life at home, about the supermarkets, the packing problems, saying anything that comes into her head. It is not like her at all.

I am driving, looking for a policeman, a traffic cop, a diversion of some sort, anything that will allow me to get rid of Lester in the back seat. I see nothing at all.

Lester says, "You have some drink?"

"No," I say.

"No liquor?"

"No. You want liquor?"

"Yes. I want liquor now." He is becoming demanding, more open in his control of the situation.

"We'll have to stop at a liquor store," I say.

"There is one on the left, up ahead."

I pull up at the curb, and get out of the car. I leave the motor running, because I plan to let him out, then jump back in the car, slam the door shut, and race off.

As Lester climbs out from the back seat, he reaches forward and turns the ignition off.

"You left the motor running," he says. He smiles innocently. He stands very close to me on the pavement beside the car.

I realize that it's only in the movies that people jump back in the car, slam the door, give the guy the finger and race off. In real life—which is unfortunately where I am right now with this guy—in real life this would never work. I couldn't get back in the car fast enough in real life. Anyway, he has turned the engine off.

Now, standing with him on the pavement, I see the knife handle protruding above his belt.

"I need money," he says.

I give him two pounds.

"Oh, mon, liquor in Jamaica *expensive,* mon," he says.

I give him five pounds. He nods, smiling.

I hate the way I feel; I hate the powerlessness and the fear. I am on the outskirts of a slum town in Jamaica, and some guy who may or may not be a convict, who may or may not have killed somebody, who may or may not intend to use that knife on me or on Terry, effectively holds us hostage on a corner in front of a liquor store at three in the afternoon while cars drive by on the busy street. And I can't seem to think of anything to do.

"Go on in and get what you want," I say, "and we'll wait out here."

Even as I say it, I feel like a fool. I don't convince myself for an instant, and I certainly don't convince Lester.

Lester starts to laugh, a high-pitched, unpleasant laugh. "Oh, *mon.* I go in that place, you drive away, mon."

"No, no. We'll wait right here."

Lester shakes his head pityingly. "Oh, mon. You think me stupid? You come with me inside."

"No, Lester."

"Yes. You come with me."

"No."

"Why not?"

"I have to stay with the car."

"Then you stay, your wife come inside with me."

"No, Lester."

"Yes," he says, and his eyes narrow. He is getting angry. Powerful tension is building. Terry, in the passenger seat, is looking over at us, following the conversation.

Lester bunches his fists. I am wondering who is inside the liquor store and whether they will help me when the fight breaks out. Lester is looking at me in an appraising way, and I can feel the tension still building, and suddenly he says, "Nice watch."

He is looking at my watch. The plastic Casio. I look at it, too.

"Very expensive, that watch, yes?"

"No, not really."

"In Jamaica, that watch expensive."

"Maybe. I don't know about that."

"Expensive watch in Jamaica," Lester says. "Imported."

"I see."

Now the tension is dissipating, because we are talking about the watch, which is all right with me. I am suddenly very interested in the watch myself.

"You let me see your watch?"

He holds out his hand. It is perfectly clear what he intends. And as far as I am concerned, he can have it if he wants it.

I say, "You can't have it, Lester."

"No, no. Just to see."

"Then you'll give it back?"

"Oh yeah, mon."

So in the end I let him convince me for a while, talk me into it, and I take the watch off, and Lester puts it on his own wrist, and during the moment he is trying to buckle the band on his wrist, I jump in the car, start the engine, and race away.

In the rearview mirror, I see him laughing and shaking his head. Then he goes into the liquor store. Then the car goes around a curve, and Lester is behind us.

And I think, *The battery was almost dead anyway.*

We are driving back over the mountains toward Ocho Rios. I've gotten past the sense of shock, past the period of shivering as if I have a fever, and now I'm angry. Really angry. Terry is trying to placate me. "I'll buy you a new watch, Michael. Anyway, it was only a Casio."

"That's not the point!"

"Well, what's the point? It was just a watch."

"Terry. You said so yourself. You were scared."

"I was a little scared, yes. Not really. I never thought he would hurt us."

"That's not how you acted."

"Well, I didn't know for sure. He said he was a guide."

Terry is one of the smartest people I have ever met, but when it suits her, she can be utterly obtuse. "Terry, he was obviously not a guide. What the hell were you thinking of?"

"I wanted to help. You needed help."

"Jesus Christ, Terry, that was a very destructive thing to do, getting involved with that guy."

"You're right," she says. "It was pretty stupid. You're right. I admit it."

"Now you're being a lawyer. I'm not trying to win the case, I'm trying to understand."

"Well, I've admitted that you are right and I've offered to buy you a new Casio; I don't know what else I can do."

"Just don't do it again!"

She looks at me as if I am crazy. Slowly it dawns on her. "You think I did that *on purpose?*"

Well, of course I did think so. And we had another furious argument about that—about whether she had.

But I consider behavior purposeful, whether the purpose

309

is acknowledged or not. Behavior is not random; it can be analyzed from the standpoint of purpose; it can be understood from the standpoint of purpose. And it seemed to me that Terry had deliberately invited a man into our lives for the purpose of making me uncomfortable. Or worse.

Terry kept insisting that Lester wouldn't have really harmed us, that he was all talk and all show with what she called "that knife of his."

But the threat was real; the next day in the *Daily Gleaner* there was a report of two German tourists whose bodies had been found some days after they were reported missing on an excursion to the Spanish Town area. The newspaper didn't say how the tourists had died, but the story seemed to suggest that the tourists had wandered into rough areas where tourists didn't usually go.

I showed Terry the story. She put the paper aside, without comment. We never discussed the Lester incident again, except when we got back home and she asked me if I wanted the Casio replaced; I said I didn't.

But I was also a participant in this episode, and in subsequent weeks I tried to understand my own behavior—in particular why, when I first saw Lester in my car, I hadn't simply let the policeman come over, gotten Lester out of the car under the eye of the cop, and gone on about my business.

All things considered, it seemed to me that I had been a passive victim in this affair with Lester. I had let it drag on, allowing the dangerous situation to continue. Why? Everything I could accuse Terry of, I could also accuse myself of. And the more I thought about it, the more it seemed to me that, if Terry had contrived this situation to make me uncomfortable, then I had prolonged the same situation in order to prove that Terry was bad, that she was wrong. We had both put ourselves in a dangerous situation in order to get at each other.

That seemed to verify, if verification were necessary, that our relationship had an unhealthy, neurotic basis. I expected that as soon as I got back to California I would break from Terry once and for all. Perhaps even in the airport, right after clearing customs. I wanted to get away from her as fast as I could.

But we didn't separate. We continued to see each other

310

all spring. We were miserable. I kept thinking, Why is this still going on?

There were no answers; this unhappy relationship just continued. I couldn't get rid of it, the way I couldn't get rid of Lester—and for the same reason. I was involved, whether I admitted it or not. Eventually I just gave in to the relationship, and waited for the end to come. It didn't come.

Finally we took a short trip to Mexico in April. Terry decided she didn't like the hotel, and she didn't like the way I was behaving. She became angry and withdrawn.

And something happened then, something just clicked—I withdrew psychologically, I uncoupled, and left her alone. I decided that I would be happy, even though she was angry and withdrawn.

So I became happy. But it was not easy to do this; it felt very awkward. It felt like heartily eating a dinner and smacking your lips, really *liking* that dinner, while across the table sat a starving person. An accusing, starving person.

It took all my effort to be happy under these circumstances, with Terry being so unhappy.

We changed hotels, but she remained unhappy—uncommunicative, sullen during meals—for four days straight. I worked hard on myself all this time, staying happy, not getting mad at her, not joining her mood. I was working as hard as if I were running a race, all day long. Constant effort to maintain my own mood, not to give in.

Each morning I would get up and meditate for an hour to keep my inner tranquillity. On the fourth morning, I went to the beach to meditate just as the sun rose, and after a time Terry woke up and came out to the beach looking for me, and when she saw me she ran toward me, and in my peaceful meditative state I turned and saw her coming toward me, her face distorted, upset and angry, her body tense, and suddenly I really *saw* her. Not in terms of what I wanted from her, or how she was affecting me, or how disappointing she was to me. Not in terms of anything to do with me at all. I just saw *her*. Another person, entirely separate from me. It was startling.

Terry must have seen something in my face, too, because she stopped running. She just looked at me for a minute, and then she turned, and went back into the hotel. And as I watched her go, I thought, *No kidding. That's the end.*

311

Because that moment—that moment of seeing each other, the moment everything stopped on the sand—was the real moment of uncoupling, and it marked the end of the relationship. There wasn't any great flash of insight. There was just . . . something. Something shifted. Something was seen. A month later we separated for good.

A Human Light Show

"Linda," said my friend Kate, "is very powerful. Linda glows in colors when she meditates. You should see her. She's a human light show."

Kate was young, and Kate was naïve. And Kate's friend Linda lived in San Diego, two hours by car. It was easy to postpone it.

Finally, one day, Kate said, "I'm going down to see Linda tomorrow. Do you want to come?"

My day was free. It would be good to get out of town. "Sure," I said.

On the way down, Kate explained that Linda was a San Diego schoolteacher in her thirties. Linda had started meditating only a year ago, but she was already very powerful. Recently a few people had begun to consult her. Poor Linda didn't know what to do about this; she was uncomfortable in her new role as a guru, still feeling her way; she didn't charge for her sessions, but Kate thought she eventually would. In fact, she thought Linda would eventually quit her job at school and become a full-time psychic. She sounded like an interesting person.

Furthermore, Kate again said, to meditate with Linda was remarkable, because Linda glowed in visible colors during the meditation. Sometimes other things happened, too. Sometimes she appeared to be of different ages, very old or very young. Sometimes parts of her body disappeared. Sometimes her body seemed to be moving or twisting. All sorts of optical effects were experienced by people meditating with Linda.

I listened to all this with private reservations. But I'd see for myself, soon enough.

Linda lived in a nondescript apartment on Mission Bay Road, in a beach area of San Diego. Inside, it was furnished with photos she had taken during vacations all over the world; like me, she had a fondness for travel. Linda was a smiling, diffident, pleasant woman. She said she would meditate with us separately. I went first.

In an adjacent bedroom, Linda sat by one wall, I sat by the bed, and we started. I hadn't meditated much since Brugh Joy's conference two years earlier. I closed my eyes to try and get centered, to block out the rumble of traffic on the street outside, the honking horns, the shouts of pedestrians.

Suddenly I felt a wave of warmth, as if somebody across the room had opened an oven door. I immediately recognized it—it was the same peaceful, warm feeling I had experienced during the group energy work at Brugh's. But that had been a group. Could she be doing this all by herself?

I opened my eyes.

Linda was sitting cross-legged, staring at me. She was vibrant. I didn't see colors, but there was great intensity about her, and the warmth that filled the room was astonishing in strength. She immediately inducted me into a powerful meditation. I felt myself expand, like a balloon inflating. It was a wonderful, tranquil feeling. Linda was staring at me. I stared back.

Linda's face was turning gray. In a few seconds it became difficult to see her features. The nose, the eyes, the mouth, were gone. It was as if somebody had pulled a gray stocking over her face. She was sitting right there, but I could no longer see her face.

I began to have trouble seeing her left shoulder, then the whole left side of her body. But the right side was fine. I found all this fascinating but not at all frightening. It was just something that was happening.

314

Suddenly I could see all her body again. Just as quickly, I began to see a stroboscopic phenomenon. Linda would be brightly lit, and the wall behind her would go black. Then she would be black, and the wall behind her would appear white. The image reversal continued back and forth in a steady, pulsating rhythm. Like breathing.

The pulsations stopped, and everything was normal for a while. Then I saw her face grow older, the cheeks sagging, the chin drooping, the eyes drained, the hair gray. She was sad and elderly for a few minutes. Then that went away.

Next her body appeared to ripple on the left side. It was as if she were water and a wave moved up it. The rippling continued for a time. I had plenty of opportunity to wonder where these illusions came from—her or me?—and what explanation there might be for them. Was this a consequence of a strong meditative state? Was this something that she had worked on? Was this merely suggestion I was responding to?

Suddenly Linda said, "You have no choice."

I paused.

"You need to realize that there is no drug you can take, no trip to another place in the world, no new person to have a relationship with. None of these things will get you where you want to go. What you are looking for isn't *out there.* You must stop looking outside. You must go *in.*"

It was pretty standard stuff, but something about the way she said it gave it new impact. Anyway, I'd long ago learned that the words are always the same, it's just whether or not you're able to hear them. The trick was to find somebody who knew how to reach you.

Something about Linda, a schoolteacher whose life was being altered like a pinball on a tilt table, made me listen to her. And the sensation of meditating with her, the peaceful, calm, detached, warm feeling, was somehow strongly confirming. It was good to feel this way.

Afterward I went to dinner with Linda and several of her friends, young people who meditated with her. They were all impressed by the visual displays you experienced with Linda. They kept talking about that. Whereas I thought the light show was a side effect. I was much more impressed with what was happening to her life, and the changes that were occurring, how it was taking place, how she was handling it. Because when you see a less experienced person,

315

you are reminded that there is a continuum of abilities, that skills are developed, and that everyone must learn to do what they do. So, whenever I would see Linda, I would feel a particular gratitude for the opportunity to watch her develop and grow into her new work.

They

I was on my own again in 1983, after more than a decade spent in marriage or otherwise exclusive relationships. Suddenly I was playing the field. It was a shock to discover how much had changed.

I was having lunch with my agent in a restaurant when a woman walked up, slapped her business card on the table, and said, "Call me." Then she turned on her heel and walked off. She was an attractive woman in her late twenties, wearing a business suit.

"Wow," I said, after she had gone. Nothing so brazen had ever happened to me.

"It's a new world," my agent said, shaking his head.

The incident was exciting, but it was also a little unnerving, so I didn't call this woman for a while. Eventually curiosity overcame me, and I called and made a date.

We met for dinner in a sushi bar. Andrea was twenty-eight; she had a degree in business administration and she worked for a commercial real-estate company. She was ambitious and levelheaded about her work; she had it all figured out, how long she would stay in this company, when she would leave, what she would do next.

She didn't ask me much about myself, and in fact didn't

seem very interested in me, except to ask where I lived, and whether my house was close to the restaurant. She was impatient during dinner, restless. I couldn't figure out why.

Finally the meal was over and I asked if she wanted tea or coffee. She shook her head. "Can't we have it at your house?"

And then I understood her impatience, her hurried indifference toward me. I was being rushed to the bedroom. Amazing! Andrea was doing to me what men supposedly did to women. I was being treated as a sex object.

At my house she announced she didn't want coffee but wanted a tour instead; she saw the bedroom and the Jacuzzi.

"Nice Jacuzzi," she said, starting to take off her clothes. "Want to join me?"

Things were going very fast. I had the strangest sense of trying to catch up, to accommodate this new pace of the eighties. It seemed we had hardly gotten into the Jacuzzi before we were in the bedroom, and it seemed that we had hardly gotten to the bedroom when she was up and getting dressed, and I was still lying there on the bed, and to my astonishment I heard myself say: "When will I see you again?"

"I'll give you a call," she said, buckling her belt.

It seemed to me she was dressing with undue haste. Did she have another date after leaving me?

"You have to go now?" I said.

"Yeah. I hate to fuck and run, but . . . big day tomorrow, I have to get my rest."

So I lay there in the bed, feeling worse and worse, while she got dressed, and pretty soon she waved goodbye, and then I heard the door slam and her car back down the driveway, and I thought, *I feel used.*

Well, I had been out of the action for a decade. My friend David had been single all during that time. The next time we played racquetball, I told him about my experience, which still troubled me.

"Yeah," he said, "I've had that, too. Where you find yourself asking her, 'When will I see you again?' You feel used after she's gone. . . ."

"Yes," I said. "I really did. I felt used. Seduced and abandoned. All of that."

318

"I know," David said, shaking his head. "It's a new world, Michael. It's all changed."

It was David's theory that feminism and the sexual revolution had actually had the effect of reversing traditional sex roles.

"Look," he said, "all of my male friends want to get married and settle down. But the women don't. The men want babies. The women don't. The men want meaningful relationships. The women want quick sex and then they want to get right back to their careers."

In keeping with this idea of reversal, David had a term for the behavior of women like Andrea: "feminine macho." David's idea was that women had seen the past years as an opportunity to behave like men—but that, in taking up certain traditional forms of male behavior, they had sometimes modified the form without understanding its underlying purpose.

"See," David said, "women think that, when men behave romantically on a one-night stand, that's hypocritical. So women won't do that. When a woman intends to have a one-night stand, she lets you know it. Bam! No illusions from her. But that doesn't feel like honesty to a man, it feels like brutality. Because, let's face it, men are the romantics. We're the ones who need the romance."

Here I am in the locker room with my friend David, who has been a Hollywood bachelor for two decades, who has gone out with so many models and actresses that he's good friends with the people who run the model agencies—here's David, suave man of the world, telling me that men are the romantics, and not women.

"No, no, no, David," I protested. "Women are romantic. Women want flowers and candy and all that stuff."

"No, they don't," David said. "Women want the respect and admiration of a man, and they know flowers are a sign of respect from a man. But they don't care about the flowers; they don't moon and ooh and aah and sigh, except for our benefit. They don't have any of those romantic feelings men think they do. Men have the romantic feelings. Women're much colder and more practical."

I disagreed.

"Okay," David said. "We're sitting in the locker room, right?"

"Right."

"Have you ever had a locker-room conversation about women—you know, the way women think we do, talking in explicit detail about what we did with our dates the night before?"

"No," I said. "I never have."

"Neither have I," David said. "But you've been accused of having such conversations by a woman?"

"Yes, sure." I couldn't count the number of times a woman had said she didn't want me talking about her to my male friends.

"You know why women think we have these explicit conversations? Because they do, that's why. Women talk about *everything.*"

I knew this was true. I had long ago learned of the frankness of women among themselves, and of their tendency to assume that men were equally frank, when, as far as I could tell, men were actually quite discreet.

"You see," David said, "each sex assumes the opposite sex is just the way they are. So women think men are explicit, and men think women are romantic. Eventually that becomes a stereotype that nobody questions. But it's not accurate at all."

David insisted on his view: women were stronger, tougher, more pragmatic, more interested in money and security, more focused on the underlying realities of any situation. Men were weaker, more romantic, more interested in the symbols than the reality—in short, living out a fantasy.

"I'm telling you," David said.

"What about the idea of the nurturing female?" I said.

"Only for children," he said. "Not for men." He shook his head sadly. "Did you ever wish a woman would send you flowers?"

The question caught me off guard. A woman send *me* flowers?

"Sure. Send you flowers, a nice note, thanks for a lovely evening, the whole bit."

It seemed such a strange idea. But as I considered it, it seemed as if it would be terrific.

"I'm telling you," David said, "we're the romantics. Work it out."

* * *

320

Working it out seemed to be the story of my life in the mid-1980s. In my private life, all the women I saw worked; often they were preoccupied with their work. During this period I went out with a reporter, a computer salesperson, a choreographer, and a composers' agent. Dinner with these women tended to be a litany of their problems at work. They assumed that the details of their jobs were as interesting to me as to them.

I was reminded of the times in the past when I had gone to dinner and monopolized the conversation with my own work problems. And, as David had said, the sex roles were now reversed. But whatever the explanation, there wasn't much romance in those dinners. On the contrary, this new equality had some decidedly dreary aspects. I used to listen to these women and think, *The only time you give your full attention is when you are talking.* When I was talking, they would glance at their watches. They were all vaguely preoccupied; they were all pressed for time; they were all playing An Important Person of Affairs. Which was fine, but it wasn't sexy: "Hey, it's nine o'clock now, I have to hit the road at ten. Do we have time to do it, or what?"

Practical, but not what I would have called a hot date.

One night I was sitting in the corner of a woman's kitchen when her roommate stormed in from a date, banging doors, shouting: "Jesus, what does a girl have to do to get *laid* these days?"

This roommate was embarrassed when she saw me sitting in the kitchen, but it led to an interesting discussion. And the most interesting thing about the discussion was that the attitudes, the frustrations, the disappointments expressed, were exactly the same as for men. In exactly the same terms. There was no difference at all.

By now I had adopted David's view of the inherent differences between the sexes, that men were the romantics and women were the pragmatists. His view that each sex saw the other as a projection of itself. I talked about this idea all the time, particularly with women.

I noticed that it always made women angry. They didn't like to hear it.

At first I thought it was because women were experienc-

321

ing so much discrimination in the workplace. Women felt they were always being told they couldn't do this, or they weren't suited for that. Or else they were just subtly bypassed in corporate hierarchies. So women were a little raw about any notion of inherent differences between the sexes, because it sounded like the setup for justifying discrimination.

But then, as I continued to listen to their complaints, I heard something else. I began to hear about "the way men are," about "the way men stick together," about "the way men are threatened by a competent woman," about "the way men are threatened by sex." About the way *they* are. About the problems *they* make for women because of the problems *they* have with intimacy or feelings or power. I heard a lot about how *they* act this way, and how *they* act that way.

I wasn't hearing about a particular man, or a particular job. Nothing was individualized. It was all abstract, all explained by a general theory of the way *they* were.

One night I was at a dinner party. The conversation was lively and far-ranging, and not at all concerned with the sexes. It was broadly social and political. But as I listened I noticed a tendency to talk about how *they* don't protect the environment, how *they* don't run the government responsibly, how *they* don't build quality products, how *they* never report the news accurately.

The basic message was that *they* were ruining the world, and there was nothing *we* could do about it.

"Wait a minute," I said. "Who is this *they* that you keep talking about?"

I got a lot of confused looks. Everyone else at the table knew who *they* were.

"Look," I said, "I don't think anything is served by imagining a world of faceless villains. There isn't any *they*. There're only people like us. If a corporation is polluting and the CEO sounds uninformed on TV, the chances are he's some guy who's in the middle of a divorce and whose kids are on drugs and he's got a lot on his mind, a big corporation to run, stockholders and board meetings and everybody pushing at him, and he's tired and pressured, this pollution issue is just one of many problems, and the government changes the regulations so often nobody can be sure whether he's breaking the law or not, and his aides aren't as smart as he'd like them to be, and they don't keep him as informed as he'd like to be, and maybe they even lie to him. This CEO doesn't want to appear like a jerk on TV. He's not happy he came off that way. But it happens, because he's just a guy trying to do his best and his best isn't always so hot. Who's any different?"

The table got silent.

"I don't know about you," I said, "but I think I'm pretty smart, and I don't always run my own life so well. I make mistakes and screw up. I do things I regret. I say things I wish I hadn't said. A lot of the people you see interviewed on TV have impossible jobs. It's only a question of how badly they'll do them. But I don't see any grand conspiracy out there. I think people are doing the best they can."

The table stayed silent.

"And what's really wrong with making *them* the problem," I said, "is that you abdicate your own responsibility. Once you say some mysterious *they* are in charge, then you're able to sit back comfortably and complain about how *they* are doing it. But maybe *they* need help. Maybe *they* need your ideas and your support and your letters and your active participation. Because you're not powerless, you are a participant in this world. It's your world, too."

So there I was, preaching at the dinner table. I got embarrassed and shut up. But in the back of my mind, I kept thinking, There's something else here. Some other way this is true. Something you haven't considered.

Back in the early 1970s, a girlfriend became exasperated with me and said, "Listen: just assume men and women are the same."

"How do you mean?" I said.

"Anything you think as a man, I think as a woman. Anything you feel, I feel."

"No, no," I said.

"Yes, yes," she said.

"Well, for example," I said, "men can just look at a woman and get turned on. The visual stimulus is enough for a man. But women aren't like that."

"Oh, really?"

"No. Women need more than the visual stimulus."

"I've certainly looked at a nice pair of buns in tight jeans and thought, 'I wouldn't mind trying *that.*'"

I thought, This is a very masculine woman. "Maybe for you," I said, "but for women in general, it doesn't work that way."

"All my girlfriends are the same," she said. "We're all bun-watchers."

She must have a lot of perverted friends, I thought. I gave another argument. "Women aren't turned on by pornography and men are."

"Oh, really?"

We went on like this for a while. She insisted that men and women were the same in their underlying behavior, and that I had a lot of wrong ideas about differences. Back in the 1970s this was pretty extreme stuff.

In subsequent years I forgot that conversation, but now, more than ten years later, it came back to me. It seemed useful to reconsider the whole business.

I still thought there were differences between men and women. It was true I didn't conceive those differences in the simplistic way I had so many years earlier. But I still thought there were differences. I wanted to know what those differences were.

Then, slowly, I began to ask a different question. Not what the differences were. Instead: What is the best way to think about men and women?

And I came to a surprising conclusion.

My old girlfriend was right.

The best way to think about men and women is to assume there are no differences between them.

I had already concluded that the best way to think about disease was to imagine that you caused it. Maybe that was literally true, and maybe it wasn't. The point was that the best strategy in dealing with your illness was to act as if you had control over it, and could change its course. That enabled you to stay in charge of your own life.

Similarly, I now thought the best way to think about the sexes was to imagine there were no differences between them. Maybe that was true and maybe it wasn't. But it was the best strategy.

Because, as I saw it, the biggest problem between the
324

sexes was the tendency to objectify the opposite sex and ultimately to become powerless before them. Both men and women did this about the opposite sex. *They* were this way or that way. *They* had this tendency. There was nothing we could do about the way *they* behaved.

When I looked back, I realized that in many instances I had failed to take action with a woman because I assumed there was nothing I could do about her conduct.

For example, whenever I lived with a woman, I knew she talked in intimate detail about our relationship with her girlfriends. I always hated that. I hated running into one of her girlfriends and thinking, *This woman knows all about me.* It felt like a terrible invasion of my privacy, of our privacy. But what could I do? Women talked with one another. Women had these special relationships.

But if I had been in a close working relationship with a man, I would have complained immediately if I found out he was talking about me with another man.

So why couldn't I say to a woman, "It makes me feel terrible that you talk to your girlfriend about us. I feel really betrayed, and I feel dismissed, too. Why do you take the most intimate parts of our relationship to a stranger? It makes me feel awful. You ask me to open up to you, but I know you're going to get on the phone tomorrow and tell all to some friend. Can't you see how that makes me feel?"

The answer, of course, was that I could say it. I just never had, because I had thought that women were inherently different from men. And in formulating that difference, I had also objectified women. They were different. They didn't have the same feelings I did. They were *they.*

Seeing Headhunters

I went to Borneo to see the Dyaks, the indigenous head-hunters of that island. After hours of flying over trackless jungle, in progressively smaller planes, I finally landed at a small inland town called Sibu, on the banks of a broad, muddy jungle river.

I checked into the Paradise Hotel, which proudly advertised hot and cold running water. I went out into the town and arranged to visit a Dyak village. I was told there were authentic villages, where the people still lived in the traditional longhouses, within two hours' travel from Sibu by boat.

I was excited to hear Dyaks were so close. I wanted to leave at once, but a boat could not be arranged until the following morning. So I was obliged to spend the rest of the day in the town.

I walked around Sibu restlessly. The air was humid and stifling. The town was small and not very interesting. I was quickly bored. I had come to see Dyaks, and now I was stuck in this tedious little town, its streets lined by the stalls of Chinese merchants. I wandered over to an open-air market near the river. The large crowd of Chinese and Malays was dressed in shorts and tee shirts, typical Western

326

clothes. There was not a Dyak to be seen. I was annoyed to be standing in the kind of crowd I could see any day in Singapore. I wanted to see Dyaks, damn it!

A little girl in a white dress stared at me while she sucked her thumb. I glared at the girl; she became frightened and reached for her father's hand. I looked at her father's hand, then his arm.

Starting at the elbow, the man's arm was covered in dark-blue tattoos.

Then, in the V-neck of his shirt, I saw more tattoos. I knew that Dyaks used tattoos for clan identification. Then I saw that the man's earlobes were pierced and pendulous; they hung down almost to his shoulders.

This man was a Dyak!

I looked at the crowd at the market, and now I saw that nearly everyone had tattoos and hanging earlobes. I had been depressed about not seeing Dyaks while I was standing in a crowd of them!

A few years earlier, during a trek in Nepal, my Sherpa guide took me to the top of a hill at a place called Ghorapani, pointed to the view and said, "The Kali-Gandaki Gorge."

"Uh-huh," I said. I was sweating and tired. It was cold. My feet hurt. I could hardly pay attention to this view.

"The Kali-Gandaki Gorge," he repeated, significantly.

"Uh-huh," I said.

What I was seeing wasn't even a gorge, it was just a big valley with snowy mountain peaks on both sides. Spectacular, but all the mountain views in Nepal are spectacular, and I was tired at the end of the day.

"The Kali-Gandaki Gorge," he said a third time. Like I still wasn't getting the point.

"Great," I said. "When's dinner?"

It wasn't until I returned home that I found out what the Kali-Gandaki Gorge is.

The Kali-Gandaki river cuts between the peaks of Dhaulagiri to the west and Annapurna 1 to the east—respectively the sixth and tenth highest mountains in the world. Both peaks rise more than four miles above the river below, making a canyon so enormous that the eye can hardly see it for what it is. It is four times as deep as the

Grand Canyon, and far wider: between the two peaks, you could roughly fit twenty Grand Canyons.

The Kali-Gandaki Gorge is the deepest canyon in the world.

That's what it is.

I'd like to go back and see it sometime.

Life on the Astral Plane

The phenomenon of trance mediumship had interested me for some years. Broadly speaking, a medium is someone who goes into an altered state of consciousness and then delivers material not otherwise available to him or her.

Some mediums become only lightly dissociated and retain their characteristic personalities, although they may claim to speak for a spirit guide or someone from "the other side." Other mediums enter a deep trance, during which they appear to be taken over entirely by a new personality that has a different name, voice, gestures, and pattern of speech. These mediums are said, in popular parlance, to be "channeling" the personality that takes over.

A century ago, mediums usually claimed to channel dead figures of greater or lesser eminence. Modern mediums are more likely to claim they channel extraterrestrials, or disembodied entities from the future, or individuals who have been reincarnated many times throughout history. So the phenomenon of channeling seems to be influenced by the broader social context in which it appears, indeed, historical studies suggest that channeling becomes prominent during times of social upheaval, and toward the end of each century. As we approach the end of our own century, it is perhaps no surprise that channeling should once more become controversial, and widely discussed.

In any case, I was eager to witness this phenomenon firsthand, but I had no opportunity until 1981, when I heard that "Dr. Kilarney" was in town. Dr. Kilarney was a nineteenth-century Irish physician channeled by a woman from Utah. I had never heard of Dr. Kilarney, but I quickly arranged a private session. It was pretty expensive, and the man I talked to on the telephone seemed very concerned about how he would be paid. It gave me a funny feeling. Nevertheless, I arranged a session the following day.

The medium turned out to be a short, slovenly woman wearing jeans and a sweatshirt. She was staying in a little house in Torrance, California. She seemed edgy, and hovered near her husband, a big, hulking fellow. They both wore a lot of Indian turquoise jewelry. I gave them my money, and then was led into a tiny back bedroom. The woman sat on an unmade bed, closed her eyes, took a few deep breaths, opened her eyes, and said, "Begorrah, and how might you be on this fine day, my son?" in a corny Irish accent.

I had spent many months in Ireland, shooting a movie, so I'd heard a lot of Irish accents. Dr. Kilarney's accent immediately struck me as fake. And her vocabulary was entirely contemporary, even though the Irish still use a lot of nineteenth-century slang in their speech. All in all, Dr. Kilarney sounded like someone from Utah pretending to be Irish.

So the persona of Dr. Kilarney wasn't convincing at all. On the other hand, the medium was clearly transformed. Her posture was erect, her eyes were bright, and her gestures were strong and direct. She had a very different energy, and the energy didn't waver. It remained exactly the same. But the information channeled wasn't very satisfactory. I was advised to be tolerant of my girlfriend, to meditate regularly, to work hard at my writing, and to take more vitamin C. I was also advised to do a series of rebirthing sessions with the woman's husband, and was handed a schedule of fees as I departed.

Thus my first personal experience with a trance medium left me entirely unconvinced. If there was anything to this phenomenon, I hadn't seen it.

In 1982 I attended a session with Ramtha, an entity channeled by a woman named J. Z. Knight. At this time Ramtha was already famous. The medium sank her head onto her chest for a few moments, and when she looked up, she was evidently different: her voice was deeper and stronger; she was tremendously vigorous and went around the room, giving advice confidently to the fifty people there. Again I was impressed by the powerful, direct manner of the medium, but this time the information seemed direct and clear as well.

I was already persuaded that psychic readings were possible, so the idea that someone might do fifty psychic readings in succession, for a whole roomful of people, didn't strike me as inconceivable. But Ramtha's energy was not the same as the energy of the psychics I had seen. Most psychics were shy, passive, or diffident. Ramtha acted like a member of the Joint Chiefs—you felt a tremendously commanding presence before you. And in the end you remembered that commanding presence long after you had forgotten exactly what was said.

But there was another quality to seeing Ramtha. There was the considerable fee, and the strict timetable, and the theatrical flourish with which the medium entered and left the room. This was star treatment and star expense, and it provoked a lot of uneasy questions about spiritualism and commerce.

So I still didn't know what to make of this trance-medium business. And then, in 1984, I heard that a trance medium named Gary was doing readings for people in Los Angeles. I arranged to meet him.

Gary was a shy, quiet, athletic man in his thirties. He explained that his method of working was not what people usually imagined when they thought of trance mediums. When he went into a trance, he said he accessed something called the Akashic Records. By looking into these records, he said he had access to any knowledge in the world, past, present, or future. This was how he explained it.

In practice, Gary lay down on a sofa, took a few deep breaths, and entered a seemingly light trance. When he began to speak, his voice was sleepy, but otherwise not strikingly different from his normal voice. He didn't open his eyes, and his body remained reclining. Gary did not dramatically take on a new persona. He just lay on the sofa and talked to you. But in his trance he spoke with uncanny confidence and disturbing psychological acuity. After he got through confronting me for an hour, he'd come out of the trance, rub his eyes, blink, and ask mildly if things had gone all right.

I liked Gary, and saw him several times, and then went on to other things.

But then, in the fall of 1985, Gary decided to teach other people how to channel for themselves. This interested me, and I arranged to learn under his direction. As it turned out, it happened quickly.

I lay on my back with my eyes closed, and Gary spoke quietly to me, guiding a meditation intended to relax me ever more deeply. Over a period of perhaps twenty minutes, my body sank into a profound relaxation, until I was no longer really aware of my limbs at all. It was as if I was at the edge of sleep. But as I relaxed further, I felt my body paradoxically start to become tense and rigid. My hands and feet felt frozen, immovable.

At the same time this rigidity set in, I became intensely aware of sounds and events around me, not only in the immediate room but also in the entire house, and the street outside. This heightened awareness was a little like the hypersensitivity that people with migraine headaches describe. It was very acute, slightly irritating.

Gary was moving around the room. I heard him moving and wished he would not, and I felt a strange kind of inner conviction, and I heard this faraway, sleepy voice say, "Gary, *sit down.*"

Gary sat down.

I couldn't see him, but I knew he had. I *felt* it.

I proceeded to tell him some things that were troubling him. I felt absolutely convinced of what I was saying: I *knew* I was right. Gary then asked me some questions about a woman he knew in Boston. I gave my impressions. All the while, some part of me was shouting, How can you know about some woman in Boston? Shut up, you're making a fool of yourself, but I gave my impressions anyway.

I say "I" gave my impressions, although that isn't quite right. I (the present writer, I) don't really know how to explain the feeling that I experience during channeling. The feeling is this:

There is an awareness present inside a stiff, tense body. The usual awareness called "Michael," my ego or whatever you want to call it, I experience as a thin coating on the

332

outside of my body, like a coat of spray paint. So "Michael" is pushed away from the center. Sometimes I imagine that "Michael" is in my big toe. It doesn't seem to matter where he is, just so he gets out of the way.

Meanwhile, in the center of the body, some other awareness is speaking and answering. This awareness has no name, no past, no embodiment, no emotions, no interests. It's just a naked awareness. And it is *very sure* of what it is saying. It speaks of Michael as if Michael were another person, or a very small part of itself. It often has to make decisions about what to say, based on its sense of what the listener can understand; these decisions are rather like translating. And sometimes the awareness has to deal with the displaced "Michael," who may suddenly start to be embarrassed by what is being said, or worried the awareness can't know what it is saying. The rest of the time "Michael" is absent, or at least not intrusive.

Now, all this may sound peculiar, but in fact during a channeling session it seems about as ordinary as cooking dinner, watching television, something like that. Only when it comes time to re-emerge is there a recognition of how deep the state really is. It is not so easy to come out of it; sometimes it takes a few minutes.

After the first time I channeled, I remembered everything that I had said in the trance state. Gary had always claimed that he never remembered what he said in a session. Now I could see he hadn't told the truth. When I confronted him, he admitted that he remembered more than he said. But he also told me, "Just wait a while."

And, sure enough, after a few more channeling sessions, I began to realize that I was losing the information. It decayed like a dream. For the first moments after I came out, I could remember the whole session easily. But immediately the memory began to fade. After an hour, I had trouble recalling it except in general terms. After a week, I didn't remember much at all. Sometimes I even forgot I had channeled for someone in the first place.

There seemed no reason to hold on to the information. It wasn't any use to me. If someone wanted to know about her boyfriend's health, what use was that to me? There was no point to keeping it in memory, and I didn't.

And the channeling awareness itself was extremely uncurious. Sometimes, when I channeled for people I knew, "Michael" would anticipate a little voyeuristic thrill, hearing the questions. But there never was a thrill. The channel was dead to gossipy feelings. Everything was just the way it was. The only effort in channeling was the effort of explanation, and the only emotion was compassion.

When I first began to channel, I wondered why it was so easy for me, and I suspected that it had some similarity to the state I am in when writing. I've spent a lot of my life writing, so that is a familiar state.

A psychiatrist friend, Judith, said, "I'm not surprised at all that you are channeling, because you must channel when you write. But who or what are you channeling? Did you ask that?"

"Who or what?"

"Well," Judith said, "is it an entity, or a spirit, or a part of yourself, or what?"

"I don't know," I said. That question had never occurred to me. I called Gary up. "What am I channeling?"

"I am teaching you to channel your higher self," Gary said.

"What's that?"

"I just call it the higher self, and it seems to be a wise part of yourself, but otherwise I don't know what it is."

I wanted more information; I called my friend Stephen. "Well," he said, "what you are doing would be called different things in different historical periods, and would be explained different ways, but the fact that you are doing it, that doesn't surprise me."

I was tremendously excited about channeling during the first couple of weeks. I channeled for Anne-Marie. I channeled for people in my office. I channeled for other friends. I tried channeling while in different physical conditions: with my eyes open, while walking around, while standing in the shower. I was very experimental; it was fun to try.

I discovered only one major disappointment. Although I could channel for other people who asked me questions, I couldn't do it for myself. This was frustrating. I felt as if I had received a wonderful inheritance that I couldn't spend on myself. Finally Lisa, in my office, said, "Tell me what questions you want asked, and I'll ask them for you."

That seemed like a strange idea, but it worked fine. The channel would talk about Michael and give all sorts of useful answers. Here is a partial transcript of one session:

Q: Why can't Michael find a house?

A: He feels his possibilities are limited, he has a feeling of hopelessness, he feels that he can't get what he wants. The image is of a car with the gas siphoned out. He drains his own energy by failing to believe he can do better.

Q: What should he do about this?

A: He needs to make a big change. He blockades himself until he finally must confront the issue; he has no choice. It would be better to confront earlier.

Q: What is his problem writing the revisions?

A: There seems to be a lot of anxiety; his assumption about any revelation is that it will be used against him, either soon or late. This is his experience from childhood, although it is not repeated for him in adulthood.

Q: Does he need to make many revisions?

A: Nothing is necessary but the changes are beneficial. He should be doing this work quickly and not be obsessive, not change unnecessary things. He should do what really strikes him and skip the trivia.

Well, this is myself talking about myself. The first time I read what came out in the session, I was surprised and slightly annoyed. The channeled information seemed correct to me. But if I was so smart, how come I wasn't so smart?

I'm still not clear about that.

Eventually the novelty of channeling wore off. Like a new car: you drive it with enthusiasm for a while, and then one day it's just a car, a thing that gets you around, a vehicle, transportation. I channeled less frequently. I stopped talking about it.

But I still understood very little about the phenomenon, and I wanted to know more. What was going on here? What was this rigid, calm, unemotional state that knew all the answers?

In part, to get some understanding of the state—or states, or whatever it was—I continued to work with Gary. We worked almost every week, trying different things. Guided imagery. Astral travel. Past-life recollection.

Sometimes I had powerful experiences, comparable to drug-induced trances. Sometimes I just had a nice meditation. Sometimes I thought, You've been in California too long, Michael, and you've gone from a perfectly okay doctor to some guy who lies on a couch while somebody puts crystals on him and you actually think it *means* something, but it's nothing but a lot of hippie-dippy airy-fairy baloney. New Age Garbage, Aquarian Abracadabra, Karmic Crap. Get out now, Michael, before it's too late. Get out before you really start to believe this stuff.

But the thing is, I was having a really interesting time. And I thought intermittent panicky skepticism was to be expected whenever you stepped off the cliff, whenever you went into some realm of experience that wasn't modeled and accepted and approved and stuck into a nice frame by society at large.

Anyway, self-doubt was nothing new to me. As it turned out, I experienced my strongest doubts about the possibility of past lives.

One day Gary proposed I do a past-life regression. I said okay. I'd never tried that. It was a trendy thing to do. I might as well get it over with. I agreed to try to recall one.

Gary induced me into an altered state with tapes and a guided meditation. When I was deeply under, he said, "Now just let images come to you, images or sensations from another lifetime."

Another Lifetime. It sounded like the title of a soap opera. Oh boy, I thought, I don't know if I can keep a straight face for this one.

"Just let it come in," Gary said.

With startling suddenness, I saw the Colosseum in Rome. But not the crumbling concentric rings that you ordinarily see in pictures. I was *beneath* the Colosseum, in the twisting passages and tiny dark rooms that the gladiators inhabited.

I was a gladiator.

"What's going on?" Gary said.

"I'm in Rome."

I smelled the odors of the arena, blood and sand and animal excrement. Above me I heard the roar of the crowd, the stomping feet. I felt the heat of the day in my tiny, oppressive cell as I waited.

About this time, a tiny voice inside my head cut in and said, *Sure, Michael, just like Kirk Douglas in* Spartacus. *How many times did you see that one? Give me a break.*

Gary said, "Where in Rome?"

"The Colosseum."

"How does it feel?"

"I'm very strong."

I was aware of my enormous body, my great physical strength. I was startled to feel genuine pleasure at having a large body, to feel proud of it and not to be embarrassed by it, as I was in real life. Here in the Colosseum, I needed this body, I needed to rely on it. But this was also a different body, hard, heavily muscled, dark-skinned. And I felt something else—a sick, tense feeling, anxiety. Adrenaline.

"I have to kill people. Kill them before they kill me."

"And how does that feel?"

"It doesn't matter, I have to do it or I will be killed. I have to kill them first. It is my job."

The voice inside my head said, *Sure, Michael, this is the perfect fantasy for you, the perfect way to explain your withdrawn and defensive nature. This isn't any past life. It's just a fantasy, and it fits you like a Freudian glove.*

Gary said, "Do you know the people you are fighting?"

"I don't want to know them. I may have to kill them."

"Are you afraid to die?"

"No."

I was surprised to realize this was true. I felt great tension but no fear. There was a kind of blankness when I considered the possibility that I might myself be killed in the future. I didn't seem to have much skill at visualizing.

"How many people have you killed?"

"It . . . doesn't matter."

There was a blankness to the past, too. No recollection of past fights in the arena. No thinking of the past at all. No future, no past. Just sitting in my cell, waiting to be called to fight. Hearing the crowd. A shout: something must have happened. Waiting.

337

"It doesn't sound like a very nice life."

I wanted to beat Gary's head in. Why didn't he shut up? What was the point of this psychological posturing? I had a job to do, plain and simple. His talk only weakened me. There weren't any choices. Kill or be killed. Everything else was crap.

"Do you have women?"

"Sometimes."

They supplied women to the fighters. Prostitutes. Hard women. Sometimes rich women came to amuse themselves.

"And how do you feel about the women?"

"I have no feeling."

There was nothing to feel. Gary didn't understand: he was speaking from another world, a soft world. Here in Rome I felt nothing except my size and my strength and my certainty that I would win. There was nothing else to feel. There was no room for anything else.

"That must not be pleasant, to have no feelings."

"There's nothing wrong with me."

"I didn't say there was."

"Why don't you shut up?" I said.

"How long have you been a gladiator?" Gary said.

"All my life."

I was a slave in Tunisia. I was sent to Rome, and when I grew so large I was sold as a gladiator. I had won many fights. I was nineteen. I had lived that long.

The voice cut in, *Make it as detailed as you want, Michael, it's still just your own fantasy, this has nothing to do with any past life.*

"What will happen to you?" Gary said.

"I will die."

"How?"

"A lion."

"What do you feel about that death?"

"I have no feeling."

And I didn't. It was an encounter, fatigue, a mistake, nothing more. There was nothing to have a feeling about. It was just animal interaction. Two animals together.

"What do you think of your life as a gladiator?"

Gary was boring. Stupid, effete, not understanding the realities. Sometimes these people came and sat with you before you fought, watching you, feeling what it was like to spend time with a man who might soon die. You were

338

supposed to make conversation. I never would. "I'm not going to talk to you any more," I said.

We ended the session.

When I came out, Gary asked me what I thought of the session. I said that it just seemed the kind of detailed fantasy any decent student of Latin could come up with on short notice. I had had four years of Latin.

"I thought it was pretty genuine," Gary said.

"Gary, I'm a *writer*, for God's sake. I make up fantasies for a living. I do it all the time. I'm good at it. This wasn't a past life."

I certainly believed that this gladiator fantasy had value—as an expression of a way I often felt. I was very clear that from time to time I felt myself in great danger from other people, that I needed to block off any feeling of sympathy toward them, because I saw myself in combat with them and needed to be able to kill them, at least symbolically, without qualms. That kind of psychological armoring was a personal problem that I was aware of. To see it take this form was not surprising.

I didn't believe it was any past life.

"I don't know, this was pretty convincing," Gary said. "Your manner was pretty convincing. Once or twice I thought you were going to hit me."

I told him I was sure it was just a fantasy.

And that is what I feel today. The kind of evidence that I have seen for clairvoyance or telepathy—evidence that leads me to accept these phenomena as unquestionably real—I have not experienced for the idea of past lives. It may be there. But I haven't experienced it. No event in my life convinces me that I have lived before.

Or, to put it another way: if the ability to enter into the persona of a long-dead person is a genuine phenomenon—if such things are really possible—it still does not necessarily imply that we are recalling past incarnations. There are other possible explanations.

One day Gary suggested I try astral travel. "Why not?" I said. I was ready for anything, except more past lives.

339

Of course, astral travel was equally trendy, but I had had more experience with the idea of "out-of-body experiences." I had done such things since childhood, when quite by accident I discovered I could shift my awareness out of my body and move it around the bedroom. The most comfortable place seemed to be a corner of the ceiling, looking down on myself. But I could also send my awareness outside, and roam around the backyard, or through the house, if I didn't mind the feeling that I was snooping on other people.

As a kid, I didn't think anything about this. It was just a way to spend time before you were sleepy. I assumed that anybody could do it. Sometimes in museums, if things got boring, I would amuse myself by trying to guess what was in the next room. But that seemed pretty ordinary, too.

One summer, after college, I had worked at Columbia Medical School. I had a dormitory room for the summer, at Physicians and Surgeons Hospital. The room was bare, nothing in it. I used to lie on the bed at night, go up to the ceiling, and look down on myself lying in bed. By then I was old enough to think this was odd. I had pejoratives to apply to it, like "dissociative state" and "schizophrenia." So I stopped doing it.

Anyway, the idea of astral travel didn't seem too alarming, and I tried it with Gary. It is, after all, just another kind of guided meditation in an altered state. I visualized my chakras glowing brightly, spinning like white spirals. Then I visualized myself leaving through my third chakra, moving up to the astral plane—which to me appeared as a misty yellow place.

So far, so good. I began to see why people so often imagined heaven as misty or cloudy. This misty astral plane was agreeable. It was peaceful to be standing here, in all this yellow mist. I felt fine.

"Do you see anybody here?" Gary said.

I looked around. I didn't see anybody.

"No."

"Stay there a minute and let's see if anybody comes."

Then I saw my grandmother, who had died while I was in medical school. She waved to me, and I waved back. I wasn't surprised to see her up here. I didn't feel any particular need to talk to her.

So I just waited around. This astral plane was rather

featureless. There weren't any palm trees or chairs or places to sit down. It was just a place. A misty yellow place.

"Do you see anybody else?" Gary said.

I didn't. Then:

"Yes. My father."

I felt worried. I hadn't had an easy time with my father. Now he was showing up while I was vulnerable, in an altered state of consciousness. I wondered what he would do, what would happen. He approached me. My father looked the same, only translucent and misty, like everything else in this place. I didn't want to have a long conversation with him. I was quite nervous.

Suddenly he embraced me.

In the instant of that embrace, I saw and felt everything in my relationship with my father, all the feelings he had had and why he had found me difficult, all the feelings I had had and why I had misunderstood him, all the love that was there between us, and all the confusion and misunderstanding that had overpowered it. I saw all the things he had done for me and all the ways he had helped me. I saw every aspect of our relationship at once, the way you can take in at a glance something small you hold in your hand. It was an instant of compassionate acceptance and love.

I burst into tears.

"What is happening now?"

"He's hugging me."

"What are you feeling?"

"It's . . . all over," I said.

What I meant was that this incredibly powerful experience had already happened, complete and total, in a fraction of a second. By the time Gary had asked me, by the time I burst into tears, it was finished. My father had gone. We never said a word. There was no need to say anything. The thing was completed.

"I'm done," I said, and opened my eyes. I had bounced right out of the trance state.

I couldn't really explain it to Gary—I couldn't really explain it to anybody—but part of my astonishment at the experience was at the speed with which it had occurred. Like most people who have had therapy, I had an expectation about the pace of psychological insights. You struggle. Things happen slowly. Years may go by without much change. You wonder if it is making any difference. You wonder if you should quit or hang in. You work and you struggle and you make your hard-won gains.

But what of this experience? In less time than I took to open my mouth to speak, something extraordinary and profound had happened to me. And I knew it would last. My relationship with my father had been resolved in a flash. There hadn't even been time to cry, and now that it was over, crying seemed after-the-fact. I had no desire to cry. The experience was already finished.

This made me wonder if my ideas about the normal speed of psychological change might be incorrect. Perhaps we could accomplish massive change in seconds, if we only knew how. Perhaps change took so long only because we did it the wrong way. Or perhaps because we expected it to take so long.

New Guinea

I am in a house made of thatched grass in Tari, a remote province in the highlands of New Guinea. Sitting around the open fire are a half-dozen muscular men, naked except for grass skirts and hornbills on their necks and sticks piercing their noses and colorful paint on their faces. Outside, I hear the leathery flapping of fruit bats moving through the night. I am staying here for the next four days and my friend Anne-Marie is asking about Rose, the woman whose house this is.

In the light of the fire, Rose picks at the bloody stump of her index finger while we eat dinner. Anne-Marie inquires whether Rose has injured herself.

"Naw," says our Australian guide, Nemo. "She cut it off."

Anne-Marie is horrified. "She cut her finger off?"

"Yeah, she got angry."

"What about?"

"Hebrew's new wife. See, Rose is Hebrew's second wife, and when he told her he was going to take a third wife, she got mad and cut off her finger. As a protest."

Hebrew, the husband, sits there by the fire. Anne-Marie asks what he felt about this.

343

"Me no liking this," Hebrew says in pidgin. He switches to English for us. "Rose better stop this foolishness or I divorce her," he says, and pounds his thigh for emphasis.

"Want to see the finger?" Nemo asks. "She kept it; you can see it if you want to."

"Maybe after dinner," Anne-Marie says.

Rose sulks and cleans the stump of her finger.

"I told her not to pick at it," Nemo says, "but I guess she knows what she's doing."

As I watch this, all I can think of is the carpeting in the elevators of the Shangri-La Hotel in Singapore.

We slept in the Shangri-La Hotel the night before. It is a very nice high-rise hotel, but because so many travelers to Singapore have crossed the international date line, they tell you the day in the carpeting. You get on the elevator and the carpeting says "TODAY IS SATURDAY—HAVE A NICE DAY." Or whatever day it is. They change the carpeting each day.

Now, one day later, we are in a thatched hut in the middle of New Guinea, surrounded by painted men. A young girl of three or four stares at me solemnly. She is Rose and Hebrew's daughter.

"How old is your daughter, Hebrew?"

"Eight," Hebrew says.

This is clearly wrong. "He doesn't know how old she is, mite," Nemo explains. "None of these blokes knows how old they are. Doesn't matter here."

For some reason this startles me more than the grass skirts and painted faces. They don't know how old they are? At the Shangri-La Hotel, one whole wall of the lobby displays digital clocks giving local time around the world. The Shangri-La Hotel has twenty-four-hour telex and secretarial services. Here the people don't know the time. They don't know their age. Their age doesn't matter to them. I have trouble conceiving a world where your age doesn't matter.

This world is not what I expected in any case. I had arranged to spend some days in a hut in a native village. I imagined a semicircle of huts in the jungle, one of which would be used by me. The visitors' hut. I expected to be smack in the middle of village life. But this hut stands alone. When I go outside, I cannot see any other huts, only surrounding fields owned by Rose where *kai-kai,* vegetables, are grown. There is apparently no village at all, but Nemo

344

explains that the "village" of the Tari people refers to the neighborhood, to all the other, similarly isolated houses in an area covering several square miles.

In fact, each Tari house and field is hidden behind massive sculpted dirt bulwarks fifteen feet high. As you drive down a road, you see only these bulwarks on all sides. With overhanging vegetation, the road is a kind of tunnel.

The ramparts are built for defense, to prevent surprise attacks. For the tribespeople of New Guinea are continually at war, and always alert to the possibility of attack. Like the Sicilians, they live in an atmosphere of perpetual vendetta.

Before we arrived, we had some vague concern for our safety. Nemo assures us there is no problem. Killings are carried out according to tribe and clan; as outsiders, we belong to no tribe or clan, and therefore are exempt from hostilities unless we happen to get in the way. Meanwhile, I have difficulty matching the cheerful personalities of the Tari men with their readiness to kill.

Anne-Marie and I retire to the next room, crawl into sleeping bags. In the light of a kerosene lantern, I look at the beautiful pattern of thatching on the walls. Mice squeak and scamper within the walls. We hear the bats flap outside, and flying foxes. In the adjacent rooms, there are arguments, crying infants. Fleas hop around in the sleeping bag, bite, fly up my nose.

Finally I manage to go to sleep. My last thought is: What am I doing here?

After Greenland, New Guinea is the largest island in the world. Its land mass is roughly equivalent to Sweden. Three million people live here. It is a mountainous country, which means there is great diversity of habits and language. People separated by intervening mountain ranges develop their own customs and language; seven thousand languages and dialects are spoken here, although pidgin is the *lingua franca*.

In fact, New Guinea consists of three entirely separate environments. There is a coastal environment, which is very like nearby Pacific islands, such as New Caledonia and New Britain. Then, in the north, there is a flat, hot jungle region, where life is organized around rivers, principally the Sepik and its tributaries. But the majority of the population lives in the mountainous interior of the New Guinea Highlands, and these people were not even known to exist until the 1930s. Although much has happened in the subsequent half-century, parts of the country remain remote. Here tribal life continues more or less as it always has.

I wanted to be among tribal people, to experience what life was like for man for thousands of years before what we call civilization, and so I have come halfway around the world and now find myself in a thatched hut in a mountain province, trying to go to sleep with fleas hopping up my nose.

I am here in New Guinea wrapped in layers of romance.

The romance of the anthropologist: I will talk to these colorful natives and learn their ways. Many of them speak English, which is a convenience for the visiting anthropologist on a tight schedule. But I quickly discover that everybody tells me a different story. This is particularly noticeable when it concerns that subject dearest to my heart, me. For example, if there is a fight in some other place, such as the city of Mount Hagen, and one of Hebrew's relatives kills someone from another tribe, then the dead man's kin may come looking for Hebrew to pay him back. Under those circumstances, am I, the innocent visitor, in danger? Most people say no. Some people shrug. Some people say yes: if the war party can't find Hebrew they will kill his wife or his children, and if they can't find the wife or children they may decide to kill me.

Naturally I am interested to learn which of these answers is correct. But I never do. I don't even find out how Hebrew will learn of a fight in Mount Hagen, which is more than a hundred miles away, over a range of rugged mountains. How does he find out?

Hebrew laughs: "Don't worry. I will hear of it."

It turns out that clans intermarry so that each village will have its spies, to report back to their families about anything that is being planned. Furthermore, children take the clans of both father and mother, so a Tari person may end up belonging to seven or eight clans. Everyone thus has multiple allegiances, and it is extremely confusing.

Then there is the romance of the visiting sophisticate, Bwana Michael in his khaki shirts with epaulets. Photographing the colorful tribal rituals with his trusty Nikon. I am particularly interested in their methods of warfare, which are traditional—axes and bows and arrows. The men avoid modern weapons such as guns, because such killings can be traced by the police. But I cannot conceive that bows and arrows are really dangerous, really lethal.

Hebrew and his friends laugh at me. One morning they show me their arrows, which are straight pieces of wood, without feathers, the tips hardened in a fire. The arrow might bring down a bird, but can such arrows really kill a person? Hebrew sets up a bamboo stalk, perhaps four inches in diameter, in the middle of a field. From a distance of fifty yards, he invites me to shoot at this slender target. But I am clumsy; the unfeathered arrows fly off in all directions.

Hebrew draws the bow. His wooden arrow entirely pierces the hard bamboo. I am stunned: that arrow would pass through a human body easily. The other men shoot in turn. They all hit this narrow target fifty yards away.

Then there is the romance of the pastoral primitive. A little time among Rousseau's noble savages. The uncorrupted natural man, unburdened by the junk of materialist civilization. Unfortunately, Hebrew and his wife fight constantly. Their infant screams. The younger children look unhappy, try to stay out of the way.

One day the betrothed wife number three shows up at the hut, armed with a baseball bat. Her arrival constitutes a provocative act; Rose immediately attacks the new wife with a kitchen knife. Friends and relatives surge in to separate the brawling women; there are shouts and traded insults; Rose's knife is taken away from her; the third wife is relieved of her baseball bat and urged to leave, but she refuses. The situation is ugly and we visitors are the audience. Nemo proposes we leave for a while, to let things cool down. We climb into the Land Cruiser. As we drive out, Rose flings herself, with her infant, on top of the car. We stop, get out, argue some more.

To a modern sensibility, all this seems to take hours. But the participants are unhurried. There is no need to resolve disputes quickly. There is no need to resolve them at all. There is no reason why we shouldn't spend all day in front of the Land Cruiser, arguing about things.

Finally the provocative third wife departs, taking her cudgel with her. Rose is calmer. We leave, going out into the countryside.

Ah, the romance of primitive nature. Unfortunately, everything in New Guinea is owned. All the land, all the trees, all the animals. If you touch or take anything, you can be killed for it. The high earthen ramparts transform the landscape into something that looks like the Maginot Line. There are no open vistas, no untouched spaces. You are in a war zone, and although people are friendly, the atmosphere is one of perpetual suspicion.

A hike to a waterfall will set things right. There's a lovely waterfall we must see. We drive to a farm, then spend half an hour finding the farmer to ask his permission to enter his lands. There is no thought of entering the lands without such permission; if we can't find the man, we must go home again.

We see a wooden sign that shows a red human hand, with the words ITAMBU NOGAT ROT. I ask what this means, and Hebrew looks at me oddly: can't I read simple English? (It means "It Taboo No Got Right"—in other words, "Keep Out.")

Finally the farmer is found, permission is granted, and we set off for the waterfall. Almost immediately we are descending a sheer forested incline. I slip and slide and stumble down this muddy jungle track. Hebrew points out local sights, the pandanus tree and something called "plenty-nut," which is like coconut, and particularly favored by the *cus-cus,* or possum. Or the "lipstick plant," a fuzzy red shell containing seeds that produce a red dye for painting the warriors.

I am grateful for all these interruptions, any excuse to catch my breath and my balance. We continue down for about an hour, but, as Hebrew says, "Down is easy. *Up* is hard." Eventually I hear the roar of the waterfall. Another fifteen minutes and the foliage is soaking wet, the ground sucking mud. We are sinking to our knees in the mud. The trail is still vertical.

At last we emerge at the base of an incredibly powerful waterfall. We cannot see it well for the dense mist it throws up. We slip over giant rocks to stand at its base, unable to speak to one another over the roar. This is not placid nature. This is raw power. It is like standing too close to the speakers at a rock concert. I am uncomfortable and soaking wet. We head back.

It takes an hour to climb back up to the top. The mud drags. My feet are heavy. Frequent stops to remove the leeches. I stagger back to the car and collapse on the seat.

"Quite a vertical country," Nemo remarks, in what I find extreme understatement. "No wonder these blokes are fit." We drive back to attend the sing-sing.

A sing-sing is what most people associate with New Guinea. Warriors paint themselves with elaborate designs, dress in traditional headgear, and dance and sing together. The Tari men have one of the most beautiful decorative motifs: the men paint their faces bright yellow, and wear elaborate headdresses involving everlasting flowers, and feathers from birds of paradise. While they are dressing, a large crowd of local people gathers. An air of expectancy settles over the watchers. Soon the sing-sing will begin.

But the dance itself is oddly disappointing. The men form lines and chant and stomp for about thirty seconds. Then they stop, talk, smoke, laugh. After a minute or two, they sing again for a brief time. Then they stop again. Then they sing again. The whole procedure, with its abrupt starts and stops, has a desultory quality that is startling to Western eyes accustomed to a performance at least as long as a three-minute popular song. But that is the way it is done, and the enthusiasm of the crowd indicates that nothing is wrong. I take pictures. By now I know many of the men, but in their paint and costumes their demeanor is entirely changed, and they pose fiercely.

When the sing-sing is over, they remove their headdresses, wrap them in plastic, and take them home to their huts. Headdresses are extremely valuable, and great care is taken with them. But the men leave the paint on their faces. That night, around the fire, they are all red and yellow as they laugh and smoke. They delight in personal ornament. During the day Hebrew will sometimes decorate his hair with small green leaves. At night he puts fireflies in his hair, so his head winks and glows like a Christmas tree.

Their makeup has a purpose: to disguise the warriors. Thus, if a warrior kills an enemy in battle, the enemy may have trouble distinguishing which warrior actually did the killing. Yet in practice everybody knows who did the killing—one more contradiction too difficult to resolve for an anthropologist on a time schedule.

But I would like to see a tribal war. I have only read anthropological accounts of these battles, which are formal affairs lasting all day. In the early morning the two sides meet at a field, and begin by prancing and exchanging insults. Later some spears and arrows will be shot. As the day continues, combat will become progressively more serious, until finally someone is killed or mortally wounded. Then everyone goes home.

If there is a battle, spectators are allowed to watch, and even to move among the warriors, snapping pictures. I say I would like to see such a battle.

One man who drove tourists in a bus told me that on a certain day he had come upon a tribal war, and all the tourists—they were Italians—piled out of the bus to take pictures. While they were taking pictures, one warrior beheaded another with an ax. Right there in front of the tourists!

But the tourists never saw it. They were preoccupied with the pageantry, the colorful costumes. They never saw the head cut off and the blood spurting and the body twitching.

But the driver saw it. "I do not like to see such things," he said. "They are too real."

In the night, when everyone is sitting around the fire, the subject of snakes comes up. Nemo describes the poisonous snakes of Australia. The Tari men listen. One of them then says he once saw a movie about snakes.

The Tari man becomes very excited as he talks about the hero in the movie, whose name was Hindy. Hindy was afraid of snakes, and in the movie he came upon a room that was entirely filled with them, crawling and hissing all over the floor. Thousands of snakes, terrible snakes. To conquer his fear, the man Hindy had to enter the room, and he did! And he fought all the snakes, until he killed them all, and he won! The Tari man says he would never enter such a room, but Hindy did. The snakes were very exciting!

I ask the man if he remembers anything else from the movie. He says no, that it was a story about a man and snakes, and the rest of the movie was just leading up to that.

So there it was, the Italian tourists taking snapshots and literally not seeing a man beheaded, and the New Guinea tribesman seeing *Raiders of the Lost Ark* and considering it a movie about a man and his snakes. The longer I stayed in New Guinea, the more profound the gap between our cultures appeared. I was losing my romantic illusions, but I wasn't getting clarity in its place. I was getting hundreds of flea bites and a lot of confusion.

Eventually I left the Highlands and went to the Sepik River, where dense clouds of mosquitoes hung in the humid air, and tribespeople looked and acted entirely different. The Sepik River people do not fight with weapons. They kill one another with sorcery.

Finally I went to the coast. On my last day in New Guinea, I dived on a sunken B-24 bomber, a relic of World War II. The wreck was overgrown with corals and quite beautiful, but the most surprising thing was its size. The airplane was so small. In the 1940s the B-24 had been a large plane. Seeing it there on the bottom was a striking reminder of how much the world has changed, and how swiftly the change continues. When I got to the surface, I asked about the plane. Did anyone know its history, how it got there, why it had crashed? No one did. There were only stories, and theories, and possibilities.

Spoon Bending

In the spring of 1985, I was invited to attend a spoon bending party. An aerospace engineer named Jack Houck had become interested in the phenomenon, and from time to time had parties at which people bent spoons. I was given a street address in southern California, and told to bring a half-dozen forks and spoons I didn't care about, since they would be bent during the evening.

It was a typical suburban California house. About a hundred people were there, mostly families with young kids. The atmosphere was festive and a little chaotic, with all the kids running around. Everybody was giggly. We were going to bend spoons!

We all threw the silverware we had brought into the center of the floor, where it made a great metal pile. Jack Houck then dumped a carton containing more silverware onto the floor, and told us what to do. He said that, in his experience, to bend spoons we needed to create an atmosphere of excitement and emotional arousal. He encouraged us to be noisy and excited.

We were supposed to choose a spoon from the pile and to ask the spoon, "Will you bend for me?" If we didn't think the spoon would respond, we should toss it back in the pile and choose another. But if we had a positive feeling about our chosen spoon, we were instructed to hold the spoon vertically and shout, "Bend! Bend!" Once intimidated by being shouted at, the spoon was to be rubbed gently between our fingers, and pretty soon it would bend.

That's what Jack Houck said.

People were looking at him pretty skeptically.

The party began: a hundred people selecting spoons and saying, "Will you bend?" and tossing them back in the pile if the feeling wasn't right. Then all around me, I heard people shouting, "Bend! Bend!" at their chosen spoons. A lot of people were laughing. It was hard not to feel self-conscious, holding up a spoon and shouting at it.

I was sitting on the floor next to Judith and Anne-Marie. They had finished shouting at their spoons, and now were rubbing them between their fingers, but nothing was happening. I was also rubbing a spoon, but nothing was happening for me, either. I felt foolish. As we rubbed, a gloom descended over the three of us.

Rubbing her spoon, Anne-Marie said, "I don't think this is going to work. This is silly. I just don't see how it can work."

I looked down at her hands. Her spoon was bending.

"Look, Anne-Marie. . . ."

Anne-Marie laughed. Her spoon was like rubber. She easily twisted the spoon into knots.

Suddenly Judith's spoon began to bend, too. She was able to bend the bowl in half. All around me, spoons were bending. My spoon remained stiff and solid. I rubbed it dutifully, but it wasn't even getting warm.

I felt annoyed. The hell with it, I thought, I'll bend it with sheer force. I tried: the neck of the spoon would bend, of course, but the bowl itself wouldn't bend. I was hurting my fingers trying. I relaxed. Perhaps it wasn't going to happen for me. Jack Houck had said a few people couldn't bend spoons. Maybe I was one.

"Congratulations," Judith said to me.

"What?"

"Congratulations."

I looked down. My spoon had begun to bend. I hadn't even realized. The metal was completely pliable, like soft plastic. It wasn't particularly hot, either, just slightly warm. I easily bent the bowl of the spoon in half, using only my fingertips. This didn't require any pressure at all, just guiding with my fingertips.

I put the bent spoon aside and tried a fork. After a few moments of rubbing, the fork twisted like a pretzel. It was easy. I bent several more spoons and forks.

Then I got bored. I didn't do any more spoon bending. I went and got coffee and a cookie. I was now far more interested in what kind of cookies they had than anything else.

Of course, spoon bending has been the focus of long-standing controversy. Uri Geller, an Israeli magician who claims psychic powers, often bends spoons, but other magicians, such as James Randi, claim that spoon bending isn't a psychic phenomenon at all, just a trick.

But I had bent a spoon, and I *knew* it wasn't a trick. I looked around the room and saw little children, eight or nine years old, bending large metal bars. They weren't trying to trick anybody. They were just little kids having a good time. Staying up past their bedtimes on a Friday night, going along with the adults, doing this silly bending stuff.

So much for controversy between magicians, I thought. Because spoon bending obviously must have some ordinary explanation, since a hundred people from all walks of life were doing it. And it was hard to feel any sort of mystery: you just rub the spoon for a while and pretty soon it gets soft, and it bends. And that's that.

The only thing I noticed is that spoon bending seemed to require a focused inattention. You had to try to get it to bend, and then you had to forget about it. Maybe talk to someone else while you rubbed the spoon. Or look around the room. Change your attention. That's when it was likely to bend. If you kept watching the spoon, worrying over it, it was less likely to bend. This inattention took learning, but you could easily do it. It was comparable in difficulty to, say, learning to count off exactly five seconds in your head. You practiced a few times, and then you could do it.

Why do spoons bend? Jack Houck had theories, but I had long since decided to concentrate on the phenomena, and not worry about the theories. So I don't know why spoons bend, but it seemed clear that almost anyone could do it. What was all the fuss about?

The party broke up around 11:00 p.m. Judith, Anne-Marie, and I went home, taking our bent spoons with us.

The next day I tried to bend one of my spoons back into its original shape. I couldn't do it, but I didn't try very hard. I showed my bent spoons to some friends, though not many. The whole thing just seemed rather ordinary.

A year later, I mentioned to an M.I.T. professor that I had bent spoons. He frowned in silence for a while. "There's a way to bend spoons," he said, "by a trick."

"I think so," I said. "But I don't know the trick."

The professor was silent for a while longer. "You *personally* bent spoons?"

"Yes."

Then he went through the whole thing. Where did I get the spoons? How did I know the spoons had not been previously "treated"? Did anyone help me to bend the spoons? Did anyone touch me while I was bending, or substitute a bent spoon into my hands. . . . He went on like this for a while. I tried to explain the quality of the room that night, and how impossible it was that everyone could have been tricked.

"So you believe the spoons bent?"

"Yes."

"Did you investigate why the spoons bent?"

"No," I said.

"You mean you experienced this extraordinary phenomenon and you didn't try to explain it?"

"No," I said.

"That's very strange," he said. "I would say that your behavior is a pathological denial of what happened to you. This incredible experience occurs and you do nothing to investigate it at all?"

"I don't see why it's pathological," I said. "I don't go investigating why everything in the world happens. For example, I know that, if I bend a wire rapidly, the wire will get hot and break—but I don't really know *why* that happens. I don't think it's my job to rush out and find out why. In this case, spoon bending, the room was full of people doing the same thing, and it seemed very ordinary. Kind of boring."

In fact, this sense of boredom seems to me often to accompany "psychic" phenomena. At first the event appears exciting and mysterious, but very quickly it becomes so mundane that it can no longer hold your interest. This seems to me to confirm the idea that so-called psychic or paranormal phenomena are misnamed. There's nothing abnormal about them. On the contrary, they're utterly normal. We've just forgotten we can do them. The minute we *do* do them, we recognize them for what they are, and we think, So what? Spoon bending is like doing the laundry, or riding a bicycle. No big deal. Not really worth much conversation.

Seeing Auras

All the religious teachings of my youth were powerful because they were inexplicable. In my family, you could discuss anything except religious matters. These were considered unarguable. The story of Joseph and his coat of many colors wasn't a story; it was a postulate. Similarly, the virgin birth of Jesus Christ—a story I had difficulty with from an early age—was not a fable or a metaphor. It had actually happened that way.

The reason why such things were possible was that they had happened a long time ago. Antiquity meant that anything they told you in Sunday school had to be taken as true, no matter how preposterous. Parting the Red Sea, and turning water to blood, the Burning Bush . . . nothing like that was going on *now*. Not even in New York City!

Many years passed before I came to know the complicating truths of pregnant nuns and whoring popes; the complex histories of the Old and New Testaments as historical documents; the anthropology of nomadic herding tribes in the Middle East; and so on. Along the way I discovered that lots of people, including my own parents, didn't believe these religious stories in any literal sense.

357

But at the time I just struggled to understand. And since the narratives seemed unbelievable, I looked at pictures.

Unfortunately, religious pictures were equally confusing. Everyone in the Sunday-school books wore a bathrobe. I had trouble imagining a world where everybody walked around that way.

And grown-up religious art, in museums, made me slightly ill. I could feel all the emotion at the service of what I felt was some kind of insanity. Those saints smiling at the sky while they were stuck full of arrows and bleeding: you couldn't tell me those people weren't crazy.

Even modern artists made me queasy. The floating rabbis of Chagall were exactly how I thought of religion—everything uprooted, swirling free, spinning, and making you nauseated, because you didn't know which end was up. I couldn't see why the floating people and animals were smiling, why they didn't find their condition horrible, like people in the tornado in *The Wizard of Oz*.

Confused, unable to understand, I eventually retreated into a world of disbelief about all things religious, and all religious images. And so, after a time, I stopped puzzling over the most perplexing feature of my childish examination of religious art—the halos that appeared over the heads of some people. The yellow circles behind the heads.

What's that?

A halo.

What's a halo?

That's what very religious people have. It's a circle of light.

Do religious people have it now?

No. Not any more.

But they had it then?

Well, artists imagined they did.

You mean religious people didn't actually have halos but artists thought they did? It was an illusion?

Well, it's how the artist is showing us that the people in the picture are very religious.

Oh.

The explanations didn't satisfy me at all. For one thing, the halos were portrayed different ways. Sometimes they were a ring above the head. Sometimes they were an orange glow coming out of the head. Sometimes only one person, like Jesus, had a halo. Sometimes everybody in the picture had a halo.

For another thing, nobody in these paintings did what I thought a normal person would do—point at the halo and say, "Wow, look, he's got a big yellow ring around his head!" The other figures in the paintings ignored the halo. Or perhaps they didn't see it.

Furthermore, there were some paintings of Jesus with no halo at all. Some artists painted halos and some didn't. The more recent artists didn't. This seemed significant. A halo was just an artistic style. It was a way of painting. Halos didn't have any reality. Maybe back in the old days people believed in such superstitions, but modern people didn't. Yellow light coming out of your head! The very idea was crazy.

I never told anybody, but I secretly looked for halos. I thought maybe our minister, Mr. Van Zanten, was religious enough to have one. I peered at him during services. Apparently not. At least, I could never see one around him. I inspected pictures of the Pope in *Life* magazine, but he never appeared to have a halo. Maybe halos didn't show up in photographs.

Sometimes I looked at my friends and, when conditions were right, I could see a whitish thing around their heads, against a uniform background like blue sky. But this was obviously an optical illusion of some kind, caused by too much staring.

I knew about other optical illusions, like the spots you saw if you closed your eyes and pressed on your eyeballs. Or about how, if you looked down at your hands against a dark surface and squinted, your fingers would seem to be twice as long and kind of streaky yellow. This was obviously some illusion caused by your eyelashes' getting in front of your eyes.

Anyway, I never saw any halos.

I finally gave up.

Occasionally, as an adult, I wondered again about halos. They were so prevalent in religious art—could they really be just an arbitrary convention? If so, why had artists settled on that particular convention? Why a circle instead of a star, or a crescent? Why yellow instead of some brighter

359

color, red or blue or green? Why did artists draw halos in the ways they did?

The simplest explanation never occurred to me: that the artists had drawn halos because everybody had one, and everybody who wanted to could see them.

The only difference is, today we don't call them halos. We call them auras.

I wanted to see auras. I felt it was time to try this. In the last few years I had come to regard most activities, even the most mysterious, as having a component of practice. Maybe by practicing a lot I could learn to see auras.

I had heard that Carolyn Conger was a good person to teach me. I attended a two-week seminar with eight other people in the high desert of California, in the spring of 1986.

Carolyn's unassuming frame house was located at the foot of desert mountains a mile high. Carolyn was very warm. "You must be Michael," she said, and gave me a hug. That was the first thing that struck me, how warm she was, and how down-to-earth.

"I reserved the big bed for you," she said, "even though you didn't tell me you were so tall. Why didn't you tell me you were tall?"

"I forgot," I said. "But you're supposed to know those things anyway." Carolyn was a famous clairvoyant.

"You're willing to trust *that?*" she said, and laughed.

I put my bags in my room, bounced on the bed, looked out the window. When I came back, there was a coyote standing right outside the living-room window. A beautiful creature, gray and white and tan.

"Oh, look at that," I said, thinking: This is a sign. This is a fabulous sign.

"Yes," Carolyn said. "The coyotes always come around this time of day. I feed 'em."

I thought: Not a sign. Oh well.

I was introduced to the other people in the group. They were mostly in their thirties and forties, practical people: a businessman from Washington, a woman computer programmer from Georgetown, an electronics engineer from Los Angeles, a housewife from Oklahoma, another from

Seattle. The oldest person was a seventy-three-year-old retired actress from San Francisco. She also had the most energy.

Carolyn's house was comfortable, although there were no pictures on the walls. Carolyn said she saw so much around people, she was distracted by pictures.

Carolyn told us she had been a sensitive from birth. As a child she had seen auras, and had asked her sister about the beautiful, shimmering colored robes that surrounded all people. Her sister said she didn't see any colors around people. Other members of her family didn't see colors, either. When Carolyn drew pictures showing glowing auras around trees, her teacher at school said, "You can do better than that." Gradually she realized she had an unusual perception that was not shared by other people.

Carolyn now had a doctorate in psychology and had worked in various programs at UCLA. She was also a self-described "techie" who took great pleasure in computers and electronic gadgets. There was nothing airy-fairy about her at all.

She was vague about what we would do during the conference. "But," she said, "if there's anything that anybody especially wants to do, let me know."

I said, "I want to see auras."

"I'll bet you do," she said, and laughed.

At six each morning a Zen monk came and meditated with us for an hour. Then we'd have breakfast, and there would be a morning session with Carolyn. After lunch most people hiked in the mountains or slept. Dinner at six, and then an evening session. It seemed similar to the way Brugh had organized his conference; indeed, Brugh and Carolyn were friends.

After the first evening session, she said, "Let's go outside." We went out onto her deck. It was about 10:00 p.m., and there was a full moon.

"Look at the mountains."

We looked at the mile-high mountains behind the house.

"Do you see anything?"

I saw mountains.

"Anything else?"

"Like what?"

"Do you see any activity? Any lights?"

I looked. I saw desert mountains, bare rock in the moonlight.

"What do you see?" I asked.

She laughed. "Oh, there's a *lot* going on. A lot of energy on the mountains."

I continued looking. I couldn't see anything more. Then, as I stared, I saw something that seemed like fireflies. Little pricks of white light. Very faint.

"I see little flashes of light."

"What else?"

I didn't see anything else.

"Any explosions? Beautiful explosions?" She had a sort of dreamy voice.

No. I didn't see any explosions at all. I was looking at a damn mountain, for Pete's sake. And I was getting suspicious. I didn't want to be talked into anything. I said so.

"You just have to relax."

I felt perfectly relaxed. I couldn't relax any more.

I scanned back and forth across the mountain ridge. And then I saw a puff of orange, like a big burst of orange powder. I stopped scanning—it was gone.

"I saw a puff of orange."

"Uh-huh. Anything else?"

"Was there a puff of orange?"

"That's the energy. Anything else?"

I looked. I saw some streaky horizontal lines. White streaky things along the mountainside.

"Yes," Carolyn said. "I call those snakes. Along the ridges?"

"Yes, along the ridges."

She nodded. "I usually see three different things," she explained. "I see pinpoints of white light, I see explosions, and I see what I call snakes."

"You're saying it's really up there?" I asked.

"Aren't you seeing it?"

"Well, it could be an optical illusion."

"What sort of optical illusion could it be?" she said.

"I don't know. Maybe low illumination from the moon, maybe something happens in the retina, you imagine you see these sparklers and things."

"Well, come out some night when there isn't a moon, and see if it's still there."

"You're saying it's there?"

"You'll have to decide for yourself."

Then she turned around and looked at the juniper bushes in her backyard. "Look at the bushes."

I looked. They seemed to be glowing in the night. Around the edges, a blue-greenish glow. But in some places it was more intense.

"That's the aura," Carolyn said.

"Trees and plants have an aura?"

"Sure."

"Well, what does it mean?" I said.

"I haven't the faintest idea," she said. "But it's there."

Carolyn was tentative in the hypotheses she formed, reluctant to create a structure that defined experiences and provided explanations. Since she ran conferences where people often had unusual experiences—experiences for which they'd want explanations—she was skilled at deflecting the questions back to the questioner.

Do crystals hold energy? She would say, "If you believe it, then it's true for you."

Is daily meditation a good thing? "If you believe it, then it's true for you."

Is there such a thing as witchcraft? "If you believe it, then it's true for you."

But she didn't deflect everything. You had to observe her carefully to see how she modulated her answers. There was a subtle scale.

Did she believe that pyramids kept food from spoiling? "I don't know. Some people do. Or did."

Did she believe in astrology? "It's fun to read in the newspapers."

Did she believe in the Bermuda Triangle? "Well . . ."

Did she believe in vampires? "No, of course not," with a laugh.

But in general she was cautious about saying what things meant. Someone asked her about the meaning of colors in auras. "I don't know what the colors mean," she said. "People have different ideas about the colors, but I don't know. I think people see the colors differently, and see disease states differently."

One night she turned down the lights in the room and got out a black cloth. She hung it over a door and asked one of the men to take off his shirt and stand against the cloth. She said, "What do you see?"

Immediately everybody in the group began to talk. "His aura is pink."

"It's pulsating."

"Stronger on the left than the right."

"He has a lot of energy in his hands."

Carolyn nodded benignly, her students performing well. She looked at me. "What about you? What do you see?"

"Nothing," I said. It was true: I saw nothing. And the more other people saw, the more I squinted and frowned and tried, the more hopeless I felt. It was frustrating to listen to the others.

"His heart chakra is very active."

"There is a bright-red band around his waist."

"He has little discharges from his knees."

Everybody else was seeing this stuff. I wasn't.

"Just relax," Carolyn said. "You have to relax. You have to not care so much."

I was beginning to not care. The whole thing was stupid. I didn't want to see auras. It was a completely worthless thing anyway. Who cared about auras? What good was it? It was just a fantasy; these people were all having a fantasy and I was much the saner not to be sharing it.

I looked away, rubbed my eyes. I give up, I thought. I looked back.

I saw a man standing against a black cloth. There was a shimmering white cloud all around him, extending out about six inches from his body. I could see it best around the shoulders and head, but I could see it everywhere else, too. It was slowly expanding and contracting, as if he were breathing. But it wasn't following his breath. It was keeping its own rhythm.

"Oh my God," I said.

Carolyn laughed.

She put another man up. This second man looked completely different. He had a cloud around him, but his was pulsating rapidly, in and out, in and out. And this man had all sorts of electrical discharges on his skin. Big sparks were shooting off his forehead into space. He had a pink-red band around his neck. His hands glowed as if he had dipped them in phosphorus.

"I don't believe it."

"Believe it," Carolyn said.

364

The other people were describing what they saw. "John has a much more rapid pulsation; his hands are very hot; he has a red ring around his neck and a lot of stuff shooting off his forehead."

They were seeing what I was seeing.

I thought, *This is fantastic! I can see auras!*

And, abruptly, I couldn't see anything any more. There was only John standing up there with his shirt off.

But now I was on to it, I had a sense of the feeling, the state you had to be in. I relaxed. I coaxed it back. I began to realize that it required a sort of inattention, the way you have to be if you are walking around with a full cup of coffee. If you stare at the coffee, you'll spill it. If you completely ignore the coffee, you'll spill it. You have to be mindful of the coffee and not worry about it, and then you can carry it anywhere. It was like that.

You had to be casual about it.

I saw the aura again. They put the first man, George, back up against the black. He was still pulsating slowly, much more slowly than John. I stared at his face. And as I stared, his face went gray, his features becoming invisible.

I asked Carolyn about this.

"Yes," she said. "That's because his aura exists in three dimensions. You are seeing the aura in front of the face, and it makes the features indistinct."

This was obviously what I had been observing with Linda, when I meditated with her a few years earlier. Things began to make sense. We watched for a while longer, and then Carolyn turned up the lights.

I could see energy all around her. She was so powerful, it was easy to see her even in the brighter light. I saw great plumes of bright green streaking around her head. Wow! Fantastic!

But the minute I got excited, I couldn't see it any more. I had to relax, and start all over.

I walked around all night seeing auras. I went out and looked at the mountain. It was active, sparks and snakes and orange puffy explosions. I looked at the trees. They were glowing. I went back inside. Everybody was glowing. It was fantastic. No wonder Carolyn didn't have pictures on her walls. This energy was much more interesting.

By the next morning I had accepted my ability to see auras. I was done with that. What next? I was sure something wonderful would follow. I was on a roll. I spent the day hiking alone in the mountains. I anticipated a wonderful experience, something really illuminating and spectacular.

I saw a couple of rabbits. They hopped away.

That was it.

Carolyn assigned a meditative exercise. "Everybody in this group can love other people. I want you to go out and love yourself. Sit under a juniper tree in the desert and meditate and love yourself. If you can."

I knew that, classically, this is a difficult meditation, but I was ready for it. I knew I could do it. Full of confidence, I went out into the desert, found a juniper bush, and sat down under it. I started to meditate. But I began to think perhaps there were ants or something in the sand. I shifted around. Also, maybe there were some snakes hanging around this juniper bush. Maybe I'd better check.

These thoughts disturbed my meditation. I couldn't concentrate. Finally I decided this was the wrong bush, so I moved to another. That bush wasn't the right one, either.

I walked deeper into the desert. I obviously needed solitude for this difficult meditation. I chose a bush, sat down beneath it, and relaxed. I saw another rabbit. It hopped away, but I knew the rabbit was still in the vicinity. Once I began to meditate, it would come hopping back and ruin my concentration. I decided to move again.

I chose a new bush. It was a little withered on one side. I sat down. Because it was withered, it didn't provide shade from the sun. I felt too hot sitting here to meditate. I thought I should move to another place.

I thought, This is ridiculous. Stay here and get on with it.

So I stayed. I tried to meditate. I couldn't do it. I had no concentration at all. Finally I gave up. I decided I would give myself love on another day.

We had two days of fasting and silence. During this time we were told not to look into anybody's eyes, or acknowledge another person in any way.

This I found incredibly difficult. I couldn't be in a room—say, the kitchen—with another person and not acknowledge his or her presence. I couldn't pretend the person wasn't there. I felt that was incredibly insulting.

The fasting wasn't hard. The silence wasn't hard. But the nonacknowledgment was brutal. Not only did I have difficulty doing it, but I also felt terribly hurt when other people did it to me. How could they ignore me this way? It was painful to be ignored.

I didn't care what the rules were. I tried to catch people's eyes, to nod and smile. But nobody else would look at me. I was miserable for the first day.

Finally I got used to it.

I liked most of the people in the conference, but a couple of them I couldn't stand. They just rubbed me the wrong way. One woman was always morose, crying and sad. I couldn't stand her being sad all the time, walking around with her Kleenex and sniffling everywhere she went. Why didn't she pull herself together and get on with her life?

And one man was a complainer. A whiner. He had lots of complaints at the moment, and lots of past complaints from his earlier life. How he'd been mistreated. How they done him wrong. He was more than willing to tell you all about it. I couldn't bear to listen to him bitch.

But by the second week I found my dislike for these people burdensome. I wanted to drop it. I went into the desert to consider why I was so annoyed by them. After all, all the others had their quirks, and I didn't seem to mind. What was it in these two people?

They probably reminded me of aspects of myself that I didn't like, but, try as I might, I couldn't see how. I certainly wasn't crying all the time. I certainly wasn't a whiner. Was I?

On the other hand, in order to drop my dislike, I'd have to decide that moping and whining were okay, after all. I just couldn't do that.

I fell into a critical mood. I began to notice things I disliked about this conference. For example, the use of jargon.

There is a specialized jargon for conferences. People don't think about a problem, they sit with it. They don't tell you something, they share. They don't have problems, they have issues. They don't help, they facilitate. They don't have a way to do something, they have a process. They don't have a lover, they have a significant other.

This jargon got on my nerves. As I sat with my issues concerning my significant other, I thought: I'd rather think about my love life. It'd be more to the point.

I started complaining to the group about all this jargon. I felt that a group of people who are committed to spiritual growth shouldn't create a specialized jargon. Jargon defined them as a group, it allowed them to feel smug and exclusive, and it got in the way of direct experience. Nobody paid attention to my point of view.

Soon after that, I began to feel that everyone was indifferent to me, that I was uncared for in my life by them, and by everyone else. I felt sad for almost two days.

And then I found that I no longer had any resentment toward anybody in the conference. They were all fine. I liked everybody fine. Even the jargon was okay with me.

I was making progress in every way but one. I had been sleeping in the desert most nights since the conference began, and I was never able to overcome an unreasoning fear of wild animals.

A few years earlier, I had definitively concluded I was not afraid of animals. But at Carolyn's, every night I curled up in my sleeping bag, the thoughts began.

First scorpions. I worried about scorpions. I hadn't seen any scorpions in the desert, but I knew they were out there. Then rattlesnakes. What if a snake crawled into my bag? It was too cold for the snakes to be out yet, but that was all the more reason why a snake would crawl into my nice warm bag.

What would I do, exactly, if I had a snake in my bag? Where would it go? Would it curl up at the bottom of the bag, near my feet?

When I'd had enough rattlesnake fantasies, I'd hear the coyotes howl, and begin to worry about coyotes.

The coyotes will not bother me, I think.

Yeah? What do you imagine you look like, in this sleeping bag? A giant salami, that's what you look like. A tasty sack of meat. Perfect for a coyote.

I don't think the coyotes will bother me.

Yeah? They might. Especially if they're rabid. You know rabid animals are unpredictable. They lose their fear of man. They'll come right up to you. And just one bite . . .

I don't think rabies is a problem here.

Yeah? If you got bitten, you'd have to have the shots; you know how you hate needles.

The shots are only shots.

They'll still hurt. And, you know, the shots don't always work. You could die anyway. And . . . what if you got bitten but didn't notice?

I would notice.

Yeah? Vampire bats have razor-sharp teeth and bite between the toes and you never wake up while they are sucking your blood.

There are no vampire bats here. Can't we go to sleep?

No. It's not safe here.

My dialogue continued like this. Each night it took about half an hour to calm myself down so I could go to sleep. And it never got any easier on subsequent nights. The final night of the conference, I woke up at midnight and heard the coyotes eating the garbage at the house next door. Crunching bones. Crunch, crunch.

You're next.

Come on, can't we just sleep? Remember the elephant in Kenya? Remember how foolish you felt?

That was then. This is now.

Crunch, crunch.

Think how comfortable you'd be back in the house. . . .

I am not going back in the house.

A nice comfortable bed . . .

I am not going back in the house.

The only reason you won't go back is you told everybody that you're not afraid of animals. Actually, you are completely full of it. You have no idea who you really are. Face it: you're terrified out here.

I am not going back in the house.

Okay. Have it your way. The coyotes will still be hungry when they finish that garbage. . . .

I am not going back in the house.

And I didn't. But the struggle never ceased. The voices inside my head kept up the dialogue. And I thought, Haven't I fought this battle already? Can't I just go to sleep? The answer was, no.

And finally, in the middle of the night, I shouted out

loud, "All right, damn it, I admit it, *I'm afraid of animals!*"
And you don't really know who you are. . . .
"And I don't really know who I am!"
With that, I fell sound asleep.

When I got home, I looked at people to see if I could still see auras. I could. It's fun to do. When the dinner parties get boring, you just look at people's auras.

But that didn't seem to be the most important thing I had gotten from being at the conference. The most important thing seemed to be that, although I knew a lot more about myself than I ever had at any earlier time in my life, I still had to admit, the way I shouted in the desert, that I didn't know who I was.

An Entity

In the spring of 1986 I was still working with Gary, the man who had taught me to channel. I continued to explore altered states with him.

I tried not to judge what was happening, but simply to accept everything as an experience. Past lives, guided meditation, astral travel: I just went along with it as an interesting time.

And I was in this general frame of mind—an interesting time, lots of doubts, and no idea what it all meant—when, at the end of one session, Gary said, "I experienced an entity around you during our work today."

"A what?"

"An entity. A dark force."

"An entity," I repeated. I was very slow about all this. I didn't get what he was saying.

"I believe it is interfering with our work," Gary said.

"What is?"

"The entity. He's attached to you. Do you have any sense of it?"

"No," I said. I was starting to feel annoyed. I felt he was telling me there was something wrong with me. And it

371

sounded bad, serious, an entity attached to me. "What is an entity, anyway?"

"Well, it could be a discarnate soul, a tramp soul."

"A tramp soul."

"Something you picked up earlier in your life, maybe at a time when you were sick, or if you drank or took a lot of drugs at some time in your life. When you're weak, these things can latch on to your field and go for a ride. And they can stay with you for years. Or it may be a thought form that you have created, I really don't know. But it's there."

I understood clearly now.

"You're saying I'm possessed."

"Well. Only in a manner of speaking."

That did it. I went crazy.

"What manner of speaking?" I was very upset. "You're saying I have a demon or something inside me! You're saying I need an exorcist!"

"Is that so bad?" Gary said calmly.

"Yes!" I shouted. "Yes! It's terrible! What am I supposed to do about it?"

"I'm not sure," Gary said. "I'll have to ask some people."

"Ask them what?"

"I know some people who have experience in these things."

"People who have been to an exorcism?"

"One, yes. Let's talk more tomorrow."

"What are you telling me? Gary, listen, I have a job, I have to write, I have to be calm, you can't just go around telling people they have entities attached to them and let's talk tomorrow!" I was shouting now, really shouting.

"Look," he said firmly. "I don't like this, either. We'll talk tomorrow. But I'm pretty sure you have an entity around you. Just don't worry about it. It's not the end of the world."

It's not the end of the world.

I was very angry. I was distracted. Who wouldn't be, to hear he had an entity bothering him? The next day I was still distracted. I couldn't write. I was angry and upset. I called Gary.

"How do you feel?" he said.

"How do you think I feel?" I said. "Terrible."

"Okay," he said. "Come over at five o'clock, and we'll have a session."

"All right," I said.

"Listen," he said. "I've asked somebody else to be there. A psychologist, if that's all right."

"Okay."

"You're sure it's all right? She won't come unless it's all right with you."

"It's fine," I said.

At five I went to Gary's apartment. It was completely transformed. The drapes were drawn. There were lighted candles everywhere. On the couch was a row of pictures of holy people, from Jesus Christ to Muktananda. There were crystals scattered around on all the tables. In the center of the room, the massage table was covered in a white cloth.

Uh-oh, I thought. *He's really going to do it. He's going to do an exorcism.*

I was introduced to a small, pretty woman with short hair named Beth. She was very calm, but there was still an underlying tension in the room. Gary seemed tense.

I was tense, too. I complained about how Gary had left me hanging with this idea of an entity, and how ridiculous I thought it all was, an entity. I mean, really, an entity.

They listened, and then Beth said in her calm way, "Well, what if it's true?"

It threw me: she was agreeing with him.

"Do *you* think I have an entity?"

"I sense something around you," she said.

"Okay," I said. That did it.

"When you're ready, why don't you lie down on the table," Gary said.

I lay down on the table. Now I was pretty nervous. I kept getting these melodramatic images of Max von Sydow and Linda Blair.

But, on the other hand, a part of me was excited. An exorcism: well, let's see what happens.

What happened was that Gary said, "I'm going to spend some time with Beth first, you just relax."

I lay there on the table with my eyes closed and relaxed. I heard Gary helping Beth to lie on a couch across the room, and heard him inducing her into an altered state. He did that by talking to her, and by playing tapes of oscillating tones. It took a while; he was really getting her deep.

Finally I heard his voice very near my ear. "Ready?"

"Ready," I said. By now I was really nervous. Some part of me was saying, This is crazy, an exorcism, you don't know what will happen, you're saying you're possessed, a demon, this is crazy. But I was determined to go on.

"Okay," Gary said, and he induced me pretty much the way he had induced Beth. Visualizing light, relaxing, visualizing moving my ego away from my center. Usually this induction took only a few minutes, but this time it seemed to go on a long while: he was getting me to go deep.

Finally Gary said, "Okay, now, Michael, I want you to visualize your body as entirely surrounded by light, so much light that anything dark will stand out against all the light."

I visualized that.

"Okay, now, Michael, do you see anything dark around your body?"

I tried to see. To my surprise, I saw a cartoon demon, a sort of Walt Disney evil spirit with wings that looked like the devil from *Fantasia*. I saw this devil right in front of me. I also saw a sort of large bug, like an ant, down near my feet. And I saw a little man about two feet high, with a hat, behind my left shoulder.

"Do you see anything?" Gary asked.

I felt ridiculous. The principal image was a cartoon devil, and I wasn't going to open my mouth and report that I saw a Walt Disney devil.

"No," I said.

Gary moved across the room. "Beth, do you have any information now?"

And I heard Beth's voice, drowsy and trance-like, reply, "There are three entities around him. There is a large creature, an insect, and a little man."

Oh my God, I thought.

Because I hadn't said anything. I was lying on a table with my eyes closed. Beth was lying on a couch across the room with her eyes closed. I had never met her before. There wasn't any way for us to communicate now, yet she was seeing what I was seeing. How was that possible?

Gary came back to my ear. "Did you hear what Beth said?"

"Yes."

"Do you have any reaction?"

"Yes," I said. I admitted she was right. I described the

374

three dark entities. By now my left neck and shoulder were starting to cramp painfully. I remembered the first time I had felt that: it was in the summer of 1968, driving home from Florida to Massachusetts. I was in medical school, I had gone to Florida for a couple of weeks with my wife, to dive and to revise a book I planned to call *The Andromeda Strain,* if it ever got finished. The work had gone well, but, driving home in my blue Volvo, my left neck and shoulder had become excruciatingly painful. The pain had lasted about five months, and gradually faded. I'd considered it tension from typing, or from driving.

"Let's talk to the little man," Gary said.

I attempted to talk to the little man. He wouldn't speak, but I sensed that he was an old and angry man beneath the sunhat, and I saw he had a fishing pole. I couldn't really see him well because he was standing behind me, behind my shoulder.

Gary asked him some questions directly, but we didn't really get very far with the little man. He was uncommunicative.

Gary asked Beth for suggestions.

"Talk to the creature in front," she said.

"But the creature is a Walt Disney devil," I said. "A cartoon devil."

"That is how he is presenting himself to you," she said. "That's what he wants you to think he is."

Gary said, "Can you talk to the creature?"

I tried. I saw him as bat-like, with glaring empty eyes. But I could talk to him, yes.

"Ask him how long he has been with you."

A long time. Years.

"Ask him where he came from."

I made him.

"When did you make him?"

When I was four years old.

"Why?"

To protect me.

"Protect you from what?"

My father.

"What about your father?"

My father wants to kill me.

I am standing outdoors, looking at a curved gravel driveway, my tricycle. My vision is low, near the gravel, at the height of the tricycle handlebars. The house behind me is narrow, two stories high. It is spring, and sunny, lots of green trees. Beyond the driveway is the road. Across the road is a high cliff, maybe a hundred feet high, of yellowish rock.

My father is recently back from the navy. He and I are going to climb the cliff. We say goodbye to my mother and cross the road and begin climbing. I am climbing first, and my father is following, so he can catch me if I fall.

We start up and I'm not scared, but pretty soon we are high, and the cliff is steep, and there is no easy path up. I don't know where to put my hands and feet next. I get scared. I look down at my father, behind me. I realize that he is scared, too, that this is more than he has bargained for. I am not safe with him. If I fall, he can't catch me.

He has lied to me. I am very frightened. The rock of the cliff is sharp, and cuts my fingers. It is brittle; it comes away in chunks in my hands.

We manage to go on. Somehow we get to the top. We have brought handkerchiefs to wave to my mother, down at the house far below. We wave to her, and then we walk down another way, a gentle way, through pine trees. My father is beside me. My heart is pounding with fear as I walk beside him.

Mount Ivy, New York, 1946.

Gary said, "You made the creature to protect you from your father?"

My father had been in the navy. He had come home, but my mother preferred me to him, and he resented me. He wanted me gone. He wanted me to fall off the cliff and die.

He hated me.

"And did the creature protect you?"

Yes.

Gary said, "Is that why you kept the creature all these years?"

I am thirteen. I have just grown taller than my father, but I am painfully thin. We are playing basketball in the back-yard. He is pushing and shoving me as we play. He often knocks me to the ground. Sometimes I want to cry.

Roslyn, New York, 1955.

"And did the creature protect you in other ways?"

Yes.

I am in high school. I am thirteen years old and six feet seven inches tall and I weigh 125 pounds. I look like a skeleton. I have grown a foot in the last year. I am the tallest person in the school, taller even than the teachers. Everybody laughs at me. The older boys sometimes chase me home from school and knock me down and sit on me and laugh at me.

But whenever that happens, whenever I am humiliated, whenever people laugh at me, I block it off. It is as if an invisible wall comes down, the rest of the world becomes dim, I can hardly hear the laughing voices. I hear a whisper in my ear. The whisper says they are jerks. I am smart and I am going to show them all. They are jerks. Anybody who laughs at me is a jerk.

"Then this creature you invented protected you from pain?"

Yes.

"The pain of growing up the way you did."

Yes.

"And later?"

In college. Yes. I could cut people dead, I could just stare at people and think, You are really an asshole, and I could reduce them to silence, make them go away.

"And later?"

Medical school. Less. Less and less with time.

"And now? Does the creature do anything for you now?"

No.

I am surprised to realize this. The images I see now are episodes in which I feel barriers, obstructions, difficulty getting past my own defenses. My own harshness.

"So are you ready to give up the creature?"

"Yes."

"Beth, how do you feel about what he is saying?"

"I don't think Michael is ready to give it up."

"Neither do I," Gary says.

I hear them with a strange detachment. I am feeling very passive, floating, just going along with the flow of images and feelings.

Gary again: "You feel the creature doesn't help you now. Let's just be sure. Does the creature do anything in your writing?"

No.

I am clear about that. The creature is defensive and protective and paranoid in a way I am struggling to be free of.

"Beth?"

"I agree."

"Does the creature do anything in your other work, movies or TV?"

I have to consider that. Sometimes collaborative work gets abrasive; people can be harsh. Sometimes my feelings get hurt, and the voice whispers soothingly.

"Yes, but I can do without it."

"Beth?"

"Yes. He can."

"Does the creature do anything in your relationship with Anne-Marie?"

I realize it does: "It lets me rest."

Sometimes when we have disagreements, when I feel falsely accused, when I feel trampled upon, I throw up an angry wall, and withdraw behind it. I can go off and sulk, or I can sit in the living room and be silently furious. But in either case I am safe, I am protected. I can rest from the struggle. Secure in my knowledge: Women, what can you do. They're all the same. They're all living out whatever Daddy did to them, and you just happen to be the latest recipient. They don't care about you, they've never even met *you*. They just use you.

And so on. Secure in righteous indignation and nice warm anger.

"Are you willing to give that up?"

"I don't know."

It is a place of my own, this angry retreat. If I gave it up, I would be much more *out there*. That might not be so comfortable.

I think of other times. The times I have wanted to give compliments, but have been afraid of also giving up a psychological advantage; the times I have wanted to say I was hurt, instead of getting mad; the times I have wanted to release anger, instead of hanging on to it for days like a security blanket; the times I have wanted to express a wish instead of a complaint.

I can see how it might be better to give it up. And, anyway, I realize I am tired of it.

"I am tired of living that way. Yes: I'll give it up."

"Beth?"

"I still don't feel he is ready."

"Neither do I," Gary says.

* * *

I still feel neutral. I am even, I am balanced, I am floating. I will take their word for it.

Gary says, "This creature has been very important in your life for a long time."

"Yes."

"I want you to thank the creature for all that it has done for you."

"Okay."

I start to do it inwardly.

"Out loud."

"Okay."

I hesitate. I feel a little stupid to be talking to a Walt Disney cartoon devil when other people can listen. I imagine that I will get formal, and say thank you to this creature. A stiff, correct statement of thanks is what I have in mind.

Suddenly my mouth opens and I hear a voice saying warmly, "I really want to thank you for everything you have done, you were loyal through a lot of hard times, and I really appreciate it, I couldn't have done it without you, I never would have made it, I would have died without you, so you have really protected me and done a wonderful thing for me."

I'm shocked I am saying this, but I am visualizing a houseguest who has been in my house for years, a relative, somebody I'm guilty about, because now I have to throw him out. And I am trying to express my true thanks, but also to be a little manipulative and get him out the door.

"I am really going to miss you," I say, "but it's time to move on, time for you to go your way and me to go mine, our paths are diverging, all good things must come to an end, but I want you to know I will never forget you, or what you have done for me."

By now I am crying. I really love this old creature, this faithful old servant. I hate to hurt his feelings. He looks lost and forlorn, but I can see he is accepting it. I am surprised at how much I love him, and how sad I feel about his departure.

I am taking leave.

"Beth?"

"I feel he is ready."

"I agree." Gary leans closer. "Michael, we are going to remove the entity now."

"What do I do?"

"Nothing. Beth will do it with me. She will do it on the astral plane."

I feel a little left out of this plan, but I am still in my passive mood. I will do whatever I am told.

Gary moves away. He is whispering to Beth. They are moving Beth to the astral plane. I can't really hear what they are saying; their voices are low. Besides, I am wrapped up in my emotions. I am crying. I am sad for this departure.

After a while I hear Beth say, "He's not coming yet."

I feel immediately that this is true.

The entity is still hanging around me.

I will have to help.

I imagine that I am standing at the door of a farmhouse. The entity is outside the screen door. It is time to say goodbye. I turn my back on it, to make it easier for it to leave. I turn away, knowing I will never see it again. I burst into sobs. But I don't turn back, to see if it is still there.

"He's not coming."

I still don't turn back. I feel that, if I remain there with my back to him, he will eventually give up and leave.

"No. Not yet."

I want to be of assistance. There must still be a connection between me and the entity, even though I can't see it. I imagine a big pair of scissors, and I use them to cut the air all around my body, severing any shadowy connections. I cut vigorously.

"He's not coming."

Perhaps I am trying too hard. Maybe I should leave it alone. Let her do it.

I can see her, on the astral plane, in misty yellow light a little above me. It's as if we are standing on an incline, or a slope, and she is a little farther up the incline, in the yellow mist. I can see her standing there, and then suddenly I can clearly see the entity.

The entity is tiny; he barely comes to her waist. He is looking up at her in a hopeful way.

He is just a little kid.

I feel an explosive burst of emotion, of sadness for this tiny thing formed in the image of his tiny creator, this frightened, forlorn child that must now leave, and I feel sad for myself, and sad to move on now, and in the instant of that burst of sadness the little kid shoots off, away into the distance.

Beth says in a flat voice, "He's gone."

* * *

Beth comes out. I come out. We sit around, dazed; Gary brings glasses of water. I look at my watch. It has taken three and a half hours. There isn't really much to say. We're all tired. Gary says, "Don't worry, he's gone. He won't be back," and tells me to be careful driving home.

I get home and tell Anne-Marie. She is very affected. But I don't tell anybody else. How many people can you tell you've had an exorcism?

Anyway, the real question is—what was the outcome? For the next few days, not much. Then I had an argument with Anne-Marie. It started in the usual way, but it quickly became different. I found myself walking around the kitchen in circles, wondering where to go. It was as if a room in our apartment had been taken away. It wasn't there any more, this particular room. I had to stay where I was and deal with her. Subsequent arguments were different, too, and after a while I began to realize that some stable change had occurred.

The other thing I noticed was that for several weeks I felt the minor and ordinary pains of life, the small momentary rejections, the people that turn away, the tiny insincerities and the trivial abuses, with the most exquisite sensitivity. They were incredibly painful. I had never felt such hurts before. But at the same time I noticed that many people were nicer to me than they had ever been before. And, in any case, in a few weeks I felt I was back to normal in my ability to roll with the punches.

A few months later I was talking with Lu, a psychologist I see sometimes. Rather hesitantly, I mentioned my experience, wondering how she would respond.

She said, "That's interesting. A lot of people are having experiences like that."

"Really?" I said.

"Oh yes. Entities are very big now."

I had to laugh.

Direct Experience

In accepting the possibility of an entity, however tentatively and briefly, I had moved pretty far from the rational, academic, intellectual traditions in which I had been raised. I was, in truth, a little nervous to think how far I had moved. So I decided to summarize the conclusions I had drawn from all these experiences, over all these years. I got out a piece of paper and listed them.

I was surprised to find there wasn't so much, after all.

1. Consciousness has legitimate dimensions not yet guessed at. The varieties of consciousness are considerably more diverse and contradictory than I had previously acknowledged. I am not persuaded that any of these states of consciousness has metaphysical meaning, any more than I am persuaded I had a real entity attached to me. I'm not convinced of entities at all. But I acknowledge that on some level the difference between a real entity and a metaphorical entity may be slight indeed. I'm obliged to remember that consciousness itself is tremendously powerful: people in every culture can become crippled or blind or even die from beliefs alone.

To me all the varieties of consciousness constitute a landscape of the mind, similar to the physical landscape of our planet. I find this landscape of consciousness rewarding to explore. I recognize that exploration of these different states is a personal interest of mine, and not everybody shares that interest.

But I feel there is more than private value in such explorations. I suspect that, in the future, studying the varieties of consciousness will have increasingly practical importance in such areas as treating illness, maintaining health, and promoting creativity.

As the practical value of altering consciousness becomes recognized, procedures to effect those alterations will become increasingly ordinary and unremarkable. The whole concept of changing states of consciousness will cease to have an exotic or a threatening aspect.

2. At least some psychic phenomena are real. Psychic phenomena are generally categorized as telepathy (communication between minds), clairvoyance (perception at a distance), precognition (perception of events before they occur), and psychokinesis (influencing objects or events by thought alone). This in fact covers a rather broad range of claims, and broadly overlapping phenomena.

I've concluded some people have the ability to know about past and future events in a manner that is not at present explicable. To me the most convincing evidence for such ability comes from rather trivial information.

I suspect everybody has a degree of psychic ability, just as everybody has a degree of athletic or artistic ability. Some people have special gifts; other people have a particular interest that leads them to develop their abilities. But the phenomenon itself is ordinary and widespread.

I have no idea of the limits of psychic ability. I don't know, for example, whether somebody can move an object simply by thinking about it. I don't even know how to go about assessing such an idea, since I have no theory to explain psychic phenomena in general.

3. There are energies associated with the human body that are not yet understood. These energies can be felt and seen, and they are related to healing, sickness, and health. Although the existence of these body energies is formally accepted in some theoretical systems, such as those of In-

dian Yogis and Chinese acupuncturists, they are not yet accepted in Western medical systems.

I suspect they will be in the near future; when that happens, medicine will recapture some traditional wisdom concerning the importance of bedside manner and hand-holding—what is now considered the "art of medicine," as opposed to the science.

This was all I concluded. And it's not really much different from what Carl Jung believed, or William James believed. It's only different from what a certain variety of incautious, unintrospective physical scientist believes. And, in their day, Jung and James found themselves at odds with this kind of scientist, too.

I went on to make a list of the things that I don't believe in, which was much longer. I don't believe in levitation, flying saucers, UFOs, ancient astronaut landing sites in Peru, the Bermuda Triangle, extraterrestrials, palmistry, numerology, astrology, psychic surgery, rebirthing, biorhythms, coincidence, or pyramid power.

And finally I made a list of beliefs about which I hold no opinion, either because evidence is lacking, or because the issue seems to me fundamentally a matter of faith. These beliefs include reincarnation, past lives, entities, poltergeists, ghosts, the yeti, the Loch Ness monster, and the power of crystals.

But, as I looked at my lists, I decided they were beside the point. I hadn't traveled with the intention of learning about anything except myself. And the real point of all this travel was not what I had come to believe or disbelieve about the wider world, but what I had learned about myself.

When I look back on my travels, I see an almost obsessive desire for experiences that would increase my self-awareness. I needed new experiences to keep shaking myself up. I don't know why this should be true for me.

In one sense, I suppose the search for new experiences represents an appetite. It's an acquired taste, in my case acquired early. From my parents I learned to perceive new experiences as fun and invigorating, and not as frightening. So this is learned behavior.

In another sense, I see my travels as a strategy for solving
384

problems in my life. Whenever things got bad, whenever my life really wasn't working, I'd get on a plane and go far away. Not to escape my problems so much as to get perspective on them. I found that this strategy worked. I returned to my life with a new sense of balance. I was able to get to the point, to stop spinning my wheels, to know what I wanted to do and how to go about doing it. I was focused and effective.

In every instance, it was because I had gone away and found out something about myself. Something I needed to know.

My own sense is that the acquisition of self-knowledge has been made more difficult by the modern world. More and more human beings live in vast urban environments, surrounded by other human beings and the creations of human beings. The natural world, the traditional source of self-interest, is increasingly absent.

Furthermore, within the last century we have come to live increasingly in a compelling world defined by electronic media. These media have evolved a pace that is utterly alien to our true natures. It is bewildering to live in a world of ten-second spots, each one urging us to buy something, to do something, or to think something. Human beings in the past were not so assaulted.

And I think that this constant assault has made us pliable in a certain unhealthy way. Cut off from direct experience, cut off from our own feelings and sometimes our own sensations, we are only too ready to adopt a viewpoint or perspective that is handed to us, and is not our own.

In 1972, I bought a house in the hills of Los Angeles. I moved into my house and was ecstatically happy for several months.

One day I mentioned to a friend that I'd bought a house in the hills. He said, "I guess the snakes don't worry you."

"What snakes?" I said.

"Rattlesnakes. The hills are full of rattlesnakes."

"Come on," I said. "Stop kidding around."

"I'm serious. Haven't you seen any?"

"No, of course not."

"Well, they're there. You have any land around your house?"

"Yes, almost an acre. On the side of a hill."

"Then you've definitely got them. Just wait. The rattlers come out when it gets dry, September-October. Just wait."

I went back to my wonderful house in a state of profound depression. I didn't have any fun at all; I just looked for snakes. I worried that snakes were sneaking into my bedroom, so I locked all the doors every night to keep the snakes out. I thought snakes might come to the swimming pool to drink the water, so I avoided the swimming pool, particularly in the heat of the day, because the snakes were probably sunning on my deck. I never walked around my property, because I was sure there were snakes in the bushes. I walked only on the little path from the garage to the house, and I peered around every corner before I turned it. But, increasingly, I didn't like to be outside at all. I became a prisoner in my own house. I had altered my entire behavior and my emotional state purely on the basis of something I had been told. I still hadn't seen any snakes. But I was now afraid.

Finally, one day, I saw my gardener tramping fearlessly around the brush at the edge of the property. I asked him about snakes. "Are there any rattlers here?"

"Oh sure," he said. "Especially September-October."

"Aren't you worried?"

"Well," he said, "I've been working here for six years, and in that time I've only seen one rattlesnake. So I'm not too worried, no."

"What'd you do when you saw the rattlesnake?"

"Killed it."

"How?"

"I went and got a shovel, came back, and killed it. It was just a rattlesnake."

"That's the only one you saw?"

"That's right."

"One snake in six years?"

"That's right."

I went and got my towel, and sat by the pool for the rest of the day. I was perfectly comfortable. One snake every six years was something to be aware of, but you didn't have to man the watchtowers every minute of your life.

So, still without ever having seen a snake, I had shifted to another perspective, and I had changed my behavior and my emotions again. Now I was a little more cautious than before, but I was relaxed.

As he was leaving, the gardener said, "You can be sure you don't have many snakes on your property."

"How do you know?"

"Because you've got so many gophers."

I had been trying for weeks to get rid of the gophers that lived in my lawn. Gophers were something new to me; they weren't found back east. Gophers were small, cute-looking rodents that created an elaborate network of underground burrows all around your property, thus turning previously solid earth into something resembling a sponge. Sometimes I'd walk out onto my lawn and fall through to my ankles. I had an image of my entire house one day sinking into the ground because the gophers had finally burrowed one tunnel too many. So I set poison, and I set traps, and I took potshots at them with an air pistol. All to no effect whatever. Each morning fresh gopher burrows crisscrossed my lawn. It was extremely frustrating. My house was Gopher National Park.

Now I realized that, if a few more of my friends the rattlesnakes took up residence around the house, this frustrating gopher problem would be solved. I began to wish for more rattlesnakes. Was there anything I could do to attract rattlesnakes to my house? Put out some favorite rattlesnake food, or perhaps dishes of water? What was wrong with my property, anyway, that the snakes would abandon it and leave me at the mercy of the gophers?

So I had still another perspective. Now I was feeling the lack of snakes, wishing for more. I had gone through all these changes—and I still had never actually seen a snake. I couldn't really say that I had experienced successive episodes of calmness, panic, and longing because I'd had some life experience that made me that way. I'd acquired some new information, but nothing really had *happened* to me.

I felt different only because I had shifted perspectives. Each shift in perspective was accompanied by a total change in my attitudes, my physiology, my behavior, my emotions. I was immediately and wholly modified by each new perspective that I adopted.

But never as a result of direct experience. Never as a result of something that had actually happened to me.

Unaccustomed to direct experience, we can come to fear it. We don't want to read a book or see a museum show until we've read the reviews so that we know what to think. We lose the confidence to perceive for ourselves. We want to know the meaning of an experience before we have it.

We become frightened of direct experience, and we will go to elaborate lengths to avoid it.

I found I liked to travel, because it got me out of my routines and my familiar patterns. The more traveling I did, the more organized I became. I kept adding things I liked to have with me on my trips. Naturally I took books to read. Then I'd take my Walkman and the tapes I liked to listen to. Pretty soon I'd also take notebooks and colored pens for drawing. Then a portable computer for writing. Then magazines for the airplane trip. And a sweater in case it got cold on the airplane. And hand cream for dry skin.

Before long traveling became a lot less fun, because now I was staggering onto airplanes, loaded down with all this stuff that I felt I had to take with me. I had made a new routine instead of escaping the old one. I wasn't getting away from the office any more: I was just carrying most of the contents of my desk on my shoulders.

So one day I decided I would get on the plane and carry nothing at all. Nothing to entertain me, nothing to save me from boredom. I stepped on the plane in a state of panic—none of my familiar stuff! What was I going to do?

It turned out I had a fine time. I read the magazines that were on the plane. I talked to people. I stared out the window. I thought about things.

It turned out I didn't need any of that stuff I thought I needed. In fact, I felt a lot more alive without it.

One of the most difficult features of direct experience is that it is unfiltered by any theories and expectations. It's hard to observe without imposing a theory to explain what we're seeing, but the trouble with theories, as Einstein said, is that they explain not only what is observed, but what *can be* observed. We start to build expectations based on our theories. And often those expectations get in the way.

Claridge's Hotel in London is famous for catering to the idiosyncrasies of its guests. If you like mineral water at your bedside every night, the staff of Claridge's will notice this, and each night you'll find the bottle of mineral water by your bed. If you like it half empty, you will find it half

388

empty. And since the staff is English, no eccentricity is too bizarre to indulge.

I lived at Claridge's for several weeks in 1978, rewriting a screenplay. I was typing and cutting and pasting the pages together. But I couldn't get an ordinary tape dispenser; I just had a plain roll of Scotch tape and a pair of scissors. Of course, every time I cut a piece of tape, the edge would fall back onto the roll, and I'd have a terrible time prying it free with my fingernails to cut another piece. Eventually I hit on the expedient of cutting long strips of tape, and running them lightly down the knobs of my desk drawers on both sides of the desk. This allowed me simply to cut between the knobs to get a piece of tape. I followed this procedure of taping the drawers for several weeks.

A year later I returned to Claridge's and checked into a room. It was a nice room, but it had a peculiarity: someone had stretched rows of Scotch tape down all the drawers of the desk in the corner.

They'd remembered! I was flattered, but I tried to imagine what the staff must have thought. Who knows why this guy likes it? But he always tapes the desk drawers shut. So make sure they're taped shut on arrival, so Mr. Crichton will be comfortable.

That's the difficulty with making theories. The original observation wasn't wrong—but the conclusion drawn was wrong.

It takes an enormous effort to avoid all theories and just see—just experience directly. But, for a time, subjective experience might benefit from a little freedom before we try to slap it into a conceptual straitjacket.

Sometimes it's better just to sit and watch.

It's surprising what you can learn that way.

I believe the experiences reported in this book are reproducible by anyone who wishes to try.

I went to Africa. You can go to Africa. You may have trouble arranging the time or the money, but everybody has trouble arranging something. I believe you can travel anywhere if you want to badly enough.

And I believe exactly the same thing is true of inner travel. You don't have to take my word about chakras or healing energy or auras. You can find out about them yourself if you want to. Don't take my word for it. Be as skeptical as you like.

Find out for yourself.

I have many friends from scientific backgrounds who accept me with amused toleration. They like me despite my views. But I have learned not to debate with them any more. Unless you are willing to experience these things yourself, even so mundane a phenomenon as meditation sounds fanciful and absurd. From my point of view, these scientists are exactly like the New Guinea tribesmen who refuse to believe the metal birds in the sky contain people. How can you argue with them? Unless they're willing to go to the airport and see for themselves, no discussion is really possible.

And, of course, if they do go to the airport, no discussion is necessary.

So, in the end, find out for yourself.

There are plenty of people around who can assist you in these inner explorations. Inner travel agents, you might consider them. Many offer organized tours lasting a day, a weekend, or two weeks. Like all travel agents, some of these people are flashy and spectacular, while others are quiet; some attract celebrities and media stars, others attract health professionals, others, people with illnesses. Some are outright frauds who don't deliver what they promise. Some are flaky and unpredictable. Some are demanding and cultish, others are open and free. Some are intellectual, some are emotional, some are rational, some are religious.

There are a lot of trips out there. It's even possible to become a conference groupie, going from one seminar to another and being a Beautiful Evolved Human Being until you start making the people around you throw up.

You may wonder how to find a person, group, or conference that's right for you. If you look around, you'll find something. And if what you find is not right, keep looking until you get what you want. I won't recommend any particular person or thing to do. But I will tell you my inner travel prejudices:

1. Be cautious around anyone who even implies he has the answer. The real gunslingers always tried to avoid pulling their guns. Same with the real gurus. Anyway, nobody has the answer for you except you.

2. Be cautious around anyone who creates proselytizing followers. In most cases, personal development is only temporarily associated with any particular group.

3. Be cautious around anyone who seems interested in your money.

390

4. Expect results. Nobody gets enlightened overnight, but if you don't get results, change your methods. Don't be afraid to experiment—nobody has the answer for you except you.

5. Trust your instincts. If it feels good, don't let others discourage you. If you smell a rat, bail out.

I've come to take a rather simple-minded view of all this. There's a natural human resistance to change. We all fall into patterns and habits that eventually constrict our lives, but which we have difficulty breaking anyway. Rilke described the problem in this simple way:

> *Whoever you are: some evening take a step*
> *out of your house, which you know so well.*
> *Enormous space is near. . . .*

Postscript: Skeptics at Cal Tech

In the spring of 1987 I met Paul MacCready, the witty and charming aeronautical engineer who in 1977 made the "Gossamer Condor," and thus achieved one of man's oldest dreams: human-powered flight. MacCready went on to make the "Gossamer Albatross," the first human-powered airplane to cross the English Channel; he also made a solar-powered airplane.

During our conversation, Paul began to talk disparagingly about psychics, people who claimed they could see auras. MacCready's view was that these people were at best deluded, and at worst fraudulent.

I disagreed, and in the ensuing discussion Paul told me that he was an active member of the Pasadena chapter of CSICOP.

The Committee for the Scientific Investigation of Claims of the Paranormal was founded in 1976 by a group of eminent philosophers, psychologists, scientists, and magicians. In its quarterly journal, *The Skeptical Inquirer,* CSICOP had had great success in debunking the claims of "paranormal" phenomena. There were CSICOP chapters all around the country, and the Pasadena chapter, which included many members of the Cal Tech faculty, was especially active. MacCready thought I should address this group.

I agreed at once. I thought it would be an interesting experience, both for me and for the audience. Paul said he would arrange an invitation for me. I went off to prepare my talk.

Because I knew very little of the work of CSICOP, I first read a selection of essays from *The Skeptical Inquirer* published in a volume called *Science Confronts the Paranormal.* [1] Many of the essays held no interest for me at all; they debunked phenomena such as biorhythms, palmistry, astrology, UFOs, and the Bermuda Triangle, which I did not believe in anyway. Other essays, such as a critique of the Loch Ness monster searches, [2] seemed uninteresting because there were no philosophical or intellectual implications.

But in several essays I was disturbed by the intemperate tone of many writers I admired; there was a tendency to attribute the basest motives to their opponents. In fact, there seemed to be a good deal of personal animosity and name-calling on all sides. For example, discussing the supposed similarities between physics and Eastern mysticism, as outlined by writers such as Fritjof Capra, Isaac Asimov observed:

> . . . If intuition is as important to the world as reason, and if the Eastern sages are as knowledgeable about the Universe as physicists are, then why not take matters in reverse? Why not use the wisdom of the East as a key to some of the unanswered questions in physics? For instance: what is the basic component making up subatomic particles that physicists call a quark? . . . .

And Asimov concluded:

> What nonsense all this supposed intuitional truth is, and how comic is the sight of the genuflections made to it by rational minds who lost their nerve.
> No, it isn't really comic; it's tragic. There has been at least one other such occasion in history, when Greek secular and rational thought bowed to the mystical aspects of Christianity, and what followed was a Dark Age.
> We can't afford another. [3]

394

Now, these were heated words, and, reading them, I began to sense there was more at stake for CSICOP than the dispassionate assessment of questionable data. Asimov himself had implicitly drawn the comparison between science and religion as competing ways of viewing the world. That, of course, opened the door to the possibility that science was a religion—a heretical position few scientists would accept. But, in reviewing the essays of CSICOP, I began to see science as battling for supremacy against perceived threats from other modes of perception.

If I was going to talk effectively to the Pasadena chapter of CSICOP, I was going to have my work cut out for me.

I began by saying that I didn't expect to change anybody's point of view by what I was going to say. It wasn't my intention to convince anybody of anything, that night in Pasadena.

I believed there was validity to certain psychic phenomena, and I knew most of my audience did not. Rather than dispute this in detail, I suggested we could all agree that history would eventually prove that either I was mistaken in my views, or they were mistaken in theirs. We could all confidently look forward to the eventual resolution of this issue.

Meanwhile, I wanted to tell this group some of the experiences that had led me to modify my own views, and to try and explain how things looked to me now. Because, I suggested, the real issue as I saw it went far beyond the relatively narrow question of "paranormal" phenomena. It went to the basic intellectual posture of science in the latter twentieth century.

I then said, Has anyone in this room had their tonsils and adenoids removed? Has anyone had a radical mastectomy for breast cancer? Has anyone been treated in an intensive care unit? Has anyone had coronary bypass surgery? Of course, many people had.

I said, Then you're all knowledgeable about superstitions, because all these procedures are examples of superstitious behavior. They are procedures carried out without scientific evidence that they produce any benefit. This society spends billions of dollars a year on superstitious medicine, and that is a problem—and an expense—far more important than astrology columns in daily newspapers, which are so vigorously attacked by the brainpower of CSI-COP.

And I added, Let's not be too quick to deny the power of superstition in our own lives. Which of us, having suffered a heart attack, would refuse to be treated in an intensive-care unit just because such units are of unproven value? We'd all take the ICU. We all do.

I then went on to mention the many cases of fraud in research science. Isaac Newton may have fudged his data;[4] certainly Gregor Mendel, father of Mendelian inheritance, did.[5] The Italian mathematician Lazzarini faked an experiment to determine the value of pi, and his result went unquestioned for more than half a century.[6] British psychologist Sir Cyril Burt invented not only his data, but research assistants to gather it.[7] In more recent years, there were cases of fraud involving William T. Summerlin of Sloan-Kettering, Dr. John Long of the Harvard Medical School, and Dr. John Darsee of the Harvard Medical School. Other cases involved a research team at the Dana Farer Cancer Institute, Dr. Robert Slutsky of the UCSD Medical School, Dr. Jeffrey Borer of Cornell University, Stephen Breuning of the University of Pittsburgh. Though most cases had come from medicine and biology, there were examples in other fields as well; three papers in the *Journal of the American Chemical Society* were recently retracted, in a case still under investigation. The extent of fraud was unknown, but I reminded the group that fraud undeniably exists in science. Thus the fact that there are some fraudulent practitioners in a field cannot be an argument to dismiss that whole field of inquiry.

Next I reminded them that science as a field does not progress in a uniquely rational manner different from other fields of human endeavor, such as business or commerce. Max Planck, who won the Nobel Prize in physics, said, "A new scientific truth does not triumph by convincing its opponents and making them see the light, but rather because its opponents eventually die, and a new generation grows up that is familiar with it."

I reminded them of the tendency of scientists in every age to think that they finally know it all. For example, the French anatomist Baron Georges Cuvier, one of the most brilliant and influential scientists of his day, announced in 1812 that "there is little hope of discovering new species of large quadrupeds." Unfortunately for Cuvier, this statement preceded the discovery of the Kodiak bear, the mountain gorilla, the okapi, the white-backed tapir, the Komodo dragon, Grant's gazelle, Grevy's zebra, the pygmy hippopotamus, and the giant panda, to name just a few large quadrupeds. Similar claims of nearly complete knowledge have been made by physicists in almost every generation; such claims have been invariably proven wrong.

I reminded them of the past failures of science to accept legitimate discoveries at the time they were made. When J. J. Thomson measured the mass and charge of the electron in 1899, many of his colleagues suspected him of fraud—or ineptitude, since he was famously clumsy around any experimental apparatus.[8] When Carl Anderson of Cal Tech discovered the positron in 1932, both Bohr and Rutherford dismissed the new finding "out of hand."[9] And the theory of continental drift, proposed by Alfred Wegener in 1922, should have been obvious to anyone who looked at a map of the world and saw how the continents could be fitted together, yet it took forty years for geologists to overcome the opposition of such eminent men as Harold Jeffreys and Maurice Ewing to this theory.

I reminded them that the rate of progress in science was highly variable. Newton's theory of gravitation stood unchallenged for more than two hundred years before the precession of the planet Mercury was found to disprove it.[10] And, conversely, hypnotism was a discredited practice for more than two hundred years, ever since a blue-ribbon panel of scientists in Paris, including Benjamin Franklin and Lavoisier, had pronounced mesmerism without merit; yet today hypnosis is unquestionably genuine and widely practiced. Thus the rate of progress within a field is no indicator of the validity of the field.

Next I pointed out the trends and fads of science, which affected scientists at every level. It was perfectly acceptable for dozens of the world's most distinguished scientists to propose that our society engage in a costly search for extraterrestrial life,[11] despite the fact that the study of extraterrestrial life is, in the words of the paleontologist George Gaylord Simpson, "a study without a subject."[12] A belief in extraterrestrial life is a speculation indistinguishable from pure faith. Few if any of those great scientists would sign their names to a proposed study of psychic phenomena,

397

because the paranormal is not fashionable in the way extra-terrestrials are. Yet there is arguably more evidence for psychic phenomena than there is for extraterrestrials.

So I was saying that, from where I stood, the enterprise of science did not look so different from other human enterprises. There was institutionalized superstition; there was fraud; there were missteps and errors; there was conservatism and plain pigheadedness; and there were fashionable trends. Observed Marcello Truzzi, a former editor of the CSICOP journal, "Scientists are not the paragons of rationality, objectivity, open-mindedness and humility that many of them might like others to believe."[13]

I was reminding the audience of this, not to discredit science, but to place the workings of science in a more realistic perspective with regard to unaccepted phenomena.

Next I said I wanted to address one of the most difficult stumbling blocks in the scientific approach to disputed phenomena. In many cases, such as so-called psychic activity, researchers came up against the argument by so-called practitioners that they couldn't reliably produce results on demand; that they couldn't work in a laboratory setting; that they were inhibited by the frowning skeptics around them; and so on. It seemed that the practitioners were defining a state-dependent phenomenon. Practitioners had to be "in the mood," and the mood was easily shaken. Traditionally, scientists found this position hard to accept. Mystical states, meditative states, trance states, were all hard for scientists to accept.

Yet everyone has firsthand knowledge of activities for which you must be "in the mood": for example, sexual intercourse, requiring lubrication in the female, erection in the male. Creative work is another state-dependent activity that cannot be reliably performed on demand, as the vast literature devoted to "courting the muse" testifies.

We know from subjective reports and from our own experience that these state-dependent phenomena are accompanied by a change in consciousness. There may be a perceived or a real change in energy and concentration; there may be a change in perception of time, and so on. Such changes vary from day to day, from person to person, and from experience to experience within the same person. The highly variable nature of the experiences, and the subjectivity of the experience, make state-dependent phenomena a difficult challenge to scientific investigation.

I would suggest to you that the scientific study of creativity has fared no better in the last century than the scientific study of psychic activity, and for much the same reasons. Yet nobody would deny that creativity exists. It is merely very hard to study.

Skeptical scientists often point out, as Carl Sagan has, that the wonders of real science far surpass the supposed wonders of fringe science. I think it is possible to invert that idea, and to say that the wonders of real consciousness far surpass what conventional science admits can exist. For example, suppose I told you that, while a group of huge men charges at you with the intention to maim you, you were required to throw a ball seventy meters to strike a one-meter target that you can't see just before you are slammed to the ground and crushed to a pulp. I doubt there is a single person in this room who could do such a thing, or would even dare attempt it. Yet we can observe this unlikely event performed every Sunday afternoon on television, during football season.

The change in consciousness necessary to execute a downfield pass in a professional football game is ordinary to us and hence unremarkable, but it at least suggests that other trained changes in consciousness, arising from other cultures and traditions, may also yield surprising results.

I earlier attempted to cover, in an informal way, some of the scientific objections to so-called paranormal phenomena. It is true that many of these beliefs are superstitions, but so are many beliefs in the more scientific world, such as the world of high-tech medicine.

It is true that many practitioners are frauds, but a proportion of working scientists are also frauds.

It is true that progress in the paranormal investigation is slow, but so is progress in many scientific fields, particularly when they are poorly funded.

It is true that some paranormal phenomena seem to be state-dependent and consciousness-related, but so are many everyday phenomena that lead to such unremarked wonders as a new painting, or a Sunday touchdown pass.

Thus, to my mind, none of these traditional scientific complaints about the paranormal seems adequate to dismiss the field from legitimate study. In looking at the matter more closely, I find three other reasons that are much more powerful grounds for dismissal.

The first is the quasi-religious discomfort these phenomena evoke in a hard scientist. In the early years of this century, Freud and Jung ended their close friendship over the issue of occult phenomena:[14] Jung was openly interested in the paranormal;[15] Freud was not. Before the split, Freud wrote Jung: "My dear son, keep a cool head, for it is better not to understand something than make such great sacrifices to understanding."[16] And Jung's enthusiastic interest in astrology, which he studied as a system of psychological projection and not as a physical reality, caused Freud to reply, "I promise to believe anything that can be made to look reasonable. I shall not do so gladly. . . ."[17]

The question is, why not? What was Freud's reluctance? Freud himself studied mythology and art without hesitation. But the occult made him uncomfortable in a way that is recognizable yet difficult to identify precisely. One can argue that the discomfort has fundamentally religious origins—origins so deep as to be untraceable except through lengthy argument, which is not relevant here.

In addition, paranormal phenomena provoke a related discomfort, which has at its core an intellectual prejudice. I would venture to say that nearly everyone here tonight has an advanced degree. We have all survived a great deal of schooling, and we are skilled in rational, linear thought. We have been trained to value such thought and the products of such thought. Thus we turn with palpable uneasiness to the occult section of the bookstore, which contains writing by all sorts of illiterate and uneducated people. These people don't share our thought systems or our sentence structures, and we are likely to see ourselves as slumming when we consider their work.

Whether we admit it or not, any person of academic standing holds certain criteria that govern the kinds of references he will cite in his writing, and for that matter the kind of subjects he will write about in the first place. I suggest that these criteria represent a powerful prejudice that has colored all formal academic consideration of the paranormal—as the unsavory reputation of Mesmer colored the assessment of his claims for hypnotism.

400

A third reason scientists are reluctant to examine para-normal phenomena is that they appear to contradict known physical laws. What is the point of studying the impossible? Only a fool would waste his time. The problem of data in conflict with existing theory cannot be overstated. Arthur Eddington once said you should never believe any experiment until it has been confirmed by theory, but this humorous view has a reality that cannot be discounted.

Indeed, the primacy of theory is conveyed by scientific history. Bronowski notes: "Charles Darwin did not invent the theory of evolution: that was known to his grandfather. What he thought of was a machinery for evolution: the mechanism of natural selection. . . . Once Darwin had proposed this [mechanism], the theory of evolution was accepted by every one; and it was thought the most natural thing in the world to call it Darwin's theory."[18]

In other words, data to support the idea of evolution—such as the fossil record—were long known; but a convincing theory to explain the data was lacking. Once Darwin provided the theory, the data were accepted.

Now consider so-called psychic phenomena, such as clairvoyance, remote-viewing, and psychokinesis. On the face of it, all these phenomena seem to be contradicted by physical theory. At least, there is no immediately available theory to account for them. And that, it seems to me, is a major reason why data to support these phenomena are denied.

What data? you may ask. Many scientists deny there are any data at all—that there is no incident or event that is properly documented, properly controlled, and therefore not subject to fraud and trickery.

Yet there are, in fact, well-studied subjects who appear to defy scientific explanation—in particular the famous medium of the last century, Mrs. Piper, who was championed by William James, professor of psychology at Harvard. Mrs. Piper was subjected to intense scrutiny for nearly a quarter of a century, but no skeptic was ever able to demonstrate fraud or trickery.

Yet the claims of fraud persisted. James wrote rather irritably, "The 'scientist' who is confident of 'fraud' here, must remember that in science as much as in common life an hypothesis must receive some positive specification and determination before it can be profitably discussed; and a fraud which is no assigned kind of fraud, but simply 'fraud'

401

at large, fraud *in abstracto,* can hardly be regarded as a specially scientific explanation of specific concrete facts."[19]

As for other scientists who continued to claim as-yet undetected fraud, James retorted, "I believe there is no source of deception in the investigation of nature which can compare with a fixed belief that certain kinds of phenomena are *impossible.* "[20]

Beyond the narrower question of whether an isolated phenomenon, such as clairvoyance or telepathy or seeing auras, actually occurs, there is a broader issue affecting science in the modern day. I refer to a certain fixity of viewpoint among scientists, a certain tendency to confuse contemporary scientific theories with the underlying reality itself.

Jacob Bronowski, one of the most eloquent commentators on the relationship of science to other human activities, always reminded us that scientific theories are a fiction. "Science, like art, is not a copy of nature but a re-creation of her."[21] Science offers a picture of the world, but its picture is not to be confused with the underlying reality itself.

Yet we all tend to confuse our fictional views with reality. I think most of us have glanced out of an airplane window while crossing the United States, and have been surprised not to see lines dividing the states, as those lines appear on a map. I myself remember the shock I felt when I first looked at live human tissue under a microscope, and found it colorless; I expected to see pink cells with purple nuclei. Yet those colors are artifacts that come from microscopic stains. Real cells have no color.

Of course I knew better, just as we all know there are no lines on the land to demarcate the states. But we forget. And, in fact, we forget with a surprising ease.

I was educated in a twentieth-century, Western, scientific-rational tradition. I was raised to think that the scientific view of the world was the correct view, and that every other view was pure superstition. I agreed with Bertrand Russell when he said, "What science cannot tell us mankind cannot know."

I had few formal experiences to contradict this view. But my later experiences have broken out of that scientific-rational perspective. I still find the scientific view useful, and I live happily within it much of the time. But I now regard science as providing an arbitrary and limited model of reality.

Because reality is always greater—much greater—than what we know, than whatever we can say about it.

Let's review why, with a simple thought experiment.

Think of a person you know well.

Now make any correct descriptive statement about that person.

George is an even-tempered man.

Now consider that statement. Is it really correct?

The chances are, as you consider it, you'll begin to remember times when George lost his temper, or was upset about something, or in a bad mood for some reason. You'll think of the exceptions.

So you must admit the statement is not quite accurate. You could modify it to say, *George is often an even-tempered man,* but that is actually just evasive. That word "often" merely says the statement is sometimes correct but sometimes not. And since it doesn't tell when the statement is not correct, it isn't very helpful.

So you'd have to be more explicit, to give a fuller statement.

George is usually an even-tempered man, except on Mondays when his favorite football team lost the day before, or when his wife had a fight with him, or when he gets tired and cranky—usually late in the week—but not always—or when his boss gives him a hard time, or when he has to rewrite a report, or when he has to go out of town . . . or when . . . or when . . .

Pretty soon you see that your descriptive statement is turning into an essay. And you still haven't covered all the things you know. It's still not complete. You could write pages and pages and you would still not be finished. In fact, it's hopeless to try to make a complete statement about George's ever-changing temper. The subject is too complicated. It was doomed from the start.

So let's start all over.

Let's make a different statement.

George is neat and orderly.

That's unquestionably true, you think. George is always neatly dressed, and his desk is always tidy.

But have you ever seen the workbench in his garage at home? What a mess! Tools scattered all around. His wife is always after him to clean it up. And what about the trunk of his car? All kinds of junk in there that he never bothers to clean out.

George is usually neat and orderly.

But by now you can see where this modification is eventually going to end up—in another essay.

So let's make a different statement, one that is both concise and complete.

George has gray hair.

That does it, you think. He has gray hair and there's no question about it.

Of course, not all of his hair is gray. Most of it is, though, especially around the temples and the back of the neck. So there's some simplification here, but it's not objectionable.

Then, too, even if George has gray hair now, he didn't a few years ago. And at some time in the future, he will no longer have gray hair, he will have white hair. So this is only a correct description of George's hair right now, at this moment in time. It isn't a description of George in some universal, invariant way.

Let's try again.

George is six feet tall.

Again, true, within the limits of measurement. He's probably not exactly six feet. He's probably somewhere between five eleven and six one. And of course he wasn't always six feet. At an earlier time he was much shorter. So this statement is only approximate, too.

George is a man.

Well, yes. But "man" is rather unspecific; it's really a culturally determined word, when you get right down to it. At birth he was not considered a man. You have to attain a certain age and position in society to be considered a man.

George is a male.

Now, that's unarguable. George is, and always was, a male. There's no way to dispute that. It is a true statement about George, both now and in the past. It is an eternal verity. It is an accurate description of the reality of George.

Of course, by "male" we mean that he has an X and a Y chromosome. But we don't know that for sure, do we? George might have an extra chromosome. He might only be *apparently* male. . . .

And so on.

* * *

There are two points about this exercise in making statements about George. The first is that every single statement we make about George can be contradicted. Why is that?

It's because our statements about George are only approximations, simplifications. The real person we call George is always more complicated than any statement we have made about him. Thus we can always refer to that real person and find in him a contradiction to what we have said.

The second point is that the statements about George that are most securely held are also the least interesting. We can't say anything comprehensive about his moods or his neatness or his complex behavior. We are on much safer ground describing the simplest aspects of his physical appearance: hair color, height, sex, and so on. There—with some qualifications of measurement error and changes over time—we can be sure of what we are saying.

But only a tailor would take pride in this fact. And, indeed, a tailor might. After making many fittings for George, and adjusting the patterns at each fitting, the tailor might eventually be able to cut a suit of clothes for George entirely in his absence, and when George came in for a final fitting the finished clothes would fit him perfectly!

This is a triumph of the art of measurement, but the clothes that fit so wonderfully are draped over a creature whom the tailor may not know at all. Nor is the tailor interested. He couldn't care less about other aspects of George. It's not his job.

On the other hand, what interests *us* most about George is not his measurements. We are most interested in precisely those other aspects, which the tailor, by definition, doesn't care about. We find it far more difficult to define those other aspects of George than the tailor does to define George's measurements.

The tailor can do his job of description perfectly. We, on the other hand, can't really describe George at all.

Now, since the tailor is so good—so clearly successful—at what he does, we might be tempted to ask the tailor, "Who is George?"

The tailor will answer, "George is a forty-four long."

And if we protest that this answer isn't really satisfactory, the tailor will reply with assurance that he is unquestionably right about George, because he can cut a whole suit of clothes that will fit George perfectly the moment he walks in the door.

This, in essence, is the problem with the scientific view of reality. Science is a kind of glorified tailoring enterprise, a method for taking measurements that describe something—reality—that may not be understood at all.

Science is very good as far as it goes. It has certainly produced powerful benefits. It would be crazy to abandon science, or to deny its validity.

But it would be equally crazy to think that reality is a forty-four long. Yet it seems as if that is what Western society has done. For hundreds of years, science has been so successful that the tailor has taken over our society. His knowledge seems so much more precise and powerful than the knowledge offered by other disciplines, such as history or psychology or art.

But in the end one can be left with a nagging sense of emptiness about the creations of science. One may even suspect that there is more to reality than measurements will ever reveal.

Let's return to the earlier problem: describing a person named George. When we looked at anything except his physical measurements, we found that it was extremely difficult to make any statement about George that could not be immediately contradicted by other statements, equally true.

Now, we might struggle with this problem for a while longer, and keep searching for incontrovertible statements about George. But eventually, after repeated failures, we may begin to suspect that there is no way we can succeed at this undertaking. The reality of George keeps slipping away from us. Whatever we say is wrong.

At that point someone who says, "Existence is beyond the power of words to define," may not sound so esoteric. This seems to be exactly what we have discovered on our own. However, this statement was made by Lao-tzu, a Chinese mystic, twenty-five centuries ago. Lao-tzu was adamant on this point, repeating it again and again: "Existence is infinite, not to be defined."

But if that is the case—if reality will always elude our definitions, just as George does—what can we do?

> There is no need to run outside
> For better seeing,
> Nor to peer from a window. Rather abide
> At the center of your being;
> For the more you leave it, the less you learn.

Lao-tzu argues that it is necessary to turn inward, toward an inner sense of reality, instead of looking outward. This would appear to be a criticism of academic undertakings, and indeed he is elsewhere explicit:

> Leave off fine learning! End the nuisance
> Of saying yes to this and perhaps to that,
> Distinctions with how little significance!
> Categorical this, categorical that,
> What slightest use are they!

Lao-tzu makes many similar statements, which seem to be opposed to scholarly learning, even to knowledge. Why does he think this way?

> People through finding something beautiful
> Think something else unbeautiful,
> Through finding one man fit
> Judge another unfit.
> Life and death, though stemming from each other,
> Seem to conflict as stages of change,
> Difficult and easy as phases of achievement,
> Long and short as measures of contrast,
> High and low as degrees of relation;
> But since the varying of tones gives music to a voice
> And what is is the was of what shall be,
> The sanest man
> Sets up no deed,
> Lays down no law,
> Takes everything that happens as it comes. . . .

He is really saying, Don't make distinctions, because every distinction simultaneously defines its opposite, and in many cases the interplay of opposites is indivisible, just as varying tones make up music. He says, If you approach the world through distinctions, you can never untangle your perceptions.

The surest test if a man be sane
Is if he accepts life whole, as it is,
Without needing by measure or touch to understand
The measureless untouchable source
Of its images. . . .

The attitude of Lao-tzu represents one way to deal with the fact that whatever we say about reality is inevitably wrong or incomplete. Lao-tzu says you must "accept life whole, as it is, without needing . . . to understand."

This attitude is in a sense antirational, and certainly anti-intellectual. But it is another perspective, clear and consistent. Although it may not be to everyone's taste, we are obliged to acknowledge that it is a genuine solution to a genuine problem.

In his day Jacob Bronowski was at some pains to address a predominantly humanistic audience, persuading them to pay attention to science by drawing connections between humanistic pursuits and scientific pursuits. Thirty years later the balance has shifted to the other side. Now it seems to me it is the scientists who need to be reminded of the similarities between their activities and those of other men, and in particular to be reminded that the rational, scientific, reductionist method is not the only route to useful truth.

I find this the most striking prejudice among the scientists I know. My friend Marvin Minsky, in a recent book, writes about mystical states in a highly critical way. He finds these states "sinister" and speaks of the "victims of these incidents." His view is expressed thus: "One can acquire certainty only by amputating inquiry. . . . To offer hospitality to paradox is like leaning toward a precipice. You can find out what it is like by falling in, but you may not be able to fall out again. Once contradiction finds a home, few minds can spurn the sense-destroying force of slogans such as 'all is one.' "[22]

Even more bluntly, Stephen Hawking says that mysticism "is a cop-out. If you find theoretical physics and mathematics too hard, you turn to mysticism."[23]

Such statements, broadly speaking, agree with Asimov's comment that intuition is for those who have "lost their nerve." Hawking takes the idea further, implying that mysticism is a procedure for those who aren't bright enough to do physics.

I disagree with this attitude. Perhaps the easiest way to state my objection is to say that I do not find the content of physics sufficient to explain the behavior of physicists themselves.

Where does the physicists' belief in consistency, in unification, come from? This belief is so strong that men and women devote their lives to proving its existence. Yet it is nothing visible in the world. What we see before us is a world of apparently disunified objects and events. The underlying unity is something we seek and find. Granted that the scientific perception of unity is not the same as the mystic's perception of unity, there is still a question: what provokes a scientist to look for unity at all? Is it just a matter of tidying up the mathematics? Does any thoughtful scientist seriously believe that purely formalistic concerns are sufficient to make him work long hours, year after year? Is science such a totally self-referential system that making inner connections between theories is the only driving force?

I think not. I suspect that scientists are driven by the sense that the world out there—reality—contains a hidden order, and the scientist is trying to elucidate the hidden order in reality. And that *impulse* is what the scientist shares with the mystic. The impulse to get to the bottom of things. To know how the world really works. To know the nature of reality.

A Nobel Prize–winning physicist wrote:

I wanted very much to learn to draw, for a reason that I kept to myself: I wanted to convey an emotion I have about the beauty of the world. It's difficult to describe because it's an emotion. It's analogous to the feeling one has in religion that has to do with a god that controls everything in the whole universe: there's a generality aspect that you feel when you think how things that appear so different and behave so differently are all run "behind the scenes" by the same organization, the same physical laws. It's an appreciation of the mathematical beauty of nature, of how she works inside: a realization that the phenomena we see result from the complexity of the inner workings between atoms; a feeling of how dramatic and wonderful it is. It's a feeling of awe—of scientific awe—which I felt could be communicated through a drawing to someone who had also had this emotion. It could remind him, for a moment, of this feeling about the glories of the universe.[24]

Some of you may recognize the writer as Richard Feynman, a distinguished member of the Cal Tech faculty. I cite the passage because it appears, in broad strokes, to express exactly the kind of unified insight that other scientists denigrate. And also because, from this most confident and unpedantic of authors, the statement is heavily qualified: Feynman says his feeling is "*analogous* to the feeling one has in religion." It's an appreciation only of the *mathematical beauty* of nature. And the awe is expressly *scientific awe,* as if scientific awe were somehow different from regular awe.

This strikes me as an oddly cautious expression of what is, I suspect, a nearly universal human emotion.

And while we are talking about Feynman's artistic career, it's worth mentioning one of the discoveries he later made. Sometime after he began drawing, he visited the Sistine Chapel. He had left behind his guidebook, so he just went around looking at the paintings. He found some of the paintings to be very good, and others to be, in his word, "junk." Back in his hotel room, he found that his judgment of the paintings agreed with the guidebook.

This was a terrific excitement to me, that I also could tell the difference between a beautiful work of art and one that's not, without being able to define it. As a scientist you always think you know what you're doing, so you tend to distrust the artist who says, "It's great," or "It's no good," and then is not able to explain to you why. . . . But here I was, sunk: I could do it, too![25]

Why does he say he was sunk? What, exactly, is sunk? Throughout his memoir, Feynman rather breezily dismisses most fields of activity other than physics. He is a man of mathematical rigor, so he finds little of interest in philosophy or art or psychology. These fields make no sense to him; the practitioners "don't know what they are talking about." Yet in the Sistine Chapel he has experienced something that sinks his conception of these other fields. Simply by doing art himself, he has acquired the ability to make perceptions about other art that agree with the formal and codified perceptions of art history.

Feynman does not discuss this remarkable incident further, although there is clearly more to be said. For one thing, his experience would seem to imply that, although he does not try to bring his critical criteria to conscious awareness, the criteria nonetheless exist. They must exist, or else he would never manage to agree with the guidebook. Second, the criteria are not arbitrary or academic, since Feynman is able to formulate those criteria simply by the experience of making pictures. The criteria of art history do indeed have something to do with the activity of making art. There is an underlying rigor to art history, which Feynman has demonstrated by reproducing its conclusions.

I am discussing this at length because it seems to me that it typifies a situation in which a tremendously bright scientist, confronted by data, even admitting the data, nevertheless does not take those data to the obvious conclusion: that there is just as much rigor to art as there is to science. It may be a different kind of rigor, but it is rigor nonetheless.

When an artist such as Jasper Johns says, "I am just trying to find a way to make pictures,"[26] he means it in exactly the same way a physicist means it when he says, "I am just trying to find a way to do physics." Like a scientist, an artist must build upon the work of his predecessors. An artist can be intimidated by the work of his predecessors, just as a scientist can be.

So for a scientist to dismiss art as some kind of formless activity in which "anything goes" means only that the scientist doesn't understand the activity of making art. He doesn't understand what he is dismissing. The scientist has only his model of what the activity of art is, and his model is wrong. It's uninformed; and it doesn't fit the data.

The extent to which scientists are uninformed about the real work of nonscientists seems to me to reach some ultimate point when scientists consider meditative states, alterations in consciousness, and the disputed psychic phenomena. If you have never experienced these things firsthand, you will naturally find the descriptions of them to be outlandish. Because these experiences are different from the experiences of ordinary consciousness. There is no great mystery here, and certainly nothing sinister. It's just different. It's another kind of consciousness.

I have known in my life one computational prodigy, and, watching him, I could not conceive how he was able to do what he did; I was simply obliged, after checking a few times, to accept that he could do it. I know one film director with a photographic memory, but he's rather tedious, given to impromptu lectures in exhaustive detail on all sorts of subjects. All that I learned is that I should never argue with him about an obscure fact, since he was invariably correct. But I couldn't conceive how he could do what he did, either.

I have a rather similar feeling around people with psychic abilities. They can do something I can't do. To them the ability is mundane, and on balance has its good and bad features.

I often hear skeptics say that, if psychic behavior was real, the psychics would be playing the stock market or the ponies. In my experience, many of them do. There is, in fact, a kind of secret level of activity in which psychics consult to major corporations and businesses. People seem to be embarrassed to admit this activity, but it takes place, just as you'd expect it to.

And I would remind you that, from one standpoint, you might expect so-called psychic behavior to exist in the first place. The eminently sensible Dr. Bronowski again:

> In science . . . the process of prediction is conscious and rational. Even in human beings this is not the only kind of prediction. Men have sound intuitions which have certainly not been analyzed into rational steps, and some of which may never be. It may be for example, as is sometimes claimed, that most people are a little better at guessing an unseen card, and some people much better, than would be a machine which merely picks its answers by chance. This would not be altogether surprising. . . . Certainly evolution has selected us rapidly because we do possess gifts of foresight much above those of other animals. . . . The rational intelligence is one such gift, and is at bottom as remarkable and as unexplained. And where ratio-

nal intelligence turns to the future, and makes infer-
ences from past experiences to an unknown tomorrow, its process is . . . a great mystery. . . .[27]

But to return to the original point, the experience of these
other forms of consciousness seems to me to be ordinary,
even mundane. These different forms of consciousness—
whether inborn gifts or trained procedures—lead to other
kinds of knowing, other perceptions of underlying order in
the world around us. They are not mathematical perceptions, but they are perceptions nonetheless. Before you dismiss these perceptions outright as fraud or fantasy, it seems
useful to experience them firsthand. If you're not willing to
experience them firsthand, you open yourself to the criticism that you dismiss what you don't understand.

And you diminish your own experience of reality.

Because, as I have said, the scientific perception of reality
is not reality itself. Even the most powerful scientific law is
not a complete description of reality. There is always more
to know.

I think it's important to be very clear about this. Feynman, whom I much admire, says of nonscientific people,
"they don't understand the world they live in." It seems to
be a favorite saying of his; he repeated it often during the
shuttle-disaster investigations.

But let's be clear: *nobody understands the world he lives
in.* Not you, not me, not Richard Feynman. We may each
understand a part, an aspect of the whole, but, in any full
or comprehensive sense, reality defies description.

And if other modes of knowing are internal, subjective,
and inherently unverifiable, that doesn't make them necessarily any less interesting or useful.

People who find numbers alien to their natures are not
fringe people in the world, the disenfranchised, the despised
ignorant who do not know how to solve differential equa-
tions and so are denied access to mathematical received
truth.

Because science alone is not enough.

Faced with a public that embraces creationism and belief in
psychic phenomena, the hard scientist is often perplexed.
The scientist sees a world of beauty and complexity, entirely

challenging enough for his rational approach. Why, he wonders, is someone else dissatisfied with his vision of the world?

Why is science not enough?

The simplest answer is that, while science is a tremendously powerful investigative procedure, it doesn't tell us what we really want to know. Max Planck put it simply: "Whence come I and whither go I? That is the great unfathomable question, the same for every one of us. Science has no answer to it."

One reason is that science can't tell you why anything happens. Feynman again, in a popular lecture on quantum electrodynamics: "While I am describing to you *how* Nature works, you won't understand *why* Nature works that way. But you see, nobody understands that. I can't explain why Nature behaves in this peculiar way."[28]

This is true, but it evades the fact that, although knowledge of how things work is sufficient to allow manipulation of nature, what human beings really want to know is why things work. Children don't ask *how* the sky is blue. They ask *why* the sky is blue.

Feynman would probably say that question has no meaning. And within the body of modern scientific thought, it does not. But it is not self-evident that this state of affairs will continue indefinitely. Physicist John Bell notes:

> The founding fathers of quantum mechanics rather prided themselves on giving up the idea of explanation. They were very proud that they dealt only with phenomena: they refused to look behind the phenomena, regarding that as the price one had to pay for coming to terms with nature. And it is a fact of history that the people who took that agnostic attitude towards the real world on the microphysical level were very successful. At the time it was a good thing to do. But I don't believe it will be so indefinitely.[29]

But, in the meantime, a mathematician observes that "the question of *why* is hardly touched by physical scientists, all the emphasis being placed on *how.* . . . The metaphysics of the cosmos is given in terms of abstract mathematics which is claimed to be absolutely devoid of goals or purposes: the reality of contemporary cosmology is a mathematical reality."[30]

414

Yet this mathematical reality is essentially arbitrary.[31] And this perception of a purposeless universe is not attained without cost. Modern science holds up its mathematical model as a triumph of reason, yet, as Hannah Arendt notes, "Modern times, dominated by technology, are characterized precisely by the fact that reason, in the sense of an originally given self-revealing contemplative understanding, is *lost,* and is replaced by a detached [technology], actively preoccupied with abstract mathematical theory and physical replication."[32]

To me there is nothing wrong with a mathematical perception of reality as long as that perception is not allowed to predominate. Because, as human beings, living our lives, making decisions for ourselves and our society, we must find meaning. And that meaning must be broadly based.

A mathematician:

> I am aware of the ingredients out of which meaning is created . . . love and language, myth, rational thought and irrational impulse, human institutions, law, history, duty, ritual, religious faith, the mystic, the transcendental, the allegorical, the aesthetic sense, play, the world as a puzzle, the world as a stage, the contemplation of life and death, the necessities imposed by physics and biology; all of these and hundreds more are avenues to meaning.[33]

This may be why Einstein once said, "Humanity has every reason to place the proclaimers of high moral standards and values above the discoverers of objective truth. What humanity owes to personalities like Buddha, Moses, and Jesus ranks for me higher than all the achievements of the enquiring and constructive mind."

The fact is that we need the insights of the mystic every bit as much as we need the insights of the scientist. Mankind is diminished when either is missing. Carl Jung said:

> The nature of the psyche reaches into obscurities far beyond the scope of our understanding. It contains as many riddles as the universe with its galactic systems, before whose majestic configurations only a mind lacking in imagination can fail to admit its own insufficiency. . . . If, therefore, from the needs of his own heart, or in accordance with the ancient lessons

415

of human wisdom, or out of respect for the psychological fact that "telepathic" perceptions occur, anyone should draw the conclusion that the psyche, in its deepest reaches, participates in a form of existence beyond time and space . . . then critical reason could counter with no other argument than the "non liquet" of science. Furthermore, he would have the inestimable advantage of conforming to a bias of the human psyche which has existed from time immemorial and is universal. Anyone who does not draw this conclusion, whether from skepticism . . . lack of courage or inadequate psychological experience or thoughtless ignorance . . . has instead the indubitable certainty of coming into conflict with the truths of his blood. . . . Deviation from the truths of the blood begets neurotic restlessness. . . . Restlessness begets meaninglessness, and the lack of meaning in life is a soul-sickness whose full extent and full import our age has not yet begun to comprehend.[34]

Thank you very much.

Well, that was my speech for the skeptics at Pasadena. But I was never invited to speak there, so I never gave it.

---

1. Kendrick Frazier, ed., *Science Confronts the Paranormal,* Buffalo, N.Y.: Prometheus, 1986.

2. R. Razadan and Alan Kielar, "Sonar and Photographic Searches for the Loch Ness Monster: A Reassessment," in Frazier, pp. 349–57.

3. Isaac Asimov, "Science and the Mountain Peak," in Frazier, p. 299.

4. See Richard S. Westfall, "Newton and the Fudge Factor," *Science,* 179 (1973): 751–58. For a full discussion of Newton's entire range of working interests, from alchemy to the Old Testament, see Westfall's definitive biography of Newton, *Never at Rest,* Cambridge: Cambridge University Press, 1981.

5. R. A. Fisher, "Has Mendel's Work Been Rediscovered?", *Annals of Science,* 1 (1936): 115–24.

6. Norman T. Gridgeman, "Geometric Probability and the Number Pi," *Scripta Mathematica,* 25 (November 1970): 183 ff.

7. See L. S. Hearnshaw, *Cyril Burt, Psychologist,* Ithaca, N.Y.: Cornell University Press, 1979.

8. Emilio Segre, *From X-Rays to Quarks: Modern Physicists and Their Discoveries,* San Francisco: Freeman, 1980, pp. 16–19.

9. Daniel J. Kevles, *The Physicists,* New York: Knopf, 1977, p. 233.

10. It may be objected that "disprove" is too strong a term, that the precession of Mercury merely provoked a modification of Newtonian mechanics, or led to the

understanding that Newtonian theory was only an approximation. Such arguments are evasive. Calling Einstein's theory of relativity a modification of Newtonian mechanics is like calling the atomic bomb a modification of gunpowder. For a sensitive consideration of the profound intellectual discomfort caused by the downfall of Newtonian mechanics, see J. Bronowski, *The Common Sense of Science,* Cambridge, Mass.: Harvard University Press, 1978.

11. Carl Sagan, "Extraterrestrial Intelligence: An International Petition," *Science,* 218 (1982): 426.

12. G. G. Simpson, "The Non Prevalence of Humanoids," *Science,* 143 (1964): 769–75.

13. Marcello Truzzi, "On the Reception of Unconventional Scientific Claims," in Seymour H. Mauskopf, ed., *The Reception of Unconventional Science,* AAAS Selected Symposium 25, Boulder, Col.: Westview Press, 1979, p. 130.

14. See C. J. Jung, *Memories, Dreams, Reflections,* New York: Random House, 1962, for the entire story.

15. Jung in fact had written his doctoral dissertation on the occult: "On the Psychology and Pathology of So-Called Occult Phenomena," in C. G. Jung, *Psychology and the Occult,* Princeton: Bollingen Series XX, 1977, pp. 6–91.

16. Cited in Jung, *Psychology,* p. vii.

17. Cited in Jung, *Psychology,* p. ix.

18. Bronowski, *Common Sense,* p. 61.

19. William James, "Review of 'A Further Record of Observations of Certain Phenomena of Trance,' by Richard Hodgson (1898)," in William James, *Essays in Psychical Research,* Cambridge, Mass.: Harvard University Press, 1986, p. 189.

20. Letter to Carl Stumpf, in *The Letters of William James,* ed. Henry James, Cambridge, Mass.: Harvard University Press, 1920, vol. 1, p. 248.

21. Bronowski, *Science and Human Values,* New York: Harper & Row, 1956, p. 20.

22. Marvin Minsky, *The Society of Mind,* New York: Simon and Schuster, 1986, p. 65.

23. Renee Weber, *Dialogues with Scientists and Sages: The Search for Unity in Science and Mysticism,* New York: Methuen, 1986, p. 210.

24. Richard Feynman, *Surely You're Joking, Mr. Feynman!,* New York: Norton, 1985, p. 261.

25. Feynman, p. 266.

26. Michael Crichton, *Jasper Johns,* New York: Abrams, 1977.

27. Bronowski, *Common Sense,* p. 109.

28. Feynman, *QED,* Princeton, N.J.: Princeton University Press, 1965, p. 10.

29. Interview with John Bell in P. C. W. Davies and J. R. Brown, eds., *The Ghost in the Atom,* Cambridge: Cambridge University Press, 1986, p. 51.

30. Philip J. Davis and Reuben Hersh, *Descartes' Dream: The World According to Mathematics,* New York: Harcourt Brace Jovanovich, 1986, p. 275.

31. Werner Heisenberg notes: "We cannot describe atomic phenomena without ambiguity in any ordinary language. . . . It would be premature, however, to insist that we should avoid the difficulty by confining ourselves to the use of mathematical language. This is no genuine way out, since we do not know how far the mathematical language can be applied to the phenomena. In the last resort, even science must rely upon ordinary language, since it is the only language in which we can be sure of really grasping the phenomena." Werner Heisenberg, *Across the Frontiers,* New York: Harper Torchbooks, 1971, p. 119.

32. Davis and Hersh, p. 294.

33. Davis and Hersh, p. 297.

34. Jung, *Psychology,* pp. 136–37.

About the Author

MICHAEL CRICHTON was born in Chicago, in 1942. He was educated at Harvard College and the Harvard Medical School, and in 1969 was a postdoctoral fellow at the Salk Institute in La Jolla, California. His novels include THE ANDROMEDA STRAIN, THE TERMINAL MAN, THE GREAT TRAIN ROBBERY, EATERS OF THE DEAD, CONGO, and SPHERE. He is the author of three works of nonfiction: FIVE PATIENTS, JASPER JOHNS, and ELECTRONIC LIFE. Among the films he has directed are WESTWORLD, COMA, and the movie version of his own THE GREAT TRAIN ROBBERY.

The Latest
By
MICHAEL CRICHTON
Will Shock
And Amaze You